P9-EMP-677

TROPIC OF FOOTBALL

Also by Rob Ruck

Steve Nelson, American Radical, with Steve Nelson and James R. Barrett

Sandlot Seasons: Sport in Black Pittsburgh

The Tropic of Baseball: Baseball in the Dominican Republic

Rooney: A Sporting Life, with Maggie Jones Patterson and Michael P. Weber

Raceball: How the Major Leagues Colonized the Black and Latin Game

TROPIC OF FOOTBALL

THE LONG AND PERILOUS JOURNEY OF SAMOANS TO THE NFL

ROB RUCK

THE
NEW
PRESS

NEW YORK
LONDON

Requests for permission to reproduce selections from this book should be mailed to: Permissions Department, The New Press, 120 Wall Street, 31st floor, New York, NY 10005.

Published in the United States by The New Press, New York, 2018
Distributed by Two Rivers Distribution

LIBRARY OF CONGRESS CATALOGING-IN-PUBLICATION DATA
Names: Ruck, Rob, 1950- author.
Title: Tropic of football : the long and perilous journey of Samoans to the
   NFL / Rob Ruck.
Description: New York : New Press, [2018] | Includes bibliographical
   references and index.
Identifiers: LCCN 2017059415| ISBN 9781620973370 (hc : alk. paper) | ISBN
   9781620973387 (ebook)
Subjects: LCSH: Football players—United States—Biography. | Football
   players—American Samoa—Biography. | National Football League. | American
   Samoa—Biography.
Classification: LCC GV939.A1 R83 2018 | DDC 796.33092—dc23 LC record available at https://lccn.loc.gov
/2017059415

The New Press publishes books that promote and enrich public discussion and understanding of the issues vital to our democracy and to a more equitable world. These books are made possible by the enthusiasm of our readers; the support of a committed group of donors, large and small; the collaboration of our many partners in the independent media and the not-for-profit sector; booksellers, who often hand-sell New Press books; librarians; and above all by our authors.

www.thenewpress.com

Book design and composition by Bookbright Media
This book was set in Fournier MT and Gotham

Printed in the United States of America

10 9 8 7 6 5 4 3 2 1

Omar *vive*!

Contents

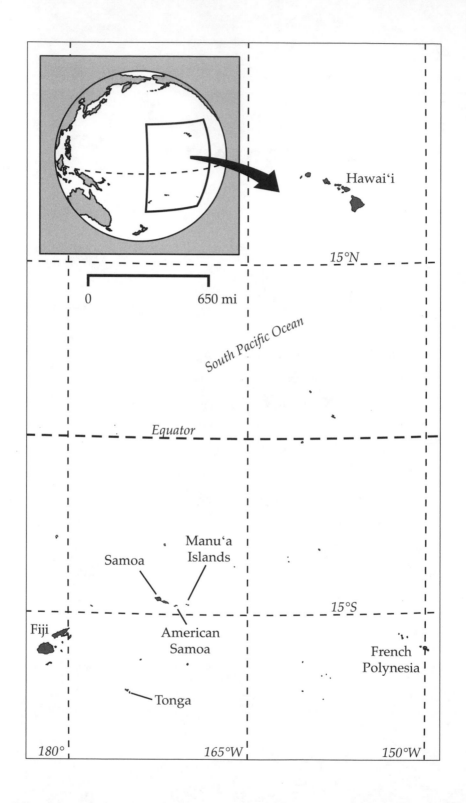

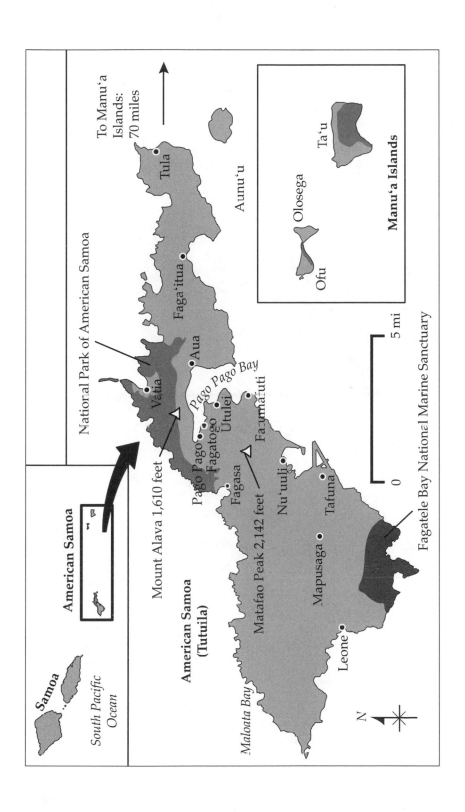

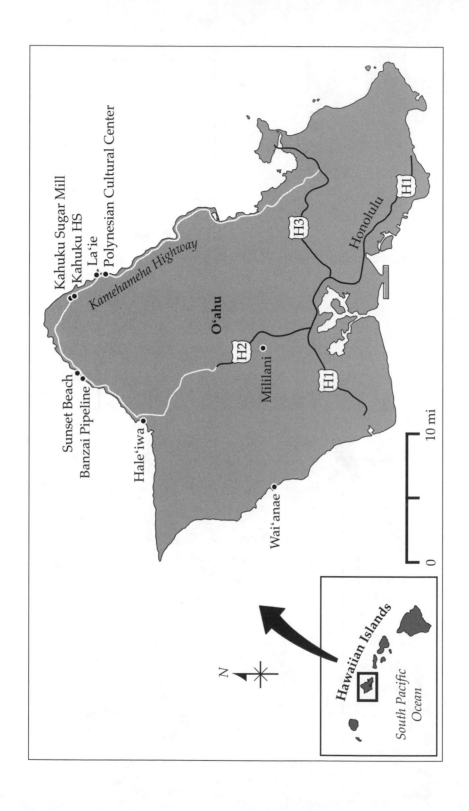

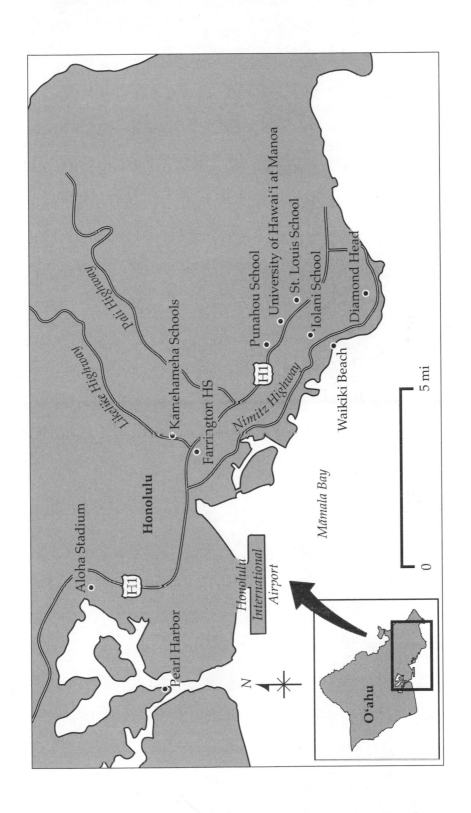

TROPIC OF FOOTBALL

Introduction

Several high school football squads cluster on the sidelines of Veterans Memorial Stadium on a July morning in 2013. Rain scuds by on its way from an angry South Pacific Ocean to the green-slathered mountains that form the spine of Tutuila, the principal island of American Samoa. It's a narrow volcanic uplift about nineteen miles long, never more than five miles wide. Suddenly, players from two schools break into *haka*, the Maori challenge appropriated by teams throughout the Pacific. Two swarms of gesticulating players advance toward each other, contorting their faces, rhythmically slapping thighs and chests, and bellowing out Samoan phrases with guttural ferocity. A few men on the sidelines shake their heads, anticipating trouble.[1]

Ryan Clark, the Pittsburgh Steelers' defensive back, glides quickly into the space between the two squads. When the players converge, Clark disappears amid the scrum. But it's all good. The players are not throwing punches; they're jumping up and down like pogo sticks, yelling and hugging, and Clark is as amped as the boys. "This *ain't* about football," Clark yells as he emerges from the celebration. "This about Samoa!"

* * *

Football in the United States is at a crossroads, the sport's future imperiled by the very physicality that's driven its popularity. The number of boys playing football in high school or on a team belonging to Pop Warner, the nation's largest youth program, plunged over the last decade as the neurological, physical, and fiscal costs of the game became more evident. More and more high schools are terminating their teams. But one group has bucked that trend—Polynesians, especially Samoans, in American Samoa, as well as in Hawai'i, California, Utah, and pockets of Texas and the Pacific Northwest where they have congregated.

No culture has produced such an extraordinary number of athletes per capita as American Samoa and its fraternal outposts in the United States.[2] The territory of American Samoa consists of Tutuila and its deepwater harbor at Pago Pago, the three islands comprising Manu'a, and a few coral atolls—just 76.1 square miles. These islands sit four thousand miles off the Pacific Coast, two-thirds of the way from Hawai'i to New Zealand, and are the only place in the world outside the United States where football has taken hold at the grass roots, the only one that sends its native sons to the NFL. In the forefront of high school football in several stateside locales, Samoans have become the most disproportionately overrepresented demographic in the NFL and Division I college football. Junior Seau's 2015 induction to the Pro Football Hall of Fame and Marcus Mariota's Heisman Trophy honors— both firsts for Samoans—herald a growing wave of talent. The men coaching at Pittsburgh Steeler Troy Polamalu's football camp on that rainy July day on Tutuila will tell you there's a tsunami of talent building in the Pacific.

Troy Polamalu brilliantly embodies that athletic aptitude. Although he settled easily into his surroundings, almost disappearing when he was off the field, the perennial Pro Bowl safety was the center of attention during a game. It wasn't just the hair, or the seemingly random way he dashed around before and during a play. It was his capacity to suddenly alter a game's outcome. Given the liberty to freelance within Hall of Fame defensive coordinator Dick LeBeau's complex schemes, Polamalu behaved intuitively but paradoxically with great forethought. Unable to anticipate what he might do on any play, opposing quarterbacks shuddered at the sight of him.

In 2010, when Pittsburgh returned to the Super Bowl for the third time during Polamalu's first ten seasons with the club, he was the NFL Defensive Player of the Year. Early that season, the Tennessee Titans had the ball on the Steelers' two-yard line with little time left to play. If the Titans got the ball into the end zone, they still had time to come back and win the game. As Titan quarterback Kerry Collins rushed into position behind center, Polamalu stood absolutely still, processing how Tennessee approached the line of scrimmage, the game situation, and what he sensed they would do. Suddenly, he took three quick steps toward the line of scrimmage and launched himself forward. He was in the air before the ball was snapped, but not yet over the line of scrimmage. Clearing Tennessee's crouching linemen by two feet, Polamalu unfurled his arms as he reached the apex of his trajectory. Plunging downward, he enveloped Collins just as the quarterback received the ball. Collins collapsed to the turf, with Polamalu on his back. As Polamalu popped up, Collins looked up from the turf and said, "Dude, that was a great play."

"He sees the game a little differently," Steelers coach Mike Tomlin said with understatement. "That's what makes him special."

For his 2013 football camp, Polamalu, who shuns the limelight off the field, has led a group of players and coaches to American Samoa on a *malaga*, a modern version of the traditional visiting party where members of an extended family pay their respects to relatives in a distant village. A *malaga* once lasted weeks, until the hosts' capacity to entertain their visitors was exhausted. This *malaga*, however, has not come to enjoy the island's hospitality so much as to serve its youth.

Polamalu's visiting party is composed of the sons and grandchildren of the "great *malaga*" of the 1950s—American Samoa's great migration to Hawai'i and the U.S. mainland, which remade the territory and created a stateside community now numbering 180,000. Theirs is an extended football family with origins on the Manu'a Islands, the ancestral home of the Polamalus, where the *tui* Manu'a, the highest chief in the islands, once ruled. Others hail from villages throughout the Samoan archipelago, O'ahu's North Shore, Honolulu's projects, and the Pacific Coast. A few are *palagi*, the cloud bursters, as Samoans called the first Caucasians who arrived in their midst, as if they had exploded out of the sky.

Football, as well as bloodlines, binds them. There's no greater fraternity in sport. These men have given their lives to the game and paid the price it exacts. When Polamalu invited them to the weeklong camp, he knew they would accept if they could. Their mutual affection is palpable. Teammate Ryan Clark isn't Samoan, but his son, Jordan, calls Polamalu Uncle Troy and watches over the Polamalu boys like an older brother. Clark was spot on: this isn't just about football; it's about *fa'a Samoa*—the way of Samoa.

The *malaga* had assembled at LAX earlier in the week to catch a flight for Honolulu. Soft-spoken and smiling, some elaborately tattooed, they gently bro-hugged. In Honolulu, others joined them, and they assembled in a circle before taking off for Pago Pago. First Polamalu, then his uncle Kennedy Polamalu, addressed the men. Most knew one another already. Kennedy, born on the day JFK died, coached in college and the NFL. Jesse Sapolu, the 49ers' former Pro Bowl lineman, is a Polynesian icon. Some of those here never made it to the NFL or did not last long in a league where careers can end abruptly. Like many islanders, several are of mixed ancestry. George Veikoso—the eclectic Polynesian musician commonly known as Fiji—completes the party. He's bigger than any of the players, and twice their age, but will lead all-night debauches that end in the hotel lobby at six in the morning with burgers and cold Vailima beer. His performance at an island-wide concert will cap the camp.

The men joke about aisle seats, a premium commodity given their size. But nobody rides first-class, not even Polamalu, his willowy wife, Theodora, or their curly-haired sons, Paisios and Ephraim, the latter named after the Greek Orthodox monk Elder Ephraim, who mentors Polamalu. If they all cannot fly first-class, none of them will. Polamalu's foundation is footing the camp's bill, but the wild-haired Steeler with sport's most incandescent smile defers to his uncle Kennedy, a seasoned coach with the acumen of a field commander, and Jesse Sapolu, the four-time Super Bowl champion whom many Samoans venerated as they came of age.

It's midnight by the time they clear customs at Tutuila's compact airport, break free of a welcoming crowd's embrace, and arrive at their hotel. But they're up at four thirty a.m.—their only chance to work out—and at the stadium, where hundreds of boys await them, before seven. Camp begins with a hymn. The Samoan players' voices rise, rich and nuanced. Each day of camp begins and ends that way, with song and prayer. There might not be a more devoutly Christian society on the planet than the one found here. Although they represent several Christian denominations, sectarianism is not a problem. *Fa'a Samoa*—the way of Samoa, infused with religiosity and military discipline—more powerful than doctrinal differences, binds a mix of Congregationalists, Catholics, Baptists, Methodists, and Mormons. At dusk, males belonging to the village society of untitled men known as "the strength of the village" blow conch shells from the backs of pickup trucks to announce *sa*—a time to go home and pray.

While the boys are primed to play, the morning is not about hitting, but thinking. They rotate through sessions about academics and life skills. Penny Semaia, whose family is from the tiny island village of Aunu'u, a ten-minute boat ride from Tutuila, had never set foot in Samoa until the night before. Since playing at the University of Pittsburgh, he has become a senior associate athletic director at the university. Along to teach life skills, he dares the boys to envision what they want to achieve and to confront the challenges to make those dreams real. Several men, their NFL careers over and futures murky, gravitate to Penny during the camp, seeking help in negotiating the treacherous post-football transition.

After the morning session, the hitting commences. While most of the men coaching at the camp are of Samoan ancestry, some grew up in the States and had little contact with American Samoa. Others are from independent Samoa, what many call the motherland. Because of late-nineteenth-century geopolitics, there are two Samoas—the football-playing U.S. territory and the rugby bastion of Samoa, which achieved its independence in 1962. But people from both polities say that they're one people with one culture.

American Samoa and Samoa never completely disentangled, and football and rugby, which came via New Zealand, remain conjoined. Boys in both Samoas grow up playing rugby, and Samoans, who number fewer than a million worldwide, have become as prominent in the game as American Samoans are in football. They're wildly overrepresented in European and Pacific leagues and at the core of New Zealand's World Cup champions, the All Blacks. Rugby, like football, has taken on a Polynesian cast, but Polamalu's camp is focused on football.

A dozen NFLers work it, surrendering the rest of their off-season to give back to the culture that made them who they are. Domata Peko, who was raised here, wears a *lavalava* wraparound over his Cincinnati Bengals shorts as he demonstrates techniques. His long hair, fluttering in the breeze, is almost as recognizable as Polamalu's. Peko, Eagles nose tackle Isa'ako

Sopoaga, and 49ers guard Mike Iupati are part of an expanding NFL contingent of players who grew up here.

The boys are dead serious about football, but they're having fun doing something they love. Smiles and laughter infuse the drills, although getting a Samoan to smile is never difficult. The coaches find the boys' commitment infectious. They're whooping and hollering, none more than Ryan Clark. He and Polamalu have been soul mates in the Steelers secondary, though both knew that the upcoming football campaign would likely be their last as teammates.[3] While Troy is quiet and reflective, Ryan is abuzz, zigzagging around the field, teaching and exhorting.

Sweat pours off the boys. Rain—which averages 125 to 300 inches a year—provides some respite, as do frequent water breaks. For most of the boys, this is their third camp of the summer, on top of daily training. Faga'itua High School coach Su'aese "Pooch" Ta'ase began workouts in February. His boys are from Tutuila's east side, where the only businesses are bush stores. The players run up the mountain each morning before chores, returning later for four-hour practices. Their school has few students, but no team outworks them. And no coach is as dedicated as Pooch, a five-foot-six-inch fireplug attired in Faga'itua red.

Pooch stresses academics, but the NFL looms larger each season and education often suffers. Many who go off island do not last long in school. Some avoid returning home. "Not finishing that degree," Cheryl Morales, the director of the Feleti Barstow Public Library, tells me, "is like getting half a tattoo. It's embarrassing to the person, his family, and his village." The traditional tattoo, a painful rite of manhood, covers much of a man's lower body. The master tattooist strikes a sharpened boar tusk with a mallet to ink its symmetrical patterns. The tattoo, done with ceremonial rigor, takes a week to complete and bears little resemblance to those adorning many young American athletes. It's considered shameful not to endure the pain and to quit before it is complete. So is returning without a degree.

For the moment, here are their heroes, whispering instructions and grabbing them in bear hugs. Domata Peko pulls a boy up by his shoulder pads after he pancakes his opponent in a blocking drill; Ryan Clark high-steps with excitement when another boy intercepts a pass. During breaks, coaches testify. Mike Iupati, a young giant with a quasi-Mohawk cut, was San Francisco's 2010 first-round draft pick. "You have an opportunity to change your family's life," the Samoan-born guard says. "There's limited opportunity in Samoa. That's a fact. This is a chance for you." Nobody thought much of Iupati's chances when he arrived at the University of Idaho as a freshman, unable to play or receive a scholarship because of a weak academic record. But he persevered in the classroom and endured injuries that prevented him from competing. By his senior year, Iupati was one of the top linemen in college football. "Don't follow temptation, especially up there," he cautions. Many Samoan youth, accustomed to strict discipline, succumb on the mainland when they're on their own. "It's hard to sacrifice eight years in school," Iupati concedes, tearing up and breaking into Samoan, the boys' default language.

By early this century, hundreds of Samoans were playing NCAA Division I football, hundreds more at junior colleges, and dozens in the NFL. About fifty Samoans from as far away as New Zealand report to NFL camps each summer. That's from a U.S. population of 235,000 Samoans—55,000 on the islands comprising American Samoa, the rest in the States, mostly Hawai'i and California.[4]

About a tenth of the Samoans currently playing college ball came directly from the territory, where the game arrived in the 1960s. But the territory is sending more native sons to the States each year. Nobody knows the actual number because nobody keeps track and because Samoans are so mobile. In the fall of 2013, more than thirty boys who played high school football on the island were on Division I rosters. Those rosters included a larger group of players who were born in American Samoa but left to play high school ball in the States. Hundreds more attend lower-division schools and junior colleges, although most never make it to a D-I school. Those who do, however, often go on to the NFL.

That makes Samoans a unique source of football talent. Of American sports, football is the most beholden to boys who grew up in the United States. Major League Baseball, the NBA, and the NHL tap other countries for more than a quarter of their player force. But football has remained almost exclusively a North American sport—except for the fast-multiplying Samoans and their island neighbors from Tonga, who picked up the game in the States.

*   *   *

Samoans' presence in football is in part a function of global capitalism reducing sport and its players to a tradeable commodity. But capitalism has never been the entire story behind excellence and meaning in sport, and certainly not the most interesting one. Though American notions about sport came along on football's South Seas journey, Samoans redefined the game's meaning and made it a way to shout their story to the world.

And that redefinition propels their success. Though Samoans are physically imposing and tough, their exploits are not the results of inherent natural superiority. What makes them so good at the sport—their discipline and warrior bearing—are the end products of a culture that resisted conquest and colonization but embraced Christianity in the 1800s and the U.S. military during World War II. No group under the U.S. flag has contributed a greater percentage of its men and women to the military.

Fa'a Samoa has created a fiercely competitive culture in which sport really is, as George Orwell wrote, war minus the shooting.[5] Samoans once prized taking heads in battle, but the *hakas* or *siva taus* they perform before games now are ceremonial and psychological. Still, the warrior spirit survives. These young men are willing to risk their bodies every time out, whether on the gridiron or the battlefields of Afghanistan and Iraq. Their capacity to overcome fear is part of what makes them so good, not some imagined genetic advantage.

But it's a bittersweet narrative. There's a cost to this devotion to football, to playing with *no fefe* (no fear). Samoan boys, who train year-round on fields blistered with volcanic pebbles and use helmets that would have been discarded long ago in the States, almost certainly incur far more neurological damage than their counterparts elsewhere. And this microculture of sporting excellence cannot conceal its lamentable public health woes. Samoans are among the most diabetic and obese people on the planet.

I went to American Samoa because I was interested in how a sport changed as it moved around the world. I also wanted to understand why a place like Samoa fostered such an extraordinary concentration of talented athletes. There's no question that global capitalism, which transformed sport from a local, noncommercial pastime that people created and organized on their own into corporate moneyball, helped to create sporting microcultures. But did sport also become so good in these settings because it mattered more to the people who lived there—not because of its bottom line but because it built social capital and forged a collective sense of purpose?

The Samoan islands gave me the chance to look at these questions in a community far away from any I've studied. I remember my first day there, sitting by the water's edge, shaking off the effects of the twenty-four hours it took to get from Pittsburgh to Pago Pago. I was trying to make sense of what I was seeing—boys hurling their bodies into one another under a scorching sun, tattooed coaches teaching in a mix of Samoan and English, and a woman wiping blood off an injured boy's leg with a Terrible Towel after he hobbled off the field before pushing him back to the fray. I was scrambling to frame American Samoa in terms I understood and instinctively compared it to the Dominican Republic.

That Caribbean nation of 10 million people currently accounts for more than a tenth of all major league baseball players and a third of those in the minors. Like American Samoa, it embraced an imported sport and made it into its own pastime, one that Dominicans came to play as well as any nationality in the world. In American Samoa, the game introduced from afar was football, not baseball; the people spoke Samoan rather than Spanish; and the island was south of the equator instead of to its north. But both American Samoa and the Dominican Republic produced disproportionate numbers of athletes who played with fury and panache. And in each culture, sport conveyed meanings that went beyond financial reward.

Before I left the island a month later, I realized my comparison with the Dominican Republic ignored how different its backstory was from that of American Samoa. Samoans were never enslaved or subjected to the demographic wipeout that affected the Americas and Hawai'i. Nor had foreign companies seized Samoans' land and controlled their labor as they did in the Caribbean. Compared to Dominicans, Samoans retained much more autonomy. *Fa'a Samoa* was rooted in a three-thousand-year history that still defined the present.

But that autonomy was under siege by Germany, Great Britain, and the United States when Robert Louis Stevenson arrived in the late nineteenth century. After the United States wound up with a few islands that became the territory of American Samoa, it largely forgot about them. The islands benefited from America's benign neglect until World War II. That conflict made the people of American Samoa into fervent patriots and offered island-ers a bridge to Hawai'i and the mainland. War also changed the territory's economy and culture—upending a traditional society and its subsistence way of life.

The closure of the island's economic mainstay—the U.S. naval base—in 1951 jump-started an exodus to Hawai'i and California. The sons and grandsons of that migration took to football, as would boys in the territory after the sport was introduced during the Cold War. These boys grew up *fa'a Samoa*; they came of age as members of an *'aiga* (an extended family), a village, and a church that demanded and received their allegiance. So did the *matai*, the chiefs who led their *'aiga*, and their parents, many of whom were members of the military. They internalized a sense of discipline and a commitment to service, which translated well when they joined a football team. So did their self-identity as warriors. They Americanized but never stopped being Samoan. Half a century after their migration off island began, Samoans are at the forefront of the sport, in large measure because they still train and play in the way of Samoa.

On the camp's final day, players scrimmage. "It's time for thud," one coach says, "but let's keep them from hurting each other." Junior Seau's shadow hangs ominously over the camp. Just a year earlier, the first Samoan in the Hall of Fame killed himself with a bullet to his chest because he could not live with the demons that came with chronic traumatic encephalopathy—the damage caused by concussive blows to the brain. Though Seau was never diagnosed with a concussion during his twenty-season pro career, his death alarmed many in the Polynesian football world. Stoic to the point of denial, many Samoans have only begrudgingly acknowledged the damage that football does to the brain. Unlike almost every high school, college, and pro squad in the United States, American Samoa's high school teams do not conduct preseason baseline concussion impact examinations, which can be used to monitor a player in case of an incident. The boys I talked with seemed unaware of the threat to their brains.

The coaches at the camp are more at peace with the physical price of having played. Many walk with difficulty, their bodies displaying the long-term effects of football's trauma. They seem prematurely aged. A few admit that they worry about the consequences of the concussions they incurred. It can trigger dementia and aberrant behavior. But most don't want to talk about it.[6]

Hours later, as the last whistle blows, the rains come. Within minutes, the field is a rice paddy. Four-year-old Paisios Polamalu twirls in the rain, his hair splayed Bob Marley–style. Everyone else retreats to the stands and teams select players to break-dance on the stage erected for Fiji's concert. Boys juke and swirl with an agility that comes from practicing traditional dance at school every year since kindergarten and walking barefoot or in *slippas*, as flip-flops are called in the Pacific. Even the linemen are nimble-footed. Their smaller teammates at the skilled positions will often add fifty or sixty pounds when they go off island and are exposed to training tables and weight rooms. That combination of size and dexterity intoxicates college coaches.

Then they sing. Someone shouts out a phrase and the squads break into a hymn they learned in childhood. The minister of education praises the coaches and remarks that tradition says that it's a blessing when it rains. She asks Polamalu to speak. Ephraim, asleep, is draped over his father's shoulder while Troy thanks the boys "for an experience we'll never forget." He does not speak long, ending, "The longer I talk, the more I'll cry." A team leads a final hymn and camp closes with a prayer.

1

God's Sweetest Work

Robert Louis Stevenson, who spent the last years of his life on the island of Upolu, in what was then German-controlled Western Samoa, once called Polynesians "God's best, at least God's sweetest, works."[1] The Scottish author, wandering the South Pacific in search of a refuge where he might write and repair his brittle health, arrived in Samoa in December 1890. He was a twitchy, chain-smoking mess, exhausted by his voyage from Hawai'i aboard a pygmy schooner built to carry copra, the dried kernel of the coconut from which oil was squeezed. Bouts of stifling heat and squalls that almost sank the ship had tormented him. For days on end, he stayed belowdecks, sitting up in his berth trying to write, coughing up blood. Entering Apia harbor on the island of Upolu, Stevenson's schooner passed by the rusting hulks of warships destroyed by a recent hurricane.

Though desperate to discover a haven, he did not expect to find one in Samoa. That changed abruptly. Unexpectedly smitten, Stevenson halted his transpacific journey and made Upolu his home. Villa Vailima, the dwelling he built on the slopes of Mount Vaea, became his Eden. But it was not enough to heal Stevenson's riddled body. He died there four years later. By then, he had come to understand Samoa like few foreigners and was loved by Samoans like no other.

Stevenson could have hardly found Samoans more simpatico; nor could he have been less enamored with Western influence on their islands. He set to work learning the language, interrogating islanders for hours about their lives and folkways. He found them merry and easygoing, "the gayest, though by far from either the most capable or the most beautiful of Polynesians." They lived on land that had been communally owned by extended families—the 'aiga—for a few thousand years. He admired their chiefs (the matai), especially the high talking chiefs, whose storytelling entranced him with its connections to a premodern past. "We [the West] are in the thick of the age of finance," Stevenson mused; "they are in a period of communism. And that makes them hard to understand."[2]

Stevenson relished his time in Samoa but feared for its future. After what he had encountered in Hawai'i—the island's loss of sovereignty, smug missionaries, and bullying by sugar plantations—he doubted imperialism's beneficence. He lamented what he saw as the unjust yet inevitable "extinction of the Polynesian Islanders by our shabby civilization." He warned Samoans gathered at Villa Vailima of a perilous future. "You and your children," he told his guests, are in danger of being "cast out into outer darkness, where shall be weeping and gnashing of teeth. . . . I have seen [these events] with my eyes—these judgments of God. I have seen them in Ireland, and I have seen them in the mountains of my own country—Scotland—and my heart was sad."[3]

Stevenson witnessed the tensions roiling Samoa, especially the conflict between Western modernity and South Pacific tradition. He tried to understand the people, an effort few Westerners made. Stevenson noted their Christian devotion—European missionaries had taken the island by storm sixty years earlier when their evangelizing schooner *The Messenger of Peace* anchored in Samoa—and praised them as hardy cricketers but was not blind to their turbulent past. He described them as "the contemporaries of our tattooed ancestors who drove their chariots on the wrong side of the Roman wall."[4] After he died, his closest friend on the island, American expat Harry J. Moors, wrote, "To [Samoans] he was a prophet; by them he was honoured as a man set apart from his fellows."[5]

But not even a prophet could have foretold Jesse Sapolu, Junior Seau, and

Troy Polamalu, much less the eruption of Samoans in Western sport. Stevenson could not anticipate what would happen when those tattooed chariot drivers jumped the wall, embraced cricket, rugby, and football, and brought their game to the West.

Joe Strong, Stevenson's feckless son-in-law, had alerted Moors that the writer, his wife, Fanny, and her son Lloyd were stopping in Samoa during their South Pacific tour. At the peak of his celebrity in 1890, Stevenson had published a dozen books in the last decade, among them *Treasure Island*, *Kidnapped*, and *The Strange Case of Dr. Jekyll and Mr. Hyde*. When the *Equator* appeared in Apia harbor, Moors, a trader, entrepreneur, and schemer from Michigan, rowed out to greet them. He knew Stevenson was heralded for his novels, but he was initially underwhelmed. Moors recalled Stevenson's sallow complexion, scraggly mustache, and bohemian demeanor. The author was barefoot, wearing a calico shirt and flannel trousers, with hair hanging down his neck. "He was not a handsome man, and yet there was something irresistibly attractive about him," Moors remembered. "The genius that was in him seemed to shine out of his face."[6]

"I needed not be told he was in indifferent health," Moors said, "for it was stamped on his face." Stevenson, high-strung and anxious, could hardly stand still. At Moors's home, Stevenson darted about, asking a jumble of questions as he leapt from one subject to another. "The long lonesome trip on the schooner had quite unnerved [him]," Moors later wrote.[7]

Moors soon became enamored of his scrawny forty-year-old houseguest, who spun tales into the night. He became Stevenson's comrade and informant. They shared a wanderlust as well as a concern for their adopted island's future. Stevenson overcame his initial misgivings about Moors, who had dealt in "blackbirds"—islanders abducted into plantation labor. He thought Moors was "not of the best character" and at first was repulsed by him, but he also found Moors greatly knowledgeable about Samoa and a likable companion.

After twenty thousand nautical miles of travel, Stevenson was reluctant to return to sea. When his health and spirits responded to his new surroundings, he impulsively decided to settle there. Upolu offered a Polynesian paradise with monthly mail ships from San Francisco via Sydney—a connection that would allow Stevenson to publish, as well as receive Belgian chocolates, wine, books, and blocks of ice. He wrote his friend Henry James: "I do not think I shall come to England more than once, and then it'll be to die." It was not just that he could no longer tolerate England's damp, cold weather. He preferred Samoa. "The sea, islands, the islanders, the island life and climate, make and keep me truly happier."[8]

Moors, whom he tasked with finding land, proposed a four-hundred-acre plot on the side of Mount Vaea that was part of a village called Vailima. Rising fifteen hundred feet above sea level, the location was cooler and less humid than Apia. Villa Vailima, the name Stevenson gave his residence, came from the five streams and waterfalls that snake through its thick forests.[9] Wild taro, bananas, breadfruit, and papaya still flourish there among banyan trees stretching hundreds of feet overhead. Flying foxes and frigate birds glide over a treetop canopy.

Stevenson paid $4,000 for the land, and considerably more to build a two-story residence with a wide veranda and imposing view. He imported prized possessions from his home in Bournemouth, then a burgeoning resort town on the south coast of England; California redwood for a ballroom; and seltzer bottles from the Magnet Bottling Company in New York for the smoking room.[10]

In the century since Stevenson settled on Upolu, Apia has sprawled up the slopes of Mount Vaea, enveloping Vailima. After his death, a succession of political figures—the German governor of Western Samoa, New Zealand's resident authority, and the Samoan head of state—lived there. In 1995, a century after Stevenson's death, Vailima became a house museum. The grandeur of Vailima's natural surroundings lends it a frozen-in-time ambience. A crown jewel for the island, it's also the name of the national beer.

The Samoan archipelago is a cluster of islands surrounded by the open sea. Savai'i and Upolu are the biggest isles in independent Samoa, while Tutuila—where Troy Polamalu's camp is held—is the largest landmass in the American territory. American Samoa also includes three smaller islands known as Manu'a, which lie sixty-eight miles east of Tutuila. All are volcanic outcroppings with a profusion of flowers and trees covering jagged hillsides. Coral reef fringes the coast, which alternates between sandy beaches and foreboding rock. Tonga and Fiji, the closest island groups, are five hundred miles away. Their inhabitants share similar cultural and linguistic characteristics with Samoans, but also a history of ferocious combat. Auckland, New Zealand, lies even farther away, eighteen hundred miles to the southwest, while Tahiti is fifteen hundred miles to the east.

After experiencing the terror of storms at sea in a seventy-six-ton ship, Stevenson appreciated the courage of the ancient Samoan navigators, who had sailed and paddled thousands of miles in outrigger canoes, orienting themselves by reading the color and texture of clouds, the ocean swells, and the flight of birds. But thousands of miles of ocean could no longer isolate Samoans from global pressures. German planters threatened village lands, warships steamed through their waters, and Western ways jeopardized *fa'a Samoa*.

Not long after settling there, Stevenson, whom everybody called Louis, took it upon himself to alert Europeans and Americans to their nations' baleful influence in the region. The years he spent exploring the South Pacific had soured him on the age of empire. In Apia, he saw the human detritus of whalers, seafaring scoundrels, and rapacious traders that had washed up on its shores and rendered the waterfront a drab, dispiriting place.

Europeans had first set eyes on Samoa in 1722, when Dutch captain Jacob Roggeveen passed by without incident on a Dutch West India Company expedition. Subsequent encounters ended badly. Sixty years later, French comte La Pérouse came upon Manu'a. "These Islanders," he declared upon arrival, "are undoubtedly the most happy inhabitants of the earth." La Pérouse found them wanting little. But before he left the islands, a dozen of his French sailors and a greater number of Samoans died at Fagasa Bay after confusion turned an exchange of goods into a battle. The massacre, missionary George Turner wrote in 1861, "branded [Samoans] for fifty years as a race of treacherous savages, whose shores ought not to be approached."[11] That reputation kept most visitors away, but not whalers or Christian missionaries, who made surprising headway.

When the Germans arrived to set up plantations in the late 1800s, they used overwhelming force. Samoan war clubs were no match for warships that could shell villages from the sea and land marines. Stevenson, offended by German bullying, crafted widely read polemics to *The Times* of London.[12] Despite readers, publishers, and an agent craving another bestselling tale of adventure, he wrote *A Footnote to History*, an account of Samoan politics and meddling by the great powers.[13]

German interest was commercial and imperial. The Deutsche Handels und Plantagen Gesellschaft der Sud See Inseln zu Hamburg, aka the Firm, was grabbing as much land as possible. Apia became the collection point for produce, especially copra. Its residue became cattle feed or was used to make coconut rock candy.[14]

When Samoans proved unwilling laborers, the Firm imported blackbirds. These men and women, mostly from Melanesia, toiled in slave-like conditions on copra, coffee, and cacao plantations. Working hand in glove with the German consul, the Firm counted on armed support from its government, which looked at the South Seas as a zone of imperial influence.

While ambivalent about annexing further territory itself, the United States was unwilling to allow German and British inroads in the region at its expense. Nor was Washington eager to see alliances form among the indigenous people of Hawai'i, Samoa, and other islands at a time when the United States and European nations were pressing one form or another of the "white man's burden" on the world.

The Pacific loomed large in the United States' future, and the islands' location raised their profile in Washington, especially at the War Department. While Hawai'i dwarfed the Samoan islands, Pago Pago offered an unsurpassed deepwater port that would extend U.S. sway in the Pacific and secure trade routes to China and Japan. Nor was Great Britain, the world's principal imperial power, without ambitions in Polynesia.[15]

Stevenson arrived after Germany gained the upper hand. Though he found each of the three powers complicit, he considered Germany the chief culprit and damned the Firm as "the head of the boil."[16] The Samoans, however, were not idyllic innocents. A notoriously contentious people, they fought with one another over land, prestige, and authority at the slightest provocation. The imperial powers, especially Germany, had inflamed matters by introducing deadlier weapons. The consequences were toxic and destabilizing.[17]

German depredations—offshore shelling and the razing of rebel villages—led to a brutal Samoan counterattack in Vailele in December 1888. Samoans killed or wounded almost half of the 140 German blue-jackets sent ashore, mutilating bodies with their war clubs, decapitating some soldiers, and cutting off the ears of others. "All of Samoa," Stevenson wrote, "drew a breath of wonder and delight. The invincible had fallen." When this humiliation prompted Germany to send warships to Apia, the United States and Great Britain responded in kind. Meanwhile, Harry Moors, the British, and the Germans armed rival Samoan factions, and blood was shed in a cascade of ambushes and battles surpassing anything in Samoan history. The Germans held the British and Americans responsible for their losses. Stevenson agreed. "Germans lay dead, the German wounded groaned in their cots; and the cartridges by which they fell had been sold by an American and brought into the country in a British [ship]."[18]

Efforts to craft a diplomatic resolution to big-power rivalries floundered. Threats and accusations, heavy-handed posturing, and a harbor full of warships made Apia a flashpoint. But before the warships could trigger a global conflict, force majeure blasted imperial aspirations out of the water.[19]

On March 15, 1889, a tempest turned deadly. As a typhoon swept toward Upolu, three German warships, the *Eber*, the *Adler*, and the *Olga*; three American vessels, the *Nipsic*, the *Vandalia*, and the *Trenton*; and a lone British ship, the *Calliope*, crowded Apia harbor. Additional German sailors were quartered in town to protect their interests from Mata'afa, a rebel chief who had assembled an army of six thousand warriors in the bush. The island was about to explode, but before it could, the skies burst with even greater violence.

When the barometer plunged, the ships' commanders did not do what their nautical instincts told them they must—leave the harbor for deeper, safer waters. To leave first would be a sign of weakness that might allow their rivals to gain the upper hand. Their posturing was foolish. Before the hurricane was over, the *Eber* had vanished beneath the sea, the *Nipsic* was beached, and the *Adler* impaled on a reef. Almost 150 sailors drowned. Samoans rescued others by forming a human chain into the sea. Only the *Calliope* escaped unscathed.[20]

At first light on March 17, Stevenson wrote that he saw "a scene of devastation . . . the beach heaped high with the debris of ships and the wreck of mountain forests." That day, he said, "the sword-arm of each of the two angry powers was broken, their formidable ships reduced to junk. . . . Both paused aghast; both had time to recognize that not the whole Samoan Archipelago was worth the loss in men and costly ships already suffered."[21]

Gale-force winds and hundred-foot-tall waves had flattened imperial conceit, and the three powers convened a month later in Berlin to avoid war over islands most of their citizens could not find on a map.[22] The sale of land to foreigners was halted, as was the importation of liquor and arms. Otherwise, Samoan interests were ignored and their sovereignty compromised. Great Britain renounced its interests in the islands in return for German acknowledgment of their suzerainty over Tonga and the Solomon Islands. Germany held on to Upolu and Savai'i, a larger if less-developed island a few miles away. These islands were regarded—at least by Europeans and Americans—as German Western Samoa.

The United States got what it wanted, the smaller, easternmost islands that would be named American Samoa. The poor cousin in every respect, it was neither as powerful, nor as profitable, nor as politically significant as Western Samoa.[23]

Stevenson, arriving in the wake of these geopolitical maneuvers, often rode his horse Jack along the coast through small villages on Upolu's scalloped coves. In contrast to Apia, which suffered from a crush of whalers, traders, planters, and foreigners fleeing the law (British consul William Churchward called it the Hell of the Pacific), the villages seemed idyllic. They hugged thin coastal flatlands at the foot of hillsides that rose abruptly into jagged mountains coated in green.

Fa'a Samoa fascinated Stevenson. Enamored with his own Scottish past, he realized that the Samoans tapped an even longer heritage. They had occupied the archipelago for three thousand years after arriving from islands to their west. People lived in *fales*, conical thatch-roofed homes open to the breeze and clustered on land that had belonged to the *'aiga* for a thousand years. Each *'aiga*, an extended grouping knit by blood, marriage, and adoption, had a guest house, and each village at least one church.

If amenable to Christianity, Samoans were indifferent to the lures of capitalism. Instead, each *'aiga* hacked out hillside plantations, cultivating taro, breadfruit, bananas, and a profusion of fruits. Men paddled into deep waters to catch bonito; women and children trapped fish and octopus or gathered sea urchins in shallow, coral-fringed coves. Between what they took from their plantations and what they harvested from the sea, Samoans enjoyed a self-sufficiency that left them disinclined to work for German planters.

A hierarchy of chiefs, the *matai*, directed *'aiga* life, which rested on communal production. The paramount high chief, chosen by consensus, governed with near total power and served as their steward. He could tell families where to build their *fales* but was not empowered to sell or otherwise dispose of 'aiga land. If there was a funeral or wedding, the *matai* told 'aiga members what to contribute in terms of food or fine mats, which were prized artistic creations woven from pandanus leaves. Moreover, the paramount chief assigned work. He sent some to the plantation, others to fish, trap marine life, or build a boat or *fale*. Afterward, he redistributed the fruits of their labor.[24]

Eager to explore local mores, Stevenson rode deep into the bush. He saw the communal ways in which land was held and the lack of want among people who could always find enough to eat from what they grew or took from the sea. He admired what he called their "loose communism." Stevenson also described Samoans as embracing "the sound and smoke of battle with delight, their ardor and bravery worthy of Waterloo and other battles on the European plains."[25]

That loose communism was a point of contention for the Germans, British, New Zealanders, and Americans who worked there. After Germany gained control of Western Samoa in the 1890s, Governor Wilhelm Solf wrote that "the natives are ignorant, they have to be instructed; they are lazy and have to learn to work; they are dirty and have to be washed." Samoans, he complained, were "savage, cruel and superstitious [and] must be soothed and illuminated."[26] But Samoans chafed at German rule. Rather than maximizing profit, *fa'a Samoa* favored reciprocity, leisure, and respect for elders.

Stevenson, who had witnessed the degradation wrought by industrialization in Great Britain, was sympathetic to Samoa's traditional ways. He saw that capitalism, a force for upheaval wherever it took hold, had found it tougher going in Samoa. Collectively owned land negated notions of private property, while *fa'a Samoa* proved resilient. Rejecting the ethos of commercialism and acquisitive individualism, Samoa was better able to withstand the demolition of indigenous culture that occurred throughout the South Seas.[27]

That resistance to the lures of the Protestant ethic troubled foreign powers seeking to bend Samoan culture to their agendas. Predisposed by prevailing racial attitudes, they tagged Polynesians as primitives. Because American Samoa was unsuited to plantation agriculture, U.S. Navy governors were less concerned with productivity and profit than German and New Zealand planters in Western Samoa, and the Navy's benevolent paternalism was tempered by fears of destroying indigenous culture. Accordingly, the United States ruled lightly.

Naval governors argued that Samoans should retain control over daily life and be Westernized slowly. "Developing the semi-civilized Samoan into a fully civilized condition must take time," Commander Benjamin Tilley reflected on Christmas Day 1900. If not, the United States "will produce a creature something like the precociously developed Negro in our country." Moreover, he feared that Samoans would become "a dependent people" if too much was done for them. Tilley favored teaching them practical, manual arts, concluding that "book knowledge will not be of much value to the present generation of native children."[28]

After visiting the territory a decade later, the Carnegie Institute's Charles Davenport warned President Woodrow Wilson not to force American modernity down Samoan throats and despoil this vigorous, if economically primitive, native population. "Our dealings with the American Indians," Davenport stressed, "illustrate the disastrous results of this procedure."[29]

U.S. Navy governors perceived Samoans as good-hearted but childish and unable to sustain effort once immediate needs were satisfied. Admiral C. B. T. Moore lamented that their willingness to feed any visitor and share whatever they had made life too easy. Because nobody was homeless or in need of food or clothing, Samoans had no incentive to aspire to a "more highly civilized" way of life.[30] Seeking to spark a Western work ethic, Moore forbade cricket matches or games between villages without his approval. But he was no more successful in suppressing the sport than the Germans and New Zealanders in Western Samoa.[31] Cricket, at least the Samoan version of the sport they called *kirikiti*, was often a flashpoint for Western frustrations with Samoan culture.

Cricket appeared on Upolu a few years before Stevenson stepped ashore. In 1881, when William Churchward arrived as the British consul, neither he nor other Brits on the island could persuade a single Samoan to join them in cricket. He found that remarkable, because on Tonga, the natives "were always ready for a game." Then, Churchward wrote, "all at once the village of Apia Samoa was seized with a most frantic desire to fathom the mysteries of the game."[32] Samoans adopted cricket, he argued, after Tongan visitors "twitted them on the subject of their ignorance of so grand an amusement." That could not stand.

A deputation of *matai* beseeched Churchward and officers aboard the HMS *Diamond*, a British corvette in the harbor, to instruct them in "the strict '*Fa'a Peritania*'—British manner—of playing cricket, for that was the version they wanted to learn, and not the '*Fa'a Tonga*'—Tongan—one." Reasoning that cricket was a British sport, the Samoans believed the British could best convey the ethos and skills of the game. "They thought that we could teach them in such a way that they might be able to beat these boasting men."

The British relished the chance to showcase their talent. In January 1883, the officers of the *Diamond*, the *Miranda*, and the flagship *Nelson* went at it on the Apia Cricket Association's new grounds. The game merited a write-up in *The Mercury*, published in Hobart, Tasmania.[33] But Samoans were not interested in aping the British style of play.

While picking up how to bowl, bat, and field from their tutors, they rejected the British recreational ideology that accompanied the game. "The quiet and serious English style did not suit them long," Churchward recalled. "One by one, innovations of their own manufacture crept into the game, until soon nothing remained of cricket, *pur et simple*, but the practice of one man bowling to another man trying to hit it." Instead, Samoan cricket meant feasting and parade, "becoming," Churchward wrote, "quite an epidemic."

Churchward marveled at how Samoans approached cricket. "The processions on match-days are fearful and wonderful to behold." Wearing outfits adopted for the sport, team members marched "in swaggering military order" to the beat of penny whistles and drums. Each player shouldered his bat "as though it 'twere a war-club, and, at the word of command from their officers, goes through an entire special manual exercise whilst *en route* to the field." The team's officers, dressed in naval uniforms with swords and cocked hats, kept the players in formation and exhorted them to display their manliness as villagers closed ranks behind those doing "battle for the credit of the village." Churchward reveled in the pageantry, with each team having "a distinct method of expressing its joy at the dismissal of an adversary from the wickets." Their displays were so elaborate that he was sure that teams drilled on their routines in private.[34]

Samoans adapted cricket, which they called *kirikiti*, so that any number could play. British teams fielded a mere eleven players, with a clear demarcation between players and spectators. Not Samoans. "I have known them to play as many as 200 odd a side," Churchward exclaimed. "The fact is, that these matches are of one town against another, in which all insist upon taking a hand. These huge meetings, as may be readily imagined, last a week or more, junketing going on the whole time, and generally wind up with a big feast."

Cricket fever spread to neighboring islands. "Age, sex and dignity alike fell under its influence, until at last there was not a village in which it was not vigorously practised to such a degree as to seriously interfere with domestic affairs." British authorities had seen this happen in Tonga, where they tried to limit cricket to one day a week. German authorities were even more appalled by its impact on production and tried to ban it entirely. They castigated the sport as a "British-induced mania." The Germans, Churchward argued, saw the Samoan love affair with cricket as "an inclination to favour things British, which it always was their studied practice to condemn and underrate, to the glorification of their own importance." While Germans suppressed the game in Apia, outlying villages paid them no mind.[35]

Churchward, constantly contending with German aspirations, was delighted that it became the "practice of the Apia men on turning out for a match to halt in front of my Consulate, and drawn up in line receive word of command, 'Salute the British Consul!' whereupon the whole line would perform a studied exercise with their bats and arms" while the village band played. Churchward relished how much this sporting homage upset the Germans, who never received such displays of respect.[36]

The Germans might have benefited from paying more attention to sport in Samoa.[37] Given how tenaciously Samoans played, they should have asked themselves: how hard would they fight? Because for Samoans, sport was often as rough as war. Both were conducted with violence and ritual. The 'aumaga, the society of untitled men known as the strength of the village, led the way in both. During times of peace, Samoans practiced war, throwing spears, fighting with clubs, wrestling, and slinging rocks. Insults, intended or not, and disputes over titles and land provoked violence. "Discord among village communities or families was a daily occurrence in former times and one might say that there was constantly something stirring on Samoa," wrote German anthropologist Augustin Kramer, "but it was always merely a local affair and no one paid any attention to it." That changed with Western intervention.[38]

Becoming a warrior defined manhood. The ultimate feat was to take a head in battle. William Pritchard saw that in 1848 as he entered Apia harbor, where his father, George, had become the British consul after serving with the London Missionary Society. The nineteen-year-old, who years later succeeded his father as consul, heard musket shots and shouting as his brig neared land. A fleet of war canoes approached. A warrior, face blackened and body oiled, stood in the bow of each canoe, shouting and whirling a club overhead, the head of a man he had slain at his feet. "The gallant warrior," Pritchard explained, was "proclaiming his own prowess and daring, and the pedigree of the enemy whose head was the trophy he exhibited."[39]

Kramer described how a warrior, carrying a head with its hair clenched in his teeth, delivered the trophy to his chief. The more distinguished heads were set atop a pile on the village green. If left unclaimed, they were given to children to play with or thrown to the dogs. Older informants told Kramer that warriors frequently devoured the toes, eyes, and hearts of those they slew to disgrace their foes and acquire their strength.[40]

When Samoans challenged another village to *kirikiti* they followed ritual preparations akin to those for going to battle. The high talking chief addressed the *'aumaga*, reminding them of village history and calling for sacrifice in the contest to come. On one occasion, in 1885, sport and war converged. A war party of two hundred men from Upolu traveled to Savai'i masquerading as a cricket team, Winchester rifles concealed underneath their cricket bats. But, Churchward noted, "as is usual in all things Samoan, no secret can be long kept," and once their cover was blown, the attack was called off.[41]

Though rugby became Samoa's national sport, *kirikiti* never disappeared, nor did its practitioners accept the dictates of British play. Students at the Malifa School organized the first cricket team in 1921. Avele College, a boarding school for boys studying agriculture, soon joined them. Students were told to bring a *kirikiti* bat along with clothing and eating utensils when reporting to school.[42] Their teachers, a mix of missionaries and New Zealanders who arrived during World War I, tried to teach cricket, not *kirikiti*, but Samoans had too thoroughly embraced their own style of play to comply.

Stevenson was no athlete, but he turned Vailima's wide front lawn into a field of play, where family, staff, and visitors came together for impromptu sessions of croquet, cricket, and rugby. For cricket balls, they used oranges.[43] Stevenson saw cricket wherever he traveled on the island, but not with the pressed white uniforms and carefully laid-out pitches redolent of London's Marylebone Cricket Club. Samoan cricket bore a closer resemblance to the traditional football (soccer) games of preindustrial England, where entire towns engaged in rough, no-holds-barred matches to celebrate festivals. "Games are popular," Stevenson wrote. "Cricket matches, where a hundred played on a side, endured at times for weeks, and ate up the country like the presence of an army."[44]

More than a century later, a young man working at Villa Vailima told me, "When I grew up, I hadn't heard of cricket. I just knew *of kirikiti*. I thought that Samoans had invented the game." He pointed to a Panama rubber tree, explaining that he and other boys made balls from its latex fiber. The *pate*, or bat, was fashioned from a breadfruit or hibiscus tree. His village, Fasito'o Uta, approached *kirikiti* with great ceremony, if less so than in his grand-parents' generation. Visiting rugby teams were welcomed with elaborate greetings, too. "Ceremony was a must for village competitions," he insisted. "Manu Samoa, our national rugby team, still has a welcoming ceremony for visiting teams."

The outbreak of war in 1914 abruptly ended German dominion over Western Samoa. When New Zealand's expeditionary force appeared in Apia harbor weeks after war began in Europe, the German governor, Erich Schultz, surrendered without a fight. Resistance, he realized, was futile. New Zealand's flag was raised at Villa Vailima, where he had resided.

Western Samoa was at peace for the duration, but no place was hit harder by the Spanish influenza pandemic that killed millions around the world. In November 1918 a steamer from Auckland arrived carrying a missionary infected with influenza. The war had just ended and ship passengers—some stricken on the journey over—joined a victory parade down Beach Road. Within forty-eight hours, people began dying. Over the next six weeks, nine thousand people succumbed—one-fifth of Western Samoa's entire population. American Samoa, however, was spared because its U.S. naval governor proactively quarantined the territory.[45]

After the war, New Zealand received a League of Nations mandate to govern Western Samoa. Germany relinquished its plantations and business interests, and the Germans who owned or managed these ventures were deported. For Samoans, little changed.

Not surprisingly, *kirikiti*—cricket—was a source of contention with New Zealand authorities, as it had been with the Germans. Imbued with a profit-maximizing spirit, officials tried to limit *kirikiti* because it interfered with plantation labor, especially when it was part of a *malaga*. A centuries-old practice, the *malaga*, or visiting party, brought an *'aiga* to another *'aiga*, where they stayed for weeks, often until the host's food supplies ran out. During *malaga*, plantations went untended, and consumption, not production, was celebrated. Samoa's New Zealand rulers considered that wasteful and archaic.[46]

Sport crystallized what anthropologist Felix Keesing described in 1934 as a basic conflict between Samoan and Western goals. Samoans sought a system of production that minimized effort and maximized leisure. "This seems to be a conscious sentiment among the Samoans, who say that life is good because it is easy," he wrote. "The ease with which the necessities of life are obtained gives much leisure time, conditions favouring the elaborate development of ceremonial and pleasure activities, in which may be appropriately included war." And cricket.[47]

But to Westerners, weeklong matches were an unforgivable indulgence that encouraged men to desert their labors. Brigadier General George Richardson—New Zealand's point man in Samoa—tried to curtail play and its accompanying *malaga* visitations. But Samoans not only ignored dictates requiring written permission to schedule matches; their loyalty to cricket fueled a campaign of mass disobedience that broke out in 1926.[48]

Robert Gibbings, an illustrator from Cork, Ireland, who began traveling the South Seas in 1929, testified to New Zealand's inability to limit *kirikiti*. "It took such a hold on the people," he observed, "that they abandoned all work on their plantations." While in an outlying village, Gibbings saw cricket played every day but Sundays for an entire fortnight. "From my house I could see three different games in progress—men's teams on my left, women's in front, and children's to my right. . . . There was a constant noise of shrieking and laughter." Not even a torrential downpour stopped play. While some women held umbrellas over their heads, most kept their eye on the ball, or the cheerleaders, a source of endless laughter. Gibbings was told that when a schooner went aground on Palmerston atoll, crew members thought they would have to fight for their lives. Instead, he said, the women on the atoll challenged them to a match of cricket. They kept their lives but lost the match.[49]

Samoans never warmed to New Zealand's mandate nor forgave its failure to protect them from the flu pandemic. But they eventually accepted their rulers' favorite sport—rugby. While cricket overwhelmed Samoa after its 1880s debut, it took global upheaval to bring rugby to the islands. Even then it was confined to Apia and close-by villages until late in the twentieth century. Though its origins in Samoa are not well documented, rugby's introduction most likely came during World War I from Kiwi troops, Marist brothers and fathers from New Zealand who began arriving afterward, and Samoans who spent time in New Zealand and brought the game back as part of their cultural baggage.

Unlike *kirikiti*, which prevailed in villages, rugby was an urban game appealing to the better-off, especially the *'afakasi* (those of mixed origins) who had contact with the world beyond Samoa. The Marists, a Catholic order in rugby's vanguard, had made substantial inroads among the *'afakasi* in Apia and on neighboring Tutuila, where they opened schools and made rugby part of the curriculum.[50]

By August 1924, enough Samoans played to field a squad versus Fiji, which stopped in Apia en route to Tonga. While Fiji's team was made up of men with Fijian surnames, the Samoan squad mixed men with European—Allen, Moors, Meredith, and MacDonald—and Samoan—Quapati, Semisi, Atiga, and Moli—names. The Fijians arrived on a Sunday afternoon and limbered up by walking from the docks to the racecourse where the match would take place. The two teams convened at seven the next morning, early enough to avoid the heat and to allow the Fijians to board their ship for Tonga and the Samoans to make it to work.[51]

As soon as play began, the five hundred to six hundred spectators realized that the Fijians, clad in all black, were more experienced ruggers. Harry W. Moors (the son of Stevenson's buddy Harry J. Moors) captained the Samoan side, which wore white and played in bare feet. A tree stood in the center of the field and puddles made the ball slippery and footing iffy, limiting sustained drives. Fiji led 3–0 at halftime after a Fijian dodged two defenders and dived over the goal line despite three Samoans hanging on to him. While spectators "barracked hard for the local team," the faster and more skilled Fijians prevailed 6–0.

"The game was played in splendid spirit," the *Samoa Times* reported. "It was hard at times, but there was no suggestion of rough and dirty play." A. S. Farebrother, who both coached the Fijians and covered the game for the *Fiji Times and Herald*, added, "Practically every man played well and there were no loafers on either side. . . . The general opinion on all sides was that the game was the cleanest and finest exhibition of football played in Samoa." In truth, it was one of the island's first exhibitions of rugby. But it conveyed the muscular Christianity that upper-class British sport cherished. After a bit of postmatch conviviality, the Fijians sailed to Nuku'alofa, promising the Samoans that they would send them results of their test matches in Tonga by radio. Organizers also agreed to send an interislands team selected from Fiji, Samoa, and Tonga to compete in New Zealand the following year.

The Fijians, after their successful warm-up in Samoa, took eight of their eleven matches in Tonga. When they stopped in Apia on their return home, an even larger crowd witnessed the rematch. This time, the Samoans held their own. Though Fiji pushed the ball forward during the first fifteen minutes, Samoa defended its goal line and Fiji could not score. As the game progressed, Fiji tired while the home team grew stronger. A pair of goals and a try sealed Samoa's victory. Rugby, however, remained a relatively exclusive pastime in Samoa for some time, confined to better-off residents in Apia. Unlike *kirikiti*, it brought islanders closer to Western culture.

Stevenson was dead by the time rugby debuted in Samoa. But during his time there, he became the people's strongest advocate and used his pen to press their case. Although his anger was directed at all foreign parties, his harshest vitriol condemned Germany. Stevenson enraged German authorities, who threatened to deport him. They impounded and burned the German translation of *A Footnote to History* when it arrived in Apia, deepening Stevenson's resolve. After the Germans imprisoned Mata'afa, the leader of the resistance, Stevenson visited him in jail. Making a public display of solidarity with anti-German *matai*, he brought the prisoners food and *kava* for ceremonial functions. Upon their release, Mata'afa's men honored Stevenson in striking fashion. By then, Robert Louis Stevenson was beloved by Samoans as Tusitala, the teller of tales.[52]

Stevenson's writing, his displays of solidarity with Samoans despite German displeasure, and his stunning lack of condescension were well received. He told his publisher to direct half of the proceeds of *A Footnote to History* to the Samoan people. "His affection for the natives of Samoa is well known," Moors wrote. "To him they were the most lovable people in all the Pacific, and they were deeply touched by his sympathetic interest in them."[53]

A charming and outgoing man unusually free of the racial prejudices of the time, Stevenson intrigued Samoans. He welcomed them to Villa Vailima, where he treated his staff with humility. When tennis, his favorite game, was played, or parties were held, which was often, all classes, castes, and races were welcome.[54]

Stevenson's support of the rebel Mata'afa endeared him to Samoans as much as it infuriated Germans. When Mata'afa's allies regained their freedom, they hacked a swath through the forest to Vailima, turning a horse path into a road that wheeled vehicles could travel. The *matai* said they cut the road because of their great love of Tusitala and his solidarity during their imprisonment. They gave the road a Samoan name, O le Ala o le Loto Alofa (the Road of the Loving Heart). Stevenson was deeply moved. He knew that Samoans furiously resisted attempts to conscript them into roadbuilding.[55]

Stevenson hosted the men who built the road at Vailima in October 1894. His remarks, delivered in English and read by his stepson Lloyd in Samoan, captured his concern. Perhaps Stevenson knew he would not live much longer; bouts of blood spitting and illness had worn him down. So had the "black dog" moods that left him depressed and unable to write.

But the feast focused his thoughts. The peace that had come about after the 1889 hurricane was fraying and Stevenson saw the handwriting on the wall, spelling out Germany's ascent. He used the ceremonial dinner to warn his guests that time was running out. If they did not reclaim their country, others surely would. "It will not continue to be yours or your children's." He beseeched them not to see their lands fall under the heel of an oppressor, as had happened in Scotland, Ireland, and O'ahu.

Attesting to his love for Samoa and its people, Stevenson said he had chosen the island as his home for the remainder of his life, and his resting spot thereafter. But, he concluded, "I see that the day is come now of the great battle . . . by which it shall be decided, whether you are to pass away like these other races of which I have been speaking, or to stand fast, and to have your children living on and honouring your memory in the land you received of your fathers. . . . Now is the time for the true champions of Samoa to stand forth." Stevenson was not calling upon his guests simply to battle the Germans and shed their blood bravely; he was imploring them to develop their island and its resources, and to engage an encroaching world on their own terms.

Stevenson had little time to see if his call to action would have an effect. He died from a stroke a few weeks later.[56] As word of his death spread, the *matai* leapt into action. The next day, they cut a trail from Vailima to the summit of Mount Vaea so that Tusitala could be buried where he hiked. Even *matai*, whose status meant they did not do such labor, chopped down trees and carried Stevenson's coffin to a grave a thousand feet above Vailima. They then issued a *tapu*, a prohibition, against firearms on Mount Vaea in Stevenson's honor.[57]

A century later, Stevenson is still revered in Samoa. Samoan novelist Albert Wendt wrote that Stevenson's *Footnote to History* revealed his "support for our struggle against the foreign powers and colonialism. . . . His views of colonialism were well ahead of his times." Henry James recognized the tragedy of Stevenson's passing in that it came while he was in his literary prime and only forty-four years of age. But, James observed, that made his life "into a fable as strange and romantic as one of his own. . . . There have been . . . for men of letters few deaths more romantically right."[58]

2

The War and America Come to Samoa

Alema Teʻo barked commands over the public address system, directing players to the next workstations. A clipboard in one hand, stopwatch in the other, he ran the camp with military precision. On the field of Memorial Stadium, hundreds of young Samoans divided into small groups dashed clockwise to the next set of coaches. A few snuck into a drill they had already completed. "They want to do that one again," Teʻo said, laughing. "They get to hit someone in it."

Manu Tuiasosopo, a porkpie hat and hipster shades providing relief from the sun, led a dozen boys through tackling drills, emphasizing footwork and physics. He crouched low to show defenders how to fend off blockers en route to the ballcarrier, something he did so well playing nose tackle at UCLA and in the NFL. Ken Niumatalolo, the first and only Samoan head coach of a Division I college program, watched intently, considering whether to adapt these drills when he returned to Annapolis to ready the Midshipmen for the Naval Academy's upcoming season. Kennedy Polamalu, the football camp's de facto chief of staff, came over to confer. He was the first, but far from the last, Polamalu to break through in football. Half a dozen of his brothers and nephews were scattered around him.

A burst of noise caught their attention. When they saw it was from the group surrounding Penny Semaia, both men grinned. The former University of Pittsburgh lineman had not intended to mix it up with the boys but couldn't help himself. Semaia came to the camp to offer life skills sessions, part of his portfolio as senior associate athletic director at his alma mater. But the boys, juiced by his remarks on the first day of camp, dragged him onto the field. And though his legs were killing him from repeatedly squatting to emphasize positioning and balance, Penny could not stop smiling or exhorting.

The two oldest coaches at the camp, Scott and Satini Puailoa, are brothers whose grandfather left the village of Nu'uuli almost a century ago to perform with the Royal Samoans, an ensemble that toured the United States. The Puailoas instructed their charges to take a knee while they talked about focus, especially during the critical seconds between plays. The boys' concentration wavered as Ryan Clark streaked by, shouting, "You just talking to each other about being Polynesian. But the black guys are doing all the work!" The players broke up—Clark had been an electric presence at the camp—but the Puailoas quickly regained their attention.

Like most of the coaches at the camp, the Puailoas grew up in the States but maintained ties to the island. They, like every coach and player here, are members of the football fraternity, perhaps the strongest clan in team sport. But they share another bond, one that emerged from their families' service in the armed forces, a union forged in World War II.

If not for that war, it's doubtful that these men would have embraced the sport that has defined their lives. Nor would American Samoa have become the tropic of football. Troy Polamalu might never have suited up for three Super Bowls or Junior Seau played a score of seasons in a league cursed by the brevity of careers. Nor would the NFL have included Jesse Sapolu, whose courage in the trenches, before and after open-heart surgery, powered the San Francisco 49ers to four championships. And it's unlikely that Samoans who grew up in Hawai'i or near California military bases would have stormed college gridirons by the late twentieth century. But World War II abruptly yanked American Samoa into the United States' orbit, introducing Americans to an exotic group of athletes, and introducing America to Samoans.

Samoa played no part in provoking the hostilities but, like much of the

South Pacific, could not escape them. The war made the United States real to Samoa; by its end the islands had changed more than in a century of European contact and decades of U.S. rule. World War II turned Samoans into fierce patriots who channeled their warrior ethos into an unsurpassed commitment to the American armed forces. That military connection transformed island life and set the stage for the great *malaga* to Hawai'i and California. There, at Farrington High School in Honolulu, Kahuku on O'ahu's North Shore, Carson High School near Los Angeles, Oceanside High north of San Diego, and more recently in American Samoa, the sons and grandsons of that great migration reduced war to its virtues—on the gridiron.

After gaining control over American Samoa in 1900, Washington promptly forgot about the territory. That had an upside. While Mexicans long lamented that they were cursed to be so far from God, yet so close to the United States, Samoans might have considered themselves blessed to be so close to God, yet far from the United States. Few parts of the United States have welcomed religion so deeply; only a few Pacific islands flying the American flag are farther away. As a result, Samoa was never squeezed too tightly by America's embrace.

Samoans initially equated U.S. sovereignty with untold American largesse and protection from Europeans. Commander Richard Meade told *matai* in 1872 that an agreement with the United States would allow the Samoan wilderness to "bloom like a Rose." Soon, "a new order [would] shine on your good people [who would] experience from the hands of the American people a liberality that will excel that of any people in the world."[1]

But after the United States gained dominion, its ardor for the islands abruptly cooled. The 1898 conflict with Spain left the United States in control of Manila, Guam, Wake Island, Midway, and Hawai'i, creating a route to Asian markets that made Samoa an afterthought.[2] Moreover, a coaling station on Tutuila was no longer necessary because U.S. fleets were converting to oil, which was safer and gave vessels greater sailing range.[3]

Because American Samoa was now an afterthought in Washington, responsibilities devolved to the Navy and Commander Benjamin Tilley, who arrived in Pago Pago in April 1899 aboard the USS *Abarenda* after a three-month voyage from Norfolk.[4] Tilley, who entered the Naval Academy when he was fifteen years old, in 1863, graduated first in his class and captured nine vessels during the 1898 war with Spain. When landside, he led the Department of Astronomy, Navigation, and Surveying at the Naval Academy.[5] Now, despite having no diplomatic training, he was made American Samoa's governor. The Navy invested him with authority to govern the islands, five thousand Samoans, and one hundred expatriates with one proviso—to "at all times conciliate and cultivate friendly relations with the natives."[6] Tilley took this to heart.

On April 17, 1900, Samoans celebrated the signing of the Deed of Cession recognizing U.S. authority. As enthused islanders gathered on a hillside, missionaries offered their blessings, the American flag was raised, and warships fired volleys. Samoans still celebrate Flag Day with rhetoric, music, and most of all, sport.

But the American government had not considered the responsibilities it was assuming. Nor did it even want much to do with the territory anymore. Other than the harbor, American Samoa hardly mattered in Washington, and Congress neither granted citizenship to Samoans nor invested funds in the island. Samoans' expectations of their wilderness blossoming like a rose withered.[7]

At least Tilley protected Samoan cultural autonomy. He allowed the *matai*, the traditional village leaders, to maintain their authority, and rather than police the island with sailors, he created the Fita Fita guard, men who shaped both territorial history and its sporting future.

Tilley's prohibition of the sale of liquor and firearms reflected his conviction that the natives "must be protected" from encroaching Western civilization.[8] He frowned on German Western Samoa, where foreign companies had gobbled up land. To foreclose that possibility, he bought up land owned by expats and issued the Native Lands Ordinance, which forbade the sale of land to foreigners. As a result, Samoans retained collective possession of land where they had resided for up to three thousand years. Even today, upwards of 90 percent of all land remains in Samoan hands.[9]

Tilley's policies meant that American Samoa did not experience the debilitating effects of Western capitalism as harshly as the rest of the South Pacific. On the other hand, Samoans wondered when the United States would fulfill its promises. They believed the Deed of Cession warranted reciprocity. A *matai* not only appropriated his subjects' labor; he also protected them and redistributed the proceeds of their work. While the Navy kept foreign powers away, Washington's gifts were not forthcoming.[10]

Meanwhile, transpacific travel to Pago Pago ceased in 1907 because there was not enough traffic to sustain it. Custom revenues crumbled and mail waited for months before leaving for the States. American Samoa languished.[11] If islanders wanted a glimpse of what Samoa might have looked like if the United States had fulfilled their expectations, they need have gone no farther than Fagatogo and the naval station. It was the most cosmopolitan part of the island, boasting the best roads and the only electricity, sewers, hospital, and school. The Navy showed motion pictures three times a week and Samoans became fans of "Tamamiki" and "Araloiti," aka Tom Mix and Harold Lloyd. America's presence was tangible in Fagatogo and nearby villages. But beyond Pago Pago, American influence was inconsequential.

That changed radically in the spring of 1940. While FDR readied the United States for a conflict most Americans wanted to ignore, the War Department began fortifying American Samoa. A thousand civilians arrived to construct gun emplacements and stretch anti-torpedo nets across Pago Pago Bay. By year's end, hundreds of Marines were on their way to Tutuila and the Fita Fita began guarding beaches and hillside lookouts.[12]

Soon, fifteen hundred Samoans were readying island defenses, working for companies with lucrative defense contracts. More funds flowed to the territory in a single year than had during four decades of naval administration as Samoans built barracks and shelters for the military buildup. Everything was built to military specs, even if it was wildly inappropriate to the environment. The new bakery's roof, for example, could withstand a snow pack twelve feet high.[13]

Months later, when Japanese Zeros swooped down on Pearl Harbor, Samoans were dressing for church. As word of the attack reached Tutuila, territorial life lurched off its moorings. After the news spread to outlying villages, scores of men wearing *lavalavas* and clutching bush knives began walking along mountain trails to the naval station in Fagatogo, looking to volunteer.[14]

Washington's attention now locked onto Samoa. Prior to the war, pleas for federal funds were rarely acknowledged.[15] But with Japan controlling most of the Pacific west of Hawai'i, making Australia and New Zealand vulnerable, American Samoa was the linchpin to Allied defenses. Pago Pago was the only way to communicate with Australia, and after the fall of the Philippines and Guam, it was one of just three U.S. bases left in the Pacific. That made holding the islands critical, no matter the cost.[16]

Days after Pearl Harbor, a Marine brigade five thousand strong was en route from San Diego aboard three commandeered Matson liners. While some of these Marines bolstered island defenses, others left to attack the Marshall and Gilbert Islands.[17] Those who stayed were ill prepared for the tropics. "My God," a medical officer said, "the towns of primitive Haiti were models of beauty, order and cleanliness in comparison [to this] drab and lifeless mudhole." Woolen uniforms, rain, and stifling heat did little to improve morale. "The place looked nothing like Dorothy Lamour singing, 'I want to See Moa of Samoa,'" one soldier lamented. "We were singing, 'I want to see No Moa of Samoa.'"[18]

In January 1942, a Japanese submarine surfaced in Pago Pago Bay and attacked the naval station. Ironically, the first round fell on a store owned by Frank Shimasaki, one of the only Japanese nationals living on Tutuila. Another salvo knocked an officer off his bicycle, but few shells reached shore. Still, Samoans prepared for a Japanese onslaught.[19]

Before long, the U.S. military presence in American Samoa grew to more than eight thousand men, surpassing the native population.[20] The island's traditional quasi-subsistence economy declined, the casualty of a formidable buildup whose aftershocks still reverberate. And while the expected Japanese invasion never came, the military's presence remade Samoan life for the duration of the war and well beyond.[21]

With the United States at war, Samoans like Troy Polamalu's grandfather, Fa'a Sasulu Sei, flooded into the Fita Fita and the newly formed First Samoan Battalion, USMC. Clad in blue *lavalavas*, white undershirts, red turbans, and cummerbunds, these barefoot soldiers were drawn from the ranks of the chiefs and their sons. Before the war, the Fita Fita maintained a presence in the villages and kept watch at the jail, which was rarely locked. Now they prepared to lead the islands' defense.[22]

Fita Fita membership became a badge of honor, even in remote Manu'a. Samoans have long considered Manu'a—the small but majestic volcanic isles of Ta'u, Olosega, and Ofu—the fount of their culture. According to legend, Samoa was created there when the paramount god Tagaloa fashioned the Manu'a Islands so that he had a place to stand amid the seas. From there, he made Savai'i, Upolu, and Tutuila as stepping-stones.[23] The Manu'a Islands burst out of the sea, with breathtakingly steep volcanic cones cloaked by clouds. Waves pound once molten rock that forms their shoreline. Most of the land is too steep to farm, but the hillsides shelter a menagerie of birds, feral pigs, skinks, geckos, and flying foxes.[24]

When it came to claims on historical and cultural primacy, Manu'a prevailed. Its *matai* held the most prestigious titles and traced their lineage to the origins of the Samoan people. Their sense of superiority about that heritage is palpable, especially the link to the *tui* Manu'a, Samoa's supreme title-holder. Troy Polamalu is among his descendants.

Commander Tilley knew little of this when he steamed sixty miles northeast from Pago Pago to Ta'u in 1901, intent on gaining consent to the cession. But the Manu'ans had ruled themselves long before Tilley's country was created and were unwilling to fly a distant power's flag.[25] When Tilley tried to persuade Tui Manu'a Elisara to accept American dominion in 1901, the chief held a *kava* (or *'ava*) ceremony for him but dismissed offers of U.S. protection. Though Tilley was accustomed to obedience from junior officers and enlisted men, the aura around the *tui* Manu'a mystified him. It rested on a higher, more sacred level than the naval chain of command. Only the *tui* Manu'a's wife could feed him, placing food in his mouth directly from her hand. Whenever he went anywhere, lesser chiefs preceded him, blowing conch shells so that all would drop to their knees and bow their foreheads to the ground. His prerogatives were absolute, his word final.

Margaret Mead, then twenty-three, spent several months on Ta'u in 1925, doing fieldwork for her dissertation at Columbia University. Her book *Coming of Age in Samoa*, based on her research there, would make Mead the most famous anthropologist ever, but it did little to alter life on Manu'a. The war, however, unleashed multiple, far-reaching changes.

The U.S. military neither fortified Manu'a nor sent thousands of Marines there, as it did in Tutuila. But it dispatched units to monitor the surrounding waters and establish radio communications.[26] More than two hundred naval personnel moved in with the 2,600 villagers, instructing them to black out their homes at night to prevent Japanese planes and ships from targeting them. Some villagers made plans to escape into the interior if attacked; others went to work for the military.[27]

Fa'a Sasulu Sei, a heavyweight boxing champ who stood five feet nine inches tall and weighed 180 pounds, was also a *tufuga*—a carpenter—on Ta'u when war broke out. Carpenters were well-respected artisans, called upon to build *fales* and *fautasi*, the longboats that Samoans had adapted from whaling boats to work the seas. "A skilled carpenter," cautioned Margaret Mead, who was engaged in fieldwork on Ta'u in 1925, "must be treated as courteously as a chief and addressed with the chief's language, the elaborate set of honorific words used to people of rank."[28] Sasulu was also a high talking chief married to a woman whose lineage descended from the *tui* Manu'a. He sat in the *fono*, the village assembly where *matai* leaned against a designated post in the *fale*. Those with the highest titles sat at posts on the seaward side of the *fale*.

Now Sasulu was Fita Fita. "They helped [the Marines] get familiarized with the island during the wartime," his oldest son remembered.[29] Until Pearl Harbor, the United States was a distant, irrelevant abstraction to men like Fa'a Sasulu Sei. But the war elevated the Fita Fita into a Pan-Samoan *'aumaga* that united the villages and brought Samoans closer to the United States. The *'aumaga*, which served as the village's war party and workforce, reflected the communal instincts girding daily life. The more powerful the *'aumaga*, the greater a village was feared. "If the *'aumaga* should disappear," Mead declared, "Samoan village life would have to be entirely reorganized, for upon the ceremonial and actual work of the young and untitled men the whole life of the village depends."[30]

With global conflict enveloping the island, the Fita Fita grew so large that almost every family had somebody in it. By war's end, it bolstered a sense of Samoan identity aligned with the distant but increasingly tangible United States. Those connections grew stronger with each subsequent generation. Almost to a man, the coaches at Polamalu's football camp were raised in families with powerful military ties.[31] Alema Te'o's father worked for the Navy; Manu Tuiasosopo's father served in it. Ken Niumatalolo's father joined the Coast Guard in Honolulu; Penny Semaia was born at Camp Pendleton to a Marine father. Kennedy Polamalu's father was Fita Fita and his older brother a Marine.

The same holds for the youth they're teaching at the camp. Their families have myriad military ties. They will join their village's *'aumaga* as a rite of manhood and many will enlist. It's their way off "the rock." For most of these boys, the overlap between team, 'aumaga, and the military reinforces the already thick communal solidarities of Samoan life.

The Polamalus were 'aumaga stalwarts on Ta'u, fighting and laboring for the village. As village warfare slackened during the twentieth century, rugby and kirikiti became surrogate competitions and the Polamalus played for their village. They exemplified the Samoan physique that caught the attention of U.S. officers. The average Fita Fita guard stood five feet eight inches tall and weighed between 150 and 170 pounds. They are "well built with very muscular arms and legs, heavy shoulders with large biceps and forearms, a small waist and well-proportioned hands," a Marine observed. Their physicality was on display at work and in play.

Fa'a Sasulu Sei vanquished both Samoans and Marines in the ring. Well muscled, with veins that stood out on sinewy arms, he embodied what one Marine meant when he wrote that guardsmen were "fast, agile," quick to respond when the pace of play shifted. Samoans became much bigger and even more rugged after the war.[32] The coaches at Polamalu's camp and their brethren in the States relish this felicitous blend of fa'a Samoa and military discipline; it's an ideal mix for football.

The islanders were not unfamiliar with Americans, but they had never encountered so many at once. Nor had jobs ever paid so well. The infusion of cash and wage labor jolted Samoans from their subsistence ways, while the troops made America tangible.[33] Within a year after the United States entered the war, the military had conscripted virtually every adult male to replace the civilian construction workers evacuated after Tutuila became the front line. Samoan men left hillside plantations unattended to serve under the Seabees. Working cheek by jowl with military personnel, they received an accelerated course in Americanization, Marine Corps–style.[34]

The Fita Fita quickly proved their bona fides, lugging gear up mountain paths while the Marines lagged behind. They were stronger than GIs, who lost weight in the tropics and suffered from the heat. Together, they blasted a lava field into submission and filled a lagoon with coral and steel bulkheads to create an airfield at Tafuna, where there was no natural stretch of flat land suitable for a mile-long runway. They drove bulldozers and trucks with gusto, ignoring road conditions and vehicular limitations, and figured out how to carry guns up hillsides that stymied the Seabees. They labored for wages from as low as 8¢ an hour to as much as 65¢ an hour.[35]

Few Samoans were unaffected by their islands' militarization. The Marines commandeered schools and ordered villagers to grow carrots, cucumbers, and lettuce—"white man's vegetables"—for the troops, fining villages that failed to comply. Because most men and many women were already working for the military, children were pulled from classrooms to tend the plantations. Soon, instruction virtually ceased as teachers enlisted or took better-paying jobs, and older students left school to work as laborers.[36] Other men joined the Navy or headed for Honolulu shipyards and docks. Few remained to farm or fish.

During a break in the camp, Alema Teʻo talked with his brother Maʻa. The elder Teʻo's coaching days were long over, but he stayed connected to the game through Alema, who founded the All Poly Camp in Utah, where players hone their skills during the summer, and his nephew Manti Teʻo, who was about to enter the NFL after a much ballyhooed career at Notre Dame that ended in a media circus.[37] Another nephew, Mike, plays for the U.S. national rugby sevens team. Maʻa resided in Mapusaga, known as the Mormon Valley because the Church of Jesus Christ of Latter-day Saints was once based there. When the Navy shut its Samoan operations after the war, the Teʻos made their way to San Francisco, where the men worked on the docks. The family moved back and forth between Hawaiʻi, California, and American Samoa, where Maʻa ultimately settled.

"I still remember the war," he said seventy years later. "There were lots of soldiers here. They took me on their shoulders and we go watch the movies outside with them." Some were teenagers, not much older than he was; a few were Mormons like his family. "I don't know what they were saying, but they played with us." Soldiers tossed footballs, swatted volleyballs, and played rugby with boys on the beach. "I remember them playing baseball and football," Teʻo said. "First time I saw a football. Yes! I enjoyed that game very much. But there was not as much football as baseball, which was very popular." The Fita Fita had fielded ball clubs since the 1920s, playing shoeless against teams from Fafatogo and the Navy.[38]

American troops bivouacked in Mapusaga, where the Navy set up a mobile hospital. Captain Eddie Rickenbacker convalesced there after his B-17 crashed en route to Australia and the crew drifted for twenty-two days. Tutuila, he wrote, had been transformed from a South Seas paradise into an ocean fortress. "The scenery is wonderful, and in many other respects the South Seas is the most attractive place in the world to fight a war. But the region has its drawbacks. The rainy season has just begun, and you have my word for it, it doesn't just rain out there, the ocean tilts up and swamps you."[39]

Te'o's uncles worked on the docks, sometimes unloading bodies from warships. "My auntie and whole lot of women love the soldiers so much that they take their laundry and wash it," Ma'a recalled. "They treat them like their sons." While in this case the "mothers" charged for doing the laundry, local women did genuinely care for many of the young Americans, who were vulnerable, scared, and far outside their comfort zone. "When they go out to war," Te'o recalled, "we have a big farewell for them." The women gave each soldier a necklace made of *teuila* (red ginger) blossoms. After the troops shipped out, villagers clustered around their only radio to track their progress. Villagers could identify when the Americans they had befriended joined an attack. "Wave 7, that was the wave that trained here," Te'o explained, referring to the invasion of the Solomon Islands. "But it never made it to shore; a lot of them died. I watched the old men cry that day." Years later, when Te'o went to the Solomons for his Latter-day Saints mission, he visited their graves and cried too. "They were so young when they lived with us. So much sacrifice they made."

At first, Marines and villagers confounded each other. Many of the troops had never left home until basic training and were overwhelmed. It was just as mind-boggling for Samoans. One Marine recalled them "staring at us as if we were strange creatures from another planet."[40] In outlying villages, protocols for military-civilian relations were ignored.[41] Some Marines moved in with families; others commandeered *fales*, forcing villagers to move up the hillsides. Samoans often welcomed soldiers into their homes and to the *to'ona'i*, the bountiful Sunday meal cooked in an *umu*, a rock-lined oven dug in the sand. And though the military still segregated African American and Caucasian soldiers, the Samoans manned beach and gun positions with white troops and shared their *fales* with officers and NCOs.[42]

Families housed small groups of soldiers and tended to their housekeeping. The soldiers' alternative was living in canvas tents that rotted in the rain and subsisting on K rations.[43] Samoans taught soldiers how to fish and climb coconut palms. They exchanged gifts and bartered, formed friendships and romances, and created children. Some Marines found a version of paradise in the villages. They did without electricity and running water but saw a splendor they had only imagined before arriving.

Marines and Samoans also met in sport. Fita Fita guardsmen played baseball and volleyball against the soldiers. Their fighters took on Marines at boxing matches that command hoped would better relations with the locals.[44]

Though Tutuila was a respite compared to what lay ahead on Guadalcanal and the Gilbert Islands, it was hardly idyllic. Skin fungi and intestinal parasites, especially hookworm, were endemic. Even worse, parasites carried by blood-sucking mosquitos spread filariasis—known as *mumu*. If left untreated, victims developed elephantiasis, an excruciatingly painful condition in which body parts swelled. A man's scrotum could expand to the size of a basketball, and legs grew to grotesque proportions, often requiring amputation. There had never been a reported case of it among the Americans stationed at the naval base, nor had it ever been diagnosed in the continental United States. Popular wisdom held that Caucasians were immune. Nevertheless, men were stricken with filariasis, and command directed island hospitals to scrub cases from the records, changing their diagnosis to something less threatening. The captain in charge at the hospital chided this as a "Hear no *mumu*, see no *mumu*, speak no *mumu*" policy.[45]

When the military eventually acknowledged filariasis, medics identified 141 cases in two months. The rate of infestation in some units was as high as 70 percent, affecting half of the 2,235 military men sent back to the States for medical treatment. Filariasis forced the Marines to close their jungle training center and send recruits to Camp Lejeune instead.[46]

When Eleanor Roosevelt visited Tutuila on August 24, 1943, her presence underscored that the war had passed by Samoa. While the Fita Fita band played, the first lady inspected the guard. She departed the next day and most U.S. troops soon followed. Most fighter pilots and their planes left, and redeployment slashed troop levels to just two thousand men. Fewer ships stopped in Pago Pago, and the number of islanders working for the military plunged. The territory became a supply depot and repair facility as well as a hospital where wounded men were sent to recover or die.[47]

Villagers said farewell to their young guests, and the nervous energy dissipated. American Samoa was returning to its backwater status, but it would never revert to what it had been before the war.[48] The U.S. military had spent millions upgrading infrastructure, building mess halls, ship repair yards, ball fields, and a hospital. The two-lane road along the water and the electrical grid remained. The mess halls and administration buildings were torn down. Alema Te'o's father and uncles helped load tons of equipment aboard ships bound for Hawai'i. Little thought was given to whether Samoans could maintain what the military abandoned. Nor did Washington ponder either the buildup's impact or demobilization's consequences. It forgot about American Samoa again.

But from a Samoan perspective, America had finally delivered the goods promised in the 1901 Deed of Cession. The war rescued Samoa from a mild prewar recession brought on by declining copra prices and slackening sales of native crafts. The island's general fund soared tenfold, and imported goods flooded the island, generating unprecedented customs duties. The alliance with the paramount high chief in Washington had finally borne fruit.[49]

Few of the men stationed there ever returned. Some never knew that they had fathered children. One historian speculated that the number of Samoan American babies conceived during the war easily topped one thousand.[50] But if Samoan women had children to remember their wartime lovers by, many of their partners had only their fading memories.

Still, the military's presence—the thousands of young Americans and dollars spent, the jobs, the contact with Western culture—was transformative. And though Samoans wondered what would happen to their wages as the military decamped, they treasured the roads left behind, valued the electricity that brought light to villages, and savored the joys of ice cream parlors and movie theaters. Some even began wearing shoes and affecting Western dress.[51]

Because of the war, farmers and fishermen had become craftsmen and mechanics. They operated bulldozers and backhoes, acquired plumbing and welding skills, and learned how to survey and draft. Adapting to construction crews with English-speaking bosses who ran strictly by the clock was a radical departure from the cadences of tropical work and time. Officers and work crew bosses lamented that Samoans could not sustain more than eight-to-ten-hour workdays. Of course, neither could the soldiers, given the weather and the torrential rain. Samoans often had to walk for up to two hours from their villages to reach work. One officer complained that Samoans had "little foresight. As long as they have sufficient food in the ground for their needs, they are satisfied."

Rather than blame Samoans for these alleged deficiencies, doctors cited the prevalence of parasitic worms and a diet consisting mostly of vegetables and lacking mineral elements. Samoans could not supplement that diet during the war because the military restricted fishing and placed mines offshore.[52] Unable to ply the ocean or cultivate their plantations, Samoans imported record amounts of food—including rice and canned beef—initiating dietary trends that worsened after the war.[53]

Diet wasn't the only change. Traditionally, Samoans handed whatever they earned to their *matai*, just as they delivered their harvest from the plantation or sea to him. The *matai* used the fruits of their labor for the *'aiga*'s collective—or his own personal—good. Wage work, however, loosened the *matai*'s authority. With construction workers' collective monthly earnings reaching $120,000 and those of women doing soldiers' laundry another $80,000, more money circulated than ever before. Moreover, these men and women received their pay directly, circumventing the *matai*.[54]

The concept of saving money meant little before the war—there wasn't much to buy. Nor could Samoans, lacking refrigeration, store their harvest or catch for times of scarcity. The exception was *masi*, breadfruit placed in leaf-lined pits, where it fermented into a pungent smelling cake-like paste that remained edible for a year and could be retrieved in times of need. But while the cash infusion and soldiers were welcome, plantation production suffered from a lack of labor. Taro and bananas were imported from Western Samoa, a harbinger of what was to come.[55]

Another change was political; a war whose objectives included making the world safe for democracy caused Samoans to question their dependent status. They had committed to the war effort and now wanted to be treated like Americans. For some of their sons and grandsons, the gridiron would become a force for their Americanization from the 1960s on.

Alema Te'o started becoming American on California's playing fields but returned to finish school at Leone High School on Tutuila's west side. "Growing up in Samoa, football was just a game to me," he recalled. The

game, however, linked him to San Francisco, the city of his birth, and to
the United States. Football offered a way for a Samoan boy to fit in. "There
weren't too many Samoans out there on the field in the 1970s, but there were
a few guys we would read about," Te'o mused. Looking around the field, he
pointed to Manu Tuiasosopo. "That's the guy we read about."

No football *'aiga* looms larger than the Tuiasosopos. In a single generation, thirteen cousins played college football, five made it to the NFL, and
another two attended training camps. Manu Tuiasosopo led the way. Chosen
by the Seattle Seahawks in the first round of the 1979 NFL draft after an All-
American career at UCLA, Manu is their paramount chief when it comes
to football. His family displays the all-around athleticism and intelligence
that so many Samoans manifest in sport. One of his sons, Marques, played
quarterback in the NFL for the Raiders and the Jets; another son, Matt, plays
major league baseball; a daughter, Leslie, coaches college volleyball.[56]

Manu's family departed Tutuila for the States in the wake of World War
II. His father, High Talking Chief Asovalu Tuiasosopo, left Vatia when he
joined the Navy, settling in Long Beach, where Manu was born in 1957. The
high talking chief's nephew, Mike Tuiasosopo, who coached with Kennedy
Polamalu at UCLA, arrived in California a few years later.[57]

But many Tuiasosopos, including Manu's grandfather, High Talking
Chief Mariota Tuiasosopo, stayed. In April 1945, with the war winding
down, Tutuila's *matai* met to discuss the territory's future. High Talking
Chief Mariota wanted the principles of freedom for which Samoans had sac-
rificed to apply to them. It was time for Washington to acknowledge their
wartime loyalty, he declared. He called for a Samoan legislature, a *fono* that
could veto the governor's decrees involving lands and *matai* titles. Along
with other *matai*, he petitioned the U.S. Congress to form such a legislature.
Their requests fell on deaf ears, initially, but Tuiasosopo became American Samoa's most forthright leader and, after a *fono* was created in 1948, its
Speaker of the House.[58]

Before Pearl Harbor, one in ten men worked for the Navy or belonged to the
Fita Fita. During the war, almost all of them did. But afterward, when wartime jobs disappeared, returning to plantations or fishing left many unsatis-
fied. Hundreds left the territory, joining the military or heading for Honolulu. Making matters worse, intense droughts and windstorms destroyed the

crops on which many subsisted. The territory's economy slowed and then, in 1951, collapsed.[59]

For centuries, Samoans had circulated freely in the archipelago. All it took was an outrigger canoe and paddlers willing to brave the sea. But few Samoans ventured much farther away, and when they did, it was usually to New Zealand. Hawai'i, not yet a state, hosted several Samoans at private schools in Honolulu, and the Mormons had brought a few to O'ahu's North Shore, but no community had coalesced on the mainland. Before World War II, American Samoa's only regular connection with the outside world was a Matson steamer that arrived once every twenty-eight days to deliver mail and supplies. After the war, it seemed as if Samoa would again become a backwater.

But the status quo changed abruptly in 1951 when the Navy relinquished control of the territory to the Department of the Interior and abandoned its base on Tutuila. The Navy's exit was the catalyst for a Samoan diaspora that would make Samoans one of the most transnational populations on the planet.[60]

By then, almost one thousand Samoan veterans had received their last readjustment allowance or exhausted their GI Bill benefits. Along with dependents, they constituted a substantial chunk of the population.[61] With the Navy's departure, wage work all but disappeared.

Mindful of the shock waves it was precipitating, the Navy announced that Samoans in the military or working for it could receive free passage to Honolulu or California and continue their military employment. Migration fever gripped the territory. When given the option of enlisting in the Navy, every one of the ninety-six Fita Fita guardsmen remaining from a wartime contingent of five hundred accepted. Even on Manu'a, the great *malaga* was under way.

As the USS *General R. L. Howze* left Pago Pago for Honolulu in June 1951, hundreds of Samoan military personnel waved good-bye to the crowds seeing them off. Once in Hawai'i, these military émigrés convinced the Navy to send a vessel for their dependents. Wives, children, and dependent relatives would be able to travel for free aboard the USS *President Jackson*. When the Navy said that it would fill the remaining berths with Samoans who secured sponsors in Hawai'i or who would commit to enlisting, hundreds rushed to get on board. When it weighed anchor, the *President Jackson* carried a thousand islanders. Others hitched rides on private yachts or paid their own way on Matson liners. Those who stayed wondered if they would ever see their friends again.[62]

By some accounts during the 1950s, more than six thousand Samoans left for the States, perhaps 15 to 25 percent of the territory's population.[63] Nobody really knows for sure, in part because so many Western Samoans arrived during the 1950s to take their places and few kept score. But many felt it simply was not possible to hold on to the kind of life to which they had become accustomed during the war.[64]

As off-island beachheads formed, migration became increasingly attractive. The human tide to Hawai'i and California has remained strong ever since. And while Honolulu was the prime beneficiary of this exodus, San Francisco, Oceanside, Los Angeles, and Seattle soon featured Samoan enclaves. The Samoan presence in the military also grew. In just one year, 1952, more than fifteen hundred Samoans enlisted. When a recruiting team arrived in 1954 to fill eighty-four naval slots, four hundred men volunteered. By the early 1970s, island authorities estimated that five hundred Samoans were leaving annually. By then, Samoans in Hawai'i and the mainland outnumbered those remaining in the territory two to one.[65]

Rather than leave for Hawai'i in the wake of the Navy pullout, the Polamalus remained on Ta'u. Several of Fa'a Sasulu Sei and Taele'ese Pomele's eleven children, including the two oldest boys, Salu and Tone, were born there. Lolo Moliga, who became American Samoa's governor in 2013, was Tone's classmate and a year behind Salu in school.[66] "They were rugged," he recalled. "We played rugby together—nothing like the rugby and football of today. The only thing is to score, no rules, but you learn how to run, handle the ball, and hit." Tone relished the hitting. "If you wanted to win," the governor said, chortling, "you make sure you had him on the team. He was husky, tall, and very tough."

The governor is surprisingly trim for a Samoan in his sixties. Manu'ans, while not spared the devastation wrought by the spread of Western diets, are slimmer than most Samoans. The only overweight people in Manu'a, the governor commented, are those who go to Tutuila. "People in Manu'a," he explained, "still get much of their food from the plantation and the sea." When he grew up there, many people looked like the Polamalus, lean and well proportioned.[67]

A master carpenter and boatbuilder, Fa'a Sasulu Sei crafted the *fales*, out-riggers, and longboats critical on an island where agriculture and fishing prevailed. "He was one of [the] original longboat builders," his son Aoata (Ao) explained, "going from village to village to build longboats," the only way from one village to another because there were no roads. Fa'a Sasulu was often gone for months, working in villages recovering from tsunamis or hurricanes. Those for whom he labored celebrated his efforts with elaborate feasts and *kava* ceremonies.[68]

The Polamalus also cultivated taro, bananas, and a bounty of coconuts, breadfruit, mangos, and vegetables. Breadfruit was more than a source of food. The Polamalus used it as an eye rinse and poles for their *fales*. Though Fa'a Sasulu did not fish, his wife's brothers shared their catch. The family lived in an open-sided house with a conical roof with mats that were lowered to keep out the rain and mosquitos, on land that belonged to the Pomele *'aiga*, Taele'ese's side of the family. Other *fales* with Pomeles and Polamalus were nearby. They sat and slept on mats woven from pandanus leaves atop a crushed coral floor. Each morning and evening, they observed *sa*, a period of devotion. Sundays revolved around church and the Sunday meal, the *to'ona'i*. Talalupe (Lupe) recalled that by the time she awoke on Sundays, her father had prepared the *umu* and foods wrapped in banana leaves were slowly cooking.[69]

The men worked in concert; it took three to handle a boat and fish for bonito, two to lasso eels on the reef, and a group to work the taro plantation.[70] Women wove mats and collected sea urchins at low tide. In the 1920s, Margaret Mead found older children disciplining younger siblings, who learned to listen and not talk back. Their socialization was so successful that children as young as six were entrusted with younger siblings. Each did chores. This sort of childhood still characterizes Samoan life and explains why Troy Polamalu, despite the inordinate attention directed his way, remains deferential to his aunts and uncles.

Recreation was communal. Men enjoyed *lafoga*, in which players slid disks made of coconut shell down mats, with the goal of knocking opponents' disks off the surface. When a family hosted an evening of play, it cooked for the players and spectators. Men and boys also played rugby on the beach, using a coconut as the ball.

But the sport that captured Manu'a best was *kirikiti*. "We played all the time," Lupe Polamalu remembered. If a team, composed of the *'aumaga* of a village, wished to play another team, it sent a representative to that village to challenge its *'aumaga*. The team, accompanied by a high talking chief and supporters, walked or rowed to the host village. Before play, the visiting high talking chief spoke at length to the hosts, delivering a *fa'a lupega*, a formal greeting that noted the lineage and importance of their hosts and their *matai*. If his remarks were deemed acceptable by village leaders, the visiting players were greeted with a *kava* ceremony and meal. The next morning the hosts served their visitors breakfast. "Then," Governor Moliga said with a smile, "they play, and after that they would have the big celebration; it would take the entire day."[71]

Or longer. Governor Moliga remembers as many as a hundred players on a side during the 1950s. Every player got a chance to bat during an inning, with an at bat lasting as long as the player hit safely. After each visitor made an out, the villagers took part in ritualized merriment. These matches, the governor stressed, were collective celebrations of village life grounded in *fa'a Samoa*. And though work roles were segregated by gender, females joined in *kirikiti*, as spectators or on the field.

But despite the power of tradition, the war had opened up vistas of what lay beyond the horizon. So did natural disasters. Typhoons periodically pounded Manu'a. In the wake of the 1957 typhoon, Fa'a Sasulu took part of his family to Tutuila. They lived in Matu'u, a tiny village hugging the western side of the island where *'aiga* connections guaranteed housing. Fa'a Sasulu worked as a carpenter for the government and cultivated a plantation. "There was no fat on him," recalled his oldest son, who worked alongside. The brood grew. Kennedy was born on Ta'u in 1963, his brother Ao on Tutuila two years later. As a boy, Ao feared that *aitu*—malevolent spirits—or bats would come and eat or carry him off if he wandered far from the *fale* or lingered outside after dark.

A year after Kennedy was born on November 22, 1963, Salu, the oldest son, became the first Polamalu to leave the territory. Salu had attended Samoana, then the island's sole public high school. In 1964, a contest selected forty-six young men and women, including Salu, to perform at the Pacific pavilion during the New York City World's Fair. Those chosen combined a facility with English, a striking appearance, and the ability to dance.

It was not the first time Samoans had performed abroad. Islanders were shamelessly paraded as South Seas primitives at an 1874 exhibit in Germany. Harry Moors, Stevenson's confidant, reprised this display of the exotic at the 1893 Chicago Columbian Exposition. But the humiliating memory of Germany made it hard for him to recruit Samoans, and few of the Chicago participants were full-blooded Samoan. That didn't stop the organizers from touting the women's mysterious beauty and the men's warrior physiques. "Their language is soft and liquid . . . the men splendidly tattooed . . . [and] fond of fame. In the past this passion has had much to do with their habit of taking the heads of their enemies, by which they secure glory and admiration from the women."[72]

But in 1964, Samoans were willing, even eager, to journey halfway around the globe. It was Salu's first time off island. He had never seen a building taller than two stories before; now he wandered Manhattan amid skyscrapers that seemed as high as the Rainmaker Mountain. Brandishing three-foot knives set ablaze, Salu spent a year doing the fire dance and parlayed the World's Fair stint into a barnstorming gig afterward. He finally settled in Honolulu, performing with Don Ho's Hawaiian revue.[73]

By then, Tone was also in Hawai'i, where he worked at the Royal Hawaiian, Waikiki's classic, pink, Moorish styled hotel. Physically precocious, Tone had talked his way into the Marine Corps when he was fifteen and wound up in Vietnam, where a bazooka shell grazed his back. A leader by dint of personality, Tone later returned to the territory and assumed a high talking chief title. But first, after returning from Vietnam, he established a family beachhead in California. Meanwhile, his brother Talati had saved enough to pay for their siblings and parents to join them.

Kennedy left in 1972, Ao two years later. When reunited in California, Kennedy, nine, no longer knew much Samoan, and Ao, seven, had yet to learn any English. "We couldn't speak to each other at first and hardly knew each other," he recalled. Nor could Kennedy talk easily to his parents, who understood little English. "The only Samoan I knew," Kennedy recalled, "were prayers." He and Ao became a package, moving among their siblings' homes, carrying their possessions in a box. Their priority was to gain a mainland education.

As Margaret Mead had noted, "Few children live continuously in one household but are always testing out other possible residences. . . . No Samoan child . . . ever has to deal with a feeling of being trapped. There are always relatives to whom one can flee."[74] The Polamalus grew up that way, switching households in a network that spread from Ta'u to Tutuila to Hawai'i to California to Oregon to Pittsburgh, and back.

After Vietnam, Tone returned to school, attending Santa Ana Junior College in the early 1970s, where he played linebacker, then the University of California, Irvine. "Tone coached us every day," Ao recalled. "He trained us but never had us playing football." Instead, Tone worked on their hand-eye coordination and footwork. "Tone took us to the track at Santa Ana and had us run," Ao explained. "Then he had us in their weight room. Then we would swim, or play racquetball, handball, or basketball, our first love." He made them stronger, faster, and durable—tough enough that Kennedy played fullback at the University of Southern California (USC; 1982–85) and Ao started at defensive tackle for Penn State's 1986 national championship squad.[75]

"Tone was very tough on us." Kennedy shrugged. "It was the Samoan way. Because we were so big, we were always playing up against older kids. If we were not playing hard or with enough passion, he would come out on the field in the middle of the game, bend us over, and kick us in the ass! They call that abuse now, but that was the way we were brought up."[76]

Tone treated his brothers like he was training them for the Marines, their sister Lupe recalled. "He was so tough on them, because he wanted the boys to come out good." Ao does not disagree. "Tone was a bull. If his backhand didn't work on us when he didn't like how we were behaving, he would put us in our room with boxing gloves and say that the one who comes out is going to get his ass whipped. He could be a mean son of a bitch."

Though the Polamalus could not afford to send Kennedy and Ao to Mater Dei High School, their neighbors, Raymond and Barbara Alvarado, whose sons David and Michael were Kennedy's and Ao's ages, could. Their boys went to Mater Dei, and the Alvarados made it possible for Kennedy and Ao to join them there. "We were the only two Samoans at Mater Dei," Kennedy recalled. "We were taken completely out of our culture and away from our church." Kennedy, embarrassed by his poor English, became shy and full of self-doubt. But teachers worked with him after school and he redoubled his efforts to become the strongest and fastest athlete at the school. By the time Kennedy was a senior in high school, he was squatting five hundred pounds, benching four hundred, and running a 4.40 forty-yard dash.

"It took its toll," Kennedy admitted. "My bones and my joints weren't ready for it. I had my first ACL tear in the eighth grade dunking a basketball and I tore the other one before junior year. Nobody lifted weights in Samoa then, but Tone had us lifting. Looking back, I think it was too early; but that's the way I was brought up. I wanted to be faster and stronger than anybody else."

Every big-time football program in the country tried to recruit him; so did some basketball schools, including Syracuse. "I jumped center even though I was only six foot, but I wanted to jump higher and shoot better than anybody else. I was jumping out of the gym!" But when he stopped growing, Kennedy realized that few Division I programs were interested in a six-foot-tall power forward. Football was his ticket to college.

By then, California Samoans like Manu Tuiasosopo were breaking through at UCLA and other western schools. Kennedy listened to announcers drawing out "Tu-i-a-so-soooooo-po!" "He was one of my idols; so was Mosi Tatupu at USC. Mosi, who was born in Pago Pago, played at the Punahou School in Honolulu, then USC, and finally in the NFL. "It was a joy for me to later recruit his son, Lofu," Kennedy recalled.[77]

After sorting through his choices, Kennedy committed to Joe Paterno at Penn State but reversed his decision when his father was stricken with coronary disease. He wanted to stay close to home and went to USC instead. To make up for it, Kennedy sent Ao to Penn State two years later.

Their oldest brother, Salu, who boxed but never played football, remained in Hawai'i until he fell in love with Shelley, a woman from Oregon visiting on spring break. They married and settled in Tenmile, Oregon, where he worked as a civil engineer. They raised three boys in the town of 150 people and eventually added a nephew, Troy, who came to stay with them.

Wherever they called home, the Polamalus lived *fa'a Samoa*, in the way of Samoa. "The shadow of nobility," Mead wrote, "falls upon the children sometimes lightly, sometimes heavily, often long before they are old enough to understand the meaning of these intrusions from the adult world."[78] Troy, born in California and raised by his mother as well as aunts and uncles, eventually decamped for his uncle and aunt's house in Oregon, thousands of miles from Samoa and with no other Samoans nearby. Nonetheless, the shadow of nobility and the way of Samoa hang over him.

3

Hawai'i: The North Shore

Hawai'i's unique sporting culture was shaped by its remoteness. Almost 2,500 miles from California, the nation's fiftieth state is comprised of an archipelago of islands, atolls, and tiny islets stretching across fifteen hundred miles. Most of these islands emerged as lava spewed upward from the ocean floor. Hawai'i's flora and fauna developed in near total isolation for millions of years. So did its sporting life, if not for so long. Few mainland teams or athletes were willing to brave days at sea or could afford flights to get there, but by the 1920s a savory blend of grassroots forces, benefiting from a felicitous climate, had begun to create a lively sporting culture, in which Samoan émigrés and their children became central figures.

Hawaiian sport encompassed private schools like 'Iolani, Punahou, Kamehameha, and Saint Louis; their less affluent public counterparts; barefoot, plantation, and military leagues; and the University of Hawai'i. Sport reflected the island's constantly evolving immigrant mix, with Filipinos gravitating to boxing and cockfighting and the Japanese to baseball.

Nonetheless, Hawaiian sport revolved around football. Private high schools were the first to organize teams. Punahou, whose alumni would include a president of the United States, Barack Obama; Kamehameha, whose campus in Kapalama was created for students of native Hawaiian ancestry; and Saint Louis, which would rule island football with dynastic verve for two decades, led the way. The private schools formed the Interscholastic League of Honolulu in 1909; while the Rural Oʻahu Secondary Schools League, organized in 1940, brought Kahuku, Waipahu, Waialua, and outlying public schools into the fold. For want of collegiate opponents, the College of Hawaiʻi (which became the University of Hawaiʻi) played these squads as well as semipro and military teams.

Most boys on sugar and pineapple plantations never finished high school, much less attended university. Barefoot football fit more easily into their proletarian lives. Sporting goods salesman A. K. Vierra conceived of it in 1922 as way to sell headgear and padding to kids in Kalihi, the Palama Settlement, and other working-class sections of Honolulu. The barefoot game, which usually set a weight limit of 135 pounds, spread to the countryside and other islands, where canneries and plantations sponsored teams. Given that most island boys had rarely worn shoes as children, barefoot football capitalized on their ability to kick and run unshod. Where native Hawaiians and Samoans competed, the weight limit was set as high as 170 pounds.

The barefoot leagues meshed with settlement house and plantation-based sports. By the early twentieth century, plantations and canneries drove the islands' economy. Most workers lived in company housing, where virtually all aspects of daily life—from where they shopped, prayed, and sought medical attention to where their children were educated—took place on plantation land. Given that few families or laborers had radios or could afford to travel, sport was either self-organized or employer sponsored.

Samoans on Oʻahu's North Shore embraced football decades before it arrived in American Samoa. At Kahuku High School, the sons and grandsons of an early-twentieth-century wave of émigrés became the core of the first mostly Samoan football squad anywhere in the world. Dethroning sugar as king in towns along the northern coast, the sport gave generations of Polynesian boys a way to come to terms with their place in the world.

Sugar shaped the North Shore and Kahuku's ascent to football's firmament. After firing up its boilers in 1890, the Kahuku Sugar Plantation began drawing workers from as far away as Europe, the Caribbean, and Asia. These proletarian wayfarers encountered Samoans, Tongans, and well-scrubbed Mormons from Utah's Great Basin who came because of the temple nearby in La'ie. Though driven by different agendas, both plantation managers and Mormon elders saw sport as a way to shape the behavior of those they recruited to work or worship. Their efforts contributed to the sporting infrastructure and ethos that would make Kahuku one of football's most gripping microcultures of excellence.

But sport here was never simply a tale of top-down manipulation, of athletics harnessed to company and church goals. Workers and their sons during sugar's heyday made sport their own. *Pau hana*, the time after work or after school, belonged to them, no matter how much the company or the church sought to control it. And during *pau hana*, they shaped Kahuku football in their own image.

Their descendants have defined Kahuku football and the North Shore ever since. Hawaiians, Samoans, Filipinos, Tahitians, Japanese, Puerto Ricans, Portuguese, Tongans, Chinese, Fijians, a few *haoles* (whites) and African Americans, and blends thereof currently populate the coastal strip extending northward to Sunset Beach. They came for work, for the church, or to surf but found common ground in sport. That's made football the North Shore's civic cement and ratcheted up the pressure on those who coach and play it.

Though he professes no interest in football, Angel Ramos knows Kahuku's sugarcane backstory better than most. He lives in a man-made swath of Eden, a modest home engulfed by a garden bursting with thousands of cacti, succulents, and snake plants. The city council named Ramos a living treasure in 1998 in recognition of his efforts to preserve the history of the immigrants who cut cane and ground it into sugar at the Kahuku Sugar Plantation. He was once a *sakada*—a contract laborer brought from the Philippines. Angel arrived in 1946, a seventeen-year-old from the Ilocos region following the path of his father's and brother's labor odysseys.[1] He worked in Maui's pineapple fields before running away to Honolulu and finding his way to Kahuku, where his father had twice gone as a *sakada*. Starting as a laboratory analyst in 1949, Angel was a journeyman machinist when the mill's giant grinders shuddered to a stop in 1971.[2]

That's when Angel Ramos became a historian. A broad smile crinkles his creased face and highlights a full head of silver-black hair. He perches atop a seat taken from the back seat of a van on the porch of his home amid birdcages and potted plants. Angel had always evinced curiosity about his surroundings and co-workers, taking photographs and talking story if given the opportunity. When the mill closed, he began retrieving discarded artifacts. "And when we have gatherings," he explained, "we tell stories about our experiences and I put that in my head, too. If you're looking for something like a book, no, I don't have that." Tapping his head, he said, "It's all in here."

Birdsong and wind chimes murmur a chorus to Angel's recollections. He has pieced together a history of the plantation from listening to his elders and passing time with documents and materials salvaged from Dumpsters. A nervous bundle of exuberance that belies his four score and some years, Angel flits from story to story, tending chickens in a cage and carp in a barrel between anecdotes.

Filipinos loomed large in Kahuku's workforce, augmented by Japanese, a few Portuguese, some Chinese, and *haoles* in supervisory positions. "They say that when we came to Hawai'i, that Lucasanos and Visaynos who come from the south of the Philippine islands don't get along. If some guy marries one—*oooh!* But here we're all Filipinos," he observed. As time went on, that new consciousness kept evolving; boys of Filipino ancestry on Kahuku's football team today think of themselves as Hawaiian or American. So do their Samoan and Tongan teammates.

Few Samoans worked on the estate in the 1950s, but their presence grew after the "great *malaga*." "There are many Samoan families here now, my goodness!" Angel exclaimed. Youth from Kahuku, as well as from Hau'ula, La'ie, and to the north where the Banzai Pipeline attracts some of the most intrepid surfers in the world, come together at Kahuku High.

The plantation, Angel explained, was organized around work camps in the fields and grouped by nationality, with men outnumbering women and scant opportunities for recreation. "So the men go to Honolulu to dance, to gamble and party. There was hardly any radio when I came to Kahuku, and only party lines with a crank telephone; maybe only seven phones in all."

"Recreation was something the people here needed, and the plantation provided that by way of sport. It keep them occupied; it entertain them, and," he said, chortling, "it keep them from Honolulu prostitutes." Kahuku's sporting life revolved around the Kahuku Athletic Association.

Mill superintendent Thomas G. S. Walker was the association's godfather. Wagging his finger, Angel declared, "He was a sportsman. That's what the old guys said. He was so good a sportsman that Filipino people would say that Mr. Walker was more devoted to sports than raising sugar!" Walker built a gymnasium for the school as well as athletic headquarters on the plantation. "He was the *patron*," Angel added. "Mr. Walker was a good man and they said that that's why he got fired—because he was so committed to sport."

The workers, especially as more women came, were not totally beholden to the mill. They fashioned their own social lives. "When people would get married," Angel protested, "they don't go to a hotel and have a reception. We do it in the camp! We slaughter a pig, and the dance is a string orchestra. It's the Filipino way." They staged boxing matches and cockfights, bet furiously, and took to sport during their scant free time.

"In the 1920s and '30s, before I came, teams from different mill departments played against other plantations and each other." Given Kahuku's isolation, the plantation furnished medical help, rudimentary housing, and firewood and kerosene for fuel and lighting. "These were the customary amenities," Angel noted, stressing that they were designed to fend off unions and make workers feel beholden.

His father had worked twelve-hour shifts inside the mill, earning a bit more than fieldworkers. It was a tough, austere life. Early union drives fizzled when the growers played nationalities off against each other. "If Japanese strike, the Filipinos work," Ramos exclaimed. "If Filipinos strike, then Japanese break the strike." When Japanese workers struck in 1894, they walked thirty-eight miles to Honolulu to protest their working conditions, and then slunk back to Kahuku in the rain after they were defeated.

In the wake of the 1909 strike that spread across the islands, the Hawaiian Sugar Planters' Association (HSPA) pushed recreation for workers. Ball fields were affordable, the HSPA argued, and "every nationality is keen for [baseball]." Corporate welfare measures, such as movies, music, and athletics, promised "magnificent results" that would raise morale and ease labor discontent. "We believe," HSPA leaders concluded, "it would be to the financial benefit of the plantation to endeavor to cultivate a spirit of contentment among the laborers."[3] Their efforts oozed with condescension. "The Filipino is something of an overgrown boy," the association's Montague Lord wrote. "He requires a certain amount of looking after. A little interest taken by the overseer in charge of his amusements, camp life, etc., will work wonders."[4]

The HSPA had anticipated the spread of factory sport programs. After obliterating industrial unionism following World War I, corporations tossed workers a few bones. Though unwilling to bargain over wages and working conditions, they gave workers restrooms, factory newspapers, English and citizenship classes, and sport. Their goals: keep their workplaces free of unions, lower absenteeism and turnover, and make employees as hardworking and loyal as possible. Though effective in the short run, these programs could forestall collective bargaining for only so long.

In 1920, when cane workers put down their machetes and millworkers refused to grind cane, they stuck together and transcended the "blood unionism" that had divided them. Nevertheless, they lost again. Afterward, plantations redoubled their recreational efforts, especially in Kahuku, which soon had one of the best-organized programs in the islands.

Kahuku, like just about everything else in Hawai'i, belonged to what was called the Big Five. An imposing oligopoly made up of Alexander and Baldwin, American Factors, C. Brewer, Castle and Cooke, and T. H. Davies, the Big Five stood in the way of workers gaining more of a say over their own lives. They monopolized sugar and pineapple production. "In no part of the United States," journalist Ray Stannard Baker argued, "is a single industry so predominant as the sugar industry is in Hawai'i." It was, he wrote, not a tropical paradise as much as "a paradise of modern industrial combination."[5]

Big Five sway over government was considerable and its control of the rural working classes nearly absolute. But Ramos was careful to distinguish Kahuku's mill superintendent, Tom Walker, from the Big Five. "No, he was not a sibling of the Big Five! The Kahuku mill was one of Big Five, of course it was; it was Alexander and Baldwin. But we know Mr. Walker was not in with those guys; he was a good man. He was too good!" If a worker's plight came to his attention, Angel said, "He would say go take care of that guy! That was what I heard and heard every time we have party and talk story; everyone pitch in and tell a story that he was so good. Oh my goodness, the workers liked him." And they knew how much Walker cared about sport.

Workers rose in time to report to their *luna*, the bosses who supervised them in the fields, at five a.m. to begin work before the sun scalded their backs. Twelve hours later, they trudged home, with little energy left for recreation. But on Tuesday nights, they rode a company train from their camp to the athletic association and watched boxing, which had special cachet among Filipinos. On days off or company sports days, they played in tournaments featuring volleyball, baseball, races, and tug-of-war, and hosted teams from other islands.

Walker was behind their sporting life. Early in 1934, he said that his vision was "to inaugurate sports in which all races can join." Citing the admirable records of company football and volleyball teams, and the triumphs of local youth, Walker asserted that "we have the material to place Kahuku well up on the athletic map." His goal was to make athletics "a major part in our Plantation policies and activities." Though Kahuku was the island's smallest mill, it featured illuminated volleyball and tennis courts, the biggest baseball diamond on Oʻahu, and the island's first golf course. Walker also recognized sport's effect on the bottom line. Promoting "sports of all kinds will not only give all of us a lot of fun but will aid in keeping the Plantation morale at its present high level."[6] In the long run, plantation support for sport contributed to Kahuku's imposing presence in football.

World War II was a game changer for Hawaiʻi's working people. By its end, they felt empowered, ready to redeem their wartime sacrifices. When 26,000 workers shut down all but one of Hawaiʻi's thirty-four plantations for seventy-nine days in 1946, they finally triumphed over a paternalistic labor system that hastened the 1954 Democratic Revolution. That ended one-party Republican Party rule, signaled the coming of age of Japanese American power on the island, and brought about more progressive policies.

Arriving in the wake of the 1946 strike, Angel Ramos embraced its legacy. "The big strike," he said with a smile, "was about getting more time for yourself. That was what we were striving for; we wanted more time for a life." He enumerated the gains: a six-day workweek, eight-hour days, higher wages, vacation leaves, and health care guaranteed through collective bargaining rather than by the intervention of the superintendent. "Since coming to Kahuku, I was a militant union man; I still cherish my learning from the union."[7]

Football was not so exalted on the North Shore when Ramos arrived. Before World War II, few boys completed high school, and the game hardly mattered. Kahuku High School's first graduating class, in 1940, numbered only sixteen students, and there were hardly enough boys to field a team. Nor was football central to the Kahuku plantation's sporting program, where Portuguese, Japanese, and Filipinos joined baseball clubs and Samoans played basketball.[8]

But after World War II, Kahuku welcomed newcomers from the South Pacific, many drawn by the Church of Jesus Christ of Latter-day Saints, and witnessed the coming-of-age of children born to earlier wayfarers. Growing up "American," they had higher expectations than following their parents into the cane fields. As their numbers grew, so did enthusiasm for high school football, which eclipsed the barefoot and barrel-weight teams the plantation fielded.

The men who coached there were as diverse a group as the North Shore's eclectic mix. During the 1940s, Mits Fujishige, a Japanese American, and Art Stranske, a Canadian expat, led the school to its first titles. But Harold Silva and Famika Anae left the greatest imprint. Silva, a Portuguese American, showed the community that Kahuku was capable of competing with the rest of Hawai'i. "He's the guy who started it all," Junior Ah You testified when Silva, his former history teacher, passed away in 2003. "He was the one who started the winning tradition at Kahuku, what has become Red Raider Nation."[9] And then, a few years after Silva left, Famika Anae came home. He became the first Samoan head football coach at any level of the game.

Silva, from O'ahu's leeward side, served in Europe during the war. Afterward, he played tackle for the University of Hawai'i, where he earned a teaching degree. He then began assisting Father Kenneth A. Bray at 'Iolani High School and stepped in as head coach when illness abruptly forced the fabled Englishman to retire in 1952. In 1956, Silva took over a Kahuku squad in total disarray and set about remaking its culture.

Silva infused Kahuku's program with Bray's tough, principled athletic code. Bray was an unlikely coaching guru. A descendant of Thomas Bray, who founded the Society for Promotion of Christian Knowledge in 1698, the Lancashire-born Bray was fifty-three when he landed on O'ahu in 1932. Although he grew up playing rugby, the Episcopal priest was in his element coaching baseball, basketball, and football at Honolulu's 'Iolani School. Tall and intense, Bray coached with the toughest form of love. He routinely played just eleven starters the entire game, and critics decried his practices as verging on cruelty. But his players became devotees, even if he kicked over their water bucket on sweltering days.[10]

Bray foreswore most earthly pleasures, using his salary to support the team and the school. He bought his players the best uniforms in the league as well as their lunches. He lived near the school with a dozen boys who accepted his ascetic discipline. On weekends, he scoured playgrounds to gauge the athletic potential of boys he might bring to 'Iolani. Introducing himself to street gangs, he won admission to the school for a few of their members. "They worshipped the ground he walked on," one 1938 alumni exclaimed. Another graduate branded these recruits criminals, there only to play ball, but even he noted that Bray changed their lives.[11]

Honolulu's private schools recruited widely, with alumni serving as bird dogs and benefactors, steering boys who could not otherwise afford school fees. Bray was prescient in seeing the athletic potential of Polynesian youth and made Alopati Lolotai his first recruit. Soon he had recruited enough Samoans to cause him to command players to refrain from speaking Samoan at practice, especially when he thought that they were talking about him. He intuited that their culture was inherently team first, ideal for his purposes. "You are not individuals greedy for individual honor," he wrote to his players, "but members of a team, eager for team achievement." 'Iolani's emphasis on *ohana*, the Hawaiian metaphor for family, resonated deeply with his Polynesian players.[12]

Like Bray, Silva demanded smart, disciplined play. After realizing he wasn't mean, but determined, the players became his partisans. "He was rough and tough, but that's the spirit of Kahuku and they don't expect anything less," explained longtime American Samoan congressman Eni Faleomavaega, who played for Silva.[13] The turnaround was stunning. After winning just one game and losing nine the year before Silva arrived, Kahuku won a title in his first season, finished second the next two years, and won again in 1959.

Hugh Yoshida, who played for Bray and Silva at 'Iolani, saw the difference Silva made for boys at Kahuku. "They were very rough at the edges because organized football had not been available there. Harold said he had to build the concept of a team at Kahuku; to bring its disparate groups together." To bolster his players' resolve, Silva left money on the locker room floor to encourage them to do the right thing. "That," Yoshida said, "was really the beginning of modern-day football at Kahuku."[14]

Hugh Yoshida and his 'Iolani teammate Larry Ginoza would become two of the island's leading coaches. Yoshida took Leilehua High in the central valley north of Honolulu to the top ranks of Hawaiian football, while Gino-za made Wai'anae on the leeward side of the island a powerhouse. "Harold didn't deviate too much from Bray," Ginoza recalled. "It was team first; nobody was better than anyone else; no flamboyance. You celebrate on the field and you would get it from Father Bray. That's what Harold tried to apply."[15]

Leo Reed, who played on Kahuku's 1956 championship team and became the school's first pro player, saw that every day at practice.[16] "I think about him all the time," Reed reflected. "He cared about his players, not like when you go up to college, where it's a meat factory." Louis Santiago lined up with Reed that season. "Coach Silva started the dynasty," Santiago affirmed. "If it weren't for him, Kahuku might still be down." When Silva took players to scout opponents in his '57 Thunderbird, Santiago absorbed his coach's comments as if they were the distilled wisdom of the ages.

Louis Santiago passed on Silva's acumen to his three sons when it came time for them to play for Kahuku.[17] Each, like their father, was an all-state selection. So were Louis's grandsons, Manti Te'o and Keala Santiago Jr. Te'o, who played for Punahou instead of Kahuku, was an All-American at Notre Dame and the San Diego Chargers' first round draft pick in 2013; his cousin Keala, one of Hawai'i's top 2015 prep players, enrolled at the University of Hawai'i after graduation. Though Santiago's sons and grandsons never played for Silva, his approach to football—passed down from fathers and uncles to sons and nephews—affected them just the same. So did Famika Anae, who returned to the North Shore a few years after Silva departed and built upon the foundation he had laid.

If Silva and Anae set Kahuku's football course, Junior Ah You epitomized the spirit and play that characterized it at its best. Though too young to play for Harold Silva, Junior suited up for Famika Anae his senior year before leaving the islands to become Arizona State's first Polynesian recruit. These days, Junior can be found baking bread in the back of Tita's Grill across the road from the high school, or schmoozing on the benches in front of his bamboo-and-wooden eatery. Lizards, roosters, and cats coexist peacefully under the restaurant's canopies; customers—a mix of students, working people, and tourists—greet Junior as he converses.

Most men who last a decade in the pros visibly bear the consequences.

Not Junior. The epitome of athleticism when he was an all-state selection in football, basketball, and track and field in the 1960s, he still is—in his sixties. "Nobody looks more like a Polynesian warrior than Junior," *Sports Illustrated*'s Richard Johnston wrote in 1976. "He has a body builder's physique, smoky eyes flanking a hawk nose in a high-cheekboned face, a Fu Manchu moustache embracing a mobile mouth full of flashing white teeth—and nobody's name sounds less like one."[18]

Junior's grandfather was a merchant from Sichuan whose seafaring ended in American Samoa in the early 1900s after he wed an island girl. One of their sons converted to Mormonism and fathered eleven children. Junior, the seventh, was born in Faleniu on Tutuila in 1948 and came with his family to La'ie when he was seven because his parents wanted to seal their children in the temple. After a career that took him across North America, he's back on the North Shore, enmeshed in church and community. While talking, Junior kneaded dough and folded batter into pans before sliding them into the oven to bake loaves of his signature coconut bread.

In 1865, the Mormons bought six thousand acres of land in Hawai'i between the Koolau mountains and the sea to free themselves of gentile contamination. La'ie had been a *pu'uhonua*, a refuge under the protection of the priests. Fugitives as well as villagers escaping the carnage of island wars found sanctuary there. Now the Mormons were seeking to make it a gathering place for South Pacific converts.

La'ie also constituted an *ahupua'a*, a wedge-shaped piece of land falling from the crest of the mountains to the reefs. Each *ahupua'a*, a political jurisdiction defined by its watershed, was a self-sustaining municipality under the authority of chiefs who served at the king's discretion. Between the sea's bounty and the timber, taro, fruits, and medicinal herbs harvested from its terraced hills and lowlands, the *ahupua'a* provided native Hawaiians with a healthy, relatively secure, life.

That way of life crumbled after Captain James Cook's ill-fated arrival in 1778 shattered the islands' epidemiological seclusion. Some researchers estimate that the native population, lacking resistance to European microbes, shrunk by more than 90 percent in the first century of contact with outsiders. The demographic disaster compromised the political legitimacy on which traditional culture rested.

The 1848 Great Mahele, a division of island land, compounded these woes when it unintentionally transferred most communally held land to private, nonnative hands. The Great Mahele was the handiwork of a land commission created by King Kamehameha III that sought to resolve land claims from both Hawaiians and foreigners. Until then, the concept of land ownership was a foreign notion; land belonged to the gods and was managed by the chiefs, who acted as its stewards. But the Great Mahele opened the way for foreigners to own land by dividing Hawaiian land into portions allotted to the king, the chiefs, and the common people. But many islanders failed to register their claims and others sold them off, allowing foreigners to take ownership. The Great Mahele upended the *ahupua'a* system and the sense of reciprocity governing relations among the king, his chiefs, and subjects. Before the Great Mahele, foreigners might lease land but never purchase it. Afterward, sugar companies and speculators gobbled it up for trifling sums. As a result, the *ahupua'a* comprising La'ie became private property purchased by the Mormons in 1865.

Nineteenth-century Latter-day Saints doctrine drew a sharp line between Caucasians and everyone else. It associated whiteness with righteous purity and the chance of spiritual reclamation, blackness with unredeemable wickedness. But the church viewed Polynesians—whom it considered neither black nor white—more ambiguously. George Cannon, an early missionary to Hawai'i, believed that Polynesians were one of Israel's lost tribes and eligible for salvation. Moreover, he felt it was the church's obligation to bring about their redemption.

Notions of the *ahupua'a* and reciprocity, much less of *pu'uhonua* and sanctuary, were only memories when the Mormons consolidated their South Pacific beachhead in 1919 by constructing a temple in La'ie. Thirty-five miles north of Honolulu, the aboriginal fishing village sat between Hau'ula to the south and Kahuku a few miles northward. The La'ie temple, the first dedicated outside the continental United States, was conceived of as a gathering place for Mormons in the South Pacific. That was a departure—church practice had called for all Mormons to gather at the temple in Utah—but Hawaiian law had curtailed the movement of Hawaiians off island due to plunging native populations.

One can hardly overstate the temple's importance to Mormons. It was the only place where the ordinances required for salvation—baptizing the dead or marriage for eternity—could be conducted and redemption sought for family members who had died before completing the sacraments. Although La'ie was a week's journey by sea from Samoa, it was much closer than Salt Lake City and became the most consequential destination for Mormons in the South Pacific.

Anthropologist Bernard Pierce called La'ie the closest approximation of a Samoan village to be found outside of Samoa. Because they were not a minority there, Samoans adapted at their own pace, albeit within the confines of a church-owned company town. With church leaders hours away in Honolulu, Samoans and Hawaiians, not *haoles*, set the tone locally.[19] La'ie's racial diversity, then an anomaly, was more of a harbinger of the church's future global demographics than Salt Lake City. A majority of Mormons now either live outside the United States or are the children of foreign-born parents.

Though the church cultivated cane on its La'ie plantation, it was not as driven by the bottom line as the Big Five sugar companies. Elsewhere in Hawai'i, sugar was king, defining the economy and workers' lives.[20] The church in La'ie was more flexible, even encouraging the cultivation of kalo, the Hawaiian staple that Samoans called taro. Most sugar companies had plowed kalo under to grow more cane. These factors made it easier for Hawaiians and Samoans to retain their own culture.[21]

While immigrants displaced Hawaiians on most plantations, almost half of La'ie's workforce was native-born.[22] Samoans held more in common with these Kanaka Maoli, as the natives were called, than taro. Their approach to land, polity, and social structure overlapped. As Japanese, Portuguese, Puerto Ricans, Filipinos, Koreans, and Chinese, as well as North Americans, arrived, Samoans blended into a simpatico Pan-Pacific town where the church's somewhat less-than-capitalist approach tempered the excesses of the plantation system.[23]

There were more than one hundred Samoans in La'ie by the 1920s. Overall, they comprised a quarter of the town's population, a critical mass whose presence attracted more émigrés, including non-Mormon Samoans.[24] Their children grew up more *fa'a Hawai'i* than *fa'a Samoa*. The only complaint Bernard Pierce heard from these young people during his 1950s fieldwork was that its athletic programs were deficient. For sport, especially football, they went up the coast to Kahuku, where Al Lolotai began his athletic career.

La'ie's Mormon elders had weaned themselves from sugar decades before the Kahuku mill closed in 1971 and had never embraced an aggressive form of capitalism in the first place. Instead, they strove to create a self-sufficient community organized around common values, remaking the economy to advance their religious agenda and minimize outside pressures. That meshed well with the sensibilities of Samoans, who settled comfortably into the town. Their numbers grew after the *President Jackson* docked in Honolulu in 1952 and three hundred of the one thousand immigrants aboard headed there. By the time Junior Ah You arrived, Samoans made up more than a third of La'ie.

But La'ie was not Samoa. The collective ownership of land that sustained Samoan society was absent. Samoans still tended garden plots and grew bread-fruit, bananas, and coconut palms, from which they squeezed coconut cream used to make *palusami*, a staple at the Sunday meal, and retained a strong communal ethos. But they were in a quasi-capitalist world now, one they entered via a church-driven political economy.[25] Many Samoans worked for the Church College of Hawai'i (now Brigham Young University–Hawai'i), the Polynesian Cultural Center, or the Hawai'i Reserves, a church-affiliated company that manages its considerable holdings.[26]

Junior Ah You's father had been the head mechanic at Tutuila's small air-port and ran a family store and buses that traveled to outlying villages. In La'ie, he worked as a mechanic for a car dealership. "We lived in a *fa'a Samoa* family and our culture was deeply rooted," Junior explained. But the Ah Yous, like most Samoan Mormons, paid even more heed to church elders than to their *matai*.

The church was consequential because of the depths of Samoan religious commitment and its centrality to their livelihood. That undermined the *matai*, whom the church sometimes criticized for levying what elders saw as exces-sive demands for funerals, weddings, and ceremonies—the practice known as *fa'a lavelave*. "The way it's done now is twisted," Junior remarked. "It's like a competition."[27] He's not the only one pushing back against a practice that devours family resources and causes some to take out loans. Still, *'aiga* and village dynamics matter to Samoans here, whether or not they're LDS.

Sport came easily to Junior. In Samoa, he played almost everything but football, which had yet to arrive. He did the same in O'ahu, where sport was a part of the "mutual nights" that the Mormons organized for young people. Junior's language skills made for a fairly smooth transition; so did the security that came from growing up in a town like Laʻie, thick with ʻaiga and LDS connections.

"I am so grateful to those who were around me in the community when I was playing, for how they embraced me, loved me, and provided for me," Junior said. Wherever he went as a youth, people exhorted him to excel in sport and avoid trouble, telling him he represented them, the village, and Hawaiʻi. "I'm getting teary-eyed thinking about it," he said. "I wonder where I would be if not for them. So when I grew up and had success and came back, I wanted to do that for kids in the community."

His grandfather, a high chief who did missionary work in Samoa for fifty years, foretold of Junior's success. Before his grandfather left for the mainland, Junior went to him. "I remember vividly the blessing he gave me— that if I kept my faith, honored my parents, was active in the church, represented my name well, and was a good servant to the community, l would find great success in sports. I started chuckling a bit when he said that; I had never played anything but Pop Warner, but that was his blessing. My goodness! Not till way later did I see what my grandfather prophesized for me."

After playing Pop Warner football in nearby Hauʻula, Junior joined Kahuku's junior varsity squad. He often watched Silva, the varsity coach, lead practice. "He was like General Patton; his voice thundered and there was no messing around. I had so much respect for him." Samoans comprised half the squad, with Hawaiians, Filipinos, and boys whose parents worked at the college making up the rest. There were even a few surfer boys from Sunset Beach. "But it was hard for them." Junior grinned. "Once surf is up, none came to practice so the coach said you either play football or surf."

When Junior's mother died of cancer his sophomore year, he went into a funk and dropped out of school. A few months later, Coach Harry "the Clown" Kahuanui, Silva's successor, came to his home. A Golden Gloves heavyweight champ and the first University of Hawaiʻi player selected for the East-West Shrine Game, the ex-Marine was bigger and tougher than his players. He was called the Clown because of his lanky body, not his demeanor. "Harry wouldn't let me quit," Junior remembered. "He told me I had a great future." Leaning on his coach, Junior returned to school, where Kahuanui worked with him one-on-one, teaching him the nuances of the game.

"Coach Kahuanui was trying to get me rough," Junior remembered. That didn't come naturally. "We were taught in the Samoan home not to talk back. No matter what they say, you shut your mouth." But Kahuanui challenged Junior during individual workouts, throwing elbows to his face and knocking him down. "Finally, I couldn't handle it anymore," Junior said, "so I started fighting back. When I did, he slammed the ball down and yelled in my face, *'About time! About time!'* If it wasn't for him," Junior reflected, "nobody would have ever heard of me in sports."

When BYU (Brigham Young University) inexplicably ignored Junior, he went to Arizona State. "I went there not knowing how I would do," he recalled, unsure that he belonged. "You hear so much about the mainland, about big *haole* guys you see on TV, but at the first practice I was shocked that none of those guys from the mainland were any better than the three of us from Hawai'i." His Hawaiian teammates, Junior reminisced, "were better than I was, but neither could stay because they didn't go to class."

Though college football was faster and more complex than high school ball, and ASU's coach Frank Kush an intensely driven man known for his outbursts, Junior's transition went smoothly. "All the *haole* and *palagi* players were freaking out because Frank scared the daylights out of them. But he knew I wasn't afraid of him. He saw that while I wasn't afraid of him, I respected the heck out of him."

Needing to generate a pass rush, Kush moved Junior to defensive end, where his athleticism and attitude compensated for his lack of size. A two-time college All-American, Junior was the MVP for both the Fiesta Bowl and the Peach Bowl.[28] Hugh Yoshida considers him Hawai'i's first breakout player of the modern era. It wasn't just his performance on the field, Yoshida testified. "People loved Junior in Arizona and here in Hawai'i because he was such a great person and made us proud." And each season, he returned home and performed as the solo fire dancer at the Polynesian Cultural Center.

By the late 1960s, most of the best island players routinely left for the mainland, where more than fifty suited up at Division I schools each season. After Duffy Daugherty called Bob Apisa the "best sophomore" in Michigan State history and Junior won All-American honors, more coaches began recruiting the islands. Consequently, the University of Hawai'i team struggled. The *Honolulu Advertiser* bemoaned Hawai'i's "balance of players problem," as far more good players left than arrived. That's still a problem for the state's flagship university. "It's always been part of the culture," Hugh Yoshida explained, "that if you want to grow, you need to go to the States.

That's a given." As the University of Hawai'i's athletic director, he often confronted that dilemma.[29]

Though the NFL's New England Patriots drafted Junior, he signed a three-year guaranteed contract with the Canadian Football League's Montreal Alouettes instead. While New England looked at Junior, who weighed 220 pounds, and thought he was better suited at linebacker, Montreal coach Marv Levy let him stay at defensive end. Junior forged a ten-year all-star career in Montreal that included two Grey Cup championships, one in which he was the MVP. He finished his career in the USFL and became the first Hawaiian inducted into the Canadian Football Hall of Fame. Given how Junior dominated wherever he played, one wonders how big a star he could have been in the NFL. But he's at peace with his decisions.

After watching coaches spend endless days in dark, smoky rooms smelling of pizza and day old coffee, Junior had no desire to coach. Instead, he returned to the North Shore and plunged into the community. He fed folks in need at Thanksgiving, spearheaded efforts to build the multipurpose Malaekahana trail linking La'ie to Kahuku, and organized annual Christmas flag football tournaments. Rather than cashing in on his celebrity, Junior provides encouragement to youth the way his elders once nurtured him. Famika Anae was one of those mentors.

Not all Kahuku coaches were like Silva, central casting's gruff mentor with a bark that cut to the bone. Famika Anae best defined Kahuku football. The brother of Al Lolotai, the first Samoan to play in the NFL, Famika was the son of a Mormon from Western Samoa who answered the call to build the La'ie temple. He was a quintessential product of La'ie's tough blend of Mormon, Samoan, and football discipline. Famika's father was no pushover either. By most accounts, Aulelio Anae was not an easy man to live with. According to family lore, Famika once ignored his instructions to tend their garden plot in order to go to practice. When he got home, Aulelio chased him around the plot, brandishing his *pelu*, a bush knife he used to garden. The *pelu* ended up stuck in Famika's leg.[30]

"My dad played because of his brother Al Lolotai," Allen Anae explained, "but my grandfather asked, 'Can you eat the football? What value can that have in your life?'"[31] A college education meant little to Aulelio. "My grandfather was all about work," Allen explained. "Because you work, you eat; that's how he thought." Nor did Aulelio care that much about retaining Samoan culture. "When the old man came here," his daughter-in-law recalled, "he said, 'We're not doing *fa'a Samoa*.'" Aulelio focused on the Mormon Church, to which he tithed, but eschewed *fa'a lavelave* and other Samoan practices.

Famika excelled in every sport he tried but baseball, where the loss of sight in one eye hampered his hitting. His brother Al showed Famika that football could take him to college and a world beyond La'ie. Famika starred at Kahuku before heading to the mainland in 1951 to play at Compton Junior College, a way station to top college programs. Two years later, after Compton won junior college's national championship, Famika became BYU's first Samoan recruit. The only player on its roster with a Polynesian surname and one of two from Hawai'i, the six-foot-tall, two-hundred-pound center anchored BYU's offensive line. When he wasn't playing football, winning boxing tournaments, or earning a degree, he was courting Alice Rice, a blond-haired student from Tacoma, Washington.

Given Utah's racial climate, Famika's marriage to Alice didn't sit well with church leaders or people on the street. "At that time," their son Allen reflected, "for the average person living in Provo, Utah, my father was black." The atmosphere was nasty enough that the Anaes left Provo soon after Famika graduated.

They moved in with the Lolotais in Redondo Beach until Famika found work in Compton. He taught and coached while Alice tended to a family that grew to seven children. But friends on the North Shore kept urging Famika to come home. "They said he needed to give back to the community," Alice explained. "Of course, his heart was here, where he grew up."[32]

La'ie and Kahuku were tiny, isolated towns in the 1960s. "The North Shore wasn't the North Shore then," Allen said. That tag emerged only after the surfing profile of a stretch north of Kahuku blew up and the pipeline became world-renowned. "Dad didn't miss a beat. He left Hawai'i on a boat in 1951 having never been off the island. Now he returns on a Pan American flight with six kids, a man on a mission." They moved into a house across from Famika's parents in La'ie, a far more tolerant town than Provo. "You didn't make much for teaching then," Alice said, smiling. Coaching paid even less, and they used Famika's stipend for athletics for Christmas gifts.[33]

But Famika was on a mission. He believed that football could make a college education possible. "He was still a young guy," Allen said, "and picked up like he never left, teaching and coaching, mentoring young men who he could relate to because they were so similar in upbringing." If Famika could make it off the island and earn a degree, so could they.

But he needed to remake the team's culture first, to take Harold Silva's work further. "My father had that North Shore vibe in him, but not when it came to football," Allen said with a chuckle. "Dad was at odds with how things naturally happened on the North Shore, where you went to work and did things at your own pace." Allen, nine when they returned, hung out at practice and became a team manager and then its starting quarterback. He saw how his dad operated. Practice began at three and if you weren't there, in pads, ready to go, "you got dinged in his personal log." Three unexcused dings and you were off the team. There was attrition his first year, including a star tailback, whose suspension incited the community's rage. "But he stuck to it," Allen affirmed, "one man reshaping how things are done on the field, reshaping the culture of the team."

Football was not yet a year-round sport, but Famika began taking his team to Lanai to pick pineapples each summer. His brother Al had initiated that practice, taking Church College of Hawai'i wrestlers to the nearby island, which James Dole had made into the world's largest pineapple plantation. The company paid them the minimum wage, and Famika and the boys went for six weeks each summer. The kids returned with money in their pockets, in shape to play. Famika knew how much that meant to boys whose families lived so humbly.

"Famika was more of a local boy than a Samoan," his wife reflected. Easygoing off the field, he made people comfortable and was able to befriend men who had a hard time making friends. "Famika was totally different than Harold Silva," Hugh Yoshida recalled. "He was more compassionate, soft-spoken. Harold was a disciplinarian; Famika was more embracing." Junior Ah You played for Famika Anae his senior year. "When he talked to you, he didn't belittle you," Junior recalled. "He made you feel your role was very important; that if you don't do your part, we won't have success." While other coaches thought Kahuku players were overly aggressive and prone to committing penalties, a view that persists, Famika channeled their rugged, competitive psyches into championship squads. Famika coached Kahuku from 1966 to 1972, winning two titles and bringing Samoan players to the fore. He also conducted clinics in American Samoa during the summer with Al Lolotai, who had moved there to organize island sport.

Unlike coaches before him, Famika understood the challenges that players from American Samoa and recently independent Samoa faced in Hawai'i. He also appreciated their background on the islands. "A Samoan boy starts hard physical labor even before he reaches school age," Famika observed. "He must climb a coconut tree 100 feet tall, barefoot and carrying a machete, tear the coconuts loose and even cut away the fronds." His players at Kahuku did chores, but not like youth in Samoa. "These kids do this every day and, after school starts, every night." Hawai'i's Samoans could climb only four or five trees, he noted, while small boys in Samoa climbed twenty of them, hiked the mountains to pick bananas, and packed out loads that weighed as much as they did. "By the time a boy is ready for high school football," he remarked, "his muscles often are as defined as those of a weight lifter."[34]

Anae realized the tensions Samoan youth faced at home. "It is very hard on a Samoan kid who doesn't do well, or what his father thinks is well. He is felt to have disgraced the family, and when he gets home he is likely to get a two-hour lecture that may end in a beating." Pride was paramount. "They see everything the kids do as an important part of promoting the culture," he said. "A loss reflects on the parents, the chiefs, and the race."

Anae channeled that fear of failure into a relentless attacking style. "Samoans are very physical people," he said. "They simply can't stand losing—either in sports or in life. They resent it when they see Caucasians or Japanese-Americans getting the best jobs, or sometimes the only jobs, and some take advantage of their physical strength to try for success along any avenue that seems open—even if it is crime."[35]

Despite the LDS's moderating influence, sport for Kahuku players meant battle. They readied themselves for games by performing the *siva tau*, the Samoan war dance. Their younger fans made Kamehameha Highway, the only way out of town, a gauntlet for opposing teams, pelting buses with gravel and coral stones from the shadows. Kahuku fed a Polynesian archetype, Allen Anae said, laughing, one in which every kid growing up in Hawai'i believed that there was a big, bad Samoan or Tongan kid who would take their lunch money or worse. "Every Polynesian who looks like the bad dude is thrown into that," he said with a sigh. Kahuku offered its football equivalent.

"Let me tell you a story," Wai'anae coach Larry Ginoza said, chortling. "When we went to Kahuku, we carried these wooden shields for the windows. We were ready for the rocks." But, he said, fighting and rock throwing happened everywhere. "They come here, to Wai'anae, they get rocked, too! Fans didn't intimidate us at Kahuku. Their team did! And besides, our own people would rock us if we lost!" Junior Ah You laughed at that. "I thought only Kahuku kids did that; one year, fans jumped the referees on the field."[36]

Famika Anae brought a touch of class and a good deal of focus to North Shore football. Vai Sikahema, who played with Anae's son Robert on BYU's 1984 national championship squad, described Famika as "Polynesian football royalty," who left a pristine pedigree and heritage for his children and players. That noble presence is on display in Waikiki. When Honolulu erected a statue of Olympian Duke Kahanamoku, its surfing emissary to the world, the sculptor used Famika's sleek and chiseled son Robert as his model.[37]

Famika Anae capped his Kahuku career against Leilehua in the 1972 OIA title game. His 1969 championship team belonged to the Rural Oʻahu Interscholastic Association, a group of country schools like Kahuku that had been built around sugar and pineapple plantations. In 1970, after five Honolulu schools joined, it became the OIA, Hawaiʻi's preeminent public school league. The Honolulu teams dominated the OIA, while schools like Kahuku and Leilehua garnered little respect until the two rural schools made it to the championship in 1972. They ignited an island-wide frenzy, and more fans jammed Honolulu Stadium to watch them play than would attend the University of Hawaiʻi versus San José State game held there two nights later. Afterward, the *Honolulu Advertiser*'s sports editor called it "the most sensational high school game seen in these parts in years."

By then, a second LDS-inspired wave of Samoans had arrived in La'ie, infusing Kahuku football with a new contingent of émigrés. Flipping through his high school yearbook, Allen Anae, the backup quarterback that 1972 season, identified his teammates. Most were Polynesian, with native-born Hawaiians a plurality. The Samoans were split between boys born locally and recent arrivals like the Finais. "Pisa Finai and his brother Paufai were born in Western Samoa," Allen recalled. "They were fresh off the boat, having to integrate into society, and football was their way. Can you imagine coming straight out of the bush, right off the plantation, having worn wrap-arounds the first five years of their life with no socialization to American society? They had never even worn underwear!" But the Finais were tough kids with enormous physical talents and Famika Anae knew how to develop them.

Their opponents in the title game, Coach Hugh Yoshida's unbeaten Leile-hua squad, had topped Kahuku 22–0 during the preseason and were heavily favored. It looked like Yoshida's team of Hawaiian and military kids would run over Kahuku, which could not stop Leilehua quarterback Alex Kaloi, a future star for the University of Hawai'i. But Leilehua could not handle the Finai brothers. Paufai returned a punt eighty-five yards for Kahuku's first score, bulled his way into the end zone for its second touchdown, and scored a third on a pass from Molia Salanoa.[38]

Although Leilehua led 22–14 in the fourth quarter, the Red Raiders' phys-icality was wearing them down. When Kahuku recovered a fumble in Leile-hua territory and scored, the gap closed to 22–20. A two-point conversion to tie the game failed, but Kahuku scored again. This time, quarterback Molia Salanoa ran into the end zone for the two-point conversion to put Kahuku up 28–22.

Their lead abruptly vanished when Leilehua came back to score and took a 29–28 lead with 1:11 left. "People were filing out of the stadium," Allen Anae said, laughing. "They thought the game was over, but that's when mir-acles happen, right?" That miracle seemed unlikely when the Finai brothers, back to receive, flubbed Leilehua's kickoff and Paufai was smothered at the five-yard line.

With no timeouts left, Molia Salanoa told his teammates, "I'm going to run around left end, so everybody block for me." They did. As Salanoa rolled to his left, his teammates blocked furiously. Seeing an opening, Salanoa streaked down the sideline until he was tackled eighty-five yards downfield at Leilehua's ten-yard line. But he had been tackled in bounds, and the clock was ticking. Totally gassed, Salanoa struggled to his feet.[39] Without time to bring on the kicking team to try a field goal, or even to huddle, Kahuku hur-riedly lined up while Leilehua's defense regrouped. "Our kids had to chase that son of a buck all the way down the field!" Yoshida recalled. "They were exhausted."

Coach Anae frantically tried to call a play from the sidelines. But before Salanoa could shout a play out, Pisa Finai, realizing that he was bigger and taller than the defender covering him, yelled to his quarterback in Samoan, "Throw 5 and out!" Salanoa obliged, rolling to his right and releasing a pass to Pisa, who was standing under the goal post. As soon as he released the ball, Salanoa was decked. "All I heard was cheering," he said afterward, "but I wasn't sure who was cheering. Then I looked into the end zone and all I could see was red-colored shirts coming over the wall. Then I knew Pisa had caught the ball."

"That's the first play he's called all season," Famika Anae said afterward. "What would I have called? Probably a sideline pattern to stop the clock. We were trying to get Molia's attention to do that but as it turned out, it was good we didn't." Anae told reporters he never doubted that they would win. Sensing their disbelief, he stated unequivocally, "We wanted it more."

"It was really painful," Hugh Yoshida said softly decades later. "But it was a classic that showcased the rural league. It became the game people always remember." Until then, only Honolulu schools had legitimacy in football. "Reflecting back," Yoshida said, "it was the start of credibility for our league and teams from other parts of the island. Kids from rural schools were considered second best. Now we're on board and the league picked up." A breakthrough for rural Hawai'i, it showcased the talent in plantation towns. But few could anticipate the Samoan surge building on the North Shore.[40]

Now the flow of boys from the North Shore to play college football is taken for granted. "I don't think there's a high school program in the United States that has benefited more from sport than Kahuku," Allen Anae argued. Eighty percent of Kahuku's current student body participates in interscholastic sports.[41] "Now we have parents thinking if I support my kids' football, and not only football but women's sports, they can get a college education," Allen observed. Maybe you can eat that football after all.

4

Al Lolotai, Charlie Ane, and Bob Apisa

Hiroshima and Nagasaki were still smoldering when the Washington Redskins assembled at Georgetown University for training camp on August 13, 1945. On the field, the Redskins belonged to Sammy Baugh, the Texas farmboy who had quarterbacked the team to three NFL championship games in the past five seasons. Most of the men crowding around him had managed to stay out of the service, avoiding conscription with defense jobs or deferments rendering them unfit for the military but not for the NFL. Others came from the league's player draft, which had lasted thirty-two rounds that year. Some had just left the service. Although the NFL offered only modest paychecks and scant security, it had survived the war and anticipated better times.

So did George Preston Marshall. Off the field, the team belonged to the flamboyant commercial laundryman. More attuned to marketing than his NFL peers, Marshall operated one of sport's most successful franchises. Because of deeply held personal prejudices as well as his conviction that the team's southern fan base would not countenance black players, Washington's roster had never included an African American. Nor had any NFL club since 1933, when Joe Lillard and Ray Kemp were the last to suit up. Marshall, who had entered the league the year before, was behind its segregation in the first place. All the more surprising, then, that a dark-skinned twenty-five-year-old free agent from Honolulu's sandlots was among the men at Marshall's Georgetown training camp.

Alopati "Al" Lolotai, Famika Anae's brother, not only made Washington's roster that fall; he was the NFL's top rookie lineman. Though he lacked the college pedigree of most players, "Sweet Lelani" Lolotai fast became one of the league's best guards.[1] After intercepting a pass and recovering a fumble against the Philadelphia Eagles in October, he began winning plaudits for both his offensive and defensive play. He kept would-be tacklers from getting to "Slinging Sammy" Baugh, while disrupting opponents when playing defense. After a midseason game, beat writer Al Costello gushed, "If there was a hero, it had to be Albert Lolotai, the Hawaiian born Samoan, a rookie who came to the club this year entirely unheralded and won his spurs as a big league performer yesterday."[2] Lolotai was a Samoan-born Hawaiian, not a Hawaiian-born Samoan, but Costello was right about his NFL bona fides. He belonged.

Lolotai never let up, and Washington returned to the championship game that December. But in a bizarre thriller, two kicks and a pass struck the goalposts at critical moments and bounced the wrong way for Washington each time, allowing the Rams, in their final season in Cleveland before decamping for Los Angeles, to win 15–14. Lolotai left the locker room with a full share of the loser's cut, $902.67.[3] Though paltry by current standards, the sum was a third of his regular-season salary, for which he had been paid $275 for each of ten games.[4]

News of Al Lolotai's breakthrough as the first Polynesian in the league went unnoticed in Samoa, and the six-foot-tall, 215-pound lineman's debut failed to draw attention to sport's impending desegregation. While Jackie Robinson's signature on a Brooklyn Dodgers contract that October heralded the sporting story of the century, Lolotai was just another anonymous lineman. Moreover, Lolotai's breakthrough did not trigger a stream of Samoans into the college or pro ranks. A decade passed before Charlie Ane and Bob Apisa followed in his footsteps. Even then, only a few of their compatriots pursued football, and Alopati Lolotai's breakthrough went largely unremarked. He would have a far more profound impact on American Samoa when he returned to the islands decades later to spread the gospel of football.

Lolotai, Ane, and Apisa defined Samoan football from the Great Depression through the tumultuous 1960s, intoxicating their brethren with a sense of what could be. Lolotai was the first, the pioneer who broke into the professional game. Ane, the second, captained an NFL championship team. And Apisa, although he never played a down in the NFL, might have been the best of all. A balky knee sabotaged his chances for a professional career, but he propelled Samoans onto football's increasingly global and televised stage.

Washington, D.C., was a long way from Alopati Lolotai's home on the North Shore of Hawai'i, even farther from his birthplace in Lauli'i, a small village outside Apia. Robert Louis Stevenson had often ridden his horse Jack through Lauli'i as he explored the island in the 1890s. But he saw neither American football nor British rugby played there; *kirikiti*—cricket Samoan-style—prevailed. Lolotai's family farmed a hillside plantation and fished the cove for octopus, fish, sea urchins, and shellfish. Alopati's adopted son still works the land, which has belonged to their *'aiga* for longer than he can remember. And while there's still no American football there, children and young men play rugby outside his home.

Alopati Lolotai left Lauli'i in 1923, when he was three. After his father died on a church mission to Savai'i, his mother, Vasati, took the children to Mapusaga, the epicenter of Mormon activities in American Samoa. She remarried, but when her second husband died, her cousin urged her to come to La'ie on O'ahu's North Shore to marry Aulelio Anae, who, like her, had been born in Western Samoa and converted to Mormonism. Vasati brought three children, Tiloi, Lesi, and Alopati, with her to La'ie. She and Aulelio had three more, including Famika, who would join his brother in shaping Samoan football.

Although no longer in his homeland, Alopati grew up Samoan strong, doing chores, walking everywhere, and eating a diet free of processed foods. Al, as he would be called, was nine years old and spoke no English when he enrolled in elementary school in Kahuku. But he quickly adapted to his new environs, internalizing the church discipline that saturated La'ie. Its stress on self-control, hierarchy, and collectivity meshed with *fa'a Samoa*.[5]

In junior high school, the charismatic Lolotai stood out. Classmates elected him president of their Future Farmers of America chapter; his football coach made him captain of the team. By the time Al was ready for high school, he had a movie matinee idol's looks and an athlete's sturdy physique. He became the first but hardly the last Samoan player to leave the North Shore for a private school.

After Lolotai was recruited by Father Bray, he spent four years at 'Iolani, where he was class president the first three years and the student body president his senior year. 'Iolani's first Samoan graduate, he led the football team to its first Interscholastic League of Honolulu title. Though far from Honolulu, La'ie celebrated the championship and the role that North Shore Samoans played that season with a luau for the team.[6] By then, Bray was providing Kahuku with football gear to form its own squad.[7]

As much as Lolotai was a product of Hawaiian schoolboy football, he reflected Father Bray's sense of muscular Christianity. Sport was about building virtue, discipline, and teamwork. Lolotai drilled that into his own children, who played at schools ranging from the University of Colorado to Yale. Most of all, Lolotai would display that ethos of muscular Christianity in his work with children and students in Hawai'i and Samoa when his playing days were done. Sport defined Lolotai's life, but education never took a back seat.

After graduating 'Iolani in 1941, Lolotai traveled to the mainland for the first time, to attend Weber Junior College in Utah. He captained the team and was an all-conference tackle.[8] Lolotai left behind a Mormon Church that was taking a more capitalistic approach to its La'ie holdings. But an increasing stress on the bottom line was not enough to allow the plantation to survive in a cutthroat commodity market where sugarcane was grown globally. The church began leasing its land and equipment to the Kahuku Sugar Plantation, where sugar prevailed.

When the United States declared war on Japan, Lolotai left Odgen, Utah, to make his way back to Hawai'i. He worked as a stevedore in San Francisco until he could book passage home. When poor eyesight prevented Lolotai from enlisting, he joined the island's territorial guard and played for the Rainbows of the Hawai'i Senior Football League. An all-star tackle, he just missed competing against Jackie Robinson, who had played for the Honolulu Bears before enlisting. Although the war chipped away at Hawai'i's isolation, just as it radically altered life in Samoa, Hawai'i's aloha spirit welcoming all participants animated island sport, and sport was more integrated than on the mainland. During the off-season, Lolotai won the state's AAU wrestling tournament heavyweight championship and a silver medal in boxing. Whether on the gridiron or in the ring, he was relentless.

Though he was playing semipro ball on the other side of the planet from Washington, Lolotai was invited to the Redskins' postwar training camp. After the season, when Washington's coach Dudley DeGroot jumped to the Los Angeles Dons of the All-America Football Conference, Lolotai went with him. Los Angeles was closer to home, and the All-America Football Conference, a newly formed rival to the NFL, was signing African Americans while the NFL lagged behind.

Although Dudley DeGroot had a PhD from Stanford and Bob Hope, Bing Crosby, Louis B. Mayer, and Don Ameche were the team's co-owners, the franchise folded after the 1949 season when the AAFC merged with the NFL. The Dons' demise mattered little to Lolotai, whose football career ended abruptly when his knee blew. He returned to school, graduating from Colorado State College in 1953, and went back to the ring. Professional wrestling helped support a family that grew to seven children.

Competing as "Alo 'Sweet' Leilani," Lolotai won several heavyweight titles over the next twenty years. Wrestling until he was fifty-eight years old, he capped his career with the NWA North American heavyweight title. But wrestling was a sideline to working in education. In 1957, Lolotai returned home to chair the Health and Physical Education Departments at the Church College of Hawai'i, which the Latter-day Saints had begun two years earlier. Judging from photographs, Lolotai was the only Polynesian on the faculty. His next stop was Honolulu, where he led the Hawai'i Kai Recreation Center and United Samoan Community Association. This work was a prelude to his return to Samoa at the end of the 1960s.[9]

While Al Lolotai was playing ball after the war, Charlie Ane was coming of age in Kapalama, a working-class section of Honolulu known as Palama. His father, "Teetai" Ane, and teammate John Samia were American Samoa's first sporting exports when they leveraged their baseball-playing ability into off-island jobs during the 1920s. Both had played in a league of sailors and Fita Fita guardsmen before the Mutual Telephone Company brought them to play for its Honolulu Commercial League team against squads of Japanese and Portuguese factory workers.[10]

"I had heard that my grandfather was a good baseball player," Kale Ane said in his office at the Punahou School, where he's the head football coach of one of the island's leading teams. "Everybody I spoke with from that era knew of Teetai Ane, which was what he was called." Teetai, a stevedore, and his family lived in Kalihi, a tough part of town near the docks where Samoans had settled. Kale often visited his grandparents on the church property they maintained in return for lodgings. His grandparents used their home's only bed while their sons slept on mats on the floor, Samoan-style.

Teetai witnessed his firstborn son, Charlie, ascend sport's ladder of success, and his three younger sons follow in their brother's wake. Charlie, born in Kapalama in 1931, had wanted to attend Kamehameha, a highly selective private school created by Bernice Pauahi Bishop, a descendant of royalty who turned down an offer to sit on the Hawaiian throne, to further education among native islanders. But the school, whose striking campus sits on the volcanic slopes overlooking the rougher neighborhood where he grew up, did not accept him. Instead, Ben Kneubuhl Jr. and fellow Punahou alumni recruited him to their alma mater, which missionaries had begun as the Oʻahu College in 1841. It was a decision with lifelong ramifications. Few choices shape Hawaiian identity more than high school, which crafts an individual's loyalties and status for life. And few schools anywhere convey that status more strongly than Punahou.

Ben Kneubuhl Jr. knew that more than most. "My father was a dinky little teenager, maybe just twelve or thirteen years old, when he ran away from home in Iowa," he said with a chuckle. "I don't think people in Iowa then knew there were oceans." After his father died and his mother remarried, Ben Kneubuhl slipped away. Riding the rails to San Francisco, he later lied about his age and joined the Navy. "The Navy didn't care how old he was," his son reflected. Kneubuhl patrolled China's Yangtze River before arriving on Tutuila as a surveyor.[11]

There, he fell in love with Atalina Pritchard, whose mother was Samoan and whose father, Alfred, was the grandson of George Pritchard, Britain's first consul in Samoa.[12] When denied permission to marry Atalina, Kneubuhl left the Navy, despite needing just another year to qualify for his pension. "That was the kind of guy he was," his son recalled. "He made up his mind and went."

They opened a general store abutting the naval station in Fagatogo, which fronted on a baseball diamond, and handled island connections for the Matson liners that docked in Pago Pago. When his oldest boys, Jim and Ben, were nine and seven, he dispatched them to Honolulu to attend Punahou. "We spoke Samoan as children," Ben explained. "That annoyed my father; it's why he sent us away so early. He didn't want us to grow up native."[13]

The two boys boarded the USS *Sierra* in 1925, clueless as to what awaited them. When they reached Honolulu before dawn on their seventh day, the ship laid anchor and waited for a pilot to take them into the harbor. "Everyone on board went out to the railing to look," Ben recalled, "and all we could see were tremendous fires." He thought Honolulu was in flames. "Then somebody told us that the fires were coming from the city dump and that they never stopped burning."

Until they graduated, Ben and Jim lived in Honolulu and returned to Samoa only during the summers. "Punahou is where I spent almost all of my younger years. Most of the kids I knew stayed there all the way through, so they were my family."[14]

Ben, fast and sure-footed after growing up barefoot on Tutuila, pole-vaulted, hurdled, and played football until a car crash disrupted his athletic career and a knee he damaged playing football ended it. Jim, who was bigger and even faster, lettered in four sports. Afterward, he attended Stanford, where he helped set a world record in the 880-meter relay in 1937.

Ben gravitated to surfing and remained connected to Punahou. "We belonged to the Punahou Athletic Club and picked up boys who we thought would be good athletes and gave them scholarships," he explained. "That's how Charlie Ane and his brothers ended up at Punahou."[15]

Punahou president John Fox was intent on admitting Polynesian students who could succeed at his school. "They had to be well-rounded and socially adept," Kale Ane said, "because they would become role models for others. So they took my dad." Charlie Ane was big and strong and had played his father Teetai's sport—baseball—as well as basketball in Palama. He had never played football before entering Punahou in 1945.[16]

When Ane enrolled at Punahou after World War II, it was an idyllic counterpoint to Palama's working-class edge. He was among the school's first Samoan students and from one of the least-advantaged backgrounds. "He said he would bring friends over to his house and they'd be eating sardines," Kale Ane explained. "They all sat down and ate them. It was just a different time, I guess. People were not so aware of the social differences between the wealthy and nonwealthy." Describing Punahou's current mix, he said, "I think that's changed. People do notice the differences now and they're embarrassed to bring people over." But Charlie exhibited what many football coaches have noticed—that Samoans often become the comfortable center of diverse cross-class groupings, especially in the locker room. They befriend everybody.

Charlie picked up football quickly and played both ways, rarely leaving the field. At the time, Saint Louis, a Marianist order school for boys, rivaled Punahou on the gridiron. Charlie began dating Marilyn Blaisdell, who attended Punahou, but whose father, Neal Blaisdell, coached Saint Louis. "In the three years Charlie played against St. Louis," she told a reporter after they married, "he accounted for most of the gray hairs in Dad's head." One season, Charlie scored the tying touchdown and then added the extra point to win the game 14–13. "He was a terror on-field but very shy in the parlor," she said with a laugh. "When he'd call on me, he was in such awe of Dad— or maybe me—that he'd just sit in the corner and scratch his head."[17]

Charlie's father-in-law, Neal Blaisdell, had starred at Saint Louis and coached before turning to politics and serving as Honolulu's mayor from 1955 until 1969. The emerging Blaisdell-Ane sporting connection included James Clark, who played for Punahou and the Washington Redskins, Herman Clark Jr., who played for the Chicago Bears, and Charlie Ane's brothers David, Danny, and Gilbert, who played at Punahou, then in college.

Graduating from Punahou in 1949, Charlie traveled to Los Angeles to play for Compton Junior College. A football powerhouse, Compton was emblematic of the junior colleges that undergirded the nation's top programs. It regularly appeared in the Junior Rose Bowl and prepared players like Hugh McElhenny and Joe Perry for NFL stardom. After winning Junior College All-American honors at tackle in 1950, Charlie joined one of football's elite programs, USC. A year later, Charles "Kale" Ane III was born. The *Los Angeles Times* touted fourteen-pound, ten-week-old Kale as already worthy of All-American status, citing his Samoan, Hawaiian, Chinese, English, and Irish ancestry.[18]

While Marilyn cared for Kale and completed her degree at USC, Charlie played ball. A devastating force on both sides of the line of scrimmage, the six-two, 260-pound single-wing quarterback bulldozed tacklers from future Hall of Fame halfback Frank Gifford's path. A mainstay on USC's 1952 squad, which beat Wisconsin in the Rose Bowl, Ane left school after his junior season. The Detroit Lions selected him as the forty-ninth player overall in the 1953 draft.

Ane joined a powerhouse squad led by quarterback Bobby Layne. The Texan was a swashbuckler with panache. "I never saw an athlete like Layne in the last minute of a game," Pittsburgh Steeler patriarch Art Rooney remarked. He might never have seen one like him off the field either. Bobby was the life of the party and demanded teammates' fiercest loyalties. Ane's blocking gave Layne time to do what he did best—improvise like a jazz musician.[19] With Layne and future Hall of Famers halfback Doak Walker and linebacker Joe Schmidt, Detroit made it to the NFL championship game three times in Ane's first five years and won twice. His teammates voted Ane, an All-Pro selection, as their captain for the 1958 and 1959 seasons. But when the Dallas Cowboys selected Ane in the 1960 expansion draft, he decided to retire. He had played on too many championship teams to start over again with the Cowboys, whose roster eked out one tie and lost eleven games in their winless first season. As he boarded a Matson liner in Los Angeles with his wife, three kids, and mother-in-law, Ane said, "I'm going home to stay. I'm through with football."[20] But he wasn't done yet.

The NFL was still decades away from becoming America's most financially successful sport, and Ane's earnings peaked at $17,500 (worth about $144,000 in 2017) his last season.[21] He had worked as a salesman during the off-season. In Honolulu, Marilyn began teaching kindergarten at Punahou, where she became a much beloved mentor, while Charlie began coaching, first for his former coach David "Pop" Eldredge at Punahou, then at Radford, Kaimuki, Damien, and St. Anthony on Maui. "My mother always said that you can't just take, you have to give back," Ane reflected. "I've been very lucky. My life has been super." So now he gave back to boys on the football field. His sons, Kale, who played at Michigan State, and Neal, who played at BYU, were among those he coached. When Kale joined the Kansas City Chiefs in 1975, he and Charlie became the first father-and-son combination from Hawai'i in the NFL. The sons carried on that ethic of service, as did their sister, Malia, a star athlete who captained the BYU volleyball team before returning to teach and become Punahou's director of Hawaiian studies.[22]

When Charlie retired at sixty-eight, Kale, who had just accepted the head coaching position at Punahou, persuaded his father to become his offensive coordinator. They made Punahou competitive again and the school won its first state championship in almost forty years in 2008, the season after Charlie died at the age of seventy-six.

Kamehameha's Rockne Freitas, who later played for the Detroit Lions, remembered Ane as "the first to show what we could do." Norm Chow, who coached in college and the NFL, seconded Freitas. Ane and Herman Clark Jr., Charlie's future brother-in-law, Chow said, "showed [that] players from Hawai'i could make an impact." They made success tangible.[23]

A handful of Samoans made their way from Hawai'i to college gridirons during the first half of the twentieth century. They played for little Saint Mary's College east of San Francisco, a team that punched above its weight in West Coast football, and better-known Stanford, USC, and BYU. These pioneers—Al Lolotai, Packard Harrington, Al Harrington, and Charlie Ane—were considered Hawaiians, which they were. They were Samoan, too.

But none of them had television broadcasting their play into the South Pacific until Bob Apisa went east to play for Duffy Daugherty's Michigan State Spartans in 1964. His on-screen athletic cameos reverberated throughout Hawai'i and American Samoa. And while a battered knee prevented Apisa from ever playing on Sundays because it slowed him down and reduced his ability to cut, the camera loved him long after his playing days were over.

If Al Lolotai came to Hawai'i because of the Mormon Church and Charlie Ane grew up there because his father played baseball, Bob Apisa journeyed to Honolulu because his father, Tailelpeua (Tai) Apisa, served in the Navy during World War II and was deployed to Korea when hostilities erupted in 1950. Afterward, he was stationed in Honolulu. In 1952, his wife and eleven children boarded the *President Jackson* in Pago Pago, joining the great *malaga* that reconfigured Samoan life.

Apisa's mother had always tried to keep her son close to their *fale* in Fagatogo, where Bob was born in 1945. The banana patch at the village's edge was forbidden territory. But neither she, his aunties, nor the threat of a whipping could keep Bob from setting out on his own. That wanderlust took him far beyond the banana patch, and when it did, his exploits on the gridiron resonated in the islands, where they entranced a generation of Samoans and Hawaiians seeking to expand their own insular horizons.[24]

"I grew up strictly *fa'a Samoa*," Apisa explained in his home in Granada Hills, in northern Los Angeles. "That's what my father knew." Tai Apisa, from Fagatogo, joined the Fita Fita guard during the 1930s and played for its baseball team. Bob's mother, Laina McMoore, was from Vatia, a village over the mountain from Pago Pago. Her mother was the matriarch of the Tuia-sosopo family, and her great-great-grandfather was a Scottish adventurer who went to sea in the nineteenth century.

Family discipline was Samoan stern, and the children complied with no questions asked. Bob had to figure out what was expected of him on his own, knowing that his elders would chastise him whenever he did not live up to their expectations. "I didn't know if I was doing anything right even though I tried," he recalled. Children were obliged to endure pain with stoicism. When Bob was five years old, his mother took the boys to the hospital to be circumcised—without the aid of anesthesia. "I remember screaming as the doctor stitched me up, then duck-walking out of the hospital. The next day, my brothers and I went to the pier to soak in salt water, going from one evil to another."

Though Bob had seen Hawai'i on a globe of the Earth, he had no expectations, only an abiding sense of wonderment, as he boarded the ship in Pago Pago in 1952. When they weighed anchor at dusk, Bob stood at the railing transfixed by hundreds of kerosene lanterns flickering against the mountainous backdrop. More than a week later, when the *President Jackson* arrived in Honolulu harbor, he saw a gigantic pineapple in the sky. It was a water tower designed in the shape of a pineapple that the Dole Company had placed on hundred-foot-tall struts atop its factory.

Bob had no understanding of electricity, had never had seen a flush toilet, and spoke no English. The family moved into Halawa Housing outside Pearl Harbor, where military dependents lived in single-story Quonset huts, six families to a building. Most of the men were in the military, often at sea, or labored on the docks. Bob's mother worked in a laundry with other Samoan women and came home with burns from working with chemicals or the machines she operated.

Relocation turned the seven-year-old's world upside down. Nothing was familiar, not even his father. Chief Petty Officer Tai Apisa had been away for two years when he appeared one day in uniform wearing spit-shined shoes, a stranger to his youngest children. Instead of working their taro patch, the Apisas now shopped at the commissary. And rather than going barefoot and wearing nothing but shorts or a *lavalava*, Bob put on shoes and a shirt to attend Pearl Harbor Kai Elementary with other military kids.

He sat bewildered while the teacher read to the class in a language he did not comprehend, taking his cues from other kids, laughing when they laughed, even though he had no idea why. Bob struggled. It didn't help that he missed several months of school and was held back a year after nearly being blinded in one eye by a rock from a slingshot.

But baseball offered an entrée, a place that had a language of its own. Bob had watched *kirikiti* on the green in Fagatogo and when he got the chance to play Little League in Honolulu, baseball seduced him. The sport might have been the American pastime, but his father brought a Samoan sensibility to the game. "When my father watched me striking out, instead of taking me aside and infusing me with knowledge, he gave me a left hand slap. I found out later that it was an embarrassment for him for me to fail." It was a trying childhood. "I was beaten so much as a young man because I fell short of expectations. It was hammered into our noggin to make sure we performed well. It was almost a curse, but at the same time it was an impetus to move on."[25]

And that he did, especially on the field where he and his brother Bill played for the CPO Chieftains, a Little League team sponsored by several chief petty officers. Meanwhile, a few years of hearing English and encouragement from empathetic teachers helped him find his stride in the classroom.

Because the Apisas lived in Halawa, Bob was supposed to attend Radford High School, which had recently opened for the children of the neighborhood's growing military population. If given a choice, he and his brother Bill would have attended a private school, but those schools ignored them. As a result, they decided to attend Farrington High School in Kalihi.

"Kalihi was a rough-and-tumble inner-city neighborhood," Apisa explained, "but I wanted to play at Farrington because it was in the best league." Radford coach John Velasco, who had starred at Farrington, signed an exemption allowing them to do so. Apisa figured that Velasco did it out of old school loyalties. "In Hawai'i, it's not where you went to college," he said. "They don't give a rat's butt about that. It's where you went to high school.

I think he knew we had potential as athletes and wanted us to do well at Farrington because he had gone there. That was our ticket."

Only a few Samoans attended Farrington, but most of them played football for coach Tom Kiyosaki, a husky World War II veteran with two Purple Hearts. As a freshman, Bob didn't know how to put on his pads, much less what to do on the field. But by his sophomore year he had bulked up and was starting in the backfield and at defensive back. Combining speed with power, he eluded or flattened would-be tacklers and began attracting attention from college recruiters. A versatile athlete, Bob won all-state honors in football, baseball, and basketball.

"I knew I had innate talent to better myself, but I didn't think of myself as a badass," he reflected about his emerging athletic aptitude. *Fa'a Samoa* meant that humility was his default attitude, not cockiness. "I thought of myself as good and that I could get better." And though it had not been easy for him as a child, Apisa realized that his upbringing, as tough as it was, had shaped his approach to sport. "My progress was based on what I was taught as a young man in my family—never be satisfied; when you are satisfied, you have not accomplished enough."

Believing he needed to become faster, Apisa worked with the track team on starts. That paid off as he started to clock 4.50 seconds over forty yards, the metric by which football coaches evaluate speed. "I screwed around with shot put that year, too, but dropped it to play baseball my junior year." When Farrington won the state title in baseball, Bob stuck with it his senior year.

The baseball team was scheduled to play a doubleheader the same the day as the prestigious Punahou Relays during his senior year. Though Bob had not thrown shot put that season, the track coach received permission from the baseball coach to pick him up between games, take him to the relays, and suit him up for the event. As long as he was entered and appeared at the meet, Farrington would receive a point.

Though the Punahou Relays and the ball games were held near each other, there was hardly any time for Bob to warm up. He didn't have a track uniform or track shoes, and simply changed tops, wearing his baseball pants, socks, and stirrups as he prepared for his first throw. Not having thrown the shot in two years, he figured he had nothing to lose. "My first throw, I just let go and my mechanics were sound. I wanted to get some height on it, even if it came right back down, but it kept going and going and going. When it hit, all I heard was the crowd going 'Wow!' and the announcer saying that 'Bob Apisa has broken the existing state record from 1956 of fifty-six feet, three and three quarter inches by half an inch.' I immediately strutted around like I knew what I was doing."[26]

By then, Apisa had sifted through thirty-four scholarship offers from schools ranging from USC to Penn State and accepted an offer to play for Duffy Daugherty at Michigan State. Farrington's assistant coach Al "Eki" Espinda, who had played at Purdue, told him, "I know you have a lot of schools recruiting you, but the Big Ten is where you want to be. If you're going to get your butt kicked, get it kicked by the best."[27] That appealed to Apisa, who headed to East Lansing in the summer of 1964, where Daugherty was challenging college football's segregation.

Michigan State had fielded black students early in the century and after World War II, when Biggie Munn became the first Big Ten coach to play an African American at quarterback, Willie Thrower from New Kensington, Pennsylvania. When Munn became the school's athletic director in 1954, Duffy Daugherty took over and began recruiting African Americans. "Biggie opened the door, but it was Duffy who blew it wide open," Larry Bielat, a former player and coach, observed.[28] More than ten African Americans suited up in 1955 when Daugherty led the Spartans to the Rose Bowl. A few years later, Ernest Green, a member of the Little Rock Nine, the African American students who braved a mob's wrath to integrate Central High School, joined the squad.[29]

By the time Apisa arrived, African Americans comprised more than a third of the team. Far more expansive in his recruiting than his peers, Daugherty sought Hawai'i's best players. Eleven islanders, several of Samoan descent, played at MSU because of Daugherty's Pineapple Pipeline. Apisa's teammates included 'Iolani's barefoot kicker Dick Kenney and Punahou quarterback Charlie Wedemeyer.

Daugherty cultivated black high school coaches in the South. They trusted him not just because he won three national championships. They believed he would educate their players, maximize their athletic potential, and treat them with respect. Between 1959 and 1972, forty-four African Americans from the South arrived in East Lansing via what was dubbed Daugherty's Underground Railroad.[30]

Willie Ray Smith's son was among them. Daugherty met Smith at a

Texas coaching clinic in the early 1960s. "Blacks weren't allowed in bars at the time," Daugherty recalled, "so I invited Willie Ray and a number of other black high school coaches up to my hotel room. I ordered a couple of cases of beer and we sat there and talked football." Southern coaches could not have gotten away with subverting the region's racial code; nor would it have mattered. Their conferences remained segregated until the 1970s. But Willie Ray Smith entrusted his son Bubba to Daugherty and sent him Gene Washington, too. Then, after receiving a call from George Webster's coach, Daugherty visited his South Carolina high school to address the student body. Smith, Washington, Webster, and Cleveland's Clinton Jones were All-Americans at Michigan State in 1965 and repeated the feat in 1966. In both seasons, Michigan State fielded a fifth All-American—Bob Apisa. The quintet of two-time All-Americans formed the core of the Spartans as they won two Big Ten titles and went 19-1-1.[31]

Apisa had never been on a field with players of this caliber. He practiced daily with four of the first eight players selected in the 1966 NFL draft—the top pick, defensive tackle Bubba Smith; the second, halfback Clinton Jones; the fifth, linebacker George Webster; and the eighth, flanker Gene Washington. Apisa's parents had always encouraged him to remain humble. Playing with and practicing against Smith et al. ensured that he would.

Nor had Apisa encountered more than a smattering of African Americans before. Now he was immersed in a high-powered athletic culture at a time when black power was gaining momentum and African Americans moving center stage in sport. "I never had black teammates in Hawai'i," he said. "But at Michigan State, we had young men from different demographics and cultures, coming from different parts of the country. There were African American kids from the South who had never played against white kids, and white kids from Fort Worth, Texas, who had never played against black kids." His voice deepening, he said, "But we came together as a team. Martin Luther King is marching in Montgomery and Selma, and we're up there as a team; Vietnam is heating up, and we're up there as a team!" Despite assassinations, escalation in Indochina, and summers that erupted in flames, they were a team. "We became brothers for life; we had each others' back. We still do.

"Being Samoan, you have a unique perspective, but you feel isolated," Apisa reflected. "If you're born white you know the expectations; if you're born black, you know the expectations. But we were born trying to figure out those expectations." That was not all he had to figure out in Michigan. Arriving with a few pairs of Levi's, sneakers, T-shirts, and his letter jacket, he was ill prepared for winter. Ken Earley, Duffy's equipment manager, found parkas and sweat suits for him. "If you went to my room," Apisa said, chuckling, "you would have thought I was the athletic director.

Freshmen could not play varsity sports then, but when Apisa became eligible for the varsity in 1965, he emerged as a key player on a team contending for the national championship. The first time he carried the ball, Apisa broke through UCLA's defense and ran twenty-one yards into the end zone, shedding two tacklers along the way. Apisa led the Big Ten in rushing touchdowns that season and the next, as he became arguably MSU's most productive fullback ever. His play was already drawing attention in the islands, but he had no idea how important he was to a young generation of Samoans until MSU played Notre Dame.

Apisa was in the visitors' locker room in South Bend in late November, preparing to play the Irish, the only remaining obstacle to an undefeated regular season. "I was being taped with Bubba Smith," he recalled. "My teammates were in a trance, preparing to do battle, and Coach Duffy was pacing the floor." Apisa heard someone urgently shouting "*Sole!*"—Samoan slang for "brother." "I said to myself, 'That's got to be a 'Sam.'" Looking up, he saw stadium guards restraining a young man. "I went over to Duffy and said, 'Coach, I think I've got a home boy over there,' and Duffy says, 'I'll take care of it from here.'"[32]

A Samoan student in Iowa had spent his last dollar to get to South Bend to see Apisa play. He couldn't afford a ticket but was determined to meet his hero and eluded security to enter the locker room. Daugherty told the guards to leave him alone and Apisa went over. "It was almost like meeting a long-lost loved one," he recalled. They embraced, and the boy, who feared he would be arrested, blurted out, "I'm so proud of you. I just wanted to watch you play." He did, sitting with players on the Michigan State bench.

"During the game I'd go on the field and do my thing and come back and we talked in Samoan," Apisa recalled. "Bubba Smith said, 'Hey sweet pea,' which is what they called me, 'what are you talking about? What you saying?'" Few sporting memories mean more to Apisa. "I felt proud as a player, proud as a Samoan, and just proud as a human being."[33]

That season, Michigan State beat its archrival the University of Michigan in Ann Arbor before a sea of one hundred thousand fans in maize and blue. Daugherty awarded the game ball to Apisa, who had been virtually unstoppable. It was the first time he received one. Exhausted, Apisa took his time showering and was among the last to leave the locker room. As he walked down the tunnel clutching the ball, a boy in a wheelchair accompanied by his father asked Apisa for an autograph. "The kid had a pen but no paper, so I signed the ball and gave it to him." Overwhelmed, the boy started crying. Ken Earley, the equipment manager, watched the interchange from the locker room door.

On New Year's Day, Michigan State played UCLA—whom the Spartans had beaten earlier that season—in the Rose Bowl. Victory would guarantee national championship honors. "We thought it was going to be another cakewalk," Apisa later confessed. The team spent two weeks in Los Angeles before the game, gradually losing focus in the city's sultry atmosphere. "Duffy could see we weren't right mentally," Apisa reflected. Though he moved the team to a monastery in the Sierra Madre for the last two nights before the game, they played poorly and fell behind 14–0.

An injury to his knee had forced Apisa to miss the three preceding games, but he scored MSU's first points on a thirty-eight-yard touchdown run. Michigan State scored again with seconds left on the clock to make it 14–12; if they scored a two-point conversion, the game would end in a 14–14 tie and preserve MSU's claim to the national title. Daugherty called for a pitchout to Apisa, who veered to his right. Running parallel to the line of scrimmage, he fought off one, then a second, tackler. The only player left with a chance to bring him down was five-foot-eight, 175-pound defensive back Bob Stiles. "I saw Stiles all the way," Apisa remembered. "My intent was to run right into or over him, and flush him into the end zone." But a defender held on to Apisa's arm, turning him sideways and off-balance as Stiles launched his body. He hit Apisa so hard that he knocked himself out, but he stopped him at the two-foot line.[34] Chastened, Michigan State demolished its opponents one after another in 1966. Their fifth game of the season came in Columbus against Ohio State. In a nasty rain with winds gusting to thirty-five miles an hour, Michigan State rallied in the fourth quarter from an 8–3 deficit when Apisa dove over the goal line on fourth and goal. The three Hawaiians—Charlie Wedemeyer, Dick Kenney, and Bob

Apisa—accounted for all eleven MSU points. The *Honolulu Star-Bulletin* bragged, "Hawaiians 11, Ohio State 8." The game kept the Spartans in the hunt for the national championship.[35]

Undefeated in their first nine games, the Spartans hosted undefeated and top-ranked Notre Dame on November 19 in a rare late-season matchup of two undefeated top-ranked teams. The much-ballyhooed game featured more than half a dozen future first-round draft picks and would attract the biggest crowd to ever see a game in East Lansing. It quickly became known as the Game of the Century.

But most of the nation would not be able to see it. Teams were allowed only one national broadcast a season and Notre Dame had already used its spot, so the game was scheduled for regional broadcast. Fans howled and fifty thousand fired off letters of protest to ABC, the network carrying the game. "This is the most universal appeal for a TV event on the part of the general public I have ever experienced," ABC Sports' Roone Arledge said. Bowing to what they called "the greatest public demand for a sports event in television history," the NCAA and ABC relented and did an end run around their own rules.[36]

But that wouldn't help Hawai'i, which could not yet receive transmission signals for live events on the mainland. Then engineers realized that Lani Bird, a communications satellite over Australia, could pick up the beam and relay it to Honolulu before it dipped over the horizon. As word spread that Hawaiians would be able to see their first live sporting event, in color, on television, sets flew off the shelves of appliance stores.

The game underscored football's uneven integration. Michigan State, which fielded twenty African American players, had elected Clinton Jones and George Webster as co-captains. Twelve African Americans, including ten from the South, started. Notre Dame had one black player, All-American and future NFL Hall of Famer Alan Page.

That's not to say that it was easy for African Americans in East Lansing, where landlords were leery of renting to the school's few black students. But six-foot-eight Bubba Smith, who had witnessed the lynching of three black men in his Beaumont, Texas, hometown, smoothed the way for students of color by dint of his performance on the field and his oversized personality. Bubba, who joined a Jewish fraternity, was voted the most popular student on campus. South Bend was less welcoming to African Americans. At a pep rally on campus in the days leading up to the game, Notre Dame students hung Bubba Smith's effigy next to a sign that said "Lynch 'em."[37]

The game ended in a 10–10 tie.[38] But that anticlimax mattered little to fans watching in Hawai'i and American Samoa. The *Honolulu Star-Bulletin* described the first-ever live broadcast as a milestone in transpacific communication, the forerunner of satellites that would expose the entire world to television.[39]

Streets were deserted before kickoff, which began at eight a.m. Pacific time, but hotel lobbies and bars with televisions were packed. Because more than half the island was watching, a pedestrian could have walked through Honolulu without missing a play, simply listening to sets tuned to the game.[40] *Star-Bulletin* sports editor Hal Wood called it a magical moment, the start of a new and golden sports era for Hawaiians.[41]

And while Hawaiians and Samoans were disappointed that Apisa saw limited action that day because his badly damaged knees would not let him play, they knew he had been indispensable in getting Michigan State there in the first place. He was a warrior, their warrior.

"When they made it a national broadcast," Apisa remembered, "they left Hawai'i out. But the government petitioned the FCC because there were three prodigal sons in the game—me, Dick Kenney, and Charlie Wedemeyer. I've been told that the whole state shut down." When Hawaiians watched *Gunsmoke*, *Mission Impossible*, even *NFL Game of the Week*, they always saw them days after their mainland broadcast. "It's my fondest memory, that I could contribute to bringing my home state into the twentieth century." And not just there. Football was coming to American Samoa, where the Game of the Century was the first ever shown, even if broadcast a week later when game films arrived. That mattered little.[42]

As a fullback who ran or blocked on every play, Apisa absorbed more punishment than his knees could sustain. Football, however, was not the only reason he was at Michigan State. "My objective," he later said, "always was to get a degree, even beyond football. . . . It was a matter of pride for me." That pride was not simply personal. "I was representing not only myself, my family and the Samoan community, but Hawai'i, too. I had three knee operations in college and it was my responsibility to all the people back home that inspired me to get up mornings when it was twenty below zero in East Lansing and walk half a mile on crutches to an eight a.m. class." For Apisa, it was about *fa'a Samoa.* "It brings a feeling of shame on your family if you don't accomplish what you set out to do. . . . A Samoan is going to see something through, right or wrong."

A two-time All-American, Apisa would have entered the NFL but for those knees. By his senior year, he could will away the pain, but not run as fast or cut as quickly anymore. Vince Lombardi, whose Green Bay Packers had won the first two Super Bowls ever in 1966 and 1967, drafted Apisa, hoping he would step in for his incomparable but aging fullback, Jim Taylor. But the injuries that slowed Apisa his senior year were not going away. Bob finished his degree, earned a master's, and began teaching in Michigan.

Had medical techniques been better, Apisa would have been a first-round NFL draft pick. Fullbacks were highly valued in the NFL, and four were chosen in the first round Apisa's year, including future Hall of Famer Larry Csonka. Apisa was as tough as Csonka running between the tackles, and better sprinting to the outside. But Apisa determined that football was over for him and moved on.

Apisa was at a club in Honolulu over the summer when a man scrutinizing him from across the bar meandered over and introduced himself as the casting director for *Hawaii Five-0*, which had debuted in 1968. "He said, 'You look like an interesting guy. Have you ever done pictures?' and gave me his card." Two days later, Apisa was at the Diamond Head studio being introduced to Jack Lord, who played the show's lead, detective Steve McGarrett. "Jack says, 'I think he'll do for us,' and the next day I'm doing a jailbird scene. Jack said, 'When I say this line, you say, 'I didn't do it.' That's how it started."[43]

Apisa returned home and began acting and working for the government. Acting was far more lucrative, especially as he began to appear frequently on *Hawaii Five-0* and *Magnum, P.I.* Moving to Los Angeles, he worked in movies where his Polynesian features allowed him to play a range of parts. Apisa also became a stunt man; he was set afire, jumped off buildings, and filmed amid stampedes and battles. At sixty-nine, he's trimmer than most ex-players and moves more fluidly. "I thank that God blessed me with a body that doesn't get overweight," he reflected. But he's had three hip replacements, one knee replacement, and shoulder surgery. He still works out but bears the damage he endured as a player and stunt man. His most recent project is a documentary to celebrate the fiftieth anniversary of the Michigan State–Notre Dame game.

At a reunion twenty years after that game, equipment manager Ken Earley, who had helped Apisa cope with Michigan winters, told him that he was going to send him something. A week later, a box arrived with a letter and a football. In the letter, Earley reminded Bob that Duffy Daugherty did not award a game ball for a tie. Instead, he had given the ball used in the Notre Dame game to Earley; it was inside the box. Earley wrote that he wanted Bob to have it to replace the game ball he had given to the boy in a wheelchair in the runway after the game with Michigan.

Apisa has kept the box, the letter, and the ball. "It's my pride and joy." But nothing means more to him than knowing that the Game of the Century had been the first broadcast in Hawai'i and American Samoa, and that it bolstered people's sense of who they were as Hawaiians and as Samoans. Ken Niumatalolo, who left the North Shore for Radford High and became the first Samoan head coach of a Division I program when he took over at the Naval Academy, put it simply: "Everybody I grew up with knew of Bob Apisa." Carter Kamana, who was part of Michigan State's Pineapple Pipeline, put his predecessor in contemporary perspective. "Bob Apisa," the Kamehameha grad said, "was Junior Seau before Junior Seau."[44]

5

American Samoa in the 1960s

In 1961, *Reader's Digest* chastised Washington, D.C., calling territorial Samoa "America's shame in the South Seas." Correspondent Clarence Hall savaged Interior Department neglect, describing government buildings rotting on their foundations, outhouses built over the water dropping feces into Pago Pago Bay, and a once bountiful island reduced to importing canned goods to cover food shortages. Hall was indignant that decades of U.S. stewardship had left teeth-jarring roads neglected since the war, a lack of water on land receiving two hundred inches of rain a year, and copious stands of coconut and banana trees ravaged by insects and disease. Public education, he wrote, was deplorable. The island's sole high school accepted twenty-four students a year, denying twice as many children an education past the eighth grade. Visiting a school held in a tiny *fale*, Hall saw a young teacher surrounded by twenty-one students spanning three grades, without books, paper, pencils, or a blackboard.[1]

Hall was not the first to point a finger at American Samoa's plight, but no one before him provoked a response. It was no secret that its infrastructure had decayed since the Navy left in 1951 and the Department of the Interior took over. When Governor Lawrence Judd resigned his post in 1953 after just five months on the island, the *Honolulu Advertiser* said his departure revealed "a tragic and little-known fact: American Samoa is in desperate straits. Its economy is virtually non-existent. Its people are unhappy and in some cases hungry."[2]

Judd's replacement, Richard Barrett Lowe, pointedly titled his Samoan memoir *Problems in Paradise*. He rued the Navy's departure, which had left American Samoa one of the most isolated and neglected places in the world. Travel from Washington, D.C., which was possible only twice a month, took four days. About the only thing that made Lowe smile was the never-ending cricket game outside the governor's house. If young men wanted to play, they beat out a staccato rhythm with two sticks on a five-gallon gasoline drum. Women beat the same drum, but with a different rhythm, to organize a match. Soon there were enough players for two teams.[3]

Earlier indictments of American neglect had been ignored, but against the backdrop of Vietnam and the Cold War, this time was different. With John F. Kennedy taking office in January 1961 and the South Pacific Conference set for Tutuila in 1963, the U.S. government suddenly remembered American Samoa. Felix Keesing, who had written perceptively about the South Pacific since the 1920s, explained why. "Small as these possessions may be, they are watched carefully by other nations . . . searching for weaknesses and mistakes in the U.S. record." In the eyes of many in the nonaligned world, American Samoa would test U.S. intentions regarding its approach to less-developed areas; the Soviet Union and China, meanwhile, were eager to exploit it as emblematic of American colonialism's shortcomings. With U.S. leadership conceiving the Cold War as a three-dimensional global chess game, even tiny American Samoa now mattered.

Three weeks after his first visit, newly appointed governor H. Rex Lee returned to Washington and testified before Congress: "For years the South Pacific has been a vacuum. Now our enemies are moving into that vacuum. Here's our chance to show the world how we can help underdeveloped peoples toward a self-sufficient life."[4] What resulted was territory building, spreading the American dream of democracy and development, mostly from the top down. Samoans, however, were granted greater control over their destiny and would soon elect their own territorial leaders. Ten million dollars flowed to the islands in a few years, generating a maelstrom of construction and institutional change in medical care, sanitation, and education.

When Clarence Hall returned in 1965, he gushed, "Somewhere on earth there may be a more spectacular example of revolutionary change in an area and its people, but in years of roving the world's far corners I have not seen it." He no longer considered American Samoa a national disgrace. Instead, he raved that this South Seas slum had become the showcase of the Pacific, the product of a magical metamorphosis.[5] In this pre–Tet Offensive heyday of the best and brightest, American Samoa was launched toward a better future. And though football was not on Washington's agenda, it became one of the decade's enduring legacies.

A few years later, in 1969, Li'a Amisone and Sikuini Seevaetasi joined students from around the island to play in what became known as the Kava Bowl. Li'a, Sikuini, and their teammates had played rugby as boys. "They knew how to hit," Amisone said with a laugh while seated at his desk in the Department of Education, where he supervises athletic programs, "and they knew how to be hit. We were very physical kids." Helmets and pads meant that they hit even harder. "For us, it was rougher than rugby," Amisone remembered. "Football channeled our physicality." And that gave it a special allure for boys becoming men. His legs are scarred from those long-ago duels. "I got them on the field at Samoana," he explained, "the one we called the Field of Champions."

Even more than serving as a rite of manhood, football connected Amisone and his friends to the United States. "Football was a way to preserve our American heritage and identity," he explained, "and people took to it because it was part of enhancing that American identity." His friend Sikuini Seevaetasi, a quarterback and Samoana High's MVP that first season, seconded the connection. "We had strong ties with the United States," the now ordained Seevaetasi explained on the grounds of the Congregational Christian Church's Kanana Fou High School, where he teaches theology. "Football meant embracing our American identity."[6]

A wave of Americanization not seen since World War II was cresting. American culture arrived with each flight of returning islanders, from American expats who came to staff the schools, and from the television station that sought to drive change on the island. The United States, no longer just a distant abstraction, became both more tangible and more mythical, an increasingly accessible destination with cachet. Youth like Amisone and

Seevaetasi, who had lived in the States, embodied these changes. At the same time, football reflected the conflicts many confronted between accepting Americanization and holding on to *fa'a Samoa*. Those tensions have shaped and roiled Samoan culture ever since.

Both Amisone and Seevaetasi had watched Bob Apisa during the historic Michigan State–Notre Dame game in 1966, even though they saw it a week after the game was played because it took that long for game films to arrive on the island. Apisa was one of them, born nearby in Fagatogo and educated at Honolulu's Farrington High, where some of their friends were enrolled. And now Amisone and Seevaetasi could play football because of the unprecedented 1960s buildup of island schools. After all, you couldn't have high school football without high schools. That institutional surge also brought Al Lolotai back to shepherd the development of sport in the territory.

When Rex Lee became governor in 1961, just a quarter of all ninth graders could continue on in school. There was only one high school, and that existed because *matai* had pressured the naval governor to turn the former Marine barracks at Utulei into one. The children of better-off, more politically connected families attended the school, which would be named Samoana. "If you missed out on a spot," Deputy Director of Samoan Affairs Sanele Tuiteleleapaga remembered, "there was only one place to go—the plantation."[7]

With the territory's median age fifteen years, demand for high school education was surging.[8] Three new high schools accommodating 370 students opened by 1968. Another two schools followed, making public education available to all and laying the foundation for scholastic sport. By 1979, 2,800 students were enrolled at six public and private high schools.[9] Teachers recruited from the States reinforced a Samoan staff that included only a few with more than a high school education themselves. The new teachers introduced English and made it the principal language of instruction by high school.

Searching for a cost-effective means to jump-start an educational reformation, Governor Lee pushed hard for a public television system. After a mile-long tramline was built so that engineers could reach transmission towers atop Mount Alava, the system debuted in 1964. Within two years, students who grew up speaking only Samoan now sat in *fales* where television broadcast as much as a third of their instruction in English. This island-wide television system reverberated far beyond the classroom. In the evening, Samoans of all ages watched Westerns, sitcoms, and sporting events. Soon many had sets of their own.

Governor Lee downplayed worries that his sweeping agenda would disturb Samoan culture. But his background at the Bureau of Indian Affairs troubled those who censured U.S. treatment of Samoans as no better than its devastating policies toward Native Americans. Others feared television's influence. After watching the first broadcast on the educational system in 1964, Brother Herman, a Catholic priest who had worked in Samoa most of his life, fumed, "At last the *palagi* has his nails into the heart of the Samoan."[10] Educational television was no panacea and did not last long on the island; educators never fully accepted it and support dwindled during the 1970s. But television was here to stay and fueled football's meteoric rise in popularity.

Most of the teachers, engineers, technicians, and staff who came to conduct this grand educational effort did their tour and left. But some expatriates decided to make their lives in Samoa. They became part of a hybrid culture with one foot in Polynesia's past, the other in America's future.

Just a few years before Lee's great experiment, George Remington visited the territory for the *Honolulu Advertiser*. Impressed by the *matai* system and the manner in which land and its wealth were shared, he wrote with admiration that "this system has been called 'Communism in its most perfect form.'" Indeed, most visitors were struck by the communal approach to property and the seemingly timeless nature of Samoan life.[11]

But America was coming on strong. A red, white, and blue sign outside a Pago Pago waterfront diner read, "Hamburgers are an American institution. It's your duty to eat them."[12] And they did, as an American diet of processed foods became standard fare. After a hurricane in 1966 flattened plantations, greater quantities of rice and flour were imported. This was the first time that many islanders had eaten rice or processed foods. Before then, Judge Satele Lili'o Ali'ita'i remarked, "I never saw a fat Samoan. The youth would come down from the hillside rippling with muscle."[13] Moreover, the *fales* destroyed by the storm were not replaced by hurricane housing—but by Western-style structures with walls and solid roofs.

Electricity reached outlying villages, where Samoans watched *The Lucy Show*, *Bonanza*, *The Wide World of Sports*, and *Davy Crockett* and listened to pop music on Armed Forces Radio. Evelyn Lili'o, the daughter of a public television educator from Virginia, remembered that when she arrived in the 1960s, boys did not wear underpants under their *lavalavas*. "They were so proud to get them," she said, laughing, "that they wore their *lavalava* so that the underwear's elastic would show!" Samoans like her husband, Judge Satele, enlisted after high school and served in Vietnam. More islanders than ever worked for the island's government, and football soon rivaled rugby in popularity.[14]

Not everybody was happy about these changes. After serving in the Peace Corps in independent Samoa, where traditional culture remained strong and people were more likely to live off the land, Rob Shaffer came to American Samoa to teach. He was taken aback by the contrast between the two Samoas. "America has totally ruined the pride and dignity in being Samoan," he told a journalist in 1973. "They have lost what is best, everything that is really good in their culture, and they adopted much of what is bad in ours."[15]

The United States, meanwhile, turned local government into the territory's economic engine and ultimately the leading employer. That slowed the drain of talent plaguing the territory. No longer would so many educated young Samoans leave for the States each year, as a majority of the first graduating class did in 1950, or join the military.[16] The American Samoa government could now offer alternative employment. But good government jobs required an education, and football became a way to get a degree. A college diploma also brought honor to the *'aiga* and enhanced a man's chances of becoming a *matai*. All of this soon placed a premium on the off-island scholarships that football might bring. But having high schools did not guarantee the emergence of sporting programs, much less football teams. That took the initiative of Samoans coming home, expatriate Americans, Mormon educators, and most of all, Al Lolotai.

The public schools became football's foundation and Al Lolotai its architect. When Milton DeMello, Honolulu's deputy superintendent of schools, became American Samoa's director of education in 1970, he brought his friend and fellow Mormon Lolotai with him as the chairman of the Department of Health, Physical Education, and Sports. After creating a sport program at BYU-Hawai'i, Lolotai had run Great Society programs during the 1960s. Returning to Tutuila for the first time since leaving for Hawai'i in the

1920s, he embraced his mandate to build sport with the same energy he had displayed playing for Father Bray at 'Iolani in the 1930s.

"Al was so humble and down to earth," Tufele Li'amatua said about the man he called his best friend.[17] "He was very charismatic—and huge! He started our sports programs out of nothing. There was nothing till Al came here." Li'amatua, a chief in Manu'a, was the director of Samoan Affairs in 2011—the culmination of a long career of territorial service. In 1977, he was elected as the territory's first lieutenant governor. Decades later, he was asked to direct Samoan Affairs, where his mission was to help *fa'a Samoa* withstand the duress of globalizing forces and keep the culture's own relentlessly competitive dynamics in check. That included resolving squabbles over *matai* titles and land ownership in the fifty-six villages that form American Samoa's bedrock. "To be honest," Li'amatua reflected, "what is keeping this culture intact is the *matai* system and land tenure—85 percent of our land is community owned."

Li'amatua was in his early seventies when we spoke in 2011. Wearing a necklace of dried shells, a yellow shirt with a striped tie, and a blue *lavalava*, he spoke tranquilly as he connected football to *fa'a Samoa*. A copy of *Thoreau on Man and Nature* and a cell phone lay on his desk; fine mats—a Samoan art form that once served as a form of currency—adorned his wall. A large photograph of Tui Manu'a Elisara staring into the camera hung on the wall. Elisara, who signed the Deed of Cession turning Manu'a into a U.S. territory in 1904, was the last man to hold the *tui* Manu'a title and the first Manu'an governor under the U.S. flag. As the *tui* Manu'a, Elisara could trace his lineage back to the supreme god, Tagaloa, who created the Samoan islands. Tufele Li'amatua's father later served as Manu'a's governor; so would he.[18]

"When I grew up on Manu'a," Li'amatua said, "and then in Fagatogo when my father came here to work for the government, there was no such word as 'football.'" Instead, he and the other boys played rugby on the field by the *fono*, where the *matai* debated village matters. "We played rugby all the time until Al Lolotai came here and began working for us. That's when 'football' became a household word."

But, he cautioned, football and other sports must be considered in the way of Samoa. "*Fa'a Samoa* is the threshold to learning and playing any sport," he emphasized. "Samoa always had its own sports, like cultivating the land— we looked at that as sport. The same with fishing. When we cultivate the land, we see who can bring in the most produce. When we fish, who can do it best? Which family could catch the most? Then we shared what we brought down from the plantation and took from the sea."

He asked if I knew of *lafoga*, the disk game. Unfurling a mat and placing it on his office floor, he slid disks carved out of coconuts toward the other end. Teams, four on a side, attempt to knock the opponents' disks off the mat while keeping their own on it—a Polynesian blend of bocce and shuffleboard. "When we played inside our *fale*, we would have to cook for all the players and spectators," he explained. "I was just a boy but would watch my father and the other men play at night. Oh, they would fight to win!"

That was the point, Li'amatua stressed. Samoans contested everything. Villages competed in fishing and cultivating the land to see which had more blessings from the sea or land. *'Aiga* and individuals competed for land and titles. Chiefs once competed to determine who could catch more pigeons.[19] Sport, Li'amatua said with a shrug, naturally reflected that fiercely competitive culture.

He talked about *fautasi* races between longboats modeled after nineteenth-century whaling boats. For more than a century, teams of up to forty men represented their villages in five-mile-long open-sea races with honor and prizes as the stakes. While contemporary *fautasi* have gone high-tech and cost hundreds of thousands of dollars to build, annual races revive village rivalries and spark island-wide celebration.

Describing how *lafoga*, *fautasi*, and *kirikiti* fit into that competitive matrix, Li'amatua concluded, "Sport has always been part of *fa'a Samoa*. But nowadays, it's cricket, rugby, and football." He returned to his friend Al Lolotai. "His legacy is the first generation of Samoan football players." When Tufele Li'amatua left to adjudicate a dispute in a village on the eastern side of the island, he insisted that I return to Tutuila and stay with his family when I did. He died unexpectedly two months later, while in Hawai'i, before I could.

Before Deputy Director Sanele Tuiteleleapaga worked alongside Li'amatua at Samoan Affairs, they collaborated when Sanele was the governor's chief of staff and Tufele the lieutenant governor. He, too, sang Al Lolotai's praises. "Al was a magnet to kids because of his reputation as the first Samoan football player," he explained. "He was the one who planted the seed."[20]

While few question how deeply Samoans contest sport, Tuiteleleapaga emphasized the role of *tautua*—service to the *'aiga*, village, and an increasingly transnational people. *Tautua* is perceived as the path to leadership, especially to selection as a *matai*, and it's fundamental to how one should live.

Born in Leone, on the island's west side, Tuiteleleapaga was fourteen when the transfer of authority to the Interior Department caused the great *malaga*. He recited the names of the ships, the *Monterey*, *Alameda*, and *President Jackson*, that carried off so many in 1951 and 1952. Tuiteleleapaga remembers standing on the docks waving good-bye to friends and family. "There was no way of knowing if any of them would come back," he said wistfully. He joined the migration, but only temporarily, to study in California. Then he returned. It was a matter of *tautua*—his education must be put to use.

"*Tautua* is at the heart of *fa'a Samoa*," Tuiteleleapaga explained, "the very tenet of our existence." He saw this as exemplified by players returning to give back to their families, villages, and teams. His remarks came weeks after Troy Polamalu's first football camp in 2011. Tuiteleleapaga characterized Troy and his wife Theodora's work with youth as *tautua*. Troy, he said, had much in common with Al Lolotai. "Al was a very humble guy. It was never about Al, but about somebody else. This Polamalu boy is very humble, too." "Humility" is a word that Samoans often bring up about Polamalu; it's high praise. During his visit, StarKist tuna cannery workers held an assembly for him; when they danced and sang, he wept. Afterward, they took him outside, where a large wooden figure of Charlie the Tuna—StarKist's icon—had long stood. The sculpture had become Troy the Tuna, replete with his long hair and Steeler uniform. I'm not sure what anthropologists—and there's no shortage of them in Samoa—would make of that, but they agree that *fa'a Samoa* shielded the islands. That's changing: global connections are severely testing *fa'a Samoa* here and among the diaspora.

The Mormons, more active than their religious rivals in organizing sports for youth, had birthed the island's first football team at the school they opened in Mapusaga to teach converts in 1903.[21] After Vaughn Hawkes joined the staff in 1963 to teach math and chemistry, he encouraged students to try flag football on the rocky field adjacent to the school where they played rugby. Appointed principal in 1967, Hawkes organized a tackle squad and solicited uniforms from Brigham Young High in Provo, Utah. Using ham radio connections, he obtained NFL game films, which were shown on the island's educational television system.

About then, former University of Utah quarterback Bill Cravens visited Nu'uuli, where his grandfather was the paramount chief. He, his wife, and their two young daughters intended to stay for a few months. They left twelve years later. Cravens, who became the government's director of economic development, helped organize a flag football league and began working with Al Lolotai. "We did a clinic and saw kids who were ready to go Division I," he recalled. "I can't say enough about their athleticism and willingness to work." There were no fat people on the island then, he said. Boys moved lightly on their feet, climbing palm trees with an ease that baffled him. While Cravens, still in peak condition, struggled to make it to the top, where the coconuts hung, boys flew past him. Young boys' feet and hands were already thickly callused. Men walked on hot, newly laid asphalt in their bare feet without flinching. Rugby had given boys an instinctive feel for football; their psyche and culture of discipline and accountability did the rest. When Vaughn Hawkes asked Cravens to teach the game at Mapusaga, he jumped at the chance.

Ma'a Te'o joined his staff. The third of nineteen children, Ma'a Te'o played rugby as a boy using a coconut for the ball. "The best time to play was when it was raining," he averred. Then you slid when tackled. The Te'os' *'aiga* land was in Pago Pago and they dutifully supported its rugby squad, but they lived in Mapusaga because of the church. Although rugby had not been as Samoanized as cricket, it was played *fa'a Samoa*. Villagers greeted visiting teams on a Friday night with a *fa'a lupega* (the formal greeting by the high talking chief), an *'ava* ceremony, and a banquet before putting them up for the night in a guest *fale*. The high talking chiefs attended the match the following day. "They were always there, to try to control the boys and keep the peace," Ma'a recalled. It didn't always work. Everybody remembers matches where the losing players or their fans provoked a fight before the game was over or started one afterward. But even when that happened, there would be another ceremony to conclude the match properly, before the visitors left bearing gifts, usually food, from their hosts.

After World War II, Ma'a's father left his job as a Navy stevedore to work at a government print shop. "But there were troubles—economic troubles—when the base shut down," Ma'a recalled. "That's when a lot of people leave."

The Teʻos went to Laʻie in 1950. Eleven-year-old Maʻa hardly spoke English, but he settled easily into the LDS community.

Maʻa saw football played in Kahuku, where coaches were planting seeds that would make the school a football powerhouse. But the Teʻos moved again before he could take part, this time to San Francisco, where an uncle lived. "It was about education," Maʻa explained. "We went there to better ourselves." San Francisco offered both superior education and athletics. "My favorite sport was baseball and I played it at my school. But the football coach saw me and said: 'You come play football,' so I did."

His uncle, a former city player of the year, had excelled at Mission High School. So did his sons and nephews. Maʻa played guard and tackle for the team, which won its first city championship in 1954. He received recruiting letters from coaches at Oregon State, San Francisco State College, and Saint Mary's, but a strike on the docks in 1957 left his father unemployed. With his older brothers on church missions, Maʻa got a job in the shipyards to help support his family.

Maʻa left football behind and in 1969 returned to American Samoa. He lived in Mapusaga and opened a bakery, settling back into ʻaiga life and paddling for his village fautasi team. Soon, Bill Cravens asked him to coach the linemen at Mapusaga. "A lot of the boys had never seen a football before," Maʻa recalled. "They did not know how to play; all they know is rugby." Nor were there many of them. "We didn't have enough boys for two teams at Mapusaga, so I trained them hard so they could last all day." His players were accustomed to hard work: they usually did chores around their fales in the morning and after practice. And they loved the game. It was more fun than weeding or heading to the plantation; and you could hit somebody. Though high school football was in its infancy, enthusiasm was building.

Facilities and equipment, however, lagged behind. "We didn't have enough helmets!" Maʻa grimaced. Players tossed their helmets to boys who were replacing them when they came off the field. One boy would wear the left shoe while a teammate wore the right; some played in their bare feet. "It didn't matter to them," Maʻa said. "They just wanted to run somebody over." Boys stuffed old flip-flops under their jerseys and pants in lieu of shoulder and kneepads. They even shared mouth guards. "It was better than nothing."

Keeping players from crossing the line between a hard hit and a cheap shot was difficult. "They knew how to hit in a dirty way, to get somebody to bleed," Ma'a confessed. Some boys relished the pain they caused. "But they all laugh about it," he reflected. "To them it was a game. And then afterwards, they become friends.

"We had to change the attitude from hurting each other to following the rules. One day we were playing Samoana and the referee stopped the game twice and said, 'Mr. Te'o, are you the coach?' I said yes. He said, 'I never see boys play so rough.'" Ma'a realized he was at fault. He had taught his linemen to slap opposing players on the ear holes of their helmets and instead of going around an opponent, to go through him. He realized that while the boys' competitive nature had driven their success, they needed to learn how to control their temper. That's still a work in progress.

Soon, Mapusaga had rivals at the Samoana and Leone high schools and Al Lolotai was back on island.[22] Lolotai was still incredibly fit. When Mel Purcell returned to the island in the 1970s and began working to build its sporting infrastructure, he played rec league basketball with Lolotai in the morning before work. "Before a game, Al would warm up at four thirty a.m. by wrestling," he recalled. "He still ran and stayed in shape." Lolotai's one concession to aging was that he no longer banged in the paint for rebounds, something for which the other players were grateful. Tusipasi Suiaunoa was a six-foot-two, 209-pound high school senior during football's first season on Tutuila. Tusi, who practiced blocking and tackling on stalks of bananas on the plantation, attended a clinic where Lolotai told him, "Get down, hit me!" "I'm thinking he's older, not wearing any pads. It seemed wrong. Next thing I know, whap! Al hit me with his forearm and I was rolling over. He was a different sort of fellow."[23]

High school football was only part of Lolotai's agenda; he organized territorial cricket and rugby leagues for Samoan Affairs and set up Amateur Athletic Union sport. He ran bingo games at the marketplace to pay for uniforms, food, and airfare when teams competed off island and solicited used equipment from college programs, figuring shoulder pads without flaps and gear that fit poorly were better than nothing.[24]

Lolotai enlisted Stan Eckert, who had played center for Southern Methodist University in the late 1950s, in his campaign to create a viable league. It was not hard to find boys who wanted to play, but capable coaches were scarce. That forced them to turn to men who knew little about the game. At Samoana, they recruited Lutero Fiso, a history teacher.

"Lutero Fiso was the head coach of just about everything at Samoana," former governor Togiola Tulafono recalled.[25] "When I came into high school, he was the volleyball coach, the basketball coach, the wrestling coach, and the rugby coach. They had a tennis club and he coached that, too." Born in Samoa but raised in Honolulu, Fiso had been an accomplished all-around athlete at Farrington High.

But while Stan Eckert did not speak Samoan, Lutero Fiso had never played football. He learned how to coach by reading about it, his wife, Ruta, said. "I never learned it!" she said with a laugh, but she paced the sidelines, drying off footballs with a towel at games along with her daughter Rita, who was voted the homecoming queen when she was ten. Football for Fiso was not about scholarships, which were not yet in the realm of possibility, but about discipline, toughness, and winning. He left football strategy to his more experienced players. "When we first played," Sikuini Seevaetasi explained with a shrug, "I would set up the plays and tell Coach Fiso what we were going to do. We coached ourselves quite a bit."[26]

Four schools fielded teams the first season: Leone, Faga'itua, Samoana, and Mapusaga. After each team had played all the others twice, Samoana was undefeated, mostly because several of its players had learned the game in Hawai'i or California. In what everyone began calling the Kava Bowl, Samoana took on a squad made up of the best players from the other teams in a game at Pago Pago field.

There was one *palagi* on the field. Riki Reinhart's family had been on the first Pan Am flight full of teachers and educational television workers during the 1960s buildup. While his parents taught school, Riki tried to make sense of his new surroundings. Sport was his entrée. He had a basketball, which few kids had, and other boys came by to play. Riki began joining them for rugby. "At first, they treated me like I was made of glass and didn't hit me. Once I learned the basic rules, I started dropping them." That gained their respect. Riki embraced the island and became close to other youth, including girls. Maybe too close. Samoan boys, incredibly protective of their sisters, punched and elbowed him in pileups on the field. "Being the only *palagi*, I was a target," Riki reminisced. "My teammates couldn't figure out how I never got killed on the field. My mind-set was that when I got a chance to hit and make a tackle, I had to go as hard as I could so that player would never forget." That was something Samoan boys understood. By his senior year at Samoana, when Lutero Fiso was molding the boys who played touch football into a tackle football squad, Riki played monster back, a linebacker with the freedom to line up wherever he thought the play was heading. By then, Riki considered Coach Fiso his Samoan dad.[27]

Fittingly, the 1969 Kava Bowl ended in a 14–14 tie. Samoan youth grow up in an 'aiga- and village-first culture. Rivalries with other 'aiga and villages are so primal that fighting between them remains ever present. But as native son Peta Anoai told me as we stood in the waters at Alega Beach, "Samoans make natural teammates; it's all for the team, just as it's all for their family and village. In truth, they are quintessential teammates."[28] When the youth of a dozen or more villages were brought together at a high school, new identities emerged that mitigated some of the internecine village strife. Those high school rivalries remain fierce, and it's a rare season unmarred by brawls on or off the field. To this day, visiting players put on their helmets as they walk to the bus after a game and lower the windows so that the opposing team's fans don't smash them with rocks as they drive off.

But football also eases those deeply embedded conflicts because the off-island success of any player redounds to all Samoans. Gabe Sewell played on the island and then at Snow College in Utah, where many Samoan boys suited up in the 1990s. After returning home, he coached at Marist, the island's Catholic high school. "You must understand that we are all connected on this island," Sewell explained. "Our kids—we are related to them. If they fail, we fail. I'll have to answer to somebody—my aunt, my uncle—if they do. But if a boy succeeds, we all succeed." Sewell did not dismiss the troubles that arise during competition. When Marist played Kanana Fou to begin the 2012 season, the game between the two religious schools was touted as the Battle of the Saints. It turned into a brawl. Still, Sewell argued, football offers boys the chance to go off island for an education and transcend these spats. "If you come back with that degree, get a great paying job, usually with the government, that elevates your family, your church, and the village," Sewell said. "You're taught from when you're little, that when you leave the island you're taking the name of the family, village, your community, with you. These boys carry the hopes and dreams of the whole island." He and others who used football to get their degrees acknowledge the pressure they felt not to fail. "You know your parents and grandparents are constantly praying for you to succeed. You cannot let them down."[29]

*　*　*

Football tactics were rudimentary, fields substandard, and equipment scant, but the fervor to play hard was apparent. That's evident on Tutuila's east side, which remains less affected by Western influence. Aside from the StarKist cannery on Pago Pago Bay, there are no commercial establishments other than a few bush stores and Tisa's Barefoot Bar at Alega Beach. Instead, small villages hug the shore along the scalloped coast. Boys there are more likely to grow up with daily chores and eating taro, breadfruit, fish, and 'aiga-grown produce. Boys from Tafuna, the biggest population concentration on the island's west side, are farther from the plantation and the sea, closer to McDonald's and KFC. Many say that's why they are the biggest boys on the island. They take cars and buses, not what Li'amatua called the "foot-mobile."

"We like to say that Faga'itua is so strong because we have not messed up the culture on the east side of the island," Lewis Wolman argued. Though neither Samoan nor Samoan-born, Wolman has lived here for most of the last thirty years. Married to a Samoan woman, he has worked hard to develop his adopted territory's capacities during a career in both the private and the public sector. "People over here live more of a Samoan lifestyle," he said in his home by Alega Beach. "We're here in our village, doing village things. We live differently. There's more fish and plantation food, and we don't have the public spaces or the choices they have in Tafuna or Pago."[30] Those east-side villages were even more traditional in the 1970s when Rob Shaffer arrived.

Shaffer's college graduation gift was a trip to Samoa, which had gained independence in 1962. Five years later, after attending grad school, Shaffer joined the Peace Corps and was posted to a remote village on Savai'i. After a two-year tour, more grad school, and another stint with the Peace Corps, he jumped the channel to American Samoa. Hired on the spot at Faga'itua in February 1972, he began teaching the next day.

He also took over coaching Faga'itua's football team. Shaffer had played varsity as a quarterback at Oceanside High School for Herb Meyer and knew more about the game than his assistants, men adept at rugby but football neophytes. His players were all heart but had little muscle memory to rely on. They had not won a game or scored a touchdown in their first three seasons of play.

Shaffer asked Meyer, his high school coach, for his playbook and ran a modified wishbone offense. Coach Meyer and other coaches in California sent used helmets, uniforms, and gear. His players looked good in their cast-off gear, but they didn't have a locker room or a weight room. Faga'itua didn't even have a field for play or practice. Most of his players had never been off island; only his quarterback and a few players spoke more than rudimentary English. And though they played rugby, most had never picked up a football before. Players were also expected to do daily chores on the plantation. "I had to meet with their fathers and ask if their kids could play," Shaffer remembered. "I told them that I really needed their sons." Sometimes, it worked. Other times, the plantation came first.[31]

Shaffer simplified the plays and taught football in a mix of Samoan and English. "They were enthusiastic," he said, "but it was rough in terms of football fundamentals. They were so raw; we worked on basic blocking and tackling and could only get so much done." Because fields were usually muddy, his players didn't want to wear their shoes. Half the time they practiced in shorts and nothing else.

"But when the ball was snapped and the lines released, talk about the pads cracking! These kids were fearless; it's amazing how tough they were." Shaffer attributes part of that to rugby, part to boys who had grown up hiking up hillsides to their family's plantation, walking almost everywhere they went. It took him a year to figure out when to allow contact at practice. Otherwise, they banged each other up so much they could barely play in games. His first year, Faga'itua didn't win a game, but it tied three and scored points, something the team had rarely accomplished. "We turned it around that year," Shaffer said. The next season, Faga'itua came in second among the four teams. A year later, they won the championship.

Every game for Faga'itua was an away game, but parents and students found ways to get to Leone, Mapusaga, and Samoana. Crowds were impassioned if often perplexed by the game, and rivalries between villages and 'aiga were difficult to contain. "The second year, we played Mapusaga," Shaffer recalled. "Their teams were always good, but we had the lead with two minutes to play when they got the ball back. It seemed like it took forty minutes to play those two minutes, and we lost in the last seconds. I still feel that the timekeeper cheated to give Mapusaga more time to score."

Shaffer was not unprepared for what came next. "Those good Mormon kids from the village surrounded our bus and started mocking my players as they got on; my kids jumped off and we had a gang war. It was pretty hard to stop." Most of the time, the antagonists were not players but fans. "They fought over ancient stuff," Shaffer reflected. But the culture was strong enough that when the village chiefs and orators stepped in, the fights stopped.

At least most of the time. Some *matai* wanted to arouse passions, not soothe them. Before a game against Leone, a talking chief asked to address Faga'itua's team and their supporters as they waited in an end zone before the kickoff. The orator, a senior *matai* carrying the fly switch and staff that symbolized his rank, declared in Samoan: "Today you're going to play a game. But enter it knowing that a hundred years ago the warriors of the eastern district would meet the warriors of the western district in battle. That is what this is—a battle! You are fighting the same battle that your ancestors fought. Do not think of this as a game. Think of this as a war!" Pumped by his exhortation, Faga'itua jumped to a 14–0 lead before losing in what Shaffer felt was another instance in which the timekeeper played a decisive role. When he complained afterward to Al Lolotai, whom he knew from Oceanside, his old friend shrugged.

This game ended without incident, but few would have been surprised if it had not. "As you know," former governor Togiola Tulafono reflected, "in the old days, games were structured after the ways we fought wars. Sporting games often replaced war games." His grandfather told him that sometimes in their village the senior boys in the *'aumaga* would tell the younger ones to get their weapons down from the ribs of the coconut palms where they were kept and go to another village to see if its *'aumaga* wanted to fight. "That's the spirit that I grew up knowing; so when we went to play, there was a little bit of a war mentality to it," Tulafono explained. "Teams did not want to lose." And when a team was losing, the captain often provoked "a little melee so that nobody could say that they lost."[32]

Sport's almost ritualized violence, however, occurred within the boundaries of *fa'a Samoa*, with attention to ceremony. Tulafono was at Samoan Affairs when its secretary, Paramount High Chief Lei'ato Tuli, hired Al Lolotai to coordinate sport. "The secretary was a sportsman—he was a cricketer and a boxer—and loved sport," he recalled. Tulafono was his administrative assistant as well as a member of the paramount chief's *'aiga*. Lei'ato Tuli told his protégé that they could bring greater harmony to island youth via sport.

"According to his vision," Tulafono explained, "sport has a great calming effect in bringing young generations together. That was his mantra: to create harmony among the younger generations. And the only way you can do that on a large scale is through sports." Lei'ato Tuli asked Al Lolotai to become his emissary and create island-wide leagues in basketball, cricket, rugby, volleyball, and softball so that youth would stay busy the entire year. "When there were fights," Tulafono remembered, "the secretary went with *matai* and reverends to make both sides talk. He asked, 'Can you get along? Can you talk? Can you get it over with and play?'"

"Whether it is war or sport, it's very ingrained in the Samoan mentality to resist domination," Tulafono emphasized. "You can see that in all generations." At Samoan Affairs, Lei'ato Tuli tried to make sport enough like war that it would bring about a greater unity among island youth, but not cross the line. By testing each other on the playing field, boys could prove their manliness and gain respect for one another and do so in the way of Samoa. "We're going to fight for our high school," former Leone coach Pati Pati attests, "but when we leave the island we represent Samoa."[33]

"It was a game that brought young people together, to get to know those from other schools," Sikuini Seevaetasi recalled about football's early years. "It built us up, unifying our people as a people—not as individual villages, but as a people."[34]

Tulafono argued that in a still warlike society, sport had the potential to mold younger generations. Sport could break down the primal barriers between villages and allow young people from different schools to know each other in a setting infused with sport's ethos. Al Lolotai advanced that project. When he died in 1990, his grand sporting project was under way but unfinished. Others spend their days working to further this vision.

Boys still meet on venues like the Field of Champions, where the first generation of players created the island game's traditions. The dirt field sits between the harbor and the mountains, under the shadow of the Rainmaker, the mountain peak that contributes to the deluge of rain that falls each year. The grass on the field has long since worn away, exposing volcanic rock. It's a tough venue. You're not only getting hit by other players; you're smashing against chunks of lava. "But if you quit or refuse to play there," said Simon Mageo, a former college player and high school coach who became an educator, "you will never, ever live it down. Your grandchildren will hear stories about your shame."[35]

6

Jesse Sapolu, Dick Tomey, and *Fa'a Samoa*

At a banquet that American Samoa governor Lolo Moliga held during Troy Polamalu's 2013 camp, chiefly protocol prevailed. In addition to serving as the territory's highest-elected officials, Moliga and his lieutenant governor, Lemanu Peleti Mauga, are *matai*, holding chiefly titles. This July evening, they act as Pan-Samoan chiefs to welcome the visiting party of coaches led by Polamalu. The governor takes the part of the territory's paramount chief, while his lieutenant governor serves as his high talking chief, who according to Samoan protocol speaks for the paramount chief at affairs of state.

The coaches come wearing *ie faitaga* (formal *lavalavas*) and Hawaiian shirts. The announcement that *ie faitaga* were required garb for the evening set off a scramble after camp was over for the day to find a store that sold ones large enough to accommodate players who have not weighed below three hundred pounds since college. Not to worry; a nearby store carried a wide selection of XXXXL garments. Still, the Carolina Panthers' six-seven All-Pro tackle Jordan Gross, entering his eleventh and final season in the NFL, can barely get his biceps through the sleeves of the shirts he tries on. His sidekick, center Ryan Kalil—who came to Samoa out of gratitude to Kennedy Polamalu, who championed his recruitment by USC—shakes his head approvingly as Penny Semaia and Mario Fatafehi, the lone Tongan at the camp, strut around in their *ie faitaga*. Clerks cover their mouths to stifle giggles at the impromptu fashion parade, and while Semaia is the only Samoan in the quartet, each appreciates the gravity of the occasion. Otherwise, they would never have made the long flights to get here on the eve of training camp for the NFL season.

Everyone quiets down as Governor Moliga heaps encomiums on Polamalu, noting that both of their families are descended from kings. Polamalu responds reluctantly. "I don't know why I am here to speak," he says softly. "The real power comes from the people. It shames me to receive these accolades." *Fa'a Samoa*, he declares, prizes humility, love, courage, and discipline. "That's what sport brings; it challenges us physically and spiritually." He ends abruptly: "I don't believe any one man should be recognized for love. Thank you."

Then the lieutenant governor delivers his remarks—a *fa'a lupega*—in the Samoan language of the chiefs, which many of the coaches born in the United States do not understand. The *fa'a lupega* is a ceremonial address to the *malaga*—the members of the traveling party, which is composed of the visiting coaches, for whom Polamalu is the informal paramount chief. Lemanu Peleti Mauga traces the lineage of different coaches, conveying respect for their families, which have deep roots in the territory as well as in football, and applauding their accomplishments in sport and work with youth. A parade of women enters and places fine mats, attire, necklaces, and packages of canned wahoo before them.

Protocol demands that when one high talking chief concludes his oration, the high talking chief representing the visiting party either accepts or rejects the *fa'a lupega* and responds in kind. But it's unclear who will speak for the coaches. While Troy Polamalu has the highest profile of any camp participant, he has internalized Samoan deference to elders and his deeply ingrained humility prevents him from stepping out of character in a moment like this. Nor does he speak the language of the chiefs, and responding in English would be unacceptable.

But then Jesse Sapolu strides to the podium, where he speaks in Samoan with the same intensity that he displayed in a football odyssey that took him from Farrington High School in Honolulu to four Super Bowls with the San Francisco 49ers. Although Troy Polamalu and the late Junior Seau are better known among football fans, neither is held in higher regard by Samoans than Sapolu, who is also a *matai*.

The king of Samoa, Malietoa Tanumafili II, conferred the title of *seiuli*, son of the king, on Sapolu during a visit he made to Upolu in 2004. As part of a documentary about Samoan football called *Polynesian Power*, ESPN had taken two players of Samoan origin to their motherland to explore football's connection to their culture. When producers asked to meet with the king to lend some oomph to the show, his representatives said that a session would be possible only if they brought Jesse Sapolu with them. Pisa Tinoisamoa and Isaac Sopoaga, the two players ESPN was featuring, meant little to the king, but Sapolu was as popular as if he captained Manu Samoa, the nation's acclaimed rugby squad.

After an exchange of gifts, the king's high talking chief spoke of what Sapolu meant to Samoa and declared that the king wished to bestow one of his own titles, the high chief title of *seiuli*, on Sapolu. "I was shocked," Sapolu recalled later. He sat there stunned, absorbing both the honor he had just been shown and the responsibilities he would assume by accepting the title. *Matai* titles come with heavy obligations, but Sapolu knew that to turn down this tribute would be "the ultimate disrespect." The appointment provoked jealousy and a backlash among other *matai*, but the king declared Sapolu was entitled to assume the rank because his mother was from the village where the title originated. That made Sapolu all the more determined to uphold the title with dignity.[1]

"Many there at the banquet knew I was a chief and part of Troy's delegation," he explained the next day. "If I kept my mouth shut, they would resent that I did not say a thank-you in our chiefly dialect. They would say what a waste of the chiefly title, the son of the king, to have conferred it on me." More important, Sapolu knew that taking part in the *fa'a lupega* would gain respect for Polamalu and the visiting coaches, demonstrating that even though they lived far from the culture, they remained Samoan to their core.[2]

But a *fa'a lupega* cannot be improvised. "It is of utmost importance in a Samoan speech to know all the descriptions of the chiefs that are in the room or venue you're speaking at," Sapolu explained. Failure to do so would label him an incompetent pretender to the title.[3] Some of the locals in the hall seem bemused by Sapolu's presence at the podium. How could an ex-ballplayer, even one whose career was marked by multiple Super Bowl victories, possibly hold his own with a high talking chief like Lemanu Peleti Mauga? But when Seuili Jesse Sapolu finished his oration, even the oldest and most skeptical guests nodded in approval of the son of the king.

* * *

By the time Jesse Sapolu arrived in the Kalihi projects in Honolulu in 1972, a sizable Samoan community had coalesced there. While Mormons created the first Samoan beachhead in Hawai'i in the early 1900s on the North Shore, the Navy brought a far greater number of émigrés to Honolulu in the 1950s. They gravitated to military housing near Pearl Harbor and neighborhoods by the docks, where many found work. Kalihi had been settled by successive waves of immigrants. When its earliest residents—Hawaiians, Chinese, and Portuguese—moved out, Japanese, Puerto Ricans, Filipinos, Koreans, Southeast Asians, and Samoans took their place. The Federated States of Micronesia has been the most recent source of newcomers.

The weeklong voyage from Pago Pago in the 1950s did little to prepare Samoans for city life. According to anthropologist Robert Franco, Samoans had almost no concept of rent and thought they would receive housing at little or no cost in Hawai'i. After all, Samoans were never homeless in Samoa. They could always stay on *'aiga* land, and they would never go hungry if the *'aiga* had food. Adjusting was a shock. Cash poor and with rudimentary English after an abrupt transition from isolated villages to a fast-growing metropolis, many ended up in public housing, especially Kuhio Park Terrace, Kalihi Valley Homes, and Mayor Wright Homes. By 1980, more than three thousand Samoans lived in these three projects, comprising about half their population and filling classrooms at nearby Farrington High School.[4]

Some, like the Sapolus, had taken the long way to Hawai'i. Jesse Sapolu's parents were Congregational Christian Church ministers, born and educated in Samoa, which New Zealand had administered since World War I. Born in 1961, the year before Samoans gained their independence, Jesse grew up in Toamua, a village near Apia. Villagers farmed and fished, living on the fringes of a wage-labor economy. As a boy, Jesse raised pigs and did daily chores with his sister. At school, he used chalk and a slate. *"Fa'a Samoa* was strong there," he recalled. "I remember each day when the young men of the village, at a certain hour, enforced *sa*. That was what I grew up with. That was what was normal for me."

Rugby was Toamua's sport, and the village's proximity to Apia meant that boys and men aspired to play in the Apia Rugby Union. "As boys we never had a ball," Sapolu remembered. "We played with a stick, in our bare feet." Teams also came to Toamua to play *kirikiti*. "Cricket was easier to play," he said, smiling. "It was a communal event, a celebration of life as much as sport." In both sports, boys wore what they always wore, their *lavalavas* and nothing else. Every now and then, black-and-white film of the All Blacks and Springboks, the national rugby teams of New Zealand and South Africa, was screened in the village. Jesse aspired to join the All Blacks.

When he was seven years old, he experienced shortness of breath while playing rugby. The problem was a small hole in his aorta, the result of rheumatic fever he had contracted when he was four years old. Because the valve did not completely close, Jesse's heart was forced to work harder, and the walls of his heart thickened. The condition often left him short of breath, feeling as if he was drowning. Jesse did not complain, but he was barred from physical education classes in the fifth, sixth, and seventh grades. Already more than six feet tall and weighing more than two hundred pounds as a seventh grader, he could only stand by the teacher's side during recess. Other boys taunted him, saying, "You are big for nothing." He resolved that if allowed to play again, he would not complain, no matter what. A stoic child, he decided that he would never voluntarily reveal the condition. When given another chance, he played through it, as he would for almost his entire career, even when heart surgery was necessary.[5]

The family left for the States in 1970 because his parents saw more opportunity there, especially for their children. Their first stop was Carson, California, where his father accepted a position as a pastor. The Sapolus had family in Los Angeles, but there were few Samoans in their neighborhood and they did not speak English. "It was tough, finding yourself in a completely foreign culture, thrown into a school without any preparation," Jesse recalled. He struggled but began learning English and gaining acceptance among his peers. "A lot of it was being good in sports," he said with a smile. Despite his enlarged heart, Jesse was a superior athlete, and, given his robust physique, nobody questioned his fitness. "When you're a good athlete, kids are more patient with you. Some befriend you." Boys went out of their way to help Jesse negotiate his new surroundings. Though he had never played basketball or football, he was fast, powerful, and tough, the best athlete whenever he stepped onto the field or court. "At that age, you learn so fast; your athleticism shows up."

An older cousin insisted that Jesse's mother take him to a flag football tryout. He was the biggest kid there and quickly chosen. Put on the line, he learned the rudiments of the game. During the second half of his first game, a teammate's father who had seen Jesse playing pickup after practice suggested that the coach try him at running back. Told to run a reverse, Jesse kept running until he was sixty yards downfield and across the goal line. He scored five times that day. After the team went undefeated en route to the league championship, Jesse no longer aspired to the All Blacks. He wanted to play football.

Unlike his American teammates, Jesse had grown up Samoan strong, working on a plantation and walking wherever he went. That experience prepared him for sport. So did his kinfolk. "I learned the instincts of the game by growing up with my cousins, who were three or four years older than me." They tested his psyche as much as his body. "They would kick my ass and I would cry and they told me to go home if I was going to be a baby." But Jesse kept coming back and cried less each time out. His cousins also taught him humility. "There was always somebody in the path down the line to remind you to respect the game."

After a year in Carson, the family moved to Honolulu, where his father became the pastor at the First Samoan Congregational Christian Church in Kalihi. Jesse moved in with an older sister and her husband in Kuhio Park Terrace, which consisted of two tough fourteen-story high-rises filled with Samoans, Filipinos, and other immigrants who had settled in Hawai'i after the war.[6] It was a difficult adjustment for many, and Jesse's family fought to hang on to *fa'a Samoa*. Reverend Sapolu's congregants shared the all-important Sunday meal, the *to'ona'i*, cooked in an *umu* at the church hall, with families contributing to the feast.

But those without a church or *'aiga* struggled. KPT, as everyone called Kuhio Park Terrace, bore little resemblance to Toamua. Teenage mothers without spouses were commonplace, and women sat on stools in project elevators and pushed the buttons for riders. "If it wasn't for these operators," Sapolu said with a shrug, "people would urinate in them. People had such low esteem." There were fights, but no gangs or guns. Still, he recalled, "It was kind of rough."

So was Jesse, at least on the field. He was soon playing for Al "Eki" Espinda at Farrington High School, which sits in the valley by the interstate bisecting Honolulu, surrounded by a sea of concrete. Kamehameha, a private school created for native Hawaiians, perches on the hillside above it. Punahou and 'Iolani, both private schools too, are not far away. While their campuses rival those of many colleges, Farrington's utilitarian buildings and playing field reflect Kalihi's socioeconomics, a mix of working people and those who have fallen through the cracks. More than half of its residents are foreign-born. Samoan, Tongan, and especially Tagalog are spoken on the street and in many homes. Kids at Farrington never expected much to be handed to them. They still don't.

Its namesake, Wallace Farrington, was the territory's governor in the 1920s. Built during the Depression, the school stood near the Houston Arena, an outdoor amphitheater seating two thousand. Though island ministers had persuaded Congress to outlaw prizefighting in the territory, bootleg boxing, as it was known, flourished. At the arena, fans could drink, bet, and watch island boys tear into each other. The Palama Settlement, where neighborhood kids swam and played, was close by. In the 1940s, its teams dominated the barefoot football leagues, which capped players' weight at 135 or 150 pounds. Few Samoans, even then, could make weight.[7]

Wally Yonamine was the first to ride sport up and out of Kalihi. Though he grew up on Maui, a football backwater, Yonamine attracted the attention of Honolulu's private schools. Rather than end up at 'Iolani or Punahou like Al Lolotai and Charlie Ane, Yonamine moved to Kalihi and enrolled at Farrington, where he starred for the school's 1944 championship squad. From there, he went to Saint Mary's College and then the San Francisco 49ers. In 1951, after turning to a more lucrative sport, baseball, Yonamine became the first foreigner to play for Japan's revered Yomiuri Giants. Over the next four decades, he was celebrated as one of Japan's best players and managers.[8]

A trickle of athletes and coaches, including Don Coryell, who launched what became known as "Air Coryell" when he took charge of the San Diego Chargers and gave Dan Fouts the chance to star in the late 1970s, emerged from Kalihi.[9] Bob Apisa first brought Farrington to the attention of mainland coaches in the 1960s when the four-sport letterman starred at Michigan State. In 1965, a year after Apisa graduated, Farrington's underdog spirit resonated throughout the island when it upset Kamehameha in the annual Thanksgiving Day football game at Honolulu Stadium, the venerable epicenter of Hawaiian football since it opened in 1926. There were enough Samoans on Farrington's squad by the 1970s that they used Samoan to communicate during games.[10]

A decade after Bob Apisa, Jesse Sapolu captained a startlingly tough contingent of Samoan players at the school. After graduation, he and teammates Falaniko, Alapati, and Petelo Noga and Nu'u Fa'aola played at the University of Hawai'i and then in the NFL. At one point, Farrington had five graduates in the NFL, the most of any high school in the nation.

"Everybody kept telling me growing up that being from Kalihi you'd never make it," Sapolu recalled. "I used that to my advantage; because I had an edge to prove people wrong."[11] Though Hawai'i was on the outer boundary of football's recruiting universe, Jesse, who had won all-state honors, was much sought after. After his five allotted recruiting trips, Arizona State and the University of Hawai'i were the two finalists. Most observers were convinced that he would end up at Arizona State, where Junior Ah You, Hawai'i's breakout player of the 1970s, had starred for Frank Kush. ASU had been ranked second in the nation the previous year and Jesse's sisters urged him to go there, figuring that it offered the best chance to make it to the NFL. "My mom, on the other hand, wanted Hawai'i," Jesse recalled. Head coach Dick Tomey had charmed her.[12]

Dick Tomey arrived in Honolulu in the middle of the summer in 1977. Hawai'i might have been as close to paradise as could be found in the United States, but it was considered a career killer for aspiring head football coaches. "Everybody else had turned the job down," Tomey acknowledged decades later as he sat at Waikiki, where he had been paddleboarding that morning. "But I had been here a number of times, vacationing with my wife and friends, and I loved it." His silver hair, light-blue island shirt, and easy smile suggest that he still does. Tomey understood why the job was so unattractive to other coaches on the rise, but he saw it as an opportunity. "If you're a little-known assistant at UCLA without a pedigree, you're not going to get a job that's acknowledged to be a great job. You're going to have to take a job that people don't think is very good and make it better. This to me, as they say in Texas, was a bird's nest on the ground."[13]

Tomey grew up in America's heartland. After graduating from DePauw University, he became an itinerant coach, starting as a graduate assistant at Miami University of Ohio and moving up the rungs at Northern Illinois, Davidson, and Kansas before reaching UCLA in 1971. He encountered Samoans there, young men like Terry Tautolo, Frank Manumaleuna, and Manu Tuiasosopo, each of whom would play in the NFL. So did Mosi Tatupu, who was on USC's 1974 NCAA championship squad, Michigan State's Kale Ane, and San José State's Wilson Faumuina, a first-round draft selection in 1977. That decade, thirteen Samoans played in the NFL.[14] There was something about these men that resonated deeply with Tomey. Indomitable players, they were exemplary teammates.

Because he had been hired late in the summer, Tomey had neither the benefit of spring practice to get to know his current players nor the chance to recruit new ones. "All we could try to do was to keep the guys we already had in the program, because they were thinking of transferring. Their coach had been fired, and they didn't know what was going on."

Hawaiʻi had never been able to keep its best players at home when schools like USC and Michigan State, or Stanford and Saint Mary's before them, came calling. Tomey faced that problem but needed to expand the school's recruiting base, too. "We knew we had to recruit differently because you're not going to get the elite athlete from LA, Seattle, Phoenix, or other places, simply because of the distance." It wasn't difficult persuading recruits to visit, but the school's remoteness dissuaded most top athletes from enrolling.

Tomey trusted his ability to see something in young men that top programs did not. "You can't get bogged down with the recruiting gurus and become worried about how many five-star guys you have, because five-star guys are not necessarily a recipe for success. It's all about evaluation—what you see in that player that others don't."

So Tomey brought young men to campus from the mainland whom the big schools had ignored; he sent some of them on to the NFL. Still, Tomey knew that he could not build a top program with them alone. "We recruited the mainland—what we knew—but we threw down a marker to the local coaches that we were going to try to keep the best kids here. We were going to spend time and energy on them." And he committed to expanding the school's geography of football recruiting.

Tomey succeeded in keeping boys who in the past would have escaped to the mainland to play for elite schools. And he brought the South Pacific to collegiate football's attention. But, he said, Jesse Sapolu was the one who turned things around. The top player on the island during his senior year in 1978, Jesse could have gone to school anywhere, but Tomey was determined to persuade him to become his cornerstone at the University of Hawaiʻi. "I told our staff that I was going to be spending a lot of time on him." He did, and it wasn't only watching practice at nearby Farrington High or attending Jesse's games on Friday nights. "I went to his dad's church on School Street for a service," Tomey recalled. Recruiting was less restricted then, allowing interactions that the NCAA has since disallowed. Tomey did not speak

Samoan and, although he had coached Samoans at UCLA, was relatively unfamiliar with the culture. But he had a preternatural affinity for it as well as guidance from Gus Hannemann, a Samoan plugged into the community.

"Jesse's sister accompanied me into the church and sat me down before her father began the service," Tomey explained. Jesse sat with his family while Tomey tried, with little success, to make sense of the service, which was held in Samoan. At one point, many people, including Jesse and his friends and family, left. "I stayed there because Reverend Sapolu was still up there and I didn't want to be disrespectful." He sat there until Jesse's sister came by and said, "Coach, service has been over for half an hour; this is the financial report."

When Tomey visited the Sapolus to make his recruiting pitch, he sat on the floor. He had done this before, reasoning that it allowed him to directly address everybody in the room. But he had no idea what an impression it made on the family, who gathered around him in chairs and on the couch. "I realized later that most people interpreted it as a show of respect. You're getting off your high horse. I did it because it seemed appropriate and felt good to me because it was easy to get the family to come down on the floor and look at the big campus map or have the kids playing. You can get people involved, feeling comfortable." At the same time, he was playing into a very Samoan tradition of keeping your head lower than others of higher rank. Tomey was implicitly showing his respect for Jesse's parents. Samoan parents, he realized, decide what's best for their sons.

Jesse was eager to join a top program, but he wanted the chance to play before his family. "In my mind," he later wrote, "I knew that when I chose my school, I would not only be playing for Farrington High School and my little town of Kalihi, but I would be representing the entire state every single time I strapped on my helmet. The pride of representing the people I grew up with far outweighed playing in the spotlight of the Pac-10 and Big Ten."[15] Not only Jesse Sapolu enrolled at the University of Hawai'i; his Farrington teammates Falaniko, Pete, and Al Noga and Nu'u Fa'aola did, too. These homegrown warriors aroused teammates and fans, making it possible for the school to compete at a higher level.

In a sport where familial connections are thick, the Nogas stood out. Some of Iosefo and Noela Noga's ten children were born on Tutuila, the rest in Kalihi after they joined the migration to O'ahu. Seven of the eight boys played at Farrington; the outlier, George, attended Saint Louis, a private

Catholic school at which Cal Lee set the standard for Hawaiian football in the 1980s and '90s. After high school, four of the Nogas traveled down the road to play for Tomey.[16]

Falaniko—Niko—arrived first. An all-state defensive lineman, Niko Noga was an eye-popping physical specimen with an outrageous blend of power and speed. He not only won the Hawaiian shot-put championship his senior year in high school; he was also among the fastest 100- and 200-meter sprinters in the state. "If you ever saw him run track," remembered Boyd Yap, an all-state running back at Kaiser High School and Noga's college teammate, "it was like watching Hercules."[17]

Rich Miano, who played for Tomey in college and became Hawai'i's associate head coach when he retired from the NFL, arrived in Hawai'i Kai, an affluent residential area on the east side of the city, after his family relocated from Brockton, Massachusetts, in 1978. He was sixteen. "I had heard of the legend of Falaniko Noga," he explained in his small coaches' office at Kaiser High School during a break in preseason workouts three decades later. "But then I saw his body and couldn't believe it." Miano, who played safety in the NFL for eleven seasons, also talked of Noga winning the shot put and competing in the sprint finals at the state tournament, a feat that still has him shaking his head in disbelief. "When we played Farrington, our best runner broke through the line, but Noga caught up with him, picked him up, and slammed him to the ground." He compared Noga's imposing athleticism to that of Heisman Trophy winner Herschel Walker. "And I'm not even sure Niko did weights," Miano exclaimed. "He was a genetic freak and had one of best careers in football in Hawai'i ever. I have never seen a more explosive athlete."[18]

Nor had Dick Tomey, who had been around football players since before Rich Miano was born. "The Nogas, first Niko, then Al, and finally Pete, looked like they had lifted weights every day of their life since they were twelve years old. But they hadn't really lifted at all. They were just cut, as naturally strong as you have ever seen."

An undersized nose guard, Niko made the Western Athletic Conference's first team his freshman year. In some games, he penetrated the line of scrimmage almost at will, sacking quarterbacks and tackling ballcarriers for losses. A crowd favorite at Hawai'i, where fans chanted "No-ga! No-ga! No-ga!" Niko played eight NFL seasons as a linebacker for the Cardinals and the Lions.

His brother Pete came next, walking on to Hawai'i's squad without a scholarship during Niko's junior year. He was shorter and lighter than his brother, but just as relentless. Pete also became an All-WAC linebacker and played in the NFL. "Pete had the most natural ability and the most natural style of running," his brother Al argued. "He was on the defensive side, but he had the speed and shifty movements of a running back."[19]

Al arrived in 1983 after his selection as an all-state defensive lineman in high school. He claims he lacked his brothers' natural talents. "But I was a hard worker and a quick learner. . . . I had to push myself over and over with hard-core training and hard-core conditioning." After redshirting his first season, he started at nose guard his freshman year and was a first-team All-WAC selection as a sophomore. As a junior, in 1986, the six-one, 254-pound Noga shattered school records, forcing six fumbles, sacking the quarterback seventeen times, and making thirty-six tackles for losses. He became the school's first Associated Press first-team All-American and joined his brother in the NFL.

After George became the fourth Noga to play for Tomey, he followed a small number of Samoans like Kahuku's Junior Ah You and 'Aiea's Duke Uperesa who entered the Canadian Football League. By then, Samoans were at the heart of Hawaiian football and coming onto the scene in California.[20]

Though the Samoan islands had been on Tomey's radar when he arrived in Hawai'i, he was too busy cultivating local talent to go there. "But I knew," he said, "that there were elite athletes in American Samoa, Tonga, Western Samoa, Australia, New Zealand, and Fiji." For almost every other coach, the lack of football in these places meant that their native sons were beyond the pale. Not Tomey.

"We knew we had to put together a more unconventional approach to recruiting." "Unconventional" understates Tomey's approach; he fashioned the biggest geographical recruitment area for any program in football history. Going where no coach had gone before, he brought in boys from Australia and New Zealand who had never played football. "They had played rugby, and we found that not having played football was not in any way a disadvantage," he recalled. "They had no bad habits. Besides, they had much better conditioning, because they run all the time and, for the most part, don't substitute." Tomey sent some of them, like Australia's Colin Scotts and New Zealand's Mark Nua, to the NFL.

One of Tomey's assistants saw Scotts playing rugby against UCLA on a touring squad. The young Aussie aspired to play for the Wallabies, the national rugby squad, like his uncle, but he was clueless about American football. "We played a showcase game against the Americans," Scotts said, "smashing them to a pulp and loving it." So did Tomey's assistant. "Next thing you know," Scotts recalled, "he is knocking on my parents' door in Sydney offering for me to be the first Australian to receive a football scholarship in the USA."

When it became apparent that Scotts didn't know how to put on his pads, a coach "asked what planet I was from." The first time Scotts ran onto the field, he remembered, "my arse pads [were] around my balls." But Tomey saw his potential. "With Scotts's obvious talent and his size, we figured we could teach him the rest." Scotts, who at fourteen pounds was reputedly the biggest baby ever born in Australia, weighed three hundred pounds and was six feet six inches tall by the time he left the university. But he could run a 4.80 forty-yard dash.

Scotts had never lifted weights or practiced. "But he took his football with us very seriously," Tomey explained. "He seemed to feel like he was representing an entire country, like someone chosen to be in the Olympics. You wouldn't believe how much he cares."

Tomey put Scotts at defensive tackle, where he knocked down passes before they crossed the line of scrimmage. "He made quarterbacks look twice before they threw the ball," Tomey said. After Scotts began celebrating quarterback sacks with a jump, others dubbed it the "Roo Hop." "I also had some free-spirited Samoans on that team, plus several other characters," Tomey said. Samoans did an abbreviated *haka* to mark a sack. "And those other guys would do something equally weird. Sometimes I used to wonder whether I was a football coach or a television choreographer."[21]

With Scotts, Sapolu, and the Nogas, Hawai'i's defense, which was ranked 123rd out of 130 Division I teams when Scotts arrived, vaulted to second best in the nation. "Never been there before and never been there after," Scotts said decades later. "Bloody proud!" The St. Louis Cardinals took him in the third round of the 1987 draft.

Scotts was a revelation for Tomey. "It dawned on me that football is not a complicated game. If a young man is courageous, physical, and has the right mental attitude, the caliber of football he had played had little to do with the kind of football player he is going to end up being." Tomey knew he would need to be patient, that a rugger with no football experience would not be able to play his first year. But if he was tough, could run, and had the right temperament, Tomey figured that "after a year or two years at the max, you're going to have yourself a real good player."

Rich Miano also saw the potential payoff in working with athletic youth from different cultures, especially Samoans. "They're so rhythmic because of their dancing and culture," he mused. "Whatever it is—the musical background, hip flexibility, great hands—you're not just talking about a big athlete who is stiff from lifting weights and who is limited in terms of skills. These kids can play." Miano had witnessed the culture's physicality and directness the day he enrolled at Kaiser High School after moving from Massachusetts. A Polynesian girl showing him around said, "By the way, the last day of school is kill *haole* day." Not knowing what a *haole* was, he asked, "What's a *haole*?" She replied, "You are a *haole*."

Miano was a diver for Kaiser's swim squad his junior year when head football coach Ron Lee saw him. Lee told his brother Cal, the team's defensive coordinator, that Miano's athleticism and demeanor were ideal for a defender and that he ought to get him on the squad. "At the first day of training camp, right out there in this locker room"—Miano gestured from the coaches' office at Kaiser—"this Samoan kid said to me: '*Haole*, move your pads before I blast you.' I didn't even want to play football. I just did it to gain friends because I wasn't accepted there at first, and all of a sudden, I'm getting intimidated by the Polynesians. And these were the guys I was going to play with in my one year of high school football!"

"He was raw, like a raw fish," Cal Lee later said. "To his credit he worked hard. When practice began, other Kaiser players made him look like a child. . . . But that was in September. It's not how you start, it's how you end."[22] And Miano ended that season by intercepting two passes in the 1979 Prep Bowl to help Kaiser upset Kamehameha High School and win the championship.

Miano walked onto the football team as a sophomore at the University of Hawai'i. "One of the Samoans came up to me and said, 'You're going to walk on and be carried off.' " But Miano became a two-time All–Western Athletic Conference defensive back and was drafted by the New York Jets in the sixth round in 1985. When he returned to Honolulu after eleven seasons in the NFL and began coaching at his alma mater, he realized how much island culture mattered to him. By then, he understood native Hawaiians' difficult history with outsiders. "But as soon as people know that you're there for their culture, that you're there for their kids, that you care for and respect them, then it's like southern culture." That ability to blend people from disparate backgrounds remains the hallmark of Hawaiian football.

Still, Miano did not romanticize his surroundings. "This is a tough culture and these kids love the violence of the sport. There are kids on this team who will run through the line of scrimmage and not run to daylight but instead run to colors. They run right at the strong safety." He saw that fierce intensity in Polynesians when he played and, later, when he coached. "The difference with these kids is that they embrace the physical; it's part of their culture. They're a physical people who love the physicality of football. It totally defines their style of play."

That made the Samoan islands all the more enticing to Tomey, and he began recruiting there. In 1982, he signed Moamoa Vaeao, his first recruit from a high school in American Samoa. Vaeao's recruitment was serendipitous. NFL veteran Duke Uperesa, who was back on the island coaching and training boys, had arranged for Tomey and Arizona State coaches to look at Taleni Wright, one of the island's better players.

By then, Moamoa Vaeao, who had starred for Samoana High in 1979 and taken a job with the immigration department, was three years out of school. The afternoon of Wright's try-out, he was heading home to Fagatogo after spending the day up in the hills chasing Tongans who had overstayed their visas. Simon Mageo, who played quarterback at Samoana after Vaeao, explained what happened next. "Moa, the homeboy, took a shortcut and was walking by the field with his immigration uniform on, wearing *slippas*. He sees these *palagi* guys with their stopwatches and there's Taleni and Duke." He stopped to ask Taleni what was taking place. The coaches saw this tall, powerfully built young man and asked who he was. Adam Rita, Tomey's assistant, remembered Vaeao from a game between players from Hawai'i and American Samoa a few years before.

When they asked Moamoa if he wanted to go to college, he said that he didn't think his father would allow it. The coaches persisted, saying, "Just run for us as fast as you can." Removing his *slippas* and tightening his *lavalava*, he took off in bare feet and clocked a 4.90-second forty-yard dash. "The coaches couldn't believe that this six-foot-three 310-pounder could run that fast, in bare feet on grass," Mageo howled. The coaches from both schools told Moamoa that they wanted him but that they were leaving the next day. They asked him to talk to his father and meet them for dinner at the Rainmaker Hotel.

"He was afraid to tell his dad," Mageo remembered. "In those days you graduate and you find a job. You're supposed to work on the farm, not play football." But Moamoa snuck away after evening prayers to meet the coaches. While Wright signed with ASU, Moa wanted to be closer to home and enrolled at Hawai'i.[23] Afterward, he returned home to coach and teach, to carry out the ethic of service—*tautua*.[24] "It was like a dream come true when I went to Hawai'i," Moamoa said later. "The main thing was I had a chance to earn a degree. That's what I tell the kids these days. Football is not your whole life, but it's a vehicle to pursue your education."

Tomey went to independent Samoa and Tonga, too. On his first trip to Samoa, he stayed at Aggie Grey's, the historic hotel built in 1933 where American servicemen relaxed during the war, and Marlon Brando, Gary Cooper, and William Holden stayed afterward. Aggie's son, Alan, who took over the hotel, was the chairman of the Apia Rugby Union and instrumental in building the game on the island. Tomey watched the *fautasi* races during May Day celebrations. "Here come forty guys who look like Joe Salave'a," the American Samoa–born lineman who starred for him at Arizona before entering the NFL, "with two boats, and those suckers are heavy, and they're carrying those boats marching toward the sea." Polynesian athletes did not have the prototypically tall and angular physique coaches coveted. "But it didn't take me long to figure out that these guys were the fastest, most powerful guys that I had ever seen. Plus they're great team guys. The thing that most people don't understand is that Samoan culture and Tongan culture are steeped in family values. And family is important to us."

Tomey kept coming back to Jesse Sapolu. "Jesse was the first player that we recruited who could have gone anywhere. He came here and then played in four Super Bowls. He helped turn things around." To Tomey, Sapolu epitomized the Samoan sporting ethic.

Sapolu not only started as a freshman at Hawai'i; he played both ways,

as an offensive guard and as a defensive lineman. Although Tomey understood the inexorable trend toward specialization in football, his squad lacked
depth. He figured he might be able to compensate by playing a few special
players like Sapolu both ways. "There were certain positions like defensive
tackle that the job was to line up and kick the other guy's butt. It wasn't that
complicated." Not if the player was Sapolu.

"He would start out of the game and I would just say: 'Stay in there.' We
played Arizona State when he was a freshman, against a heck of a team—
they had Mark Malone, Ron Brown, Jim Jeffcoat. They had all these guys but
they scored only one touchdown against us. Jesse started to come out of the
game in the first quarter and I told him to stay in. He was strong enough to
play with those guys; some guys aren't but Jesse was." Hawai'i won 27–19.

Sapolu laughed quietly when asked about playing both ways. When
pressed, he acknowledged the physical and intellectual demands required to
master two positions and play most of a game's snaps. "There is nobody in
the trenches doing that," he conceded. It's different from cornerbacks who
might also play as a wide receiver. "Half the time, they're not hitting anybody." Doctors monitored Jesse's heart, but if anything, he played with a
motor that never seemed to stop.

Jesse won all-conference and All-American recognition, and Hawai'i
finally became a top-twenty team. Tomey kept the state's best players on the
island and held his own recruiting on the mainland. When he left a decade
later, he had won more games than any head coach in the school's history.
And he had done so with a team built around Polynesians, especially Samoans. His first teams had about twenty Polynesian players, including a Kalihi
core of Sapolu, the Nogas, and Nu'u Fa'aola. Many more came later; no college team has fielded as many Polynesians.

Football, which requires precise, coordinated action on each play, fosters
one of sport's tightest fraternities, especially among Polynesians steeped in
fa'a Samoa. "It is a brotherhood," Tomey attests, "and the guys become such
great teammates because of the emphasis on family within the entire Polynesian community, maybe no more anywhere than in the Samoan community.
On a football team you want to create a family, and with Jesse or Al Noga,
their entire family embraces that idea.

"That's what struck me the most about these kids—their family orienta-
tion, their willingness to give themselves to the team, their unselfishness,

their willingness to work hard, and their toughness." Tomey knew that was a rare combination. "You're looking for guys who want to be part of something good, something great, rather than being the whole show." Tomey's affinity for Samoans persuaded him to recruit boys other programs bypassed. "There are so many guys that are not Troy Polamalus out of high school," he protested, "but you give them three years and coach the daylights out of them, and nurture them as people, and you've got yourselves a tremendous player."

Tomey did not believe that football was especially complicated. "What trips teams up is when players got too territorial about their ethnicity, their position, or their class. We would talk story with each other and let people know who we are." "Talking story" is the island's pidgin phrase for getting to know somebody. It's a deeply ingrained tradition, especially among Polynesians. Tomey brought the team to his house and took them to a park near Waikiki at the end of spring practice each year where the Hawaiian pop duo Cecilio and Kapono performed for them. "C&K, that's what everyone called them, played a song called 'Friends,'" he recalled. "That's what a team ought to be."

Tomey saw that Samoan culture encouraged an all-embracing sense of fraternity and conducted clinics in American Samoa funded by the State Department. No university had ever done that. "We made a trip every year, to American Samoa, to Samoa, to Tonga, and further south." The players and coaches held clinics in the villages, imparting skill and technique. They were tangible role models who embodied what football could mean in terms of education and career.

Tomey quickly realized that he was not the center of attention. "If some *haole* coach talks, they're going to listen and be respectful. But it was the players who got to them; it was what Jesse had to say, it was what Mark Tuinei and Al Noga, not Dick Tomey, had to say. When those guys were speaking there was a laser-like focus on them. Kids were not missing a word because those guys had walked in their shoes."

Jesse Sapolu was on Tomey's first trip to American Samoa. He stayed with relatives and slept on a mat in a *fale* the first night but joined the team at the Rainmaker Hotel the next day. "He couldn't handle sleeping on a mat," Tomey said, chuckling. But Sapolu was part of an emerging vanguard. "It was clear way back then," Tomey said, "that as time went on, there were going to be more and more players from this little corner of the world."

Nobody coached more of them than Tomey. Over the course of his career he mentored well over a hundred Samoans, many who played professionally. Whenever Tomey visited Samoan households, he could say he had coached a relative. "I can't recall a home where if you looked far enough, there wasn't somebody, because it's a small island; everybody is connected." He realized that how he treated a young man became common knowledge within the Polynesian community. "I know this, if you mistreat an athlete, if you recruit an athlete from Pago Pago or Honolulu or Oceanside and mistreat him, or don't do a very good job mentoring that athlete, the entire Polynesian community knows that."

After taking football at the University of Hawai'i to where it had never been before, to bowl games and national recognition, Tomey moved on to the University of Arizona, where he was the conference coach of the year, as he had been at Hawai'i. There, too, he led the team to more victories than any previous football coach at the school. And the flow of Samoan and Polynesian players eager to learn from him continued. During his tenure at the two schools, he did more than any other figure to expand the geography of American football to include the South Pacific.

Each time I've been in American Samoa, somebody brings up Dick Tomey's last trip there, one in which he was in the air far longer than he was on the island. It came after Joe Salave'a's junior year at Arizona. Joe had been a special player for Tomey at Arizona. Born in Leone, he moved to Oceanside, California, and lived with relatives during high school. Because he was negotiating school and SAT exams in a second language while learning how to play football, Joe was an academic partial qualifier at Arizona his freshman year. Once he became comfortable, Joe thrived academically and graduated after three and a half semesters with a year of eligibility left. He had excelled on the field, too, starting on the defensive line and winning All–Pac 10 conference honors. Most expected that having earned his degree, Joe would forgo his senior year and enter the NFL draft.

Instead, he opted to return to school, take graduate courses, and play his senior year. "His dad, Miki Salave'a, was a principal in American Samoa and I went there to thank the family for Joe coming back to Arizona," Tomey explained. "If you're going to Pago Pago, you stay either two hours or three days, and I wanted to stay for two hours." Even today, flights between Honolulu and American Samoa occur only two or three times a week. The Honolulu flight arrives on Tutuila at nine thirty p.m. and returns to Honolulu at midnight. Tomey arrived late one evening and the Salave'a family and a couple of high school coaches came out to the airport to greet him. Tomey wanted the Salave'as to know how much he thought of Joe and how grateful he was for their trust in him. A couple of hours later, he was on the plane back to Honolulu and then Arizona.

By this point, Tomey was not only fabled throughout the South Pacific for opening doors for Polynesian players; he was a folk hero in the Samoan community writ large. Gus Hannemann gladly attested to that. Born in Nu'uuli, Gus graduated from Farrington High School in 1955, just as more Samoans were coming to Hawai'i.

Gus's father worked three jobs and never owned a home, but one of his sons, Mufi, became Honolulu's mayor and Gus worked for the American Samoa government. "There's a certain way to Dick Tomey," he emphasized, "a down-to-earth approach. He was not only interested in his boys winning football games, but in their character. He knew that football is not enough; it's a ticket." Gus schooled Tomey in Samoan culture and accompanied him to Tutuila. "They went crazy when I did." After a big greeting at the airport, *matai* held a *kava* ceremony for them. "It's just the way he talks; what a gentleman he is!"

At the University of Hawai'i, two cultures—Samoan and Hawaiian—came together. Their standard-bearer, Jesse Sapolu, articulated what that meant to him. "Being of Samoan ancestry and raised in Hawai'i," he said, "I feel very blessed and honored to be part of two proud cultures. " Respect and modesty were of utmost importance in both. "It is a high priority," Sapolu emphasized, "to represent yourself, your family, and your people with humility." That brought respect, he said, but if you were not humble, your accomplishments "mean absolutely nothing."[25] His playing days over, Sapolu now serves as Samoan football's high talking chief.

Tui Manu'a Elisara. Manu'a's paramount chief held the *tui* Manu'a title. Its first holder was said to have descended from Tagaloa, the supreme god who created the islands. Tui Manu'a Elisara, who signed the deed ceding Manu'a to the United States in 1904, was the last to hold the title. Courtesy of the Polynesian Photo Archives, American Samoa.

Robert Louis Stevenson and paramount chief Tuimaleali'ifano. Before his death in 1894, Stevenson warned chiefs gathered at Vailima of the existential threat they faced from abroad. "Now," he said, "is the time for the true champions of Samoa to stand forth." Samoans called him Tusitala, the teller of tales. Courtesy of the Alexander Turnbull Library, Wellington, New Zealand.

These women and men are preparing 'ava, a mildly stimulating drink to be shared by those taking part in the 'ava ceremony. The preparation of 'ava and its role during the ceremony are highly ritualized. Courtesy of the Polynesian Photo Archives, American Samoa.

A *fale*. The *fale* was once the standard island dwelling. Poles held up its thatched roof and mats could be lowered to ward off rain and mosquitoes. Each village has a *fale* where the *fono*, the gathering of its chiefs, and *'ava* ceremonies are held. Courtesy of the Polynesian Photo Archives.

Fita Fita guards. The Navy organized the Fita Fita in 1900. Their ranks expanded during World War II when surprising numbers of Samoans enlisted. That tradition of service has continued ever since; Samoans are as overrepresented in the military as they are in football. Courtesy of the National Park Service, Springfield Armory National Historic Site, TEMP-625.

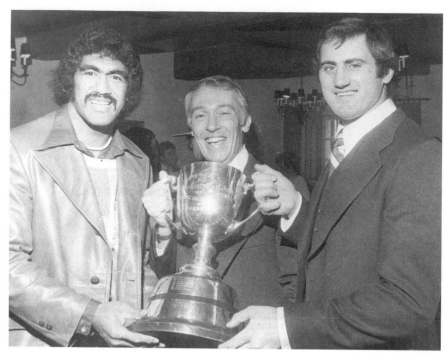

Junior Ah You, Coach Marv Levy, and CFL Hall of Famer Peter Dalla Riva. Samoan-born, La'ie-bred Ah You starred for Kahuku High, Arizona State, and the Canadian Football League's Montreal Alouettes. Hugh Yoshida called the two-time college All-American Hawai'i's first breakout player of the modern era. Here, he receives the 1974 Grey Cup MVP award with his coach Marv Levy and teammate and CFL Hall of Famer Peter Dalla Riva. Courtesy of the Montreal Alouettes.

Jesse Sapolu. Samoan-born Jesse Sapolu captained Farrington High's squad and starred at the University of Hawai'i before winning four Super Bowls with the 49ers. In 2004, Samoa's king conferred the *matai* title of *seiuli*, son of the king, on him. Since retiring, Sapolu has become an advocate for Samoan and Polynesian players. Courtesy of the University of Hawai'i.

Al and Pete Noga on the beach on Oʻahu. Seven of Iosefo and Noela Noga's eight boys played at Farrington High, the eighth at Saint Louis. Four starred at the University of Hawaiʻi. Al (left) became the school's first All-American while Pete was an All–Western Athletic Conference linebacker. They and brother Niko played in the NFL. Courtesy of the University of Hawaiʻi.

Falaniko Noga. Niko Noga (#54) was an eye-popping athlete who won the Hawaiian shot-put championship in high school and was among the fastest sprinters in the state. "If you ever saw him run track," remembered Boyd Yap, an all-state running back at Kaiser High and Noga's college teammate, "it was like watching Hercules." Courtesy of the University of Hawai'i.

Dick Tomey. After arriving at the University of Hawai'i in 1977, Dick Tomey stretched recruiting to Samoa and beyond. He won more games than any coach in school history, with Polynesians like Jesse Sapolu and the Noga brothers at the core of his squads. Courtesy of the University of Hawai'i.

The Paopaos: Anthony "Tony" Paopao, Joseph Paopao, Loia "Junior" Paopao, Michael "Mickey" Paopao (left to right); seated: Alipati "Bucky" Paopao. Five Paopao brothers starred for Herb Meyer in Oceanside, part of the first wave of Samoans to emerge in California football. Many of their sons and nephews also played. Few families anywhere have had such an impact on a town's sporting life. Courtesy of the Paopao family.

Okland Salavaʻe (left) and Sal Aunese. Okland Salavaʻe grew up on Tutuila but attended high school in Oceanside, along with Junior Seau. His best friend at Colorado University was Sal Aunese, who was also from Oceanside. Salavaʻe coached Tafuna High to several island championships; Aunese, who led Colorado's resurgence in the late 1980s, died at twenty-one from cancer. Courtesy of the University of Colorado Sports Information.

Herb Meyer and players celebrating after the California Interscholastic Federation championship game. From 1959 to 2003, Herb Meyer coached at Oceanside High and El Camino, winning a then record 338 games. His teams heralded the arrival of Samoans in California football. Meyer was California's Coach of the Year on three occasions and the National Coach of the Year twice. Courtesy of Herb Meyer.

John Carroll. Carroll returned Oceanside football to the glory it enjoyed when Herb Meyer coached there. The Pirates won two state championships during his tenure and more than 75 percent of their games. Like Meyer, Carroll had Samoans at the core of his squads. Photo by Zach Cordner.

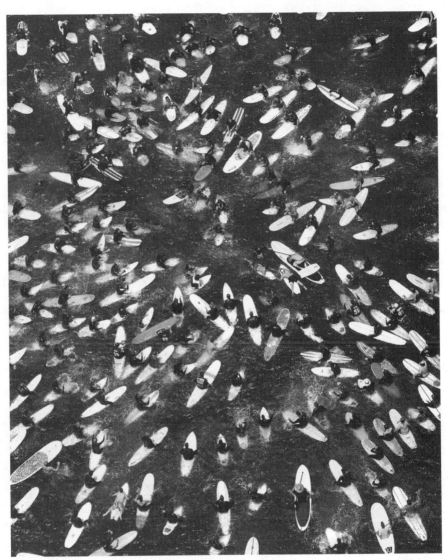

A tribute to Junior Seau. Four days after Junior Seau's death on May 2, 2012, hundreds of his friends remembered him by paddling out into the ocean in front of his home on the Strand, the street by the sea in Oceanside, California, where he lived most of his life. Photo by Howard Lipin, *Union Tribune*, San Diego, © U-T San Diego/ZUMAPRESS.com.

Kahuku *haka*. Kahuku High's team, largely comprised of boys with Samoan, Tongan, and Hawaiian ancestors, performs a *haka* before their homecoming game versus Leilehua in 2014. The Maori war dance energizes them and their fans while attempting to intimidate their opponents. Photo by Jonathan Canlas.

Troy and Theodora Polamalu at 'ava ceremony. Shaun Nua, who grew up on Tutuila and played with Troy Polamalu on the Pittsburgh Steelers' Super Bowl championship team in February 2006, interprets for Troy and Theodora Polamalu during an 'ava ceremony. Photo by Chris Baldwin.

Boys begin Troy and Theodora Polamalu Foundation's summer camp with prayer. When high school players on Tutuila pray and sing before and after each session at the Polamalu Foundation's summer camp, it's easy to see why Robert Louis Stevenson called Polynesians "God's best, at least his sweetest, works." Photo by Chris Baldwin.

NFL veterans in *lavalavas* at the Troy and Theodora Polamalu Foundation's summer camp. Samoans who played and coached in college and the NFL often return to American Samoa to work with boys trying to leverage football into college scholarships and careers. These men coached at the Polamalu summer camp on Tutuila. Photo by Chris Baldwin.

Troy Polamalu and his sons. Troy and Theodora Polamalu brought their sons, Paisios and Ephraim, with them to American Samoa, where their Fa'a Samoa Initiative has expanded from a focus on football to include volleyball, academic and life skills, and medical efforts. Photo by Chris Baldwin.

Domata Peko and Troy Polamalu. Domata Peko was born in Los Angeles but went to high school in American Samoa, where he played more rugby than football until his senior year. Since graduating as a sociology major from Michigan State, Peko has played more than ten seasons in the NFL. Photo by Chris Baldwin.

Boys doing *haka* at the Troy and Theodora Polamalu Foundation's summer camp. Samoans grow up learning traditional dance, and many teams perform a *haka*, a Maori ritual to prepare for combat, or a *siva tau*, the traditional Samoan war dance, before a game. Rugby and football teams throughout the Pacific have appropriated the pregame display. Photo by Chris Baldwin.

7

Fa'a Kalifonia: Oceanside, California

After days at sea en route from Honolulu, Junior Paopao remembers riding a double-decker bus from San Francisco down the Pacific Coast Highway in the spring of 1960. Few forget their first look at Big Sur swooping to the surf below. Junior and his brothers and sisters were in America now, this time to stay, on their way to Oceanside, California.[1]

Seven of the ten Paopao siblings had been born in American Samoa. But in 1955, the family joined the great migration off island after USMC sergeant Loia Paopao was dispatched to Camp H. M. Smith in Honolulu. Two years later, the Paopaos traveled to the mainland, but only for a few months when Sergeant Paopao was stationed at Camp Pendleton in Oceanside. His sixth son, Tony, who was born there, was forever after the California Kid. Before long, they were back in Honolulu, living in military housing near Pearl Harbor. Mickey, the youngest, was born there months before the territory gained statehood on August 21, 1959. And now, as the sixties dawned, they arrived in California, the state about to redefine American culture.

For the seven brothers—Paul, Ben, Buck, Junior, Joe, Tony, and Mickey—who ranged from seventeen to one in age, this was the beginning of a wonderful adventure. The geography of military bases and service affiliations dictated where Samoans took up residence on the mainland. The Paopaos were in Oceanside because of Camp Pendleton, which had become the Marines' principal Pacific Coast base since its hurried construction during World War II. Had Loia Paopao, who joined the Marines during the war and rose through the ranks to staff sergeant, been in the Navy, the Paopaos might have ended up in Long Beach or San Francisco. If he was Army, they could have gone to Fort Lewis near Tacoma. Another enclave took shape in Carson near Los Angeles. Instead, the Paopaos sunk deep roots in Oceanside, and though six of the boys played and coached football throughout the United States and Canada, the town remains their home.

In Oceanside, Samoans encountered American consumerism and surfer culture in a once-sleepy beach town thirty-five miles north of San Diego. The Paopaos and the other Samoan families who settled nearby in the 1950s and 1960s—the Poumeles, Molifuas, Godinets, and Seaus—were the vanguard of a Samoan influx that grew to more than five thousand. They made Oceanside the southernmost beachhead of *fa'a Kalifonia*, "in the way of California."

Along with their brethren along the Pacific Coast, they led Samoans to new prominence on the mainland and, within a decade or two, in football. The first Samoans in college and professional football—Al Lolotai, Charlie Ane, Famika Anae, Bob Apisa, Leo Reed, Ray Schoenke, and Junior Ah You—had been from Hawai'i. But in the 1970s, when thirteen Samoans entered the NFL, California came to the fore. Mosi Tatupu, born in American Samoa and educated at Punahou, was a member of USC's national championship team before his fourteen-season NFL career; Long Beach–born, UCLA-educated Manu Tuiasosopo was selected in the draft's first round by the Seattle Seahawks and won a Super Bowl with the San Francisco 49ers; San José State's Wilson Faumuina, who was born in American Samoa but attended high school in San Francisco, went to the Atlanta Falcons with their first-round pick in 1977; and Oceanside High's Joe Paopao began an illustrious career in the Canadian Football League (CFL) that's not over yet.[2]

They came from big families, and most Samoans who made it very far in football had brothers, cousins, or sons who also played. The Anes, Tuiasosopos, Tautolos, and Uperesas are evidence that when a Samoan turns professional, one or more of his brothers most likely will make a similar leap. In Oceanside, no family better exemplified that trend than the Paopaos. Across three generations and six decades, more than a score of them played and coached the game; others are sure to follow. Through marriage and blood, they seem related to almost every Samoan in the game. "My great-grandfather was married five times," Tony Paopao said with a laugh, "and it's a small island. He was a doctor; I think he made a lot of house calls."

"It's not like the Smiths—there are a thousand different Smith families," Mike Tuiasosopo pointed out. "The Tuisasosopos are one family; so are the Paopaos and the Polamalus." And they're big families. Given that *'aiga* connections are flexible—a young man or woman can align with either a father's or a mother's *'aiga*—the thickness of familial connections among Samoans is almost unrivaled.[3]

As the Paopaos, Tuiasosopos, and other Samoans won respect in football, the game became ever more central to Samoan boys growing up in what became the most populous state in the union. Soon, the Paopaos and their neighbors on the east side of Oceanside joined the Samoan wave in football. And as they made it, younger boys like Sal Aunese, Okland Salave'a, Pulu Poumele, and most of all Junior Seau, were caught up in their wake.

But the transition from living *fa'a Samoa* to living *fa'a Kalifonia* could be bewildering. The Paopaos, Tuiasosopos, Polamalus, and other football-playing Samoan boys were reared *fa'a Samoa* and successfully navigated *fa'a Kalifonia*. Many of their sons and nephews did too. But it became tougher for later generations, and many succumbed to the temptations of American-ization. During the 1980s, Oceanside's Samoan elders were blindsided by the emergence of single-headed households, teenage pregnancy, gangs, and youth who had strayed far from *fa'a Samoa*. Football has managed to maintain its grip on the Samoan psyche, but it's unclear how much longer it will.

Football's perfect storm swept through Oceanside in the 1960s. While coach Herb Meyer provided structure and consistency, the Marines dictated an extraordinary level of discipline and respect, and the Samoan boys who tried out for the Oceanside High squad brought an abiding sense of toughness and teamwork. By the time Herb Meyer retired in 2003, he had won more high school games than any coach in California history and Oceanside had emerged as a microculture of football excellence. From the 1960s on, Samoan ballplayers spearheaded Oceanside squads.

Only a few Samoans had arrived in this quiet vacation village by the time Meyer had graduated from Oceanside High, class of 1953, starred at Pomona

College—"the Harvard of the West"—and returned to coach as John Simcox's lone assistant. If an Oceanside boy wasn't surfing in those days, he most
likely played football. In Meyer's first season, 1958, more than 150 students
played varsity, junior varsity, or freshman football. It was a rough season, as
Oceanside went 2-6, and got rougher when the reason for the uncharacteris-
tically poor record became evident: John Simcox was terminally ill.[4]

Simcox resigned his position after the season and died months later; the
football field at Oceanside now bears his name, and his alma mater, San Diego
State, gives out the John Simcox Most Valuable Player Award each season.
Herb Meyer, who had graduated college only two years before, took over.
His selection dismayed a local sportswriter who complained that Oceanside
needed a football coach, not a biology teacher. Teaching human physiology,
however, paid the bills for Meyer and his family; he received only $106 his
first year as an assistant football coach, and not much more as the head coach.

Consternation turned to celebration when Oceanside tied for the section championship in Meyer's first season and won five titles in his first six
years. Oceanside was not supposed to compete with Southern California's
top programs, but it was beating them. Meyer realized that they had arrived
the night Oceanside upset a highly favored parochial school team from San
Diego. He was woken four times by telephone calls from incredulous sportswriters wanting to verify the score coming in over the wire.

Oceanside reigned over football in northern San Diego County, winning
seven league titles, completing two undefeated seasons, and sending a slew
of players to college. Several of them made it to the NFL. Others played
major league baseball, including Chris Chambliss, the top pick in the 1970
MLB draft, and Gary Thomasson, who was reunited with Chambliss on the
New York Yankees' 1978 World Series championship squad. Chambliss won
major league baseball's Rookie of the Year award in 1971; the next year his
Oceanside teammate Willie Buchanon was the NFL's defensive Rookie of
the Year. No high school had ever pulled that off.

Under Meyer's tutelage, football reigned as the town's most popular sport.
Meanwhile, Oceanside's population tripled to 76,700 between 1960 and 1980.
Weather favored physical culture and the town's increasingly diverse demographics contributed a variety of boys and body types to the team. Local
rivalries brought out Oceanside's competitive best; the struggle to win starting positions made players better each day at practice. Meyer, an astute ana-

lyst of the game and an effective motivator, built a staff that got bigger and better.

By the time Samoans started enrolling in the 1960s, Meyer commanded a juggernaut. "They called them FOBs—fresh off the boat," Meyer said, "because they came from Samoa and there wasn't any football over there in those days." They were as raw as could be. "They didn't know anything about the game," he explained. "You had to teach them everything. But they were very aggressive. They would grin while knocking the crap out of you and it was clear they were having a good time doing it." Technically, though, they were far behind their stateside teammates.

"When the late 1960s rolled around," Herb Meyer explained, "Samoan boys had been in the elementary system and some had played Pop Warner football. They were becoming more acclimated to American football, so we could coach them a little quicker. By then, they were a big part of what we were doing."

Samoans infused Oceanside's football teams with resiliency, energy, and determination as Meyer built not one but two of the most exceptional programs in high school football, first at Oceanside, then at El Camino High. And from 1963 until he retired in 2003, he always had at least one Paopao playing for him.

If the 1951 closure of the Navy base pushed islanders out of American Samoa, Camp Pendleton brought them to Oceanside, where Samoan life marched to military cadence. Men were often gone for tours in Vietnam; women worked on base and shopped at the commissary. Loia Paopao was a Marine, as were the fathers in most Samoan households during the 1950s and 1960s. His wife, Tina, worked at the camp laundry and picked up hours on weekends at the industrial laundry in town. While her husband was fighting a war in Vietnam the United States could not win, she kept her brood on the straight and narrow. "The moms carried the broomstick," Tony Paopao said, chuckling. "Mother was the discipline in our family. I think that's true in most Samoan families. When our mom said jump, you better jump. You didn't play around."

At Oceanside games, mothers channeled the spirit of island rugby. "When we got behind when I was playing or coaching," Junior said, "the moms would come out on the field and literally start a fight." They did not understand football very well, but those were their boys out there and somebody was hitting them. "When their sons were being tackled, they were ready to go on the field to help them out," Junior said with a chuckle. Both he and Tony dissolved into tears of laughter recalling Mrs. Tialavea, who was ready to fight whenever her sons or daughters were involved.

Both Loia and Tina Paopao were born in American Samoa. Loia was from Aua, which sits at the foot of Mount Pioa—the Rainmaker—on the eastern edge of Pago Pago Bay. He joined Aua's 'aumaga when he came of age and played for its rugby team, with many a match ending in a fight between teams or their fans. Loia was twenty-three when World War II changed the trajectory of his life. Instead of following his father and uncles up the hillside to the plantation, or working the seas in a *paopao*, a small outrigger canoe, he joined the Fita Fita. When the guard disbanded after the war, Loia entered the Marine Corps.

Tina was from Leone. Her cousin Francis Tuitele had transformed Leone's football team into the island's top squad in the 1980s. "Coach Tuitele said, 'Do this, do that,' but you couldn't understand most of what he said," Pati Pati recalled. "But the words 'Hit! Bam! Smack!' came through. He would say you were born to hit."[5] That his players understood. After the war, Tina and Loia married, baptized their children at the Catholic church in Aua, and left the island when Loia was shipped to Honolulu, joining the exodus that made Samoans a thoroughly transnational people. "When we moved here in 1960," Junior Paopao said, "there must have been fewer than ten Samoan families. The only kids I knew were on the football team." Not for long. After brief stints in military housing at the Sterling Homes, the Paopaos and other Samoan families gravitated to the east side, living with African American, Filipino, and Hispanic families near the high school and close to the beach.

By the 1960s, the Paopaos, Poumeles, Molifuas, Godinets, Seaus, and other families drawn by Camp Pendleton had boosted Oceanside's Samoan population above three thousand.[6] They were a close-knit community; family and church were its pillars, football not far behind for their sons.

Their children lived with one foot in the world of their parents and the other in the world they encountered outside their homes. Most children growing up knew Samoan because it was spoken at home and in church. "That's all that Mom and Dad spoke at home," Junior Paopao recalled. His father became fluent in English because of the military; his mother could get by but preferred Samoan. She made herself understood perfectly to the children, who internalized her ethos of hard work and discipline.

"Mom worked two jobs," Tony recalled, rattling off the names of his friends' mothers who worked with her on the base or in town. "And Dad worked all the time. That meant that our mother and our friends' mothers had lots of responsibility because the dads were gone overseas." Vietnam reverberated in their homes; Sergeant Loia Paopao did multiple tours there.

The Paopaos lived in two rooms; the parents had one, the sisters the other. "The boys slept wherever we could," Junior said with a laugh, "the floor, the couch; that's how it was." When the sisters left home after they married, the boys picked up their household chores in addition to their own. One did the laundry; another cooked; a third did bathrooms. "Our wives are eternally grateful for that," Tony added.

While there was little discretionary spending, the boys felt secure. "Mom made all our clothes and nobody got anything different," Junior explained. "When we went out together, we looked like triplets," Tony exclaimed. "We got the fifty-cent-special haircuts where you would wear your beanies to school the next week to cover the maltreatment of your hair. It was always the same haircut every time."

They shopped at the commissary, eating lots of chicken and drinking Kool-Aid or Tang. "Thank God for the commissary; that's how we could eat," Tony added. "And when they said eat, you better eat because if you didn't you were out of luck. There were never any leftovers. But we never felt poor." The boys entertained themselves; a ball and a tree limb became their basketball court. They collected spare bicycle parts and constructed their own bike, declaring victory if they could get a few hundred feet before their contraption fell apart.

Brought up in the Catholic Church, they served as altar boys and attended six thirty mass on Saturday morning even if they had played the night before. The church played an even bigger role in California than it had in American Samoa. The children learned traditional dance and celebrated festivals there. It became a surrogate *'aiga*, transmitting culture along with scripture. "Religion is the core and fabric of our culture," Tony said, "and we carried on as the elders brought it to us."

*   *   *

If family and church grounded the Paopaos in *fa'a Samoa*, football offered a chance to bask in American culture. Six of the seven brothers played, and all but one of them starred at Oceanside. Given how many of their sons and grandsons played, it's easy to see why the Paopaos are considered the first family of Oceanside football. Paul, the oldest, never had the chance to play for Herb Meyer because the family arrived in the spring of his senior year. But he was the first Paopao to pick up the game, making the varsity at Honolulu's Radford High on a squad of boys whose fathers were stationed nearby. In California, Paul enrolled at Oceanside-Carlsbad Junior College (which became MiraCosta College) and primed the family pipeline. In 1961, he was the first of four Paopaos to win a South Central Conference title at Mira-Costa; the next season, he led the squad in rushing. Though Paul could have played Division I football, he didn't connect it to education as much as his brothers would, and left the game. While he never suited up for Oceanside High, his son Paul Jr. and grandson Tofi were both chosen as San Diego County's Player of the Year.

Ben Paopao, the next brother, was the outlier; he eschewed football. But Alipati "Buck" Paopao, the third brother, was ready to emulate Paul. By contemporary football standards, the Paopaos were not especially big, ranging from five-nine to six-one in height. But they were quick and relentless and played both ways. Buck, the first Paopao Herb Meyer encountered, was also the first of the five brothers to wear a jersey with the number 41.

"Buck was the wildest of them all," Meyer recalled. Early on, Meyer benched Buck because he had gotten into trouble. Meyer was at home that evening when Sergeant Paopao rapped on his door. "There was Papa Paopao," Meyer recalled. "He wasn't real tall but he filled the whole doorway and he was upset. He came to tell me that that was not how Buck was going to act and that I had his permission to do whatever it took to keep him in line. He would back up whatever I did or said." The sergeant's message was clear; corporal punishment was acceptable in Samoan households and Coach Meyer was free to administer it as he saw fit. Meyer described Samoan boys wearing stocking caps to school because their heads had been shaved. "With all that hair," he reasoned, "that was bad news." Meyer later realized that boys who did not respond to these admonishments were shipped back to the islands to let the family settle them down.

Meyer also witnessed the role that shame played. Because Buck's misbehavior shamed his entire family, it was a powerful incentive for him to fall into line. It also sent a message to his brothers. "After that," Meyer said with a grin, "I never had any more trouble with Buck, and I didn't have to beat him up, either." Nor did he have problems with Buck's younger brothers.

Buck was a running back until Meyer switched him to quarterback his senior year, in the fall of 1965. Buck had matured and his scrambling abilities complemented Meyer's single-wing offense, where the quarterback often ran or blocked. Buck's kid brother Junior was on the varsity and Meyer knew he had to find a place to play him. Underclassmen made the varsity only if they were going to start; Junior did so as a sophomore. At six-one, 190 pounds, he was already one of the best players.

By then, Samoans were moving center stage in Oceanside football. As Oceanside rolled to one triumph after another, on their way to the 1965 championship, the Samoan presence on the team was undeniable. In addition to Junior and Buck Paopao, there were two Samoan juniors on the varsity, Mao Fuimaono and Larry Faumuina, and four other seniors, Fi Maluia, Tasi Mudd, George Molifua, and Smitty McMoore. The press dubbed them the Samoan Victory Eight. Seven of them started and played both ways; the eighth handled kicking duties. They were one-sixth of Oceanside's team, its leaders on the field and in the locker room. Averaging 173 pounds, the Victory Eight won because of a relentless physicality that belied their size. Meyer just called it toughness.[7]

The Victory Eight made an indelible impression on Meyer. George Molifua's mother was the daughter and last surviving princess of High Chief Paleopoi Mauga, who had signed the Deed of Cession with the United States in 1900, and Tasi Mudd came from a line of high chiefs.[8] These men kept winning wherever they played, and when they came home, they assumed leadership positions. George and Wally Molifua and Buck and Junior Paopao won championships at MiraCosta. George joined the LDS Church and served on the Human Rights Commission. Wally played for the Hawaiian Islanders in the World Football League and became Oceanside High's first Samoan teacher. Teammate Larry Faumuina was the town's first Samoan policeman.[9]

Buck Paopao followed Paul to MiraCosta, which featured Oceanside players and was a stepping-stone to four-year schools. He was the team's MVP during MiraCosta's 1968 championship season, beating out his brother Junior and the hypertalented Willie Buchanon. At Southern Utah University, Buck became a larger-than-life figure. "He broke all their records as a passer," Meyer said, "but broke all the other records in town, too, because he liked that hard stuff and Samoans don't go good with hard stuff." Buck was no saint, though brother Tony remembered him as the one "you naturally turned to" when you had serious matters to discuss. Still, Meyer reckoned, Buck gravitated to trouble, especially when drinking.

Buck went to camp with the Green Bay Packers but did not make the squad. So he followed the well-trod Samoan path into the military, where he became a paratrooper. After the service, he played in the Pacific Northwest's semipro leagues. Before television seized control of football, U.S. and Canadian cities far from the NFL's eastern and midwestern markets fielded their own teams. In 1977, Buck was the Northwest International Football League's Player of the Year. Bulked up to 234 pounds, he was bigger than opposing linebackers but faster than defensive backs. When he could no longer play football, Buck worked as a roofer during Southern California's housing boom.

Junior, next up, was the biggest and best Paopao so far. He bulled his way into the lineup as a sophomore, an almost unheard-of feat at Oceanside, and stayed there until he became the third Paopao to attend MiraCosta. There, he reunited with brother Buck and Willie Buchanon to win the conference title. MiraCosta coach Bill Corcoran could hardly contain his happiness over the stream of Oceanside players, especially the four Paopaos, who played for him. "It seems like every time a Paopao shows up," he remarked, "we win a title. The nice thing about them, though, is that they just aren't good football players; they are also gentlemen." Gentlemen, he might have added, who hit very hard. One season at MiraCosta, Junior and his Oceanside teammates Wally Molifua and Willie Buchanon won Desert Conference defensive honors. Another year, Corcoran fielded three sets of Oceanside brothers, including Buck and Junior Paopao and George and Henry Molifua.[10]

Junior's next stop was San José State, where he started as an undersized defensive tackle. The problem was that Junior wanted to play middle linebacker, a position for which he was better suited. When San José's coaches refused to shift him from tackle, Junior returned to MiraCosta to complete his associate's degree over the summer, enrolled at San Diego State, and walked onto the team. With his starting linebacking corps returning, Coach Don Coryell told Junior that if he wanted a scholarship he had to crack the lineup. After two ferocious days of practice, Assistant Coach Donnie Rea exclaimed, "I've never seen anyone go 1-on-1 with a guard like that. He just destroys the guard. He hits him with that forearm and destroys him." Coach Coryell was similarly impressed. "He's broken three helmets in 1-on-1 drills," he said. "He's big, strong, and fast." And he was Coryell's starting middle linebacker from then on.[11] After San Diego State, Junior spent time with the Chicago Bears and the Washington Redskins and in the CFL before turning to coaching.[12]

At San Diego State, Junior was one of three Samoans whose father was a Marine from the village of Aua in American Samoa. Another, six-foot-seven guard Taetafe "Tuffy" Avii, offered a glimpse of the Samoan wide-bodies beginning to appear on NFL rosters. He weighed about four hundred pounds when San Diego signed him; the Chargers weren't sure exactly what Tuffy weighed because their scales did not go high enough.[13]

By then, Junior's brother Joe was crafting a career that's still under way. Even though Joe initially shied away from football because his brothers seemed so much better at it than he was, he had little choice but to play. His older brothers made sure of that, challenging their kid brother to join the daily fray. They made Joe a football player, toughening him up and passing on what they learned from Coach Meyer—stance, footwork, consistency, and effort. "Everything I know about playing quarterback I owe to Buck," Joe said after surpassing his brother at the position.[14]

Although Joe led Oceanside to two championships, he received scholarship offers from only Rice and Utah. So he followed his brothers to MiraCosta and then played at Long Beach State University. Joe rewrote the schools' record books but went undrafted and took a job stocking goods at J. C. Penney for $2.65 an hour.

His career seemed to be at a dead-end when he attended a free agent CFL tryout camp with two hundred other wannabes in Huntington. After the first day, the British Columbia Lions invited Joe to camp but did not guarantee a roster spot. "I was lucky," he recounted, "they were looking for a quarterback." Joe made the squad and a year later, when the starting quarterback was injured, took over.

He was a sensation in Vancouver, where a 1980 poll found him the city's most popular athlete, recognized for his off-the-field demeanor almost as much as his flair for winning. Paopao was heralded as Canadian football's

"Throwin' Samoan." "His passes are poetic and when he is unable to pass he runs with elusive abandon," Earl McRae gushed during the 1981 season, when Paopao led the Lions to their best start ever.[15] He threw deep with precision, completed passes with defenders hanging on to him, and most of all, won.

"In this business," Paopao told McRae, "it's so easy to forget who you are and where you came from. I'm a simple man with simple tastes. We never had much back home and I never expected much and I don't want to take all the good things that are happening to me for granted."

For seven seasons in Vancouver and another four in Saskatchewan and Ottawa, Paopao was a crowd-pleaser with a solid reputation. "Humility and decency are perhaps the best explanation for the amazing, improbable rise of Joe Paopao," McRae reasoned. Retiring as a player in 1990, he has since coached for eight teams. Like his brothers, his sons played in Oceanside, too.

Anthony Paopao, who arrived two years after Joe, surpassed his brothers in high school. Carrying the brunt of the Oceanside Pirates' offense, he posted near-record numbers for a high school player during the 1970s. At six-one and 190 pounds, Tony was a Prep All-American his junior year, the Avocado League MVP, and the center of growing media attention. The Paopaos were by now a football brand. "Any time I hear the name Paopao, I know my team is in for a tough game," remarked Escondido coach Chick Embrey.[16]

For a band of brothers forced to wear beanies to school to conceal their "fifty-cent haircuts," they made up for it during the 1970s. The sports pages featured them with luxuriant Samoan 'fros. In a 1973 shot, their freak flags flying, the six brothers smiled radiantly in a pose sure to have exasperated a few grizzled Marines.[17]

Though leery of singling out individual players, Herb Meyer could not hold back about Tony, who spearheaded his offense as a ballcarrier and steadied his defense at middle linebacker. "Anthony Paopao is the best running back we've had at Oceanside High School in the 15 years that I've been coaching here," Meyer declared. "The only person who could be compared with him is C. R. Roberts." Coming from Meyer, that was high praise.[18]

"Much has been written about Anthony," Meyer told reporters. "He's a super kid who works hard and he isn't a prima donna by any means. He's not only a fine running back, but a pretty good linebacker. Let's face it, he's a super-athlete with a great football future."[19] Meyer saw Tony as the product of his family and Samoan culture. "He's got a lot of native football ability," he said. "Like children from some families have native intelligence or some have musical ability, the boys from the Paopao family have talents for football. When someone from a family like that is continuously confronted with a subject daily he either makes rapid progress or rejects it." Even as a freshman, Meyer said, Tony was very mature and possessed unusual football sense. "He has continued to develop that talent, rather than tend to get by and float on it like some high school athletes."[20]

Highly recruited, Tony roomed with Manu Tuiasosopo on his recruiting trip to UCLA. They both enrolled, but after his freshman season, Tony transferred to California Lutheran, where he became the focal point of the offense. He followed Junior and Joe into the pros, playing with Seattle and in the USFL, but left a more enduring mark as a coach. For thirty seasons, half of them with Herb Meyer, he mentored hundreds of young men, some of whom played professionally, others who became coaches.

By the time the youngest brother, Mickey, enrolled at Oceanside, the Paopaos were synonymous with scholarships and championships. Mickey might have been the most Americanized member of the family, the most affected by *fa'a Kalifonia*. He grew up during urban rebellions and the Summer of Love, when a Beach Boys ambience clashed with Ronald Reagan's law-and-order regime in Sacramento. "During the Vietnam War," former San Diego sports editor Steve Scholfield reflected, "Oceanside was a wild-ass, tough town." Some of the discipline that had characterized Oceanside of the 1950s and early 1960s had given way.

"Mickey was the clown of all the brothers," Tony recalled, "the jokester. When I was a freshman and he was in seventh grade, Mom said he had to be with me wherever I went. So when I went to my next basketball game, Mickey sat with the cheerleaders in the front of the bus, telling them he was a junior in high school." Chatting them up, Mickey had a date before they got off the bus.

Though Mickey wasn't very tall, he weighed more than two hundred pounds. "He was round like a bowling bowl," Junior explained. But when the ball was snapped, he penetrated the backfield and often sacked the quarterback or stopped the ballcarrier in his tracks. Mickey was quick, powerful, and full of pizzazz. He played nose tackle on defense, quarterback on offense.

"On the option," Tony howled, "it took four or five guys to tackle him." Mickey, who returned a punt sixty-four yards in a playoff game at Chargers Stadium, was agile, and his basketball IQ was high enough that he played point guard.

In 1975, Mickey played quarterback during Herb Meyer's final championship season at Oceanside. By then, the town had grown too big to accommodate all of its students at just one campus. "My last year at Oceanside," Meyer recalled, "we had five football teams; a varsity with fifty to fifty-five players; a JV team of about forty-five players made up of juniors, some immature seniors, and outstanding sophomores—they only played varsity if they could start; a sophomore team that played JV teams from small schools around the county; and two freshman teams with about 130 kids." Close to three thousand students were enrolled at the high school, which had split into two campuses. One of the facilities became El Camino High in 1976.

Meyer, who taught human physiology and served as the athletic director as well as the football and baseball coach, was already based on the El Camino campus. It wasn't an easy decision to leave Oceanside, a school where he was legendary. "But I figured if I went over to El Camino I could start from scratch with the physiology curriculum and the whole athletic program, including football." Most of his coaches went with him. So did many of the rising seniors on the team, because seniors could choose where to finish their high school education. Mickey Paopao was among them.

"Mickey was an all-world linebacker at 215 pounds and our backup quarterback that final season at Oceanside—quick as a cat." Meyer figured Mickey would be his quarterback at El Camino in 1976, but when players weighed in at summer practice, Mickey would not step onto the scales. "You could tell by looking at him that he had put on a lot of weight," Meyer said. "I told him he had to weigh in if he wanted to get his uniform. It was the only time that I ever saw him cry." Mickey was up to 265 pounds. Meyer told him he was too fat and out of shape to play quarterback.

Chastened, Mickey got himself into shape even if he never became svelte. He had an outstanding season and was all-conference at linebacker as El Camino won the title in its first season of play. Meyer inserted him at quarterback in a few games, where, he said with a chuckle, "Mickey saved our butts. He was more physical than other kids, and I sent him in at key times. In the semifinals, he saved our fanny. Mickey—and his brothers—were a major, major part of our success."

Though Mickey had a scholarship to San Diego State University, he could not control his appetite. "When they got on him for his weight," Herb Meyer said, grimacing, "he quit and came back to Oceanside and played in a band. He was very, very popular, but he kept getting bigger and bigger till he passed away." Mickey worked at the Oceanside Boys and Girls Club; his forte was talking kids out of gangs, which had begun appearing in the 1980s. He moved back home and cared for his mother, performing with his band, Island Society, at clubs on the beach. Mickey's health deteriorated after an automobile accident; in October 1995, he died of a heart attack in his sleep.[21]

More than twelve hundred people attended his funeral, spilling out of the center where services were held. Many teammates, including the Los Angeles Raiders' Dokie Williams and the San Francisco 49ers' Toussaint Tyler, attended. So did Mickey's close friend Junior Seau, then in his sixth NFL season with the San Diego Chargers. After returning from an away game, Seau made it to Oceanside in time to join the Samoan men who began cooking at five that morning for the ceremonial feasting that would occur after services.

The youngest of the seven brothers, Mickey was thirty-six.

After Mickey graduated in 1976, the torch was passed to the second generation of Samoan boys, and Herb Meyer's El Camino teams did not miss a beat. They were every bit as good as if not better than the ones he fielded at Oceanside. These boys had come of age emulating the Paopaos, Molifuas, Godinets, and Seaus, who had branded Oceanside football with Samoan fervor. Meyer never had a huge number of Samoan boys, but they made a disproportionate impact on the field and in the locker room.

When asked why Samoans excelled, Meyer eschewed genetically based explanations and downplayed the oft-heard warrior theory, addressing instead their cultural and psychological makeup. "They're not more talented but they put forth a greater physical effort than the other boys," he argued. "They utilize a greater percentage of their ability." Meyer did not dismiss physical differences among the ever-changing mix of racial groups on his teams, but he saw cultural differences as more salient.

"I always used to say that we got our toughness from the Samoans because they were so physical and our speed from the black kids. The white kids had to fight back in self-defense and that was pretty much the melting pot of our teams. We always had a couple of Hispanics who started who were athletically gifted or highly motivated to play, but they didn't dominate like the Samoans and some of the black kids did."

Meyer's 1965 team and its Samoan Victory Eight personified toughness. According to Steve Scholfield, nobody was tougher than George Molifua. The veteran sports editor had always wanted to identify the toughest kid to come out of Oceanside and figured it had to be Molifua. As young boys in Pago Pago, George and Wally Molifua walked up the hillside with their grandfather to his taro patch in the morning, listening to stories of *'aiga* lineage and island ways. Like the Paopaos, they left for Honolulu in the 1950s and came to Oceanside in 1963. Two years later, George and Wally were winning accolades on the ball field.

"George was only about five-eight, but he weighed 280 pounds," Scholfield recalled. "When he was in high school, a nineteen-year-old Marine had a beef with him." The Marine showed up on the school grounds and clocked George with a Coke bottle in the back of his head. It was almost fatal—for the Marine. George, hardly fazed, threw him to the ground, broke his jaw, and dislocated his shoulder. Finally, the principal intervened, saying, "George, I think that's enough."[22]

Meyer had only a few African American players in the 1950s, but the ones who played underscored how dramatically integration was reshaping sport. C. R. Roberts, one of the first African Americans at Oceanside, became a symbol of racial change when he starred for USC. In 1956, Roberts rushed for 251 yards in a handful of carries to lead the Trojans over the University of Texas in Austin. The game marked the first time that an African American competed against white players in the state. Roberts, like Dokie Williams and Toussaint Tyler, was among a number of Meyer's African American grads who played professionally. None was better than Willie Buchanon, who won All-American honors at San Diego State University. The seventh pick in the 1972 draft, Buchanon was the NFL's defensive Rookie of the Year en route to an All-Pro career.

"For Samoans, football is a good outlet," Meyer argued. "It's a way to express oneself physically within a set of rules." And it played to their strengths. Football demands more coordination, discipline, and teamwork than other team sports. Each play requires synchronized motion at lightning speed by eleven players. That called for discipline. "For the most part," Meyer said, "and I know it's an over-simplification, but I always used to say that Samoans were more willing to submit to discipline." They were willing to repeat a play in practice until their coaches were satisfied they could execute it in games. On the other hand, Meyer said, "The Samoan kids who were rebelling against the cultural discipline or got involved with alcohol stayed away from football."[23]

Bill Corcoran, who coached many Oceanside graduates at MiraCosta, said simply that his Samoan players were tough kids. "They're like the player of 30 years ago—completely devoted to playing football."[24] A coach's dream.

Meyer said that most people wanted to talk about their size. "Not all of them were all that big, but most are bigger than average-sized Caucasians," he observed. "The best had tremendous reflexes that, defensively, allowed them to get from point A to point B quickly once they understood the rudiments of the game." And players like Junior Paopao, who closed so quickly that he made tackles most thought impossible, simply had uncanny instincts.

"When Junior played for me," Meyer explained, "we had just instituted a six-one defense, with Junior as our monster back. You put your strong safety to the wide side of the field and played with three deep instead of four deep. We had developed that as our base defense and Junior was our middle linebacker. I had a guy come up to me who was a very good football coach that we had played against for years. He says, 'I don't understand how you have so much success running that defense because you don't have anybody covering the weak-side flat. You're three deep and you don't have an outside linebacker.' I said our middle linebacker covers that. He said, 'He can't!' I said, 'You know that and I know that but our middle linebacker doesn't know that. And I'm not telling him.' Junior just made plays."

Meyer, who knew what to do with toughness, was a critical reason for their success. Coaching matters in all sport, but boys are more likely to learn the basics of baseball or basketball on their own than those of tackle football. Given football's specialized positions, large rosters, sophisticated techniques, and imposing playbooks, coaches have an immeasurable impact. Meyer assembled a skilled staff while constructing a sporting environment that meshed with his players' sense of family and culture. He turned their unyielding physicality into sustained athletic excellence and scholarships. Meyer did so by addressing his players as individuals willing to commit to the team as well as to his code of rectitude. Most coaches strive for similar goals; Meyer more often than not attained them and treated his players, and then their sons and grandsons, with consistency.

Meyer's standards applied to all players, regardless of their background or abilities. "We wanted to win, but there's a right way and a wrong way to do anything." His mantra was that if you did things the right way, winning would take care of itself. And if a boy did not do things the right way, he did not play, no matter how good he was. On several occasions, Meyer benched star players before playoff games because they had not lived up to team expectations. That code worked well, especially with Samoans.

Steve Scholfield, who covered scholastic football, lauded Meyer's demeanor, even as his squad pounded opponents into submission. "I never recall an Oceanside or El Camino team having a personal foul called on them, never." The coaches were a steadying influence that was reinforced by their families. Scholfield visited the Paopaos on a Monday night and found the boys in the living room. *Monday Night Football* was under way, but the television was off. When Scholfield asked why, he was told that no one could watch until Joe finished his homework. "Those were Papa Paopao's rules."

Samoans, who embraced the concept of a team, were its emotional core. "When we went out on the field, one of our Samoans would lead a chant," Meyer said. "I don't know if it was a war chant or what it was, but they would hoot and holler." Their fervor and willingness to go hard at practice and in games energized teammates. Samoans might have been a distinct minority in Oceanside, but the Paopaos felt that they were accepted. "To me," Tony Paopao said, laughing, "the Caucasians were the minority when I went to school. It was such a melting pot. We associated with everybody—Filipinos, Caucasians, Samoans, blacks, Hispanics. I didn't feel discriminated against."

Many who worked with Meyer internalized his coaching ethos, including Tony and Junior Paopao. When asked about their family's secret for success, they replied in unison: "We're blessed with God-given talent. But I don't think we're any different than any other Samoan family. Like them, we were raised by our parents to work hard." And then both turned to their great fortune to have played for and coached with Herb Meyer. "I keep reflecting on Coach Meyer," Tony said. "Talent doesn't matter without hard work, and Coach showed us what that meant as football players and as human beings. He taught us that you're not going to get there by going halfway; that's how Mom and Dad brought us up, and that was Coach Meyer."

More than thirty of Meyer's former players, including a dozen Samoans, played professionally. Junior, Joe, and Tony Paopao and a score of their teammates later coached with him at Oceanside or El Camino. They were his co-coaches, Meyer insisted, not his assistants.

When Meyer retired after forty-five seasons as head coach of Oceanside and then El Camino, he had won more high school games—338—than any coach in California's history. That mark has been surpassed, but he's still the only one to reach one hundred victories at two different schools. El Camino was also only the second high school in NFL history to have two players from the same school become first-round draft picks in the same year, when Detroit picked Brian Westbrook fifth and Atlanta selected Mike Booker eleventh in 1996.

Meyer was California's Coach of the Year on three occasions and the National Coach of the Year twice and was inducted into multiple Halls of Fame. But what matters most to him is what he meant to the boys he helped coach into manhood. Meyer teared up twice when we talked, the first time when discussing his first wife's death. The other instance was when talking about letters from former students.

Their message was simple: that they could not find the words to convey the impact he had on making them who they became. "I can remember way back during Vietnam, I got a letter from a kid who said, 'Coach, you wouldn't believe the difference between kids who played football and kids who did not. . . . When you've got to dig in because you could be overrun, I want a football player next to me because he's not going to give up.'" That's what he wanted to get across, Meyer affirmed. "Football is part of your education; there are going to be hard times and anybody who is going to be successful knows that." For Meyer, adversity defined a person. "When you're knocked on your butt, what are you going to do?"

Over forty-five seasons, Meyer coached five Paopao brothers and a score of their sons and grandsons, as well as many Faasougas, Maluias, Molifuas, McMoores, Toluaos, Tialaveas, Meyers, Godinets, and Seaus. But he never had the chance to mentor future Hall of Famer Junior Seau. Neither did Oceanside coach John Carroll. Nor did either of them coach Sal Aunese. But it would be hard to find two young men who would mean more to Samoans in Oceanside and beyond than Sal and Junior.

8

Kalifonia Dreaming

"The further they move away from here or Western Samoa," Mel Purcell told me on my first morning in American Samoa in 2011, "the further they move from what is the true culture. They learn distorted values." Purcell has gone as far away as a man born in Samoa could go, to Hawai'i, across the United States, back to the South Pacific, and finally, of all places, to Iraq. He's since come full circle. Returning to American Samoa in 1979, Purcell has nurtured football there, advancing its international profile while trying to anchor it and the boys who play it in *fa'a Samoa*.[1]

But he's concerned about island youth, especially those who leave to play at junior colleges. Liberated from the restraints of family and village, many cannot handle their new freedom. By some estimates, half don't make it through their first year off island.

For Purcell, that's a reflection of larger cultural tensions. He frowns when the full *pe'a* becomes a tattooed band on the shoulder. "The language of tattoo remains the same over the centuries," he declared. "To remain true to your culture is to hold on to your communal land, the purity of chiefly titles, and the tattoo. They're the triangular pillar of Samoan culture." Yet each has been buffeted by change. As a high talking chief with a cosmopolitan résumé, Purcell is all too familiar with globalization's corrosive effects on *fa'a Samoa*.

He became a high talking chief after a stint in Iraq in 2004. Two sons were among the first to go directly from island football to Division I schools, and a daughter studied on a volleyball scholarship. Each graduated: one son played professionally and coached; the other served in Iraq. "I wanted my kids to get a degree," Purcell explained. Sport was how they could do that. Many on the island share his mind-set, in which education matters more than the lure of the NFL. "The greater success comes when they are walking across the stage with degree in hand," Purcell insisted, "not on the field."

He offered a proverb. Noah, wanting to see if his ark was near land, let loose a bird. When it did not return, he released another that came back with a leaf. Translated from Samoan, the proverb says that the pigeon that was let go has returned. "The boy or girl who gets that degree," he continued, "is a pigeon who comes back with a leaf."[2]

But Purcell is worried and wipes sweat off his brow with a Terrible Towel, an artifact of Troy Polamalu's visit the month before, draping it over a knee. He is anxious about boys growing up in American Samoa holding on to a culture that roots them in their *'aiga* and knows the challenge is even more daunting off island. American Samoa, of course, is not an idyllic paradise. Ice—methamphetamine—has become a problem and street culture's coarser aspects are evident, though life there still moves at a slower pace. But *fa'a Samoa* is more stressed in Samoan enclaves in California, Seattle, Utah, and Texas. How this plays out will shape Samoans' trajectory in football.

Oceanside is far from American Samoa, farther than Farrington High in Honolulu or Kahuku on O'ahu's North Shore, where Samoans blend into a Pan-Polynesian culture. There are about as many people in Oceanside—175,000 in 2013—as there are Samoans in the United States and American Samoa combined. And more Samoans live in California alone, some 60,000, than live in American Samoa.[3] The state has produced the lion's share of Samoan players, but Samoans there have not done well overall when measured in terms of health, income, and education. Americanization has weakened the collective tenets of Samoan culture—the foundation for much of what was good and secure in life—and left later generations in peril.

An upbeat, optimistic mood permeated the early years of Samoan migration to the mainland as the New Deal and World War II's economic jolt ushered in a golden age for working-class Americans. But with deindustrialization, the rise of the global assembly line, and growing inequality, that prosperity crumbled in the 1970s. Many families lost ground or came undone. "Oceanside was down and dirty when I came here in the 1980s," recalled Kristi Hawthorne, who heads the local historical society. Elsewhere in California, matters were worse.

Pulu Poumele, born in 1972, came of age in the 1980s when gangs and crack seized hold of the nation's psyche. In some towns, Samoans became synonymous with trouble. "They weren't easy times," Pulu acknowledged in the classroom where he teaches special needs children. "But what helped me was that the core group of Samoan guys I hung out with had a goal. Every single one of the guys wanted to go to college; we wanted to play football and get a scholarship." For the most part, that's what they did.

Given that his father, Talo Galeai Poumele, was a gunnery sergeant in the Marines and a reverend in the Congregational Christian Church, and that Pulu was the youngest of eight children with three football-playing brothers, he grew up old-school. His upbringing resembled that of the Paopaos, who came of age in the 1960s, more than that of Samoan boys who now play at Oceanside. Boys today are often generations away from American Samoa and tenuously tied to *fa'a Samoa*.

"My grandfather was very strict—his way or the highway—and my dad was entrenched in military discipline," Pulu emphasized. "If you didn't get up to eat breakfast at six a.m. you didn't eat breakfast." On family days, Sergeant Poumele marched the children in a line from their east-side home to the destination du jour while following along in the car.

"We spent most of our time at church—bingo, singing practice, learning traditional dance," Pulu said. "The culture was heavy at the time, so a lot of the things that we did in the home stemmed from what they did in the islands." His grandfather observed *sa*, and services and Bible reading were in Samoan. So was conversation at home. "It was all *fa'a Samoa*," Pulu remembered. He even grew up with *kirikiti*. "It was huge!" During the 1960s and '70s, cricket teams from Samoan enclaves traveled to tournaments around the state, with all of *kirikiti*'s attendant mirth.[4]

But Samoan life was evolving. The *'aiga*, all-powerful in the islands, adapted to mainland realities. It was more ad hoc, less of a daily presence, and not as beholden to centralized *matai* control. Nor did village life translate easily to California. By the 1980s, new civic organizations filled some of the vacuum, while churches hosted Samoan ceremonies and assumed secular and social roles.[5]

But it wasn't just parents and the church that helped Pulu navigate growing up in California. His peers were critical to his development. For them, football was both an escape from their parents' world and a way to gain respect within it. They grew up with a strong desire to never shame their parents or dishonor the family name. At the same time, they sought access to a world that their parents hesitated to embrace. Football offered admission. "We pushed each other, whether it was running or working out, we pushed each other to work hard. I went to my buddy's house at six in the morning, knocked on his window, and said, 'Let's go. Let's run.'" They set goals, to become team leaders and get to college.

Boys just a few years older offered them an alluring vision of who they could become. They saw them at church and family gatherings and were related to each other in multiple ways. And while these boys knew of Manu Tuiasosopo, Jesse Sapolu, and Samoans who had broken through in the 1970s and '80s, they had two fearless role models right there in Oceanside: Sal Aunese and Junior Seau.

"Manu and Jesse were very well-known," Pulu explained, "but Sal and Junior made it real to us. They didn't have to say anything; you just had to look in Sal or Junior's face to know that this guy is a leader. When they came along, it clicked in many of our heads that we can get an education out of this. It made me want to be like them, to achieve that goal."

As far as football players go, Siasau "Sal" Aunese wasn't much to look at; quarterbacks aren't supposed to be five foot ten and stumpy. Sal wasn't even very fast. But that didn't bother his teammates, not when he juked defenders off their feet or ran through them; not when he executed the option as if he were put on earth to do just that; and not when he set their considerable bulk on his shoulders and willed them to victory. Aunese had presence; he was confident, brash, and tough, but humble just the same.

On the other hand, it was hard take your eyes off Tiaina "Junior" Seau. He was chiseled, six feet three inches tall, and more than two hundred pounds of fast-twitch muscle, perhaps the greatest athlete to ever come out of

San Diego County. His senior year Seau was San Diego's Player of the Year in both football and basketball. Like Aunese, he was indomitable and zealously committed to teammates. If there was trouble on or off the field, you knew that he and Sal had your back.

Born eight months apart, Aunese and Seau were cousins and lived down the street from each other. Sal, born in May 1968, followed his brothers to nearby Vista High. A high school All-American quarterback, he led Vista to the state championship, destroying Helix 35–7 to cap an undefeated season in 1985. Junior, born in January 1969, trailed his brothers to Oceanside. A *Parade* All-American in 1986, he lifted Oceanside out of the slump it fell into after Herb Meyer decamped for El Camino in 1976.

"For me," Pulu Poumele avowed, "Junior Seau and Sal Aunese were the two who had a profound effect in terms of football and what it could do in terms of an education." Pulu's older brothers had played for Herb Meyer, but they had not looked at football as a way to college. "But we saw what you could do with it. We took that direction and ran with it."

Junior was especially important to Pulu. The Seaus and Poumeles were related and Junior's father had lived with the family when he first came to Oceanside. After Junior was born, Tiaina and Luisa Mauga Seau took their family back to American Samoa. When they returned, Junior struggled in the classroom until he picked up English. His father was the rare Oceanside Samoan man who was not in the military at that time. He worked at a rubber factory and as a custodian at El Camino High, where he ran Coach Meyer's equipment room. Junior's mother worked at Camp Pendleton's commissary and, like Pulu's mother, did shifts at the Newcomb industrial laundry in town.

When Pulu was a freshman at Oceanside, Sal and Junior were highly recruited high school seniors. Their scholarships made his goals seem more tangible, and he redoubled his efforts to use football to get his education. By then, every Samoan boy playing football in Oceanside and its environs wanted to be like Sal or Junior. Aunese was magnetic—in the locker room, on the field, or on the street. He could scramble when a play broke down and turn a loss into a big gain. Junior was revered and feared for his stubborn will and athleticism. He lettered in three sports and was such a rare player that when *Parade* magazine named him to its high school All-American squad, they labeled him as an "athlete" rather than reduce his contributions to a single position.

In 1985, Sal's senior year in high school, University of Colorado football was in free fall. Coach Bill McCartney, desperate to resurrect his floundering team, ditched his playbook and adopted an up-tempo, option-based offense. He then went looking for a quarterback tough and savvy enough to run it, somebody like Sal Aunese. McCartney dispatched Les Miles, his top recruiter, to reel him in. "He probably was the best player I ever signed," Miles later said.[6]

Miles also brought back Okland Salave'a. Okland was drawn to Sal, who, like Junior, was tough and charismatic and made teammates believe in themselves. "Sal and Seau were just different," Okland said. "When you have either one of those guys on the team, you believe you can win."

But college began on a downbeat for Aunese, who failed to qualify academically because of his SAT scores. Nor did Okland Salave'a. Okland, from American Samoa, wound up in Oceanside after an aunt persuaded his parents—both educators—that he would be better served by its schools. Both he and Sal had difficulty with standardized testing, mostly because they had spoken Samoan growing up. They sat out the season, unable to play or practice with the team, feeling like outsiders. They could not even stand on the sidelines during games. Instead, they worked out on their own and bonded during their exile. Junior Seau would face similar problems at USC.

While Okland and Sal, the squad's only Polynesians, proved themselves academically, the team struggled, with players in trouble. "White kids didn't mix well with black kids, and me and Sal were caught in the middle," he explained. "We're not white, we're not black, but in that community you're either white or black. There's no in-between."

They roomed together and when Sal announced he was going out late at night, Okland didn't think twice. When Sal wasn't there in the morning, Okland figured he was already up and out. Sal, however, had been spending nights elsewhere. He had become friends with the coach's daughter, Kristy McCartney, who lived down the hall.

"We couldn't wait for spring ball freshman year," Okland said. Both would soon start. Sal became the field general the Buffaloes needed to change their demeanor and style of play and Okland bulked up his now six-foot-six frame to line up against Oklahoma's and Nebraska's behemoth offensive linemen. After not playing for more than a year and a half, Sal joined the huddle in the third game in 1987. He carried for 60 yards the first time he touched the ball, and ran again on the next play, gaining 185 yards in a Colorado victory. The Buffaloes won seven games that season and Aunese was named the Big Eight's Newcomer of the Year. As Colorado began beating ranked teams, the two Samoans brought teammates together in the locker room.

But that spring, after an altercation on campus, Sal spent two weeks in jail. "Aunese was very, very competitive," Coach McCartney remembered, "maybe like a fullback would be, wants to hit you in the mouth." From Sal's perspective, he was standing up for himself and friends when challenged. Junior Seau felt the same way about his friends. In a basketball game against El Camino his senior year, Junior decked an opponent during an on-court scuffle. He showed up at El Camino's general assembly two days later and apologized for his part in the fight. "Honor is a very big part of Samoan culture and Junior felt he had let everyone down," Oceanside's athletic director, Pat Kimbrel, said afterward.[7] Like Junior, Sal was chastened by his encounter.

By the 1988 season opener, Sal was in total command of the team; his swagger in the huddle and cadence at the line of scrimmage jazzed teammates. They beat nationally ranked Iowa in triple-digit heat early in the season when Aunese rallied them in the fourth quarter. For McCartney, the win on the road heralded his program's turnabout. After Aunese lit up Oregon State in the next game and threw the winning touchdown against Colorado State with thirteen seconds left to play a week later, Colorado was 4-0 and nationally ranked. Coach McCartney was at home the evening of the comeback against Colorado State, savoring the win, when Kristy came to see him.

She was pregnant; Sal was the father. When a stunned McCartney asked his quarterback the next day whether he would be with his daughter during the pregnancy, Sal said he was not going to marry Kristy. McCartney, a devout Christian conservative who later founded Promise Keepers, blamed himself for not spending enough time with his daughter. He was devastated that she would bear a child out of wedlock. But, as the coach, he needed Sal to win.

Oklahoma State crushed Colorado the following week, and the team lurched through their remaining games. Finishing 8-4, they played in the Freedom Bowl against BYU, a school that heavily recruited Polynesians. The game was held at Angels Stadium, an easy drive from Oceanside, and Sal's family and Oceanside fans showed up en masse. They could hardly believe what transpired on the field that day. Sal had the worst game of his life. Clumsy and slow afoot, he could not do what he had almost always done, mount the winning drive or at least lose with panache.

When Sal returned to campus in January 1989 to begin winter conditioning, something was terribly wrong. The irrepressible team leader who wore short-sleeved jerseys to practice in freezing weather was tired and shaky, unable to complete workouts. He began coughing uncontrollably and vomiting blood. Okland insisted he see a doctor before they and friends left to visit a teammate's mother in Alabama for spring break. They waited for Sal during his appointment, but when he emerged, he said he needed to stay for more tests. So Okland and his teammates hit the road. Coach McCartney called the next morning, telling them to return to Boulder. Sal had inoperable stomach cancer; he had six months.

Okland was near tears recalling that day. On the interminable drive back, they discussed who should see Sal first and what to say. But when they arrived at his room, Sal was cracking jokes to family and friends. And though he and Kristy had fallen out during her pregnancy, Sal was at the hospital when his son, T. C. McCartney, was born that April.

Sal made it to camp that summer to address his teammates, and watched their games from a private box. By then, Sal had lost fifty pounds and his health was rapidly deteriorating. He left the third game that season before it was over and was watching at home when the television announcer said he had been chosen the Player of the Game. A week later, on September 23, 1989, with Kristy and T. C. in his hospital room, Sal Aunese succumbed. He was twenty-one.

"It was an awful period," Okland said. "I just wanted to quit; I didn't want to play football." But Colorado visited the University of Washington in Seattle the next week. Moments before kickoff, the players knelt on the field, each raising an arm in silent salute to the sky. Colorado won, with Okland batting down a pass and blocking a field goal. When asked about his friend afterward, he could not speak without crying.

Undefeated during the regular season, Colorado played Notre Dame in the Orange Bowl. Though they lost, the Buffaloes were declared national co-champions. Years later, Les Miles, who had recruited Sal Aunese to Colorado in 1986, and led LSU to the national championship in 2008, invited T. C. McCartney to walk on to his team at LSU. And twenty years after

Colorado played the University of Washington and saluted Sal in the first game after he died, T. C. ran onto the same field in Seattle with his teammates and saluted the father he had never known.

"We were very close," Junior Seau, then a junior at USC, said after Aunese's death. "I talk to him every day. I say: 'Sal, here we go again.' And I know he's up there listening."[8] Junior followed his brothers, cousins, and uncles—an assortment of Seaus, Molifuas, Poumeles, and Godinets—to Oceanside even though he could have attended El Camino High, the county's top football program. He played tight end and linebacker, threw shot put, and was an intimidating presence on the basketball court, where few defenders could stop him from driving to the hoop. Junior's work ethic was daunting; he ran sprints and cone drills on his own in the morning before two-a-day summer workouts and challenged teammates to keep up with him. He saw himself as an heir to the school's Samoan tradition, one that the Paopaos and a generation of Samoans had helped to create. "When I saw what Tony [Paopao] did," he later said, "I knew anything was possible in life."[9]

Tony Paopao coached Junior only once, in an all-star game. He recalled Junior knocking a trash-talking player out with one punch at practice that week. "He had only one speed—all out. He was going at it so hard in practice that we had to try to slow him down. We put three guys on him to try to block him," Tony said, giggling, "but they couldn't do it."[10]

In the spring of Junior's senior year, Oceanside High retired his number, 11. He was only the third player to be so honored. The first was the incomparable running back C. R. Roberts, who went on to play for USC and the 49ers; the second, a Samoan fullback named Arthur Hemingway, whose father was a Marine sergeant. When Junior was told he would join Roberts and Hemingway by having his number retired at the assembly where he would receive his *Parade* All-American award, he was stunned. "I was in the clouds."[11] Junior's next stop was the University of Southern California, where both Roberts and Hemingway had gone.

College football Hall of Fame coach John Robinson had recruited Arthur Hemingway to USC in 1978. "We really thought he was going to have a great career," Robinson reflected. "He just had everything going for him." He did, until a teenager in a stolen car, police in pursuit, ran the vehicle up on the sidewalk and smashed into Hemingway, who was heading for a burger on his third night at training camp. After weeks in a coma, Hemingway underwent twenty-one operations, including two brain surgeries. He never regained his ability to walk and his speech remained slurred.

But more than a decade later, Hemingway returned to USC and graduated with a degree in English. After completing a master's degree in education, he coached at Oceanside and Rancho Buena Vista and established a foundation that gave scholarships to students with disabilities. "When he was recruited, everybody looked at him to be the next Mosi Tatupu, and he had all the attributes and skills to be that," Ronnie Lott, the former USC safety and Hall of Famer said when Hemingway died thirty years after the accident.[12] "[Hemingway] was one of the brightest prospects we recruited," Robinson remembered, "a great-looking kid and a real leader at his school. He had a devastating smile." Robinson said the Trojans had envisioned Hemingway succeeding Tatupu, another Samoan fullback, who would play fourteen NFL seasons. "Arthur's potential was unlimited," Robinson said. "I thought he was going to have a great career for us. I was so impressed by the guy."[13]

Junior was impressive in his own right but, like Aunese, could not reach the required score on his SATs—he was ten points below the 700 cutoff—and sat out his freshman year as a Prop 48 student. Junior felt like a pariah; for the first time since grade school, he was off the team. The setback only motivated him to work even harder. That spring he won USC's annual contest of strength, physical endurance, and speed—the "Superman" contest—beating out every other player on the football team.

An ankle injury limited his play the following season, but Junior more than made up for it during his sophomore and junior years. No longer playing tight end, he focused on linebacker, where he displayed versatility unheard of in an era of increasing specialization. Few defenders are on the field for all defensive snaps, as game situations dictate frequent substitutions. Most play precisely defined positions. But Seau could play anywhere. In a game against Stanford, switching among four positions—nose guard, tackle, defensive end, and linebacker—he never left the field on defense.

An All-American with nineteen sacks his junior year, Junior played in the Rose Bowl on January 1, 1990, as USC beat Michigan. Rather than risk injury his senior year, he declared for the NFL draft and was taken by the San Diego Chargers in the first round.

Seau played with a controlled fury that could spin out of control. Some criticized him for freelancing on the field and leaving his team vulnerable when he gambled, but most lauded his performance week after week, season after season. He never took plays off, and he dominated games like few other defenders. Seau's NFL career was extraordinary; he was selected to twelve consecutive Pro Bowls, rarely missed a start, and played twenty seasons. "Junior Seau broke the mold, as big and fast and athletic as he was," Tony Paopao recalled. "He was the guy to me; the best athlete to come out of here."

His San Diego coach Bobby Ross said that Seau "could have played any position in the NFL with the possible exception of quarterback. He was that talented an athlete." When the Chargers made the Super Bowl for the only time in franchise history, his teammates knew he was the biggest reason why. "Not even close," Rodney Harrison said. "He was the catalyst, the emotional leader, the spiritual leader, the best player. . . . He made [teammates] believe and did something a lot of people didn't think we could do . . . beat Pittsburgh at Pittsburgh."[14]

It's hard to assess how badly football damaged Seau. During those twenty NFL seasons, he was never diagnosed with a concussion, which on the face of it is preposterous. But he received multiple injections of painkillers and anti-inflammatory drugs, underwent more than a dozen surgeries, and played with fractured bones. From Junior's perspective, that's who he was; that's what he did. In the 1995 AFC Championship game in Pittsburgh, despite a pinched nerve in his neck, Junior made sixteen tackles to upset the Steelers.

Life off the field was hardly sublime. Like Aunese, Junior Seau fathered a child when he was in college and became enmeshed in a fractious paternity suit because he was too immature to take on fatherhood's responsibilities. Antonio, his younger brother, served time as an accomplice to attempted murder after taking a baseball bat to another kid's head in a gang fight.

Some athletes turn their backs on their community once they've made it. Not Seau. Oceanside was his home and sanctuary and he remained rooted there. A couple of years into his professional career, he created a foundation to work with youth, especially those who had been neglected and were vulnerable to abuse. Junior worked with his cousins at the Oceanside Boys and Girls Club, fed hundreds at Thanksgiving, initiated a "Shop with a Jock" program, and gave out scholarships. Overall, he put millions back into the community.

After retiring days before turning forty-one, Junior lived on the Strand, the street by the ocean. He maintained a frightening level of fitness, working out with Marines from Pendleton on the beach and looking like he could still play. Junior rode the waves in front of his house when the surf was up and sat on his porch afterward, strumming his ukulele. Kids followed him along the beach, where he led them in impromptu workouts. While his commitment to the community was exemplary, Junior's peace of mind was fracturing. He slipped into rages, abused Ambien and alcohol, and gambled compulsively at Vegas casinos. The transition from football frightened him.

Junior had earned millions during his career. He had invested in a number of restaurants but they were hemorrhaging money, and pleas for monetary help dogged him wherever he went. The worse his finances became, the more risks he took. Jay Michael Auwae, a Marine with whom Junior worked out, was with him in Vegas when he won $800,000 just hours after arriving in town. "Let's go home," Auwae urged, "surf, chill, pay some bills." Instead, Junior was enticed back to the tables that evening and lost it all. He dropped another half million the next morning.[15]

In October 2010, a few hours after his release from jail for allegedly assaulting his girlfriend, he drove his car off a hundred-foot-high bluff, flipping the Cadillac Escalade but walking away unscathed. Then, on May 2, 2012, he went into a guest room in his home on the Strand, closed the door, lay down on the bed, and shot himself in the chest. Postmortem tests revealed chronic traumatic encephalopathy, brain damage almost certainly caused by concussive and subconcussive blows from playing football for almost three decades. CTE, of course, has been conclusively linked to the sort of behavior that Junior exhibited before his suicide, including depression, mood swings, and outbursts.[16]

The football world was stunned; Oceanside went into mourning. People congregated on the Strand, weeping. To most people, Junior was an upbeat, generous, fun-loving guy who, unlike most successful people, had remained close to his roots. Surfers paddled out en masse to pay homage in front of his home, players at Oceanside broke into a *haka* in his memory during a break between classes, and the town grieved the passing of their favorite son. In 2015, when he became eligible for election to the Hall of Fame, Junior Seau was the first Samoan to be so honored.

Penny Semaia was born near Camp Pendleton in 1981 but grew up in Utica, New York, where his mother took her children to live with her sister when he was four years old. A few years later, when Penny found out that he was Samoan, he hopped a bus to the public library and tried to read the only book about his homeland he could find—Margaret Mead's *Coming of Age in Samoa*. He didn't get very far with it, but in junior high, Penny discovered Junior Seau—"the man I would consider my Superman"—on the cover of an issue of *Sports Illustrated* in the school library. "Mesmerized by the story, I was even more engulfed because I found out that we were the same ethnicity." Penny began carrying himself the way that Seau did. "He was the player and person I wanted to be." And then his aunt told him they were related; both the Seaus and the Semaias were from the tiny island of Aunuʻu, which lies a few hundred yards north of Tutuila. If Junior would push his body past his limits, if Junior would close his restaurant and feed Oceanside's bereft on Thanksgiving, Penny would work just as hard at honing his body and game, making sure to give back to the community, too.[17] That led to four years on Pitt's defensive line, a degree in anthropology, and an ongoing commitment to sport and community both in the United States and in American Samoa. Like Sal Aunese, Junior Seau touched a generation of Samoan boys.

By the 1990s, not even the combined discipline of *faʻa Samoa* and the Marine Corps could ward off the damaging effects of a changing global economy and Americanization. As the U.S. economy stagnated in the mid-1970s and manufacturing gave ground, and as a fiscal crisis hit American cities and family structure collapsed, Samoans' purchase on the American dream slipped.

Fewer Samoans born in the States followed their parents into the military. And Samoans did not fare well with jobs, income, and other measures of well-being. "The problems of Samoans are the basic ones of poverty," Beverly Yip, the executive director of the Pan Asian Union in San Diego, pointed out in 1981. "Those are overcrowding, lack of income, and lack of education. Of all the Asian groups, they have the greatest problems."[18] A Department of Labor study confirmed her observations, finding Samoans among the most disadvantaged of any ethnic group. "Samoan youth," it concluded, "are experiencing particular difficulties in school and in accessing the labor market." Given the lack of an entrepreneurial culture in American Samoa, it was no surprise that few owned businesses or that disproportionate numbers held unskilled positions as laborers, nurse's aides, and factory workers. Upward mobility lagged.[19]

While demographers had a hard time counting just how many Samoans resided on the mainland, researchers knew they were confronting harder times. Their population was younger than longer-established Asian or Pacific Islander groups, and their households averaged twice as many people in them. Given how Samoans lived rent-free in the islands on 'aiga land, that was not of particular concern. The Paopao boys did not think twice about sleeping wherever they could in their home; nor did Junior Seau and his brothers mind spending nights on the concrete floor in their garage alongside the washing machine. But other issues took a toll. Samoans faced higher levels of unemployment and dropout rates than anybody else. They had the lowest per capita income, with a third of all families making less than what the Department of Agriculture considered necessary to escape poverty.

Something else was happening before their eyes. Samoan bodies were getting bigger and bigger. Surveys reported a startlingly rapid increase in body mass. The level of obesity among Samoans in California, researchers reported, "is as great as any known in the world." The farther away from the islands and the more they lived in cities, the heavier Samoans became.[20]

The generations born in the States were, as Mel Purcell feared, moving further away from Samoan culture. That's hardly surprising; no immigrant group to the United States remains unchanged for long. Though the first generation holds on to language and traditional practices, both weaken over time. Samoans were no different. People lost their grasp of Samoan lineage and language; many retreated from 'aiga obligations. Though transnational citizens, moving among U.S. cities, Hawai'i, and American Samoa, and priding themselves on their three-thousand-year heritage of fa'a Samoa, Samoans were now a tiny minority in a culturally heterogeneous world moving at frightening speed.

By the 1980s, Oceanside's Samoan community had dispersed from their east-side enclave. Many moved to Mesa Margarita, what's called the Back Gate because it's located by the back gate of Camp Pendleton. Others spread inland to Vista, Rancho Buena Vista, the Tri-Cities, and parts of San Diego, as Oceanside and its environs witnessed substantial population growth.

Samoans, few in number, were also marrying outside the Samoan community. "You cannot be as entrenched in Samoan culture when that happens," Pulu Poumele pointed out. In his household, two different cultures coexist. "My wife is Caucasian; her upbringing is different than mine." That's not the way it was in his parents' household, where the clash of Samoan and

American cultures was muted. But he knew many former Samoan players who married non-Samoan women they met on campuses where Samoans were a tiny minority. The effects of intermarriage became more pronounced with the arrival of the third and fourth generations of Samoans in Oceanside.

After playing in the NFL and CFL, Poumele began coaching. The boys he currently works with in Oceanside are less likely to live in two-parent households or to have grown up with *fa'a Samoa* as pronounced as it was for his generation. "There are things they are going through that we didn't go through," Pulu observed. "I wonder if they know where *fa'a Samoa* is coming from, if they know the sacrifices that people had gone through to get here."

"I never wanted to do anything to disappoint Mom and Dad; that was the big thing for me, knowing what they had gone through. I never wanted to put them in a bad light." For Pulu and his peers, representing the family name was paramount. "We took pride in that; it's not Pulu Poumele, it's Poumele." The elders reinforced that message constantly. "It's the same deal on the football field," he said. "You represent Oceanside. I don't know if these guys are missing something or they are just more Americanized."

Pulu's upbringing played out for him in football. "I think football was an extension of what we were already going through in regards to the culture—the respect and the work ethic we saw in the home all the time." Pulu recalled taking direction, doing chores, and working as a team with his sisters and brothers. "We would work toward a common goal. A lot of that transcends to football. If we are asking you to sweep the floor, sweep the floor." Switching to coach-talk, he continued, "If we are asking you to contain on a play, keep contain. That's all it is."

But Pulu sees a different mood in homes where no father is present, finances are sketchy, and the parent or parents are painfully young. He's not the only one witnessing a slow undoing of that which the first families prized—a sense of family and pride in *'aiga*. "Almost all of our kids had both parents," Herb Meyer recalled, "and many of them grew up in military households."[21]

Meyer was struck by the intense sense of shame Samoan players experienced when they did something wrong. "Sometimes, if a kid made a bad mistake you had to really work to get him back. You could tell him it's all right but they were really, really bothered when they did something wrong. They didn't get over it in just a couple of minutes." That shame was a powerful motivator for boys Meyer coached, like the Paopaos, Poumeles, Godinets, Seaus, and Molifuas, who were raised in households where Samoan and military culture fused.

That's no longer the case. "Today's world is a me world," Meyer said, where team, family, and the sense of representing something bigger than oneself no longer seem relevant. Many of the boys seeking playing time at Oceanside these days live in households where a parent is missing, and the grown-up in charge is working a low-wage job, struggling to hold things together.

Junior and Tony Paopao were part of the first generation and better able than most to negotiate cultural change in their children's lives. But they cringe at the issues now confronting youth. "Kids here, they're exposed to a lot of things," Tony Paopao lamented, "including fast foods, which is why they're so big." Like many Samoan Americans, he has witnessed the scourge of obesity and diabetes. "And there's often no guidance or leadership, no mom or dad, at home."

Tony's son Jordan graduated from San Diego State University with a degree in accounting and coach Jim Harbaugh solidly in his corner. Harbaugh described the 290-pound Mid-Major All-American as possessing "incredible balance, great feet and toughness," but was even more impressed with Jordan's demeanor. As a five-foot-ten-inch lineman, Jordan was hardly big enough to play professionally no matter his skill set. Although offered accounting positions, he followed his first love, football. Harbaugh hired him as his recruiting assistant when he took a job at Stanford, his next stop on a coaching carousel that continued with the San Francisco 49ers and then the University of Michigan. Jordan is now the tight ends coach at the University of Washington in Seattle. But few Samoan Americans boys do as well as Jordan, much less so quickly. Many peers Jordan knew growing up fell by the academic wayside and ended in dead-end jobs. A few drifted into gangs.

"When I was going to school," his uncle Junior Paopao recalled, "there were only a few gangs." The Posoles and Mescaleros recruited Hispanic Americans and the Hell's Angels attracted white bikers, but the thought of a Samoan gang was ludicrous. Then in the 1980s, the Bloods and the Crips, African American gangs from Los Angeles, made inroads in Oceanside, boosting the number of local gangs to eleven. When a Samoan gang appeared in the Back Gate area, the Paopao brothers were incredulous. "We could never figure out how a Samoan guy would get involved unless he didn't have parents," Tony Paopao said. "In the old days, you would send a kid back home to the island to get straightened out. We were raised to try to be open-minded, and mixed in with Hispanics and blacks. We wish these kids could understand what we did, but it's out of control. I'm one of those who thinks we're losing the battle."

That battle—a low-intensity conflict—smolders in classrooms, in kitchens, and on the field. Much of it plays out near Camp Pendleton. Today the neighborhood is home to the Deep Valley Bloods, a Samoan gang. Though few youth join gangs, most negotiate childhood with their presence close at hand, and membership offers protection from rivals. But Samoans make up a small percentage of overall gang activity in Oceanside according to local police, who listed two with Samoan affiliations. Although these gangs do not directly affect everyday life in readily apparent ways, they have fostered fear and violence, including several deaths, one involving a police officer working as a liaison to the Samoan community who was killed by gang members.[22]

Though outsiders from more troubled cities might consider this a trifling gang profile, it has shamed Samoan community leaders like Wayne Godinet, a member of one of Oceanside's earliest Samoan families. Like his brothers and cousins, including Junior Seau, Godinet played ball at Oceanside; since then he has worked as a community activist. He and other elders have intervened to try to prevent matters from spiraling out of control. "These fourth-generation kids are getting so good at riding the fence," Godinet observed in 2008. "When the sun goes down, they can hang with the bad crowd and in the morning, they're real good at meeting their family duties. I mean, some of these kids change into their [gang] colors on the bus on the way to school."

Like Mel Purcell, Godinet draws strength from traditional Samoan culture while fretting over how hard it is to maintain that way of life in California. "Over there," he says in reference to the islands, "it's more of a communal mind-set, like an extended family. Everybody supports each other. Now, they do the same thing here, but it's hard here because in a village it's more controlled, and church is an everyday venue." Godinet has worked tirelessly for the Oceanside Boys and Girls Club and other Samoan groups and serves as a go-between with local government. His take on the community is hardly an academic one; he's as deeply embedded as possible. He's promoted

Oceanside's Sister City relationship with Pago Pago and visits often. "Over here," Godinet said, "it's a capitalist society. You snooze, you lose. So it's pretty aggressive." He believes that youth anchored in tradition better resist the lure of gangs, but he knows that conveying that tradition requires his generation to engage with them.

Many Samoan children growing up in California never experience the warmth and sustenance that pervade the Paopao family, or for that matter, the Polamalus and Tuiasosopos. There's symmetry to Kennedy Polamalu's and Mike Tuiasosopo's football careers. Both were born in American Samoa in 1963 and left before starting school. Though they have always had *'aiga* ties there, their lives in California, education at Mater Dei High and USC for Kennedy, at Banning High and Pacific Lutheran for Mike, and subsequent careers have been first-world all the way. The first two Samoans to coach in the Pac-12, both were on the staff at UCLA in 2014. Like every Samoan veteran of the football wars I've encountered, they are concerned.

"*Fa'a Samoa* is having a real hard time in California," Kennedy said during a break at UCLA's training camp in the San Bernadino Mountains. "I'm very worried about where it's going. We have been blessed in our Polamalu family," he acknowledged. He, his brother Ao, and a dozen or more nephews and nieces either played professionally or used sport to get their degrees. "There's a confidence level that comes with having that degree," the USC history major noted. "Doors open up." It instills a confidence that carries over. "We're not all Troy. I'm not guaranteeing the NFL for these kids; we're just guaranteeing an education." That's what his neighbor made possible for Kennedy and Ao when he sent them to Mater Dei. But even the Polamalus have witnessed family fall into trouble, including Troy.

Though his family hails from Manu'a, Troy was born in California. His mother, Suila, uncles Kennedy and Ao and aunties Lupe and Moana joined an older uncle, Tone, in Santa Ana before he was born. "There were twelve of us in two bedrooms," Ao Polamalu recalled. Suila married Tommy Aumua. While the marriage produced five children, it was not a happy one and Tommy left. Troy's siblings could not escape the influence of Santa Ana's gangs; nor completely could he. *Fa'a Samoa* was becoming *fa'a Kalifonia*, with street culture winning out. Troy's salvation was Tenmile, Oregon, a town of 150 people where his oldest uncle lived.

After visiting, he begged to stay and Suila realized that Oregon would be better for her youngest child. Samoans never took to the notion of the nuclear family; families readily send offspring to live with an auntie, uncle, or sibling. Salu and Shelley Polamalu laid down the ground rules for their Oregon home, and Troy bought into them, blossoming academically and athletically.

By then, his uncle Kennedy had played at USC and Ao at Penn State. When Troy graduated, Kennedy was coaching at USC, which offered a scholarship. An All-American, he was drafted by Pittsburgh in 2003; a decade later, he was in the twilight of a career that will almost certainly end with his bust in Canton, Ohio.

"We've had ones who have gone into gangs," Kennedy said. "We couldn't straighten them out, but they've all come through. Those who served time in jail are now working, contributing to society and making their lives and their children's lives better. Our family has remained strong. When someone in our family needs something we all come together in the *fa'a Samoa* way."

Mike Tuiasosopo echoed Kennedy's sentiments. "It's a scary culture," he conceded. He sees more and more boys in single-parent homes, without the backing and guidance that the Tuiasosopo *'aiga* offered. "If you're in a community like Carson or Oceanside, the roots are deep. It feels like it's a village in some ways, because you have that extended family, but if you are out of those circles . . . ," he said without finishing his sentence. "Now you're getting these third, fourth, and fifth generations here. I wouldn't say it's watered down, but *fa'a Samoa* has dropped off."

Meanwhile, it's quite possible that football has reached its apogee. Few doubt that the NFL has displaced Major League Baseball as the nation's principal sporting spectacle or that football drives the NCAA and most high school athletic programs. But the number of boys playing football nationally has fallen precipitously since the 1970s. At first, those numbers reflected deindustrialization and the collapse of mill and mining towns. Then the rise of alternative sports, especially soccer, lacrosse, cross-country, and crew, lured potential players away from football. Finally, consciousness of the sport's potential to damage brains as well as bodies reached a tipping point.

Traditional football states like Pennsylvania, Ohio, and Michigan witnessed double-digit drops by the 1990s, foreshadowing a decline that spread across the country. The falloff began in youth football. Pop Warner football, which counts more boys among its ranks than any other program, saw its numbers plunge by 9.5 percent between 2010 and 2012, its largest decline ever. Nationally, tackle football among boys six to twelve years old dropped by almost 20 percent between 2009 and 2015 before experiencing a slight uptick in 2016.[23] Accordingly, the number of boys playing high school football fell five times in the last six years. Only wrestling saw a greater decline during the 2014–15 school year.[24]

Even in western Pennsylvania, once football's fertile crescent, high school teams are fielding smaller squads, with freshman teams all but disappearing. In the 1960s, most of the region's high schools had a freshman squad; in 2016, only 18 of 122 Western Pennsylvania Interscholastic Athletic League teams still fielded one, down from 88 in 2002. Although football remains the region's dominant sport, the numbers are down at every level.

Fear of concussions has driven the decline.[25] A 2014 Bloomberg Politics study reported that half of all parents responding did not want their sons playing because the risks were too great. While 43 percent said they would encourage their sons to do so, few thought the sport's popularity would rise. When broken down by income and education, the poll revealed that better-off, better-educated respondents were the most dubious about playing football.[26] Another poll done that year found that a majority favored banning contact prior to high school.[27]

Youth football is frantically experimenting with reforms. Leery of lawsuits and falling numbers, Pop Warner banned kickoffs in 2016 to reduce concussive blows; its three youngest divisions now begin games with the ball at the thirty-five-yard line and place it there after each score. Ramping up safety measures, it sidelines players when a head injury is suspected and has banned drills in which players line up more than three yards from each other and go at it with full speed. It also reduced the amount of practice when contact is permissible from a third to a quarter of the time.[28]

Programs adopting no-tackling policies have seen their under-eleven players' numbers soar while the ranks of youth tackle teams thin. The 2016 USA Football Participation Survey reported that flag football was the fastest-growing sport among children age six through fourteen in recent years, rising almost five times as fast as tackle. Where extensively promoted, flag football numbers have exploded.[29]

Tackle football remains the strongest among youth from lower socioeconomic backgrounds. In the United States, that means more and more African Americans in the game. A 2016 HBO Real Sports / Marist Poll found that more Caucasian and Hispanic adults (43 percent) are less likely to let their kids play because of the possible trauma to their brains than African Americans (28 percent). Among black families, better-off black households were more leery of the game. Given Samoan Americans' class background, it's no surprise that football remains much stronger in its ranks.[30]

Not even Oceanside, where parents dropped sons off on a mid-August morning for summer practice, has been immune from the game's erosion. Boys greet teammates who walked from nearby neighborhoods or arrived on skateboards or bikes. Though the number on the field swelled to more than one hundred, even this bastion of the game has witnessed shrinking numbers. In the 1970s, when the first generation of Paopaos was cementing their family's reputation, Oceanside fielded five teams with close to two hundred players. In recent years, head coach John Carroll considers a varsity of about forty-five players, a junior varsity of fifty, and a freshman team of sixty as a good count. But he was down thirty players overall from that lower threshold when workouts began in 2014.

"I don't know if it's the concussion mania, Junior Seau, or what—I would like to think it's an overreaction," Carroll said. For this coach, male culture is still a physical culture. "What's the most physical thing you can do and not break the law and get in trouble?" he asked rhetorically. "Hit somebody on a football field!" He dismissed state legislation limiting practice, especially in the summer, as unnecessary. "Hell week has become heck week!" he grumbled. "It's the wussification of the male physical nature." Pointing to the alarming rise in single-headed households, Carroll asked where else are boys raised by mothers who are overwhelmed by their own lives able to get the male mentoring that football provides.

If any coach in San Diego's North County could be compared with Herb Meyer, it's Carroll. As he entered his twenty-sixth season at Oceanside in 2014, Carroll's teams had won more than 75 percent of their games and made it to the San Diego Section semifinals twenty consecutive seasons, winning twelve times and playing in the finals for the last ten. Its seven section titles in a row between 2004 and 2010 included state championships in 2007 and 2009. Carroll reminds people of what Meyer did at Oceanside and El Camino during his historic tenure as head coach of Oceanside's two high schools.[31]

Oceanside football had slumped after Meyer left for El Camino in 1976; not even Junior Seau's presence on the team could restore the school's glory years. When Junior played quarterback as a fifteen-year-old, Oceanside won only two games. The team improved when he switched to linebacker and tight end but did not regain its mojo. Nor did Carroll revive the program overnight when he arrived. But once on track, Oceanside began winning with numbing consistency, a steadiness that defined Carroll's tenure.

Oceanside's success, he argues, rests on three factors: talent, continuity, and community support. "You have to have a talent pool," he explained in his office, "players who are willing to perform physically and emotionally, kids who do what you ask, who not only play with passion and energy, but practice that way." Samoans have exemplified that ethos at Oceanside since the early 1960s. "Samoans bring energy, which is why they naturally become leaders," Carroll said. "People gravitate to them because they have a huge passion for the game and play with high emotion and enthusiasm. That's alluring for a boy who is a quiet and reserved kid." Their size and physical strength, he added, win respect, and nobody challenges their intensity or work ethic.

Coaches like Carroll appreciate that Samoan boys come to sport without a sense of entitlement. "They don't have their own rooms; they share," he emphasized. "It's nice to be in a culture of people who don't want things given to them, and I hope that stays." When asked if Samoans have played an undue role on his teams, Carroll walked over to a wall on which one of his coaches has pasted newspaper stories about the players he respects the most and pointed at the faces. Most were Samoan.

"Percentagewise, our school is only 1 percent Samoan," Carroll noted. "Other schools think we have a ton of Samoans but we'll have fewer than fifty on campus, male and female. But let's say you have twenty-five Samoan males on campus, then twenty are playing football, and ten of twenty who play football are really good." He looked over the varsity roster and determined that ten of the forty were Samoan, mostly of mixed origins. Comparable numbers of Hispanic, African American, and Caucasian boys complete the varsity. Given that Hispanics account for 60 percent of the student body, Samoans were enormously overrepresented. Other schools, Carroll said with a laugh, "think we have a bunch of black kids because some of our skill kids are black. They think we have a bunch of Samoans, and they think we have a lot of military." The reality, he countered, is that few of the soldiers at Camp Pendleton these days are old enough to have children in high school. Nor were there that many African American or Samoan students at Oceanside. Carroll jokes with his players that he remembers when Samoans were big. "We have had a run of tiny, short Samoans in the last three, four years, but they're excellent leaders and excellent football players." He smiled like the Cheshire cat when noting that his freshmen players are returning Samoan size to the team.

Carroll believes that football can build community. "I'm for *E pluribus unum*—from many one," he declared. "And that's football. You're taking your Hispanic, Samoan, black, and white cultures and putting them together on a football team and they're going to share an experience. There's nothing better at doing that, except maybe the military during the draft." The best get to play, he insisted, regardless of color or class. Moreover, he stressed football's inclusivity. "There is no other sport that requires so many people to participate or where every size fits. You can have the lanky tall kid, the stocky muscular kid, the big heavyset kid; there isn't a body type, a one-size-fits-all football player."

Football players practice more and play less than athletes in other sports. They spend more time with each other in a culture of male toughness. And, Carroll concluded, "your success lies in how everyone around you does their job." Every member of a team shares in that success. "Even the worst guys have a role; they're going to be your scout guys. They're the guys that get the other guys ready and share in the victory, too, even if they don't see the field." That bond, Carroll argues, is something many boys don't have at home. "It becomes family if it's done right."

I saw several of the freshmen who made Carroll smile at practice that morning. While some were no bigger than the water polo team members training a mile away at the beach, others towered over their classmates. One boy who just turned fourteen stood six feet six inches tall and weighed 307 pounds, according to his auntie, who watched the boys practice from a lawn chair on the sidelines. "I come out to support my nephew," Dee Ioane explained. Breaking into a wide smile, she added, "They're all my nephews. We try to teach them the *fa'a Samoa*, but a lot of things change."

Dee Ioane has remained connected to the islands and seemed to know every Samoan family in Oceanside. On her mother's side, she is related to Chief Mauga, who signed the Deed of Cession a century ago. On her father's, she's connected to the Tuisasosopos. Ioane dispensed advice to a father of another player regarding the team's chiropractor, as well as diet and how to build bulk. "Feed him taro!" she exclaimed. It would be better than the fast food available across the street from the school, where, Carroll said with a grimace, you can order the "ninety-nine-cent heart attack."

Carroll argued that California football had evolved because of two demographic shifts: the desegregation of the schools, which led to more African American players, and the emergence of Samoans. "Those ethnic groups have elevated the level and quality of play at our campus, and elsewhere," he said. Disproportionately, Samoans were his team's leaders. "They all learned to dance, to do the *haka*; they're not afraid to have attention drawn to them, to get up in front of a group."

Oceanside football continues to benefit from the Samoans who have made the town their home. When asked about how good his team was going to be in an upcoming season, Herb Meyer would answer, "Let me see what the boat brings in." Fewer Samoans arrive by boat in Oceanside these days, but John Carroll need not worry. According to Junior and Tony Paopao, "There's another wave on the way that's in the third and sixth grades. They're our grandchildren."

John Carroll will not be there to coach them. After leading Oceanside to a 14-1 record during the season and losing to Folsom in the state championship, he announced his retirement. Carroll had overcome physical injuries in past seasons but had endured blot clots and trauma to his brain resulting from a fall while playing the scout team's quarterback position during practice. "This injury was different than the others," he said. "I pushed and fought, but it just wasn't getting better. . . . I wanted to teach until I was sixty and coach until they buried me on the field. But, as they say, 'Man makes plans and God laughs.'"[32]

9

Back in Hawai'i: Where Football Still Matters

Samoan boys who played together as kids stare warily at one another across the line of scrimmage. Once teammates, they're now opponents. Some are related by blood, several attend church together, and many share *'aiga* connections that stretch across the Pacific to Samoa. A few weeks ago, they laughed with one another at the Sadie Hawkins dance at the Kahuku High gym. And when night falls, they all return to the North Shore.

But for next few hours on this November evening, those friendships won't matter. Some of these boys have suited up for the 2014 state championship semifinal game at Honolulu's Aloha Stadium for Kahuku High School, others for Punahou. Almost half of Kahuku's players are Samoan, as are a dozen or more players on Punahou's roster, including six starters who would have been playing for Kahuku's Red Raiders if not for the lure of an elite, private school education.

In Hawai'i, it's where you went to high school that matters. A primal sense of self that formed in high school endures, often outweighing college and other signifiers of identity. It's telling that coaches at most schools are working where they once played. Most of them wouldn't have it any other way.

An education at Punahou is difficult to reject. Still, it wasn't easy for any of these boys to leave the North Shore and play for Punahou's "Buffnblu," as the team is nicknamed, instead of the team for which so many of their fathers played. And rising before dawn to catch a bus or carpool for the hour-plus ride to Honolulu, and returning in the dark after practice, is not for everyone.

Semisi Uluave, six foot six and 315 pounds, anchors Punahou's offensive line; his cousin Siotame Uluave does the same for Kahuku. "It would have been easier not having to get up at 4:30 every morning," Semisi confessed. "We all have our second thoughts, especially when times get tough." Punahou academics are not for the faint of heart. "We would want to run away from our problems and just go home," Semisi admitted. "It's tough to be 'those guys' because we don't want to be separated from the pack like that."[1] Several current Kahuku players tried private schools but returned.

Just how good would Kahuku be if the North Shore boys who play at Punahou and other private schools had stayed home and played for the Red Raiders? "It would be a different ballgame," Uluave declared. "Kahuku would probably be a feared machine." Punahou assistant coach Reggie Torres giddily sketched out the possible lineups Kahuku could have fielded, exclaiming, "It would be amazing what you could do." Torres ought to know; he coached Kahuku last season.[2]

Coaching football in Hawai'i is not for the timid. Coaches' decisions are scrutinized with an intensity that exceeds most everything else in island life. And no position is more freighted with politics and more terrifying to hold than that of Kahuku's head coach.

If the players are alike except for their uniforms, the students on opposing sides of Aloha Stadium are a different matter. They don't look alike, talk alike, or shop at the same stores. Kahuku's students are mostly Polynesian, with Hawaiian, Samoan, Tongan, and Filipino backgrounds; more of the Punahou scholars are of Japanese, Chinese, and *haole* descent. After the game, Kahuku students will ride back to the North Shore in the backs of pickups; not many Punahou kids roll that way.

It often seems as if everybody gangs up on Punahou at sporting matches—it's like rooting against Duke in college basketball—and enough Punahou students grew up with a sense of entitlement to give credence to their persona of privilege. Many won the fallopian sweepstakes and were born to well-to-do families. They'll soon be at Stanford or the Ivies. Others are smart, hardworking kids from tougher circumstances who will do amazing things someday. Kahuku youth, for their part, are underdogs; nobody considers them privileged or expects much of them, except on the gridiron.

About the only thing the two schools have in common other than the Samoan players on the field is a chant Kahuku students initiated in the fourth quarter. "We got spirit, yes, we do! We got spirit, how about you?" Punahou fans responded with the same chant but at greater volume. Kahuku roared back at them and Punahou matched their intensity a second time. After a third round of back-and-forth, they broke into applause—for themselves and each other. At least for a moment, sport transcended class. But after the game, they return to different tax brackets.

The players on the field, and not just the Samoans, share something else: the belief that school is family and teammates brothers. That's strong at Kahuku as well as at Punahou, if in different ways. Though crashing into each other on every snap, they belong to one of the most intense fraternities in team sport—the Polynesian-centered brotherhood of football. Their coaches, Punahou's Kale Ane and Kahuku's Lee Leslie, are part of that fraternity, as are their assistants. Kale Ane could hardly be more representative of Hawaiian football; Charlie Ane, the second Samoan in the NFL, is his father. Lee Leslie is an outsider. His father left him in an orphanage after his mother died giving birth to him and he's spent most of his life in Idaho and Utah. But both are committed to their players, football, and family.

Semisi Uluave pass protects for quarterback Ephraim Tuliloa and blocks for fullback Wayne Taulapapa. These three North Shore Samoans played with many Kahuku boys on the La'ie Park Raiders, a Big Boyz squad, until entering high school. They're the core of Kale Ane's offensive juggernaut. Going into tonight's game, Tuliloa had thrown only two interceptions all season and Taulapapa had run defenses ragged as Punahou averaged forty-eight points per game.

The game is hard fought. Mouthpieces fly when players collide and ball-carriers refuse to go down until flung to the turf by a pack of tacklers. The teams combine for fourteen turnovers, many the result of crunching hits after a ballcarrier has been stopped in his tracks but keeps trying to go forward.

Punahou started with a roar when Kanawai Noa returned the opening kickoff eighty-seven yards for a touchdown. It looked like they might trample Kahuku when on Punahou's first play from scrimmage, Semisi Uluave drove the Kahuku defender in front of him eleven yards downfield. "It's the fastest I've seen him go all year," Lee Leslie said of his defensive lineman, "in either direction. It was alarming."

But Kahuku's defense, long one of the island's best, stiffened. Led by Salanoa-Alo Wily, a six-two, 270-pound all-state Defender of the Year who does double duty at fullback and will play for the University of Nevada, Las Vegas (UNLV) in college, it kept Taulapapa in check and put Tuliloa on the ground. They reduced Punahou to a negative four yards rushing for the game and intercepted Tuliloa three times. After the kick return, Punahou's only points came on field goals.

Kahuku led 10–7 late in the fourth quarter when a Punahou field goal tied the game. Headed to overtime, Kahuku was flagged for consecutive defensive pass interferences, allowing Punahou to kick the game-winning field goal with seconds left to play. I've heard about the refs' seeming animus against Kahuku for years; now it seems to be playing out before my eyes. A *Star-Advertiser* reporter, displaying restraint, called the pass interference penalties questionable. Even some Punahou fans agreed.[3] But the score stood.

Some observers lampooned the semifinal as Kahuku versus Kahuku too. The other semifinal game—Mililani versus Farrington—also featured heavily Samoan lineups. The four teams' rosters underscore the extent to which Samoans have risen to the heights of Hawaiian football. Though Samoans comprise less than 3 percent of the state's population, they have become the most prominent players in the state's most popular sport. It's been that way for the state's best teams since the 1980s, when Cal Lee brought Samoan players to national prominence.[4]

Cal Kamaloloikalani Lee has long been an outlier, but never one who could be ignored. Forging a storied career in Hawaiian football at a school other than his alma mater, he forced other coaches to scrutinize what he was doing. Lee attended Kalani but made his reputation—and that of Hawaiian high school football—at the Saint Louis School. His father and two brothers attended Saint Louis, a Marianist boys' school. When asked why he didn't enroll at Saint Louis too, Lee shrugged. "You've got to get good grades to go there."[5] But years later, Lee set the standard for competitive excellence in island football as Saint Louis's head coach. For two decades, until he stepped away in 2001, Lee challenged every man coaching high school football in Hawai'i to match Saint Louis's performance.

Other coaches responded, and not just on the field. Like Lee, they began holding off-season conditioning sessions, attending clinics on the mainland, instituting strength and weight training, and cultivating community-based feeder programs to develop kids who would enroll at their schools. To win, they had to confront how Lee had built Saint Louis football into the state's best program and challenge him on terrain he ruled with near absolute authority. In time, they came to terms with Lee's influence, even if few would ever beat him. Out of that competition, Saint Louis, Farrington, Punahou, Kahuku, Radford, Roosevelt, and other schools created an enduring culture of football excellence.

A native Hawaiian, Lee played at Kalani, class of '64, with teammates of Hawaiian and Portuguese extraction. None were Samoan. Though Farrington's Bob Apisa was climbing football's ladder, few Samoans had emerged on local gridirons. After Kalani, Lee played linebacker at Willamette University in Oregon, where he was the school's only two-time All-American. Spearheading the defense, Lee led Willamette to a number three national ranking. He stuck around afterward as a graduate assistant before becoming Saint Louis's head coach in 1972 when he was twenty-five. "I lasted a year," he said with a laugh. Saint Louis won two, tied one, and lost seven games. "But I learned. I learned what you got to do."[6]

The following year, he became his brother Ron's defensive coordinator at Kaiser High. In their seventh season, the school won the 1979 Prep Bowl, what everyone regarded as the state championship. Rich Miano was on that team, as were several Polynesians.

Cal Lee then returned to Saint Louis. This time, he stayed—for twenty-one years. Under Lee, the Crusaders won fourteen Prep Bowls, eighteen Interscholastic League of Honolulu titles, and the first official state championship in 1999. His overall record: 241 victories, 32 defeats, and 5 ties. His tenure included a fifty-five-game winning streak that stretched over six seasons, a 15-1-1 record versus teams from the mainland, and two selections as the National High School Coach of the Year. More than one hundred of his players won Division I scholarships; several made it to the NFL.

"You don't think about it when you're going through it," Lee reflected. He was too busy keeping the team in orbit to bask in its glory. "I didn't think about the wins; I thought about the losses and why did we lose. Even when we won, and the streak was going on, I kept thinking about how we could get better; you couldn't relax." Trying to account for Saint Louis's success, Lee ticked off the usual suspects—coaches and players. "You can't do it by yourself," he offered. There are too many boys at different positions for a single coach to teach.

"Then you need players," Lee said. "Bottom line—nobody wins without good players. And if you don't have those players, what're you going to do? If you don't have the big, fast, stronger players, you better make them stronger." He played boys who weighed 155 pounds on the defensive line his first year. "We stressed that you've got to have confidence in your team. And if you don't have the size, you better be confident in the fact that you were strong." Accordingly, he emphasized weight training. Few teams lifted then, which gave Saint Louis a chance to outmuscle bigger opponents.

Entering the weight room, players walked by their names on a board where clips marked how much they could lift. Those who stuck with football pushed hard to raise those numbers. Even Lee was astonished by what happened next. "Everybody is looking for the edge, and more time in the weight room is one way to get it. Once we got it going, we had to chase kids out! How beautiful is that? I'm not telling the kids to lift weights after practice. They're saying, 'Coach, can you open the weight room?' They bought into it."

As Saint Louis won, the school attracted students for football as well as its academic reputation. Many players were from Catholic families on the outer islands who sent their sons to Honolulu to live with relatives during the term. Saint Louis's mission to educate and challenge boys from diverse backgrounds meant that it sought youth from lower socioeconomic strata. They were a diverse lot of co-religionists. When Lee began coaching Saint Louis, there were *haoles*, Filipinos, Portuguese, a small number of Polynesians and Hawaiians, but no Samoans. That changed. Closing his eyes, Lee traced the evolving ethnic makeup of his starting lineups in the 1980s. By decade's end, Polynesian names were commonplace.

As a private school, Saint Louis could recruit students from anywhere, including working-class kids from Kalihi's projects, the North Shore, and Wai'anae. "That was the beauty of his program," coach Hugh Yoshida observed. "Cal Lee made it a jumping-off place if boys wanted to go to the next level. Kids would migrate there because of football, to play for him, and that skewed the whole structure in the state of Hawai'i, taking away the best from all the other schools who would have stayed home."[7] Yoshida's point was driven home when I asked three men in Honolulu one day whether there had been many Samoans in the neighborhoods where they grew up. In each case, the answer was yes. When I asked if their high school football team had been good, they laughed and said no; the best Samoan kids in their neighborhoods had gone to Saint Louis to play for Lee.

Honolulu's private schools have recruited boys from comparable backgrounds since Father Bray brought Al Lolotai to 'Iolani in the 1930s. Their capacity to recruit has long been a source of contention; public schools resented losing top players and believed that private schools had an unfair advantage. But the social capital they afford is undeniable.

During the 1960s, high school football was the most acclaimed sport in the islands, overshadowing college ball.[8] By the 1970s, high schools had divided into two leagues, the ILH (Interscholastic League of Honolulu) for private schools, and the OIA (O'ahu Interscholastic Association) for public institutions. In 1973, the winners of the two leagues began meeting in an informal state championship called the Prep Bowl. Cal Lee owned it from 1986 through 1998. When the two leagues created a new state championship tournament in 1999, he won that, too.[9]

Lee was an outlier in another respect—his teams loved to throw. "Everybody was running the ball back then," he said, "but we couldn't pound anybody." Kahuku and Farrington sought to control the ball, putting their best players on defense, keeping scores low, and rushing until they wore opponents down. Taking their cues from Mouse Davis and June Jones's run-and-shoot offense at Portland State, Ron and Cal Lee brought a passing attack to Kaiser and later Saint Louis. "We beat everybody—public schools, private schools—by throwing the ball and that was because of June and Mouse,"

Lee testified. The approach, then novel, is still exceptional in Hawai'i, where teams have stuck to a power game.

Lee, who watched San Diego powerhouse Morse High visit the islands and crush teams, scheduled teams from the mainland. "We had to play teams like that to get better," he reasoned. "You can't stay here in your own little comfy hole." He took games with teams from Georgia, Arkansas, Japan, American Samoa, even mighty De La Salle High School, which went undefeated between 1991 and 2004. "Who am I to turn someone down?" Lee asked. "I never turned anybody down." He understood that competition raised the overall level of play. "We had some tough games; we just didn't roll over anybody," Lee remembered. "We had games you were just happy to be a part of."

Samoans became central to football's culture. By Lee's second go at Saint Louis, Jesse Sapolu, the Nogas, and Nu'u Fa'aola were at the University of Hawai'i, and Manu Tuiasosopo, Mosi Tatupo, and Kale Ane in the NFL. Lee loved their physicality and attitude. He raved about one of his Samoan players who built brick walls with his father during the summer. "That's what they do, carry rocks and build walls. This boy works a full day, so he can't come to summer practice. He'd like to come to practice; it would be easier!" His affection for players past and present is palpable.

But winning took its toll. "It grows on you in the sense that it becomes a monster," Lee reflected. "The season ends and you should be happy, but you're thinking about the next year and what you have to do to get better. It really was a monster." Lee stepped aside in 2001. After a year as Saint Louis's athletic director, he left the school and coached the Hawaiian Islanders in the Arena Football League. Although Lee had declined offers to coach in college, June Jones persuaded him to join his staff at the University of Hawai'i in 2003. Lee's reign at Saint Louis, with fourteen consecutive Prep Bowl titles, will likely never be equaled. But by then a new colossus was rising at Kahuku.

The Kahuku sugar estate has been reduced to a vestige of the roaring plant that once belched smoke and filled the air with the molasses-scented fumes of bagasse, the pulp that remains after sugar is extracted from cane. A posh resort, Turtle Bay, replaced the cane fields that grew to the water's edge; food trucks offering shave ice and garlic shrimp now occupy the land where the mill stood. But while sugar has fallen from its perch atop the North Shore, Kahuku football remains on an extraordinary ascent.

It's been a long time coming. Amid the swarm of players and coaches milling about the Kahuku locker room at Aloha Stadium before a playoff game, Tanoai Reed was hard to miss. Garbed in leather leggings, his face daubed with war paint, Tanoai prepared to lead the Red Raiders onto the field as their Warrior, a role he assumed during the season. While his *American Gladiators* physique is striking, his backstory is more intriguing.

Though born in Honolulu, Tanoai lived in Los Angeles until dispatched to his grandmother's house in Laʻie the summer before ninth grade, in 1987. At summer's end, he realized it was a one-way ticket. His parents had entrusted Tanoai to the care of his grandmother, Vaitai Tanoai Reed, the matriarch of Laʻie's Samoan community. Vaitai had come to Laʻie as a two-year-old when her grandfather Tatua and his cousins journeyed there to build the temple and establish a Samoan community. When I visited Tanoai there a few days later, he found a photograph of these early émigrés, a small group of men and women who had converted to the LDS Church in Western Samoa. Their descendants—Reeds, Anaes, Salanoas, Maivias, et al.—would write the bruising, ultimately triumphant, story of Kahuku football.[10]

Vaitai Reed spoke only Samoan to Tanoai. "She raised me," he said. "She gave me wisdom. She was my mother and my father growing up." Pressured to assimilate on the mainland, his father's generation had pulled back from traditional culture and language. "They grew up *faʻa palagi*," in the way of white people, Tanoai said, "but my grandmother taught me the *faʻa Samoa*." She taught him well. Tanoai learned the language and served at ceremonial gatherings held in Vaitai's carport. He helped prepare the *kava* and assumed a *matai* title when he was older.

Both the Mormon Church and *faʻa Samoa* loomed large in daily life. Although the *matai* system has waned, its influence now largely relegated to funerals and weddings, most Samoans in Laʻie still belong to *ʻaiga* that connect them to relatives scattered around the world. Vaitai was intensely committed to the church and *faʻa Samoa*. Tanoai attended LDS services before school early each morning, while learning *faʻa Samoa* from his grandmother afterward. Though the church projects an image of stern compliance with its strictures, Vaitai was not alone in choosing which church prohibitions to obey and which to ignore. When they tended the family graveyard, she would tell the kids, "Go away now; I'm going to puff the magic dragon."

"The church has its rules and its expectations," Tanoai observed, "but we have our free agency to do what we want. I don't believe the Lord will face me one day and ask why I got this tattoo if he knows it was for my family." The tattoo depicts the near death and miraculous rescue of Vaitai's uncles who were swept overboard during their voyage from Samoa to Hawai'i. The LDS code frowns on tattoos, but many Samoan members have them anyway. "People say that you are born with a tattoo," Tanoai said. "The artist pulls it out. It's a reflection of *mana* [an inner spiritual essence], of what's inside you." A free thinker, Tanoai concluded, "For me, my culture trumps my religion; religion is what's taught to me but my culture is in my blood."

So was football, especially Kahuku football. "Football was the foundation of my family, and my grandmother told me: 'You're going to play for Kahuku.'" Tanoai's father and uncles had played in college. One uncle, a former All-American nose tackle plagued by bipolar disorder, lived with Vaitai and Tanoai in La'ie. "He was so excited to teach me how to play that he got me in a three-point stance, and *whap!* knocked me on my back." His 320-pound uncle unleashed elbows and stiff arms as he tossed Tanoai around the yard. When he took him to the wrestling room, he ripped the cartilage in Tanoai's knee in a takedown seconds after they stepped on the mat.

Vaitai was just as eager to see Tanoai develop, but less hands-on. "She trained me; anytime I was home and doing nothing, she said 'ten laps' and had me run around. She would drop me off at the weight room, say 'go lift barbell,' and come back three hours later, or have me in the backyard hitting banana trees. She was always working me out." And feeding him. Tanoai weighed 150 pounds when he arrived, 190 as a sophomore, 240 as a junior, and 275 his senior year. One summer, he bused to Honolulu to train with George Perry, an organized crime figure committed to physical culture. His backyard gym mixed guys working for the syndicate with some of the island's best players.

Given his athletic pedigree, much was expected of Tanoai, who couldn't even figure out where his pads went at his first practice. But by his junior year, scholarship offers were pouring in. By then, Tanoai was a Kahuku Red Raider for life. So was Vaitai. "My grandmother was the biggest Red Raider fan," he said. "She went to every game, yelling and shaking her pom-poms. I played O line and when I pulled to block, I could hear her yelling: 'Here he comes! Get that stretcher out!' I remember running downfield laughing." With Tanoai an all-state lineman, Kahuku won the public school title in 1989 before losing to Cal Lee and Saint Louis in the state championship.

After graduating with a 3.5 GPA, Tanoai went to the University of Hawai'i, where his grandmother could see him play. One spring, he conducted clinics with Samoan teammates on Tutuila. He loved football, and Hawai'i won the WAC championship in 1992 with a team filled with Samoans, but the summer before his senior year, Tanoai and his cousin (and UH teammate) Dewey Reed were hired on the set of *Waterworld*, the Kevin Costner production filming in Hawai'i.

Tanoai and Dewey hung out with the stuntmen. "They were gung-ho cowboys, full of testosterone," Tanoai recalled. "It felt like a football team with the camaraderie so tight." He extricated his new friends from fights in local bars and they took a liking to him. One asked if he could ride a Jet Ski. Though he had never ridden one, Tanoai said sure and learned on the job. "I grew up on food stamps with Grandma and had never seen a hundred-dollar bill in my life. I got my first paycheck, about $5,000 for two weeks, and I was like, I'm getting paid this to ride Jet Skis and crash them and jump them and shoot fake guns. I can't believe it." By the time Hell Week, the infamous beginning to summer football, began, Tanoai decided to forgo it and become a stunt man. "I thought maybe this was what I was called to do."

Tanoai got his Screen Actors Guild card and moved to Los Angeles, but finding his way in Hollywood was another matter. "There were a thousand stuntmen looking for work, hungry, more skilled than I was." He lived out of his truck, worked as a bouncer, and detailed cars before moving back to Hawai'i. There, he got into trouble but managed to stay out of court.

When Tanoai met Suzanne, the Kamehameha grad he would marry, he returned to LA to give stunt work another shot. This time, he had headshots made and snuck onto studio lots to promote himself. Things broke his way in 2001 when he ran into somebody with whom he had worked on *Waterworld* who said the stuntmen were talking about him because he looked so much like Dwayne Johnson, who was filming *The Scorpion King*. Tanoai has been the Rock's body double and stunt man ever since.

About the same age, Tanoai and Dwayne share Western Samoan roots, *'aiga* connections, and tattoos. Their great-grandparents were brother and sister, and once, when Dwayne's grandfather, pro wrestler Peter Maivia, was being thrashed in the ring, Tanoai's grandmother Vaitai intervened and began whacking Peter's foe in the head with her shoe. Peter's tag-team partner was Al Lolotai; not surprisingly, the Reeds, Anaes, Maivias, and Lolotais are related.

Dwayne "the Rock" Johnson, who also played football, was on the University of Miami's 1991 championship squad. After a stint in the CFL, he became the third generation of his family to wrestle professionally, performing as Rocky Maivia in the World Wrestling Federation. He was one of the most commercially successful wrestlers ever when he jumped to Hollywood.

"When I met Dwayne on *The Scorpion King*," Tanoai recalled, "he didn't know much about Samoan culture and said he wished he knew as much as I did. I said it doesn't have to be like that." Tanoai began introducing him "back to the culture." A few years later, they got tattoos together. A year after that, the Samoan head of state honored Johnson with the *matai* title of *seiuli*, the same one he conferred on Jesse Sapolu.

Tanoai and the Rock have worked together on a score of projects, with Tanoai performing as his body double in fights and stunts. He's been blown up, run over, and hurt more times in more movies and television shows than he can remember. In 2008, Tanoai took center stage, appearing on *American Gladiators* as Toa, the Samoan word for warrior.

But just as Tanoai's parents sent him to La'ie when he entered high school, he and Suzanne wanted their son, Samson, to grow up there too. They moved back in 2012. "One of my missions coming home was to give back to my school and community; it's my *tautua*." When asked to become the Red Raider Warrior, he assumed the role with the same pride he takes in his film work. And just as his grandmother wanted him to play for Kahuku, Tanoai wanted his son, Samson, to be a Red Raider. Samson Reed could have gone the private school route and joined his teammates on the La'ie Park Raiders (the local Big Boyz squad) who went to Saint Louis. Weighing the three hours of daily commuting and the diminishing of ties with his community, Samson stuck with Kahuku, and Tanoai could hardly be happier.

He's working with others to rehabilitate the school's football facilities. Other schools have passionate followings, Tanoai argued, but no community is more intensely engaged than Kahuku. "We're the only school surrounded by a community; at Saint Louis and in Honolulu, you're all spread out. Not here." Nor can many schools match Kahuku's multigenerational football families. "You could take my roster and my son's roster and you'll see the same names." That makes football a critical part of North Shore identity. "The Kahuku Red Raiders represent everybody in the community, so when we win, we feel like it's us that has won. When we lose, our whole community feels it was in a battle with some other community and we all lost."

While Tanoai believes that the wins and the losses "belong" to the kids, he knows that "everybody is a coach here." Kahuku coach Lee Leslie seconds that. "I'll have a 285-pound woman walk up to me and say, 'Why so much cover two last week! Maybe use the nickel package.'"[11]

Social media has intensified and often vulgarized the emotional discussion that rages around the team. But sport has brought people together despite its capacity to provoke outrage. "Football is the binding factor among all the communities," Tanoai pointed out. "There are kids from Sunset who play football and they're part of the team. Now you'll see them over at some Samoan family's house for a get-together. You would never have seen them there before."

When Tanoai played, almost three-quarters of the team had some Samoan ancestry. Few Tongans played then, but both he and Junior Ah You note that they're coming on strong. His generation of players, he argues, was in better condition. "We were big, 270, 290 pounds, but we were built. We didn't have big guts sticking out; we were athletes." He grimaced when talking about current players' diet and girth.

At Kahuku, Tanoai played for Doug Semones, who was more Dennis Hopper than Vince Lombardi. A Mohawk-coiffed, Mormon-reared free spirit who bit off the head of a snake while a student at Cal Lutheran to jazz his teammates, Semones coached Kahuku from 1989 through 1995. Semones demanded fitness. "He was young and fired up, hungry. We had to run a mile in full pads before practice with linemen doing it under eight minutes, linebackers and backs under seven, or you did it again."

For somebody who works on the cutting edge of twenty-first-century pop culture, Tanoai Reed remains committed to the past. "I will get the full *pe'a* [the traditional tattoo]," he said. "It's been calling to me." Men usually get the *pe'a* with a partner to share the agony, and he has invited the Rock to join him. The *pe'a* takes about two weeks, five hours a day. "It's a pain you can't compare to anything," Tanoai said. And he knows pain from stunts that went awry. He intends to build a traditional *fale* in back of his house and have the tattoo done there. His grandmother would smile at that.

Kahuku became a good team in the 1990s, at times an exceptionally good team. If not for Saint Louis, it would have been state champ. But Cal Lee's squad had been unbeatable in the playoffs since 1986. When Kahuku's Red Raiders met the Saint Louis Crusaders in the Prep Bowl in 1989, 1993, 1994, 1995, 1998, and 1999, they lost each time. "Kahuku was our best competition," Lee said.

Doug Semones pushed Kahuku to the state championship four times. But each time, they fell to Cal Lee's Saint Louis School juggernaut. When Kahuku lost 27–26 in Semones's last season in 1995, it was the closest any team had come to beating Saint Louis since the parochial school's championship streak began in 1986.

Semones took an assistant coach's position at the University of Hawai'i after the 1995 season, leaving behind a staff of ten men, each of whom had played at Kahuku. "They're committed to the kids and they can talk story with them about when they played here, on the same field, against the same teams," Semones said. So could many in the community. Almost everybody had family who had played for the Red Raiders. Few teams anywhere had such intense local support. During the playoffs, families brought meals to feed the boys after practice.[12]

After a selection process that drew more scrutiny than local elections, Siuaki Livai, who had coached at Kahuku for eight seasons, became the new head coach. The Tongan émigré was ten when he arrived in La'ie in 1971. "Everybody wants to come to America," he said in the classroom where he teaches math. For some Tongans, the attraction was the Mormon Church, but for Livai, born on the island of Ewa, America was "the land of opportunity, where education and jobs other than farming could be found." Livai's parents had entrusted him to an auntie and uncle unable to have children of their own who joined the fledging Tongan migration to Laʻie. There were only about forty Tongans in Laʻie then, divided between students at the college and labor missionaries brought to build LDS infrastructure. While his adoptive father, who had been a principal in Tonga, ran a fruit stand on Kamehameha Highway, Livai left for school at five each morning to attend Sunset Beach Christian School, across the road from where the Pipeline's monster waves crash the shore, north of Kahuku. And education, even more than football, has driven Livai ever since.[13]

Livai, who grew up playing rugby, joined Pop Warner football and entered Kahuku High, class of '78. Almost all his teammates were Polynesian, mostly native Hawaiians and Samoans, including Famika Anae's sons. "There were only a few Tongans on the team and I don't remember any Tongan or Samoan surfers," he said, laughing. Nor were there many *haole* surfer boys from Sunset Beach. Livai played running back and linebacker but knew that education, not football, would define his future. After college, he returned home to teach and soon to coach with Doug Semones.

As head coach, he tapped into the resilience and pride that had driven Kahuku since Harold Silva and Famika Anae coached there. Livai supervised team study halls and took players camping, as well as to play games and attend clinics in Utah. The North Shore by then was the hub of a transoceanic circuit of families flowing from the Samoan and Tongan islands to Hawaiʻi and the U.S. mainland. Although Kahuku was losing kids to private schools in Honolulu, other boys transferred in to be a part of the program or because their families wanted to live in Laʻie.[14]

"That was Livai's problem—losing kids to other schools!" Waiʻanae coach Larry Ginoza exclaimed. "That's what happens when you have a big honeypot. People are gonna come and try to get some." But Kahuku's success made it easier to keep kids from leaving for private schools. "I didn't mind Cal Lee picking up boys from around the world," Livai exclaimed years later. "I minded him picking boys from Kahuku and I had to put a stop to that. I went to the homes of families and told them their sons had to come here." He remonstrated and argued and could not persuade all of them, but over time, fewer kids left. They found that Livai would work the phones and land scholarship offers for them. "I had to take away [Cal Lee's] strength to have the chance to beat him."

The North Shore was the first stop for many South Pacific immigrants who had *'aiga* connections there and found the pace easier to handle than the turmoil of a city. Livai, a first-generation immigrant, began working with these Samoan-born boys. Some, like Toniuolevaiavea Fonoti, wound up in the NFL.

Football was gentler than what Toniu, ten when he arrived, experienced at home. "My dad was huge into punishment," he said after becoming the youngest second-round NFL pick ever in 2003. "I got hit every day. His work belt was the worst." Toniu realized later that he released "that hatred I was feeling inside . . . onto the field." After two seasons at Kahuku, he moved in with an auntie in Oceanside to absorb Herb Meyer's coaching at El Camino High and test himself against California-grade competition. Meyer was impressed with Toniu but didn't have him for long. "We thought he would have been one of the best linemen who ever played for us," Meyer said.[15]

Toniu returned to Kahuku in time for Livai's first year as head coach. When Kahuku went 2-6, it was almost his last. But they improved to 8-3 and then 12-1 Toniu's senior year. That year, the offensive line averaged 283 pounds. "Everybody in the state knows we run the ball," Livai said. "Our goal every year is to improve the passing game to give a balanced look. But I know [opponents] aren't fooled."[16]

Toniu went to Nebraska, where he became an All-American whose ability to pancake defenders was unrivaled. No Cornhusker offensive lineman ever flattened as many opponents in a single game, season, or career. After Toniu was drafted, Nebraska coaches told Herb Meyer that if he had come back his senior year, he would have been the best lineman ever at a school known for its offensive linemen.[17]

Kahuku's fortunes were on the rise, but that didn't mean coaches let up. Players braved Livai's Hell Week, a five-day on-campus ordeal during which the players left only once, to scrimmage Saint Louis. Arriving Sunday night, they slept in the gym. Awakened at six a.m., they endured four practices in ninety-degree heat, four meetings, weight lifting, and sprints.

After meals provided by churches and businesses, they cleaned the cafeteria. The next day brought more of the same. "The coaches," slot-back Marcus Salanoa groaned, "own us for a week." Marcus, whose father quarterbacked Kahuku's 1972 title-winning team, got no sympathy at home. Meanwhile the staff stayed up past midnight watching tapes and planning the next day's punishing regimen.[18]

After losing to Saint Louis in 1998 and 1999, Kahuku tried again in 2000. "Everybody was talking about Saint Louis and cutting us down," Livai acknowledged, especially after Saint Louis destroyed Wai'anae in the semi-finals. "I told my guys if we don't believe in ourselves, let's just stay home and save everybody the trouble."[19]

Few opponents could stop Kahuku's relentless running game, and some years, every starting offensive lineman won a D-I scholarship. "But we lost the Prep Bowl each year because Cal Lee stacked the line and beat us," Livai explained. "To win, we had to make them respect the pass. Cal Lee pushed us to get better." So that 2000 season, Livai took to the air. Kahuku lost twice that season, once to a team from Utah by one point, the other time to Larry Ginoza's Wai'anae squad.[20]

"But I fooled Cal Lee," Livai said with great satisfaction more than a decade later. "He looked at our losses to prepare and scouted us when we used the spread offense. I was setting it up that way. We came out in the Prep Bowl using the Power I formation with two tight ends, and the Double Power I with three running backs behind the quarterback. There were no wide receivers on the field." And play after play, Kahuku ran the ball. Lee chuckled when I related Livai's remarks. "I never heard that before, but it worked."[21]

Junior Ah You was at Aloha Stadium for that 2000 championship game. "Kahuku did the *haka* before the game," he recalled. "It was the first time I had ever seen it before a game and I saw the fear they put in their opponents. The players were so passionate, so hyped, like they were walking on air. In all the years I've played I had never seen anything like it. There was no way they were going to lose. I had goose bumps watching them. In fact, I feel them now."[22]

Saint Louis had not trailed in a championship game since 1995, but Kahu-ku scored first. Saint Louis tied the game, and when Kahuku scored again,

Saint Louis came right back to even the score. A change in eligibility proto-col for the new state tournament meant that Saint Louis was without three all-state defenders for the game because they had exhausted their eligibility. That helped Kahuku outrush Saint Louis by a margin of 270 to 65 yards, and score on three consecutive ten-play possessions in the second half, during which they threw once. Meanwhile, their defense, led by future Pittsburgh Steeler Chris Kemoeatu's two fumble recoveries and a smothering second-ary, was steadfast. When the gun sounded, Kahuku had won 26–20. The king was dead!

While the vanquished Crusaders stood on the field and applauded the vic-tors, sportswriters took stock of Saint Louis's legacy. "Through its success, Saint Louis has given overdue national visibility to Hawai'i football," Ferd Lewis observed. Its incredible winning streak and the number of grads who excelled in college "helped to open eyes beyond these shores and opened the door for college scholarships to many more deserving players."[23]

Lee had goaded other coaches and teams, especially those like Kahuku whose competitive passions burned the hottest. "Coach Lee pushed us to get better," Kahuku coach Siuaki Livai said years later.[24] As a caravan of buses, cars, and pickups snaked its way northward, crowds gathered along the blacktopped road to applaud. The buses stopped in each town along the way so that players could perform a *haka*. They passed victory signs and placards with their names and jersey numbers draped on utility poles. It was after midnight when the convoy pulled into the school parking lot, where thousands, many shaking red and white pompoms, roared their approval. Many stayed up all night, drinking *kava*, barbecuing, replaying the game, and basking in a sense of fulfillment, long deferred.[25]

It normally took Junior Ah You five to ten minutes to get from his home to the school. But with cars stopped on the highway as people danced and performed their own renditions of the team's *haka*, it took him two hours.

Pauline Masaniai, a Kahuku grad then teaching at the school, was caught in the same delirious gridlock of fans returning from Honolulu. "I remem-ber those years when we went to the stadium to play Saint Louis and would come back with our hopes deflated. I was in the stands when we won that first game against them." As she described the response along the way back as people who had watched the game on television now lined the highway awaiting the victory caravan, tears slid down her face. "It seems ridiculous, why we put football up like that, but we do."[26]

The victory resonated beyond the North Shore. For public schools, it was sport's "Democratic Revolution." A rural district imbued with a plantation past and a century of missionary influence had conquered an impregnable private institution. "That game changed the course of Hawai'i high school sports for the better because it gave all schools—especially the public schools—renewed hope and optimism," High School Athletic Association director Keith Amemiya reflected. Kahuku would reprise its victory, winning in 2001, 2003, 2005, and 2006. Three of those wins came against Saint Louis, the other one against Punahou. "There was no longer this aura of invincibility," Amemiya said, "and it wasn't just football. The public schools have ended [private school] dominance in many sports since then."[27]

Meanwhile, players internalized Livai's standards. "I think the biggest thing was discipline," Inoke Funaki reflected about Kahuku's turnaround. "I know it's a vague word. You can't really put a finger on it, but it's a day-to-day thing." Funaki was the quarterback during the breakthrough 2000 championship season. He had grown up thinking that Kahuku, for which his older brother played, was cursed, bound to make mistakes that cost them the title. But Livai changed the team's culture. "He was always reminding us about penalties, always cracking down on us about the littlest things, because the little things always hurt Kahuku in the past," Funaki said. Livai kept them focused on each step, from breaking huddle to sustaining blocks.[28]

Decrying the practice of keeping boys eligible at all costs, Livai argued that he would get the best from them only if they applied themselves in school. If need be, he intervened personally, driving to Chris Kemoeatu's home and those of other students to get them up for school or SAT exams. Livai simplified the game for them, but once they mastered the basics to his satisfaction, he diversified the offensive and defensive schemes. "You need their brain to dig deeper if you want to open up options for players. I diversified everything; I simplified it to diversify it. When you make it simpler you can throw more out there."

Pauline Masaniai taught alongside Livai before becoming Kahuku's principal. "Siuaki was a unique person," she explained. "He fought for those scholarships and spent hours on the phone with college coaches. He figured how to get kids to clinics and camps on the mainland because he knew that's where the recruiters were."[29] Livai learned how to game the system to place players in the right academic and athletic settings.

Livai backed Masaniai's predecessor, Lea Albert, when she unilaterally raised academic eligibility standards (what became known as the Kahuku Rule) despite opposition from the community and the OIA, which stuck with the lower threshold. When the state raised its standards, Kahuku set an even higher GPA for student eligibility. "If a coach is not invested in academics," Masaniai argued, "the number of athletic scholarships goes down." Livai was totally invested in both football and education, and more students than ever before found that football was their ticket to college.

And the sport became ever more popular. In 2003, three hundred boys and one girl out of twelve hundred students tried out. Although half of them quit during the rigorous preseason, 167 played JV or varsity ball that year. "I didn't cut anyone," Livai explained. "It was an opportunity to belong to a positive organization, to a community with structure, and that benefited their academics."[30]

The team's success resonated beyond the school; no institution brought more cohesion to the area. "They are the pride of the North Shore. This is the only high school for twenty miles each way," Livai pointed out. "People here know everyone who has played for Kahuku past and present. . . . Their support means so much to us. They get off work and they're tired, but they still make the trip to Honolulu. What we do means a lot to them, and we want to show them how much we respect that."[31]

Cal Lee saw the significance of Kahuku's 2000 victory. "It got the monkey off their back." Kahuku was recognized as the best team in the state, something that matters in Hawai'i. It also got another monkey—the monkey of inflated expectations—off Lee's back. But as journalists Dave Reardon and Paul Honda pointed out, that monkey, needing a place to go, jumped atop Siuaki Livai and refused to budge.[32]

No matter what Kahuku did on the field, fans were insatiable. They expected the team to win and do so with pizzazz. Meanwhile, Livai expanded his portfolio beyond the North Shore. Mindful of his roots and those of his students, Livai brought Tongan boys living on the North Shore to Tonga to play football in the Kingdom Bowl. The first was held to honor the king of Tonga, His Majesty Taufaʻahau Tupou IV, on his birthday in 2002. During that trip, American Samoa's governor, Togiola Tulafono, suggested that Livai also bring Samoan players from Hawaiʻi to American Samoa. With Tulafono's support and community buy-in from the territory, the Samoa Bowl began in 2003. Volleyball, wildly popular in American Samoa, where boys and girls play outside every evening on dirt courts, was later added to offer young women exposure to mainland coaches and the chance of scholarships. Teams from California and Australia also began participating.[33]

"The success we've had at Kahuku High School is for all Polynesians," Livai declared. Their achievements reflected a Polynesian ethic that drew strength from their transoceanic roots. But Livai's off-island activities provoked criticism from locals who wanted him to focus exclusively on Kahuku. Nevertheless, he was committed to these programs, which brought a thousand Tongan and Samoan youths to the islands where their families were from.

After stumbling to a 6-3 record in 2002, Kahuku rebounded and went undefeated in 2003. Recognition came to the team, the school, and their coach. Livai was honored five times as Hawaiʻi's Coach of the Year, twice as the National Coach of the Year, and once as the state's Coach of the Decade. Kahuku ranked among the leading high schools nationally for the number of players earning scholarships. Some years, more than three-fourths of all senior players landed scholarships. In 2004 and 2005, Kahuku led all high schools in the number of graduates playing Division I football. Signing days became community celebrations, with players paying homage to their parents and the North Shore as they inked their letters of intent. "That's the ultimate goal, to move on to college," Livai reflected. "Football is just a vehicle."[34]

Kahuku kept winning, but some carped about the style in which it triumphed. Accusations of recruiting and ineligible players dogged Livai, as they will any coach who wins so consistently. And after Kahuku was crowned state champ for the fourth time in 2005, he left, while still on top. Five Kahuku players played in the NFL that season; no high school had more; eleven seniors signed Division I offers.

Livai's respect for Cal Lee only grew during those years. He called Lee's record "amazing," after Kahuku won four state championships in six years. "What I found out was that it is easier to get there than to maintain it year after year."[35]

"The pressure of being the Kahuku football coach is unbelievable," Kahuku's athletic director, Joe Whitford, said when Livai stepped aside. "It took a toll on his family. Every activity they did, it pertained to football, whether they liked it or not. No matter what you do, you're not going to please an entire community."[36]

"I promised my wife the past few years, every year, that it would be my last," Livai said. "I've been neglecting responsibilities at home with my family." With a dozen family members including foster children as well as Back to the Roots, his nonprofit organization that connects youth to their Tongan and Samoan heritage, and football games in Samoa or Tonga, those responsibilities were daunting.

And the pressure to keep Kahuku at the top only intensified. While his commitment to sport remained strong, Livai later said, "I blame myself for football becoming god in this little town. It's misleading kids, interfering with academics. Like I said, I blame myself. When I became coach, we had never won a state championship." Many championships later, Livai said, sighing, "I wish they would see reality."[37]

Livai had felt as if he was riding a tiger as Kahuku's head coach, holding tight so he wouldn't be thrown off and devoured. When he leapt off the tiger's back, Reggie Torres jumped on. Torres, who played cornerback and wrestled when he was a Red Raider, had worked his way through the ranks, coaching judo, wrestling, and JV football, before joining the varsity staff. In 2006, after a contentious search with nineteen applicants, he took over a team whose supporters questioned anything short of the state title.[38]

Torres didn't know it when we talked in the summer of 2013, but he was entering his final season as Kahuku's coach. And even if he had, his focus on preparing for the oncoming season would hardly have changed. Though the season runs only August through November, football at Kahuku demands year-round effort.

When Reggie was a player in the mid-1980s, he and teammates spent summers on Lanai. "It wasn't mandatory but the coach encouraged it and almost all football players went." They worked night shifts till one in the morning. "After breakfast, we would train, have intramurals, take a nap, and go off to work. We came back tougher, slimmer, and conditioned. We were in awesome shape." After football season, Reggie wrestled. After wrestling, he ran track.

Nowadays, coaches urge players to participate in winter sports to stay competitive, and push them in the weight room to prepare for the next season. There's no longer any downtime. In January, boys lift. In February, it's speed work and conditioning. Then it's spring practice and readying themselves for camp in late July. "The older kids understand what they need to do to stay successful," Torres argued. "If they play for us for one year, they know. They know that if they don't train with us, they won't survive spring ball."

When Torres played, Samoans were the squad's core, playing the skill positions as well as manning the lines. "There were more Samoans then, fewer Tongans," he said in the utilitarian room that served as his office. It's jammed with the equipment and supplies necessary to maintain 150 players on the field.

Though camp is a few weeks off, players are engaged in voluntary compulsory workouts. That is, if they expect to make it through training camp and have a chance to play, these workouts are critical. Few survive without them. Nodding to the adjoining weight room, where boys squatted, jerked, and pressed weights, grunting as rivulets of sweat dripped to the mat, he said, "There are more Tongans now, almost as many as there are Samoans."

The past spring, 120 boys started spring workouts; 80 made it to the end. More will show up when summer camp begins, including some newly arrived from Samoa and Tonga. There's never a shortage. "They pare themselves down," Torres explained. "We don't have to cut anybody. Our summer workouts and the reality of our program make some kids realize this isn't for them."

And that might be why so many are Samoan, Tongan, or Hawaiian. Hard work doesn't dissuade them. "Our success is because of our work effort," Torres kept saying. Many Polynesian boys cultivate land in the hills that the LDS provides their families or work construction with their fathers; physical exertion does not faze them. "They come naturally strong and when you put them in the weight room and they learn technique, it shows."

"We can push them, not baby them." But that's only one of the reasons that Torres relies so much on Polynesians. "What makes them so good at football is that they're fearless," he argued. "They hate losing. They grow up respectful, disciplined, and when they misbehave, I'll sit down with dad and the kid gets a licking afterwards."

"Do you know why colleges love Polys in their programs?" he asked. "The difference between the Poly kid and any other kid is not that they're stronger or faster but that they bring teams together. For them, the team is family; other kids circulate around them." Recruiters say they need Polynesians because they're locker room leaders whose demeanor rubs off on other players. "And they'll battle," Torres declared. "They shut their mouths and just battle."

Other than two white defensive backs and two African Americans on the JV, his players are Samoan, Tongan, Hawaiian, or a combination of Caucasian, Japanese, Filipino, or African ancestors. Between ten and twenty each season are fresh from American Samoa, Samoa, or Tonga. "They're stronger," Torres stated. "Their problem is the language barrier, but other kids bring them into the team, into the family."

"Some Poly kids struggle, especially those who come without English. We're not the smartest; we're not like kids in the private schools. Some have learning disabilities. We just try to keep it simple." That means running the ball. "We run the I formation while others run the pistol or spread, but we're going to get our four or five yards. We come right at you, and do it again and again." Usually by the third quarter, Kahuku's opponents are tiring, bent over with their hands on their knees, and Kahuku's backs aren't gaining five yards but twenty. "We load up our defense, keep scores down, and in the fourth quarter, you see the separation between them and us."

Most players are churched, with Mormons predominating. "There's a moral upbringing that's part of all the churches' culture here," Torres observed, "but kids are kids. There's still going to be rascals even with the church; they're going to be temperamental."

Though the North Shore was never entirely insulated from the pressures bedeviling Samoans in Honolulu, its Mormon culture tempered the stress. Samoan families have remained stronger and more intact here; many are from independent Samoa, which has Westernized more slowly than American

Samoa. Elsewhere in Hawai'i, Samoans, especially youth, were incarcerated or in gangs at much higher rates than the population at large. More women led households and many felt helpless to control their children.[39]

Meanwhile, Mormon influence countered the growth of an underclass. Youth seek to stay worthy in the eyes of the elders; males are ordained at age twelve, a religious connection reinforced as they get older. Many look forward to serving on a mission. But historian Matt Kester cautioned against caricaturing the Samoan experience in La'ie. Samoan Mormons have not adopted all of the church's strictures; many ignore its admonitions against tattoos and drinking 'ava.[40]

The fortunes and behavior of the team transcend religious differences among students and affect the entire school. "We go to different churches and we have all these cliques—North Shore Boys, surfers, Tongans, Hawaiians, Samoans—on campus, but football unites us," Torres declared. "When football is great, behavior on campus is great. When football's not going well, the campus has problems. I tell you, I just love the kids here." Principal Pauline Masaniai tells me the same.

For Torres, like Livai, getting kids to college is almost as important as winning. A dozen or more receive scholarships each year. Torres rattles off some of their names, noting how they fared in college. The list would be longer but for the stream of boys who accept private school offers and play elsewhere. In 2012, when Punahou defeated Kahuku for the title, its team included Manti Te'o and several boys who otherwise would have suited up for Torres.

Kahuku has held its own despite the private schools' ability to attract students from afar, redshirt players so that they are often nineteen their senior year, and offer social capital students can tap long after graduation. "They take our kids." Torres shrugged. "They recruit heavily on this side of the island." But he's not backing down. "We've taken teams without that much talent and yet we win. We went against a Punahou team that was packed, bigger than us, with more talent. But we had a great senior class; we kept coming at them and we beat them." That senior class was rooted in a bedrock of *fa'a Samoa*, Mormonism, and *anga fakatonga* (in the way of Tonga). It's ironic that after being replaced at Kahuku, Torres took an assistant's position at Punahou. He was on the winning sidelines again in November 2014 when

Punahou beat Kahuku in the state semifinals—this time wearing Punahou's Buffnblu, not Kahuku red.

Many of the Kahuku boys and several Punahou kids had played Big Boyz football together. While Pop Warner introduces boys to tackle football, its weight limits exclude many Polynesians. When Kalani Soren and Doc Taula's sons turned ten in 2001, they were already too big for Pop Warner. So Soren and Taula began training them at La'ie Park, near Soren's Hukilau Cafe, where locals and visitors stop for generous breakfasts and lunches. Three nephews joined them that first year; twenty boys showed up the following season. They soon created a tackle football league that spread across the state, with dozens of teams playing fall and spring seasons. Other youth leagues for kids who weigh too much for Pop Warner have copied their approach around the island.[41]

Big Boyz teams became feeder programs for local schools. The La'ie Park Raiders field several age-based squads; some of the players, like a six-foot-three, 280-pound seventh grader, are eye-catching. Without Big Boyz, he and many other boys wouldn't have played organized football until high school.

The La'ie Park Raiders work closely with Kahuku's coaches. "We give them our schemes and invite their coaches to our practices and to sit down with us," Torres explained. "That's good for us." Lee Leslie, Torres's successor, added, "Another reason that Kahuku is amazing is the Big Boyz program here; they play a fall season and a spring season, so they get two seasons a year for two, three years, and then they come up to high school." That introduces them to technique, terminology, and hitting. It also deepens their commitment to the sport. "When my group came to the ninth grade in 2007," Taula said, "twenty started as ninth graders and twenty-six moved up to the varsity."

Kahuku coaches—and there are more than thirty of them including the JV staff—also work with the Big Boyz. Most coaches are unpaid; others receive a small stipend. Many go out of pocket to cover expenses. That degree of commitment—from players, coaches, and the community—explains why Kahuku has reached the pinnacle of football in Hawai'i. "With that community," Cal Lee said with a smile, "you're born and you're raised to become a Red Raider."[42]

*　*　*

A week after Kahuku's last-minute loss to Punahou, Lee Leslie sat in his classroom and talked with players and assistant coaches about a season that had ended one game too soon. The loss to Punahou in the waning moments of the 2014 state championship semifinal rankled, even though Kahuku had surpassed what could reasonably have been expected of them that season.

But the Red Raiders could not overcome the loss of boys who would have played for them if not for the appeal of a Punahou education. Compounding the problem, Kahuku's losses had been Punahou's gains. Instead of Semisi Uluave opening up holes for Wayne Taulapapa and pass protecting for Ephraim Tuliloa for Kahuku, all three suited up for Punahou. And not just them; several other top Punahou players were from the North Shore and would have played for Kahuku if they had stayed home. That Kahuku played so well despite these losses is probably why his fellow coaches voted Lee Leslie the Coach of the Year. Besides, those men know how difficult it is to coach at Kahuku, where anything short of a title just won't do. "They all know what it's like here," Leslie said, grimacing.

Leslie, who has played and coached at all levels and won a score of titles in football and other sports, is still processing his time on the North Shore. "I wanted something to really sink my teeth into," he said, laughing, when asked why he took a job so far from home and out of his comfort zone. "I get here and holy crap! I had no idea what I was doing. It's just a whole different culture."[43]

Leslie, who had seen his share of racist behavior toward minorities on the mainland, saw the tables turned when he arrived on the North Shore and found that not everybody welcomed him. But he spoke at LDS firesides, small informal gatherings held in the evenings, and showed his bona fides on the practice field. "That helped," he said. It allowed him to shed some of his outsider, *haole* identity and be seen instead as somebody committed to their children and the community.

Kahuku is nothing like Idaho and Utah, where Leslie lived and worked most of his life. "I spend all my days in a classroom with forty kids and they're all brown. It's just a whole different world than I ever anticipated." But you only need to watch him interact with the youth he teaches to know how much he loves them and their passion for football.

Still, it's been frustrating. Funding and resources for the football program have not met his expectations, and his salary did not allow his wife to join him on O'ahu, where housing is costly. He slept in his truck for a few weeks after arriving in early June and had not been back to Idaho to see his wife since. He'll return soon, in time to see the youngest of his three sons come back from a two-year LDS mission.

As much as it hurts to have been separated from family, Leslie is enamored with the people and the culture on the North Shore. "Having lived here for seven months, I'm part of it now. It's an experience everyone should have because it expands your horizons." Polynesian players had intrigued him since he encountered them on the mainland while coaching in college. He can't say enough about their humility, or their sense of family, which he had missed as a child.

Leslie's mother died as he was born, and his father, only nineteen, couldn't cope with three children on his own. The kids spent several years in an orphanage, leaving only to visit with their maternal grandparents on weekends. But when *Bonanza* was over on Sunday nights, it was time to return to "that big scary place." Finally, his grandparents gained custody and life improved.

Leslie reconnected with his father, whom he described as a high-strung, hot-blooded man who married fifteen times and drank too much. After watching him slug one of those wives at a Fourth of July party, Leslie joined the Mormon Church. He had dated a girl who was LDS in high school and was attracted to her family's warmth. "I saw the Brady Bunch every time I went over to see her. I listened to her dad lead prayer at dinner, and before I left, we had family prayer where you got down on your knees." Leslie did not want to become like his father. "I had that blood in me and couldn't allow that to happen," he explained. "LDS gave me a blueprint to what I wanted." Family, the Mormon Church, and football have shaped his life ever since. "I am so rich in family, which I didn't have as a kid."

Part of that family is now Polynesian, made up of the young men he coaches, the girls and boys he teaches, the men and women he works with at the school, and their families. "They're so humble," he stressed, "but once it's time to fight, look out. As far as blowing their own horn individually, I never see it. But as a group, when they do the *haka*, it's intimidating." Or as

Jesse Markham, a close observer of football here, said, "The Poly kids lay the wood every time; they're the toughest."[44] For somebody who has been around football for most of his fifty-five years, Leslie is enthralled by the Polynesian passion for the game. "One of the reasons I came is because of the spirit of these people." Their work ethic wows him. "I've never seen kids work harder or longer at practice and conditioning. My boys on the mainland would never run as much as we ran these kids."

But Leslie finds the culture's monomaniacal focus on football problematic. "For them," Leslie said, "nothing matters more in life than football. I try to teach a well-rounded approach, so that they get an education, too. But their dad says, 'You've got to win that football game.' If I say to a boy, 'You can't play in that game unless you've got a 2.5,' the father says, 'You give me the name of the guy who says you can't play.'" Leslie knows that almost all of his players' fathers played for Kahuku. "They can't let it go." Perhaps that's why he told his coaches as they gathered in the runway to the field at Aloha Stadium before the semifinal game to "keep [the players] up. Have a blast! Show them what being good teammates is about."

He's met with resistance—especially from those who were angry about Reggie Torres's dismissal despite winning three state titles, or favored Siuaki Livai's return, or thought Leslie passed too much instead of running the ball down opponents' throats, or wanted him to play their boys more or at other positions, or because he is not only an outsider to the North Shore but a *haole* as well. Several Kahuku stalwarts tell me that Leslie will be gone at season's end, no matter the outcome in the playoffs. Leslie isn't sure himself. "It's the most politicized background I've been around," Leslie concluded after thinking about the dozen or more places he's coached. "These men around here, some will want to fight you." Take one look at Leslie, a robust man who stands well over six feet tall and looks like he could still play, and you realize what that willingness to fight means.

"They feel like they're the have-nots who will kick your ass," Leslie offered. Pausing for a beat, he added, "But they're always going to invite anybody walking by to eat with them. If you're hungry, people take care of you. We're not like that as Caucasians; we take care of ours but not others." He made another observation about Polynesians and football. "The white guy is always intimidated by the black players, but the blacks are intimidated by the Polynesians—big-time. Everybody is." That works wonders in the locker room. "When there are problems in the ranks you always go to one of your Samoans and say, 'I want all of this crap to stop.'" That's usually enough said.

Leslie knew that rebuilding Kahuku, which had gone 6-5 the year before he arrived, would be a challenge. They had been hemorrhaging talent to the private schools for years, and Cal Lee's recent return to Saint Louis would only make that loss of talent more severe. He quickly saw that he didn't have the horses up front, that his defensive linemen did not measure up physically with those of other schools, which had two or three kids who towered above Kahuku's biggest kids. "I knew early on that this was going to be a train wreck." Kahuku's early-season record, he explained, was deceptive. They won but had not played stiff competition.

Leslie made adjustments and Kahuku threw the ball more than ever, even though his quarterback was better suited to play tight end. "I'm a quarterback, but if we had the kids that we once had, the ones now at Punahou, I would run the ball thirty, forty times a game, because there's nothing more humbling than not being able to stop the run." But they didn't have those kids. "So I tried to make it happen other ways."

Leslie paused, knowing that, in the end, they had come up short in making it happen against Punahou. And he's uncertain about next season. He's tired of days that stretch from six in the morning until ten at night, of a disconnect with school leadership over its support, and of having anxiety dreams about dying far from his family. "I'm not saying I'm not coming back; I'm leaving it in the Lord's hands for now."

Leslie finally got home for spring break and the decision was clear. "I just chose my family," he told reporters after announcing he would not return for another season. "I was away from them for 257 days and I never thought I could do that. I finally got to meet my sixth granddaughter and I just got a lump in my throat and I didn't feel like I could leave them again," he said. "I loved my time at Kahuku . . . those kids are second to none in the country."[45]

Leslie had perceived his mandate at Kahuku as dual: winning championships and bolstering academics. He refurbished the locker room, worked with former NFL lineman Ma'ake Kemoeatu and Tanoai Reed to raise funds to improve facilities, and let the players know that he was serious about education. "Kahuku will put fourteen kids in college again next year," Leslie pointed out. Five will attend Division I schools on scholarship; most of the rest will attend junior colleges.

When asked about who might replace him, Leslie said, "I am crossing my fingers and hoping that Maʻake Kemoeatu can step up and take the job. He is the greatest player to come through Kahuku and he is exactly the role model those kids need. The job screams for a local person who knows the culture and he is perfect." Whether or not Kemoeatu is the best player to emerge from Kahuku is debatable, but Leslie was right that finding somebody who knows the North Shore culture was imperative.[46]

There was no shortage of men seeking the Kahuku position; more than thirty applied, including several who had coached at Kahuku. One of them was Siuaki Livai, who had placed Kahuku on the football map; others had coached college and brought impressive résumés to the table. As commentators noted, the Kahuku job was as high profile as the head coaching position at the University of Hawaiʻi.

The chosen one, Vavae Tata, had left the island after graduating from Saint Louis in the spring of 1994. A two-time all-state defensive lineman, Tata was one of five football-playing brothers from Honolulu's Kalihi projects. Though Kalihi underwent a long-needed facelift in 2013, the projects were a drab collection of austere two-story low-rises and two towers with 555 units when the Tatas lived there. Each boy was all-state and played in college. Three of them were on Oregon's 1994 Rose Bowl team, one played at Nebraska, and Vavae anchored the defensive line at UCLA. After realizing that he didn't have his heart in the business world, Tata began coaching. His last stop before returning to Oʻahu was Vanderbilt. "This isn't a one-, two- or four-year decision," he said when his hiring was announced. "This is a lifetime commitment from me."[47] But he will need to win for that to happen.

Tata, like Leslie, stressed academics as the most important part of his job. "Football has an expiration date. It's really all about what comes after and what you do with your education," he said. Academic issues have hurt Kahuku when players became ineligible because they could not maintain the school's standards, and scholarships disappear for kids who can't qualify in the classroom.

When asked about his style of play, Tata said, "We will be a mini-Stanford. Everything Stanford does on offense and defense is what we'll be doing. That will be our DNA and our branding." That went down well with Kahuku partisans, who want to ram the ball down opponents' throats and put the toughest players on defense.

Tata's model is Cal Lee's Saint Louis program, the one he and his brothers played for. Under Lee, he explained, "There wasn't any drop off when the JV players came up to varsity. The varsity and JV had the same system and the same language and the same type of coaching, and there was so much continuity. The JV teams won championships and the varsity teams won championships. Cal surrounded himself with a great staff and created a winning program." Like Leslie and Torres, Tata will extend that synergy to the La'ie Park Raiders, the Big Boyz program where many of Kahuku's, Punahou's, and Saint Louis's players first played tackle football. But he's got competition for those players, including his former mentor, Cal Lee.

"I'm blessed," Tata said as the gravity of his new position set in. "I get to do what I'm passionate about, coach football. I get to reach out and show [these boys] that there's a huge world out there and that they can make it." Referring to his childhood in the Kalihi projects, he argued, "If someone from Mayor Wright housing, Building 29-A, can make it, why can't you?"[48] (Tata's lifetime commitment lasted two seasons. While undefeated in 2015, when they beat Saint Louis to win the state championship, Kahuku lost to Bishop Gorman from Las Vegas during the 2016 regular season and was crushed by Saint Louis in the title game. And Tata was soon gone.)[49]

When Kahuku played Saint Louis in 2015, Vavae Tata coached against Cal Lee, the man for whom he once played, and who had returned to Saint Louis in time for the 2014 season. That's already shaken up island football.

In 2011, after a decade at the University of Hawai'i, Cal Lee lost his job when a new coach, Norm Chow, did not keep him on the staff. Lee returned to where he played, Kalani High, and became its defensive coordinator. He wasn't looking for another head-coaching position, but Saint Louis, which last won the state championship in 2010, when Marcus Mariota was a senior, needed him. It wasn't just that its football team was no longer winning titles; the school itself was in trouble. Enrollments had plunged, causing deficits. Many connected with Saint Louis saw Lee as the panacea for their existential woes and implored him to come back. "Besides, I had a lot of aloha for the school," he said. "But it wasn't easy coming back and starting again; this is a young man's game." To help, he brought along his brother Ron, an offensive mastermind.

Saint Louis faced Mililani (the ultimate state champions), California powerhouse St. John Bosco, and Punahou in their first three games in 2014 and suffered humiliating defeats each time. But Lee's players responded to his coaching. They went undefeated the rest of the season and narrowly lost to Punahou in a rematch in the playoffs.

Lee's quarterback, Tua Tagovailoa, threw for more than 2,500 yards and thirty-three touchdowns, with just three interceptions, while rushing for 576 yards and scoring eight additional touchdowns in 2014. After Marcus Mariota, then a freshman, showed interest in him at a Saint Louis football camp when he was in the fourth grade, Tagovailoa has modeled his game and demeanor after the 2014 Heisman Trophy winner and number two pick in the 2015 NFL draft, who now starts for the Tennessee Titans. "Tua Tagovailoa is as good as any sophomore we've ever had," Lee said. "He's never satisfied." Tagovailoa, who like Mariota is Samoan, committed to SEC powerhouse Alabama during his senior year.

One of Lee's first hires when he returned to Saint Louis was Wes Tufaga, a Laʻie native and the state's co–Defensive Player of the Year in 1996, which marked one of three state championships he helped win at Saint Louis before heading to Utah. Tufaga brought his son to Saint Louis along with five of his Laʻie Park Raiders Big Boyz teammates. The six were among Saint Louis's best junior varsity players in 2014 and became major contributors afterward.[50]

Saint Louis is not the only private school that recruits from Kahuku's Big Boyz program. Some public schools also find a way of enrolling their boys. Given how extended Samoan and Tongan families are, it's not difficult to find a relative who lives in a public school district where that boy can reside. "It's not fair to stop kids," Siuaki Livai argues. "Every parent wants kids to be in a program to be exposed." But he knows that hurts Kahuku. "Big Boyz is the fishing grounds for everybody." You can expect Punahou, Saint Louis, and other schools to have a few lines in the water. And you can expect to see Samoans leading Kahuku, Punahou, Saint Louis, Farrington, Mililani, and other schools for years to come.

Livai, Lee's longtime Kahuku foil, pointed out how much better Saint Louis was at season's end and declared, "My punch line for the future of Hawaiian football is that the Lee brothers are back and will turn the program around. You just wait and see." That's a refrain I hear around the island. Nobody in Hawaiian football would dare underestimate Cal Lee's ability to win. As Lee Leslie put it, "Cal Lee is back and the future is unknown."

10

David and Goliath

It's Faga'itua versus Tafuna, American Samoa's David against the island's Goliath. Faga'itua, the smallest, most rural, and in some ways most Samoan of high schools, sits on the eastern side of Tutuila. Tafuna, easily the biggest, most urban, and most cosmopolitan island school, stands on its sprawling west side. When they clash on the gridiron, it's *fa'a Samoa*'s past confronting *fa'a Samoa*'s future.

The seniors on Tafuna's 2013 team had never experienced defeat, not on the junior varsity or during their three varsity seasons. That 2013 squad toyed with opponents, averaging sixty points a game. The 2014 team was a few games away from matching its feat. The common denominator for the unrivaled skein of victories is coach Okland Salave'a, the former University of Colorado star whose two best friends in football were Junior Seau and Sal Aunese. And though Faga'itua battled hard before losing 38–34 the first time they met, early in September 2014, Tafuna hasn't lost this season either.

Tafuna, which opened in 1982 with one hundred students, is the newest of American Samoa's five public high schools and now enrolls twelve hundred students. The team practices on a rippled grass expanse in the middle of the campus. Faga'itua, whose student body is a bit over five hundred, practices at the old rugby field by Pago Pago Bay. It's never had its own field, and Onesosopo Park's uneven turf is replete with sand traps, volcanic stubble, pools of water, and Samoan-sized toads big enough to bring a runner down.

I arrived for practice at Onesosopo early on Tuesday, November 4, 2014—early because I had not reset my watch after arriving late the night before on one of the two flights from Honolulu that fly here each week. I wanted to talk with Coach Su'aese "Pooch" Ta'ase and watch his Faga'itua boys ready themselves for the final regular-season game, a rematch with Tafuna scheduled for that Thursday.

Pooch wasn't there when practice began. It's Election Day and he went to vote after classes let out at Faga'itua, where he's the vice principal. By nightfall, when the ballots were counted, the balance of political power in the territory had shifted. Aumua Amata became the first woman elected to the U.S. Congress as American Samoa's nonvoting representative, toppling Eni Faleomavaega, who had been in office since 1988. Her election reflected the congressman's recent illness, shifting alliances among 'aiga voting blocs that cast ballots for candidates favored by their matai, and the entry of women and youth in island politics.

Pooch's boys believe that the balance of power is about to shift in island football, too. They say they lost to Tafuna in their first encounter because they made too many mistakes. Though Pooch was not yet at practice, they began without him. Forming a circle, they held hands and sang a hymn, then prayed. A few late arrivals sprinted toward their teammates to join them. When they broke their huddle, they held their helmets high in the sky and shouted as one.

Practice always begins with prayer. The boys are not that big, although few are as small as their 132-pound free safety. And there aren't that many of them. But they are as spirited as can be, even in warm-ups, which are accompanied by the defensive coach's guttural grunts and exclamations. The players punctuated every action with a rhythmic clap. They moved fluidly, despite wearing cleats and helmets as they strode across the rough surface.

They started dancing as children, barefoot, often in sand, and haven't stopped. Frequent ceremonies call for ensemble dances in which people move in unison, shouting and clapping to the beat. It makes these boys not only light on their feet, but balanced as they walk and run.

I'm reminded of comments by His Highness Tui Atua Tupua Tamasese

Efi, independent Samoa's head of state, after he met with Troy Polamalu during his second football camp. "If you look very closely at our culture, there is a Greek appreciation of the body. You see that in the dancing, the walking, the sitting, and how we balance. It's supposed to reflect a symmetry. If a man sits there and looks like a clumsy frog, like me," he said with a laugh, "there's a dysfunction, a disconnect."[1] These boys, despite wearing football gear and negotiating treacherous footing, moved with grace, at least until the hitting started.

It's overcast and a red flag with the school's name and Vikings logo snapped in the wind blowing off the bay. A dog hobbled by; many dogs limp here, the result of encounters with cars. In this most competitive of cultures, even dogs participate. They crouch low by the roadside and sprint after vehicles intruding on their village. They would do better chasing away *aitu*, the invisible spirits that one boy tells me only dogs can see.

Onesosopo Park is at one end of Pago Pago Bay, on the road to the island's east side, where village life endures. There are almost no businesses from here to the road's end in Tula. The offshore rock outcroppings covered with vegetation that shoot straight out of the sea at Futu'mafuti are visible on the westernmost edge of the bay. The StarKist cannery is closer, with purse seiners riding low in the water waiting to be unloaded. You can almost smell the whiff of tuna. The wooden statue of StarKist's iconic Charlie the Tuna is back on its perch by the cannery's main gate. On two of my trips here, it had been replaced by one of Troy Polamalu. Troy the Tuna was back in 2015 when Polamalu returned to hold his third football camp.

When Pooch arrived, we chatted briefly before he blew a whistle and his charges came running. Taking a knee, they gathered close around him. At thirty-eight, he's American Samoa's senior coach and has won the most titles in island history. He announced how happy he was for a boy whose SATs just came and were back high enough to qualify for NCAA play. That's no small feat for youth who begin learning English in the fourth grade. "I believe what we are doing is working," Pooch exclaimed. "You juniors need to pass the SATs now. It creates opportunities for you. This is a big game, but the SATs are more important. We'll play Tafuna again." No matter who wins their regular-season rematch, it's likely they'll meet in the title game.

Pooch explained that he was uploading video of players on "Hudl," an online system that the Polamalu Foundation made available to coaches. It allows recruiters to access game footage. Though more college coaches are willing to brave flights to get here and some hold clinics on the island, it's not easy for Polynesians to gain exposure. When coaches inquire about players, Pooch stressed, they always ask first whether they will be eligible. "Not all of you did that well on the SATs," he said with deadpan delivery, "but nobody got below 200 points." They laughed; you get that many points for signing your name.

Pooch reviewed what he wanted to accomplish at practice, then said that they could see there's a "Caucasian" present. When he explained what I'm doing, they applauded respectfully. Pooch then asked if I wanted to say something; it was a rhetorical question. He knew I would not reject the chain of command, where the head coach sits at the top. I told the boys they represent the heart of Samoan football, or at least I tried to get that across.

I had spoken with several before practice. They're polite, according me deference, even to one so out of place. Their game against Tafuna will be played Thursday afternoon—despite the heat; SATs are on Saturday and night games are discouraged. "If we play at night," Lafaele Simanu explained, "we get rocked on the way back." Even after a day game, they know the drill: put on your helmet and lower the bus windows to reduce the chances of shattering glass on the way out of Dodge. While fights on the field are few, fans often lose control. It's long been that way.

Lafaele, tall and thin, plays several defensive positions, shifting from end to linebacker to safety in the course of a game. With only thirty-five boys on the squad, several play both ways. Given the heat, humidity, and up-tempo, no-huddle offense Pooch runs, that's demanding. They do it without complaint. Pooch has them training all year round and this is definitely not Kvetchistan, where the culture of complaint prevails.

The boys are accustomed to physical labor, with chores in the morning and again after practice. Given that they live in villages down the coast or over the mountain from Onesosopo Park, it will be dark when they get home. The sun sets early this close to the equator, and it might take an hour to return home. Many boys work their families' hillside plantations and prepare the *umu* for the Sunday *to'ona'i*. "We still live in our culture out here," Lafaele told me. "We live in our Samoan ways. We're not allowed to go out at night that long. Football," he added softly, "is in our culture. We're aggressive."

The east side of the island has been losing population. Some boys born and raised there attend Tafuna because their parents believe it offers more academically. Tafuna is also home to many from independent Samoa, Korea, Fiji, China, the Philippines, and Tonga, as well as the children of Samoans returning from the military and the States. The Manuʻa Islands have also lost residents to Tafuna. About a thousand people remain on its three islands, which are difficult to reach from Tutuila. Overall, population and power have shifted from Pago Pago Bay and Leone, the two traditional centers, to Tafuna.

Unlike the east side, Tafuna has substantial property not owned by an ʻaiga. People can buy plots and build, even rent, dwellings there. As a result, ʻaiga authority, a pillar of faʻa Samoa, has weakened. Village councils are less influential, and many live outside the matai system. That means less of the social control that prevails in east-side villages, and more burglaries and crimes. "The traditional faʻa Samoa has broken down," Police Chief Bill Halleck observed. "The ʻaiga presence just isn't as strong in Tafuna. It's not really a village where you have one chief who can go speak to the families and say cut it out."

Many of the youth who cause trouble, Halleck said, are from independent Samoa. Halleck, whose grandfather Max was the patriarch of one of Tutuila's most powerful families, grew up in a village at a time when faʻa Samoa went unchallenged. So did Satele Liliʻo Aliʻitaʻi, an ex-Marine who became a judge and more recently the paramount chief for the village of Alofau, where Mel Purcell is his high talking chief. "Most of the kids we see in court live in Tafuna but are from Upolu," Satele explained. "The problem is that there is no village or ʻaiga controlling them."[2] But, Halleck, declared, "They are Samoans; they are our brothers and sisters. They just come from there."

Overall, Halleck noted, the level of crime is much, much lower than in the States, where he worked for decades with law enforcement and the DEA. But he's apprehensive about youth exposed to faʻa Amerika and their influence on peers once they return. As early as 2001, customs officials were busting smugglers bringing in methamphetamine on small boats. Police began raiding meth labs and arresting people strung out by the drug and acting violently. The National Drug Intelligence Center judged ice to be a far more serious threat than islanders' consumption of marijuana, most of which was brought in across the channel from Samoa or grown in the hills, and rarely led to violence. Meth use has risen since that 2001 assessment. While use of drugs is disturbing in a traditional culture absorbing the shocks of globalization, per capita consumption lags behind that of the United States. That does not allay Halleck's concerns; his officers do not carry weapons except in extraordinary circumstances, and though firearms are rarely used and handguns illegal in the territory, he fears for his officers more than he once did.

Tafuna doesn't have a monopoly on island violence, especially when it comes to the sexual and child abuse that traditionally has been hidden from public scrutiny. "These cases may involve ministers of their own church and respected leaders of communities, and to avoid embarrassment, a lot of them would keep it hush-hush," Halleck said. Or as one woman told me, "It's a very contradictory way of life. They are holy rollers on Sunday and when in church, but the level of corruption in government and cheating on wives, beating of children, and sexual abuse is really high." But she and Halleck believe that these problems are being addressed more than in the past and offenders increasingly brought to court. "Families," Halleck said, "are thinking more now about stopping the problem than contributing to it by hiding it. A lot of these offenders have been arrested and prosecuted."

Tafuna High, I'm told, has become the island's top public school and now attracts students returning to the island the way that Samoana High once did. But if better academically, it's less cohesive socially. There are more fights and drugs, more of the social issues that have surfaced on the island, though in far more muted forms than in the States. When talking about Tafuna students, the Faga'itua players have trouble finding a direct English translation but suggest they are "outsiders," youth who did not fit in and are prone to trouble. And in two days, they'll tangle in a game in which personal, family, school, and village identities form part of the stakes.

Pooch is as east side as they come, brought up in 'Aoa, a village of three hundred people over the mountain on Tutuila's north shore. His father was an electrician and his mother taught, but the family depended on their plantation and what it took from the sea. Wanting their sons to know more than the village, their parents sought a stateside education for them. So when Pooch was nine years old, they sent him and brothers Tupulua and Ola'ese to live with an aunt in San Jose, California. Pooch looked up to Tupulua, aka Bonecrusher or Bone. In 'Aoa, that meant following Tupulua, five years older, to the plantation to weed and carry back taro in handwoven baskets on a pole across his shoulders.

In San Jose, emulating Bone meant sport, at least at first. "Football was something I did because my older brother did it and I wanted to be like him," Pooch recalled. Bone starred in high school. "But we didn't have the money for me to register for Pop Warner football. I watched but couldn't participate." So Bone, intent on toughening his kid brother, coached him. "He would get pads on and let me hit him as hard as I could," Pooch said. "I learned my work ethic from him."

Pooch took English as a second language classes with Hispanic children and got an education, but not the one his parents intended. Instead, he began hanging around older boys and joined the Sons of Samoa, a gang on San Jose's east side. They offered him tutorials in the workings of the marketplace. Gang members ditched his given name and called him Pooch. He was the gang's youngest member, a *lavalava*-wearing corner boy in the crack trade. Pooch escaped notice for a while but was eventually busted and did six months at the Boys Ranch.

When his parents came to California for Bone's graduation and Pooch's release from detention, they took their sons back home. Ola'ese—perhaps the best athlete in the family, taller and physically gifted—returned to the mainland to play college football. But a Halloween incident that turned violent ended with him doing twenty-five years to life in prison.

Pooch found his gang persona didn't cut it back on Tutuila's east side. When he got in trouble, he received a whuppin' from an uncle, a police officer. "That was the best thing," Pooch reflected, "coming home. But I don't regret any of what happened in San Jose because it made me understand what is right and wrong. When we came back in the eighth grade, it wasn't gangs anymore; it was more village."

Gangs were not an option on the island. Parents, aunties, and uncles, much less *matai*, reverends, and the *'aumaga*, put such behavior beyond the pale. Instead, boys played rugby, going at it with all the ferocity they could muster. "The toughness was there," Pooch recalled. "Here's an eighth-grade kid who had just been incarcerated. I'm not scared of anybody."

"After school, we played rugby down on the beach with the older guys; it was much tougher than football. All I did was tackle!" They played rugby and *kirikiti* in the village, at church functions, and on Memorial and Flag

Day. "My dad would say, 'Stop football and go up the plantation!'" Pooch complied, but, he said, grimacing, "I used it as my workout! I would run the hills up and down from the plantation; I would lift weights. What I did on the plantation, growing taro and preparing the *umu*, that taught me hard work and discipline."

Pooch and Bone were not the only ones sent back because they had joined gangs. Boys from Los Angeles and Oʻahu now became classmates and ultimately teammates at Fagaʻitua, where they submerged their gang identities in football. "We put the red colors, the blue colors, to the side; we were a football team, and one of the best in 1994," Pooch declared. No longer wearing the blue gang colors of the Sons of Samoa, he's resplendent in Fagaʻitua red.

Pio Grohse, Pooch's high school coach, had led the village rugby squad in Aua. Like other Aua youth, Pio finished high school in Oceanside, California, where he lived with an uncle, a Marine sergeant major who inspected chores with white gloves. While Pio couldn't wait to escape his uncle's authority, he internalized his discipline when it came to teaching and coaching. After a stint in the Army and a degree from Southern Utah University, Pio returned to the island to teach and coach.

Except for a year in college, Pio had never played football, but he had played and coached rugby. He scoured old football magazines and coaching catalogues to learn offensive and defensive setups, and visited a friend coaching at Kahuku, returning with the Red Raiders playbook. The Fagaʻitua Vikings have channeled Kahuku's defensive-minded strategy ever since.

Pio's sporting approach had been shaped mostly by rugby. "Nowadays, they teach you skills in rugby," he said as we sat under an awning in Aua as rain crashed down. "Then it was all muscle; the stronger teams won. But the games always ended in fights." So along with making them run and lift weights, Pio preached toughness. "I told them they had to be tough to play. A lot of time," he admitted, "we ended up fighting whenever we played rugby. Football," Pio reflected, "is not as rough as rugby, but fights stopped football games too. *Faʻa Samoa* makes an imprint on our lives and how we play our sports. It's our pride; we don't want to be defeated. To make sure nothing happens, our high talking chief would speak to us before the game and our *matai* would come and watch." That sometimes held passions in check.

When the rain stopped, roosters and a gospel choir singing in Samoan at the church across the road could be heard. As I left, Pio remarked that he had seen a different sort of discipline in Pooch than in other boys, something that made him a leader. Like other youth, Pooch walked in his bare feet and practiced dance at school, but few boys ran mountains and lifted weights on their own. Fagaʻitua had long been the league's doormat. But with Bone as the offensive coordinator and Pooch a gung ho leader who did everything but punt, players came together as a team in 1994, Pooch's senior year.

Dissension had reduced the squad to eighteen players when the first half of the season went poorly. "But we had so much commitment on that team among those who were left," Pooch recalled in his crammed office, which is part of Fagaʻitua's open-sided gym. "We were getting up and working out in the morning. That last half of the season, it was about us believing. Nobody else believed in us, but we beat Samoana, and then we tied Leone." Pooch quarterbacked the offense and rallied the defense. They finished second to Leone, which had Spencer and Gabe Reid, brothers who played at BYU and were among the first to go from the island to the NFL.

Pooch had been thinking vaguely of college but didn't know how to make that happen. Eugene Reid, Spencer and Gabe's dad, did. The Reids were one of the island's oldest ʻafakasi families and had long brokered off-shore relations. Eugene interceded, connecting Pooch to Keith Uperesa, who had just become the first Samoan head coach in college football at Snow College in Ephraim, Utah. Pooch knew that Keith, who had played at the Punahou School, at BYU, and in the NFL, was related to Duke Uperesa, who was back on island coaching and training boys after playing in the Canadian Football League. And Alema Teʻo, who was from Tutuila, was Snow's linebackers coach. But he had no idea where Snow was or what to expect there.

Arriving in Salt Lake City airport, Pooch told a cabbie to take him to Snow. The driver laughed and said that would cost $300, far more money than Pooch had. So Alema Teʻo drove up to Salt Lake City and got Pooch, who arrived late to camp. "He shows up at the first day of practice," Keith Uperesa remembered, "and nobody knows who he is. He's just a little kid who happens to have been coached by my cousin Duke. So he gets there, gets outfitted, and gets his first opportunity." Uperesa was overseeing a running drill; after it was over, players were returning to the huddle. "Out of nowhere," Uperesa exclaimed, "Pooch comes flying and spears our starting center in the back. This big strong kid drops down and my first words ever to Pooch were, 'Get out! Get off this field!' I look at Alema, Alema looks at me, and he gives Pooch a look."

Pooch cringed recalling that day. "I wanted to prove myself. I just want to go out there and play. Everything is going fast; the play is over and I'm so jacked up and I come out of nowhere and there's this lineman just standing there and I crack him from the back. You should have seen Coach Ups. He stares at me and yells, 'Hey you! Get your butt out of here!'"

Pooch, Alema, and Keith laugh about it now, but Pooch was shaken. "I want to play so bad but I figure I'm out of there." He sat in the locker room, uncertain if he was through. "I came so far, so far from Mom and Dad, so far from home, and I don't know if it's over. Then coach Ups comes in and says, 'Don't let your parents down.'"

"We sat down," Uperesa remembered, "and we got into our *fa'a Samoa* culture. Pooch was very humble, very respectful. I said, 'You're one phone call away. Back in the village, I'd tattoo your ass. Now I just make a phone call and you're gone.'" He continued. "'I'm Polynesian and I'll be the hardest on you Polynesians.' But from that day forward, he probably became the most inspirational player that I've ever had—at any level, any program.

"From the day he stepped on our campus and got kicked off till where he is now," Uperesa said with a shake of his head, "is a phenomenal story. He was just trying to make an impression, to show he could hit, and I did the same thing. I made an impression. I knew we had to bring this kid back into the fold, because there was something very special about him. He was what you envision as a coach, a humble young man who is respectful and going to do what he set out to do—get his education. He told me he would go back to Samoa and give back and he's done all of that and more." Snow was becoming something special too. Uperesa made it the go-to school for Polynesians, including several from American Samoa, who could adjust to academics and football under his tutelage before entering a Division I program.

Pooch learned more than playing football from Uperesa. "That lesson I learned from coach Ups was to be fair and to be disciplined," Pooch concluded. "Even to this day when I discipline guys I tell them there's nobody who is above the team. Everybody is the same. I learned that from Coach Ups; Keith was always fair with us."

He saw that even-handedness when days before a bowl game, Uperesa threw Snow's All-American Tongan linebacker off the team for kicking a teammate after he knocked him to the ground during a fight while playing basketball. "Mind you," Pooch explained, "it's three days before a bowl game and he's your All-American. You just lost three sacks for that game. But we had another kid, from American Samoa, and Coach Ups said to him, 'You're up.'"

A majority of Snow's roster of 120 players by Uperesa's second season was Polynesian; it soon became a critical way station for Polynesians from as far away as Tonga and New Zealand. "Within our Polynesian group," Uperesa said, "we had cliques, but probably the most respected group we had on campus were the kids from American Samoa; not from Hawai'i, not from California or Utah, but from Samoa. They needed to be guided, they needed help because they were behind in education, but it was more a communications barrier than anything else."

Pooch, Snow's starting middle linebacker, became their emotional leader. "He was very vocal, but his vocal is all positive; it was never to belittle, to put himself above others. The kids from Samoa for the most part are all like that. In the two years I was there I had a front seven, four-three defense, where five of the seven were from the island of American Samoa. All got D-I scholarships and all graduated."[3]

After Snow, Pooch went to Louisiana Tech on a full scholarship and studied sociology. "I promised my family I wouldn't come back till I finished my degree; I stayed there that summer, stayed through the winter bloc, and finished in the spring. Everybody's fantasy is the NFL, but I wanted to get that paper."

Pooch was severely undersized for a Division I linebacker. "But I had that warrior pride and I practiced hard knowing that I might only get one play on special teams. What more could I ask? They're paying for my degree, and I'm going to get everything out of it every day." He was one of two Polynesians on campus. "When we said we were from Samoa, they thought we were from Somalia, so we started saying we were from Hawai'i." He was the scout team's Player of the Year both seasons at Louisiana Tech. His last game came against USC, when Troy Polamalu was a sophomore. The Trojans crushed the Bulldogs, 45–19. Though they went different ways, Pooch and Troy have reunited on the island. On my first day in American Samoa in 2011, Mel Purcell told me that Pooch had taken coaching here into the future. He's done that by staying true to the past—and playing Kahuku-style football.

* * *

Okland Salave'a, a decade older than Pooch, was already an assistant coach at Leone when Pooch played for Faga'itua. At six-six, he towers over Pooch, who is five-six on a good day. Okland looks like he could still play; his arms are muscled ropes and broad shoulders emphasize his body's V shape. I don't know if I've ever seen somebody carry 340 pounds so well. The *pe'a* (traditional tattoo) covers his lower body.

"We grew up very *fa'a Samoa* in our family, like Pooch did," Okland said, "but on the other side of the island." Though born in Carson, California, in 1967, when his father, Miki, was stationed there, Okland grew up in Leone on Tutuila's west side, where the Salave'a family has long worked the land and fished. Miki became an educator and a *matai*.

Okland played rugby on the beach, using a breadfruit for the ball. "There was not much thinking involved," he recalled. "It was just brute strength, running into your friend and trying to make it to the try line." Between playing rugby, eating traditional foods, and doing plantation chores, Okland and his brother Joe grew up fit and lean. "When I look at photos of us then," Okland said wistfully, "we were slim. It is sad to see the change when new things were added to our way of life, like fast foods and sweetened drinks. I see former students that I taught and I cannot believe my eyes."[4]

Okland hiked the mountain to gather coconuts for the family's bakery and to feed their pigs. "The good eating pigs," he explained, "are the ones that eat the coconut." If he was lucky, he found enough on the ground to fill the handwoven baskets he carried back down. Otherwise, he climbed as high as fifty feet to knock coconuts loose, developing enormous strength in his legs and arms. "There's no margin for error in climbing a coconut tree," Okland observed. He sometimes offered older boys candy to ascend for him. He also tended the taro patch, gathered bananas, and prepared the *umu*.

With no Pop Warner or junior varsity football, Okland didn't try football until his freshman year at Leone High. "My first experience was with older kids who wanted to show how tough they were." That dissuaded many boys, but Okland, already six-two and 201 pounds, was plenty tough himself. And he loved the game. "When you're growing up and get a brand-new bike," he explained, "you want to ride it all the time. That's the feeling I got playing football; I wanted to play all the time." After his sophomore year, the Salave'as attended a funeral in Oceanside, California. Okland's aunt, Avalua

Tuisee, convinced his parents that he should stay with her to finish school. Okland needed no convincing.

But he was ill prepared. "It was very difficult for me," Okland remembered. "Everything was in English; it forces you to learn on the go." Okland's transition to football came easier; he spoke football fluently and played both ways on the line. His best friend on the team was Junior Seau, who lived nearby and befriended this kid from Samoa. "I could tell right away that Junior was special—fiery—that's the first thing I noticed about him," Okland recalled. "He never liked to lose."

After high school, Okland joined Sal Aunese at the University of Colorado. They revitalized the Buffaloes, but Okland's joy was tempered by the death of Aunese when he was just twenty-one. After graduating, Okland tried out with the Chargers, who had made his high school buddy Junior Seau their top draft pick that season. But Okland balked at switching to tight end and returned home. Now he calls his decision "stupid pride" and regrets that Polynesians then lacked mentors to guide them through the NFL maze. "I stress to the kids that the decisions you make *now* affect your future."

He returned home and began teaching at Leone. Okland remembers coaching against Pooch, an undersized quarterback who roused his teammates to play better than anyone thought possible. Pooch is still convincing east-side boys to smash expectations, and Okland has nothing but respect for him. "The thing about Faga'itua is that all they have is that football team. Next to that there's just family. And that's why Faga'itua is always on top. They believe in one another, in their brotherhood, and they believe in Pooch. They believe in what he is doing and that's not common."

While other schools change coaches almost yearly, Pooch and Okland bring unusual consistency to their teams. "Pooch has done a lot over there, and not just in football," Okland argued. "That's what is keeping them on top. When he became head coach, that's when the changes came; Pooch brought new ideas and energy, and got the community to believe in him, year after year."

Okland has done much the same at Tafuna. No team on the island has ever been so dominant for so long, or sent as many kids to college. Almost every senior on the previous year's team, acclaimed as the best to ever play here, went to college on scholarship. A few entered Division I programs and one, Destiny Vaeao, made the NFL. Most attended junior colleges, which many

believe allows them to acclimate to the States and college. But not all graduating seniors qualify academically, and many cannot afford the costs of college not covered by scholarships. Others simply cannot handle the new environment. "The big problem is that they're on their own when they go off,"
Okland reasoned. "They're so used to getting instruction from their parents."

Okland acknowledged that football has come far on the island, but lamented the lack of resources. "Faga'itua has no field," he said. "Kids live everywhere on that side of the island and don't have rides home after practice.
American Samoa is just scratching the surface to help these kids. There's
no funding for football; all the equipment, everything we do to help kids,
we pretty much do on our own." Players and their families struggle to raise
money to attend off-island camps. "They're very important for those kids,"
Okland stressed. "Just like me, you want to see a different world."

Beauty Tuiasosopo, Tafuna's principal, paid no attention to sport while
growing up. Her father, a minister, made sure she came straight home after
school. "Now," Beauty said, smiling, "I have no choice."[5] She's an ardent
fan. For her, football's benefits go beyond winning games. When football
is going well, she observed, there are fewer problems at school. I heard that
point first from Elia Savali, an educator who was born on Manu'a and brought
up in Fagatogo, Honolulu, and Los Angeles.

Almost sixty, Elia Savali defies physical limitations. As the 2012 football
season approached, he stepped in to resurrect a flagging program at Samoana High. I found him that 2012 preseason on the field, stepping in to show
players how to fulfill their assignments on particular plays. Savali and the
Samoana Sharks have been at it for more than two hours. Humidity is near
100 percent, the sun unrelenting, and the temperature in the eighties. His
shirt is soaked with sweat, but the principal/coach is all over the offensive
unit, barking at players in a mix of Samoan and English. Taking the snap
from center, Savali pivots to his right, fakes a handoff, drifts back a few steps,
and rifles a pass into the flat. He's tapping what's left of the physique and
athleticism that made him a top high school pole-vaulter and stalwart on
village teams.

Elia knew little about football before coaching at Samoana in 1979. Later,
at Faga'itua, he assisted Duke Uperesa, who revolutionized offensive sche-
ma on the island, and then took over as head coach. Elia learned by asking
questions and observing Dick Tomey at summer practices at the University

of Hawai'i when he was completing his master's degree there. With help from his mentor, Li'a Amisone, he led Faga'itua to the school's first football title in 1988.

Elia became a Department of Education troubleshooter, assigned to schools facing problems. He was asked to step in at Samoana a month before the new school year began. "The football team sets the tempo at each school," he observed. "If the football team does well, the whole school year seems to pan out smoothly." Elia saw that wherever he taught. If football players are acting out, he said, "it's tough, but when they are the ones who are breaking trouble up, it's very easy."[6] Football players are the most visible athletes on campus and constitute a large chunk of the student body. If they behave well, other students usually do, too. At Tafuna, Principal Tuiasosopo credited Okland and his staff with instilling discipline, ensuring that players value education, and making them role models. It's a different vision of the student athlete than the cocky BMOC stereotype that often prevails in the States.

While unwilling to concede that *fa'a Samoa* has weakened in Tafuna, Tuiasosopo described the school as more diverse and cosmopolitan, with a tenth or more of the students from independent Samoa, Korea, the Philippines, and elsewhere. She, too, calls on village leaders to intervene when on-campus fights—now often provoked by Facebook comments—occur between kids from different villages. And she knows that the threat of calling a student's mother can overwhelm a chiseled football warrior's defiance. "Football," she concluded, "not only reduces problems but gives excitement to kids to make them want to come to school, even if they're not playing."

Beauty applauded Okland as the architect of Tafuna's ascent. Coaches are hardly paid for what amounts to a year-round job, and Okland works nights as a baggage handler at the airport to supplement his teaching salary. He lives in 'Ili'ili, a neighborhood where most land is privately owned, close to the school. He coaches because it is his *tautua*, his way to help. "I'm very happy that I came back," he said, although he admits he would entertain offers to coach in college, like his brother Joe.

But Okland is focused on the island at present. Once a member of the village *'aumaga*, he has traditional tattoos visible below his *lavalava*. He endured ten painful days as the tattooist hammered a sharpened boar tooth into his skin. But that was not as painful for him as it is to watch a boy fail. "If football doesn't get better here, a lot of these kids will end up doing nothing else; without football for young boys I don't know what else there will be for them." That hurt endures far longer than the pain of the tattoo.

It's finally game day, time to see if the training that began weeks after last season's title game and continued ever since will pay off. Faga'itua's bus and trucks bearing fans arrived at Veterans Memorial Stadium in Tafuna well before the three p.m. kickoff. Though the island is small, driving is slow, and it's an hour's drive from Faga'itua. There are far too many vehicles for the roads to handle, and speed limits rarely exceed twenty miles per hour.

Faga'itua's players sat cross-legged in five rows under a canopy and clapped rhythmically in response to Coach Pooch's remarks, delivered in Samoan. He introduced me again but didn't ask me to impart any game-day advice; good move. Then principal Elvis Liufau, who once coached the school to a title, spoke in English. A reverend who is a *matai* and Pooch's cousin led them in prayer and they sang a hymn.

As a pickup drove the perimeter of the field, a boy standing in the truck's bed tossed yard markers onto the ground. Girls in red *lavalavas* with the Faga'itua emblem set up water tables behind the benches. But nobody sits during the game. Instead, players and coaches crowd the sidelines. Faga'itua's jerseys are faded and full of tiny holes, their shoes scuffed, and their helmets well past the point where they would pass inspection in the States.

By now, I'm a familiar face to the boys, easy to pick out. They offer hand-shakes and call me "Coach." A girl brought me a water bottle, something that happens everywhere I go. It's a keep-the-*palagi*-hydrated policy. Breaking into offense, defense, and special teams, they ran through plays.

When it was three o'clock and time to kick off, Tafuna was nowhere to be found. Their school is a brief walk away, prompting a coach to shake his head and say they were playing mind games. Faga'itua's players returned to the canopy and Pooch reviewed signals he'll send in from the sidelines. He tapped his hat, brushed his forearm, and crossed his arms as players shouted the calls. He then began to work them, speaking of family. "Your moms and dads are here. They're the most important people in your lives. Your aunties and uncles are out here today." He switched midsentence between Samoan and English. "I know that our key players will show up today, but how about the role players?" Pointing at boys, he asked them if they would step up if a starter needed a break or went down with an injury. "I'm proud that all of

you have registered for the SATs on Saturday," he interjected before returning to the game.

"This is why we run up Masefau," he said, referring to their early-morning
three-mile runs up Masefau hill during the summer. "You win in the fourth
quarter, when they're tired." That is, if the game gets to the fourth quarter.
"You must do whatever it takes, whatever it takes! The legal way, of course."
The boys laughed.

They ate bananas and drank juice and waited, but Tafuna still did not
arrive. George Tafua, an assistant coach who played for the school and now
has two boys on the squad, told me that most players are connected to somebody who bled for this team. "That's part of the drive. The majority of players have had family who played for Faga'itua."

A small boy, his forearms taped for action, stood next to Pooch. It's his
brother's girlfriend's son, Cornelius. The team's flag-bearer, Cornelius
clutched a pole with a red banner bigger than he is. He's turning six today
and the players sang a bilingual version of "Happy Birthday." They love to
sing and their voices are as sweet as a boys' choir. On the field, however,
they channel their inner thugs. Cornelius beamed; if there's practice at seven
thirty in the morning during the summer, he's the first to arrive. He lives to
lead the team onto the field.

An hour later, Tafuna arrives. They swaggered off their bus for a brief but
spirited warm-up. Before taking the field, they huddled and shouted, "Protect this house!" Under Armour ought to listen up. Given that they haven't
lost a game in going on four years, it's hard to begrudge their swagger. After
downing the kickoff in the end zone, Tafuna ran its first play off tackle.
When a safety misjudged the ballcarrier's angle and missed the tackle, the
Tafuna runner didn't stop running until he crossed the goal line. Goliath was
looking like Goliath. Tafuna players were chippy and threw a few punches.
Sometimes personal fouls were called, but mostly not. A few veteran observers with no dog in this fight thought that Tafuna was getting away with too
many cheap shots and voiced apprehension. Faga'itua responded to Tafuna's
score by advancing to the one-yard line but failed to score on fourth and
goal, and the ball turned over to Tafuna.

Samoan kids like to hit; scratch that, they love to hit. Ballcarriers absorbed
body blows from multiple players who delight in piling into a runner after
his forward progress has been slowed. Faga'itua stood its ground, despite

an enormous size differential. Tafuna's offensive linemen outweighed Faga'itua's defensive linemen by thirty to fifty pounds per player. From the sidelines, the hits seemed devastating; violent thuds sent players hard to the ground. They either popped back up or limped off.

Cheerleaders worked the crowds. Some were female, others male, and many were *fa'afafine*, males who chose to live "in the way of women." *Fafas*, long accepted and respected here, are the majority on some cheer squads. Earlier that season, the island's sole athletic trainer, Florence Salesa said, laughing, a Nu'uuli Vo-Tech player looked at his team's cheerleaders and remarked to the boy next to him, "How cool! We have all three genders on the squad."

After a Faga'itua player fumbled when hit by four Tafuna defenders long after his forward progress had been stopped but no whistle was blown, Tafuna scored again. Flags began flying after egregious misconduct, but it was too late for the refs to regain control.[7]

In the second quarter, his squad behind 20–0, Faga'itua's Oly Ta'ase was flagged for punching a Tafuna player who had flipped off his teammates and cursed at Pooch. When Pooch remonstrated with the ref that the Tafuna player had provoked Oly, who is his nephew, another ref threw a second flag. While refs huddled and the players went to the sidelines, fans crowded the field. A mother smacked her son in the chest and unleashed a torrent of maternal advice. Many mothers are bigger than their sons. Tragically, when these boys stop training four hours a day, year-round, and become more sedentary, many will blow up in size. Some parents shouted and gestured at the refs; others scolded their sons or tried to make peace. Suddenly, a man in a black T-shirt and *lavalava* weighing well over three hundred pounds barreled toward the field, intent on making his point. It was Pooch's relative, the reverend who had delivered the pregame prayer. Half a dozen fans and players intervened, diverting him from the refs. When the police arrived and began to arrest a boy, his sister jumped between them. A policeman grabbed her, but another brother knocked him away with a body block. You protect your family, not just your house, in Samoa.

Frowning, Li'a Amisone strode toward the refs. Amisone, who played in the Kava Bowl forty years ago, is a director at the Department of Education. He told the officials that the game was over; this violence could not be tolerated. Tafuna, ahead at the time, was awarded the victory.

Pooch assembled his players on the sidelines, where parents and fans encircled them. He was distraught, and tears slid down his face as he apologized, to the players, to their parents, to his principal, to the school, to the east side. Mortified, he exclaimed that this shame would never happen again. "This is not what we teach our kids. I take full blame for this."

Breaking into Samoan, he told the players, "I think I should step aside; it is time to let another man coach you." His players, horrified, shouted, "No, Coach, no!" They could not imagine anybody else coaching Faga'itua. Recovering his composure and switching back to English, Pooch said, "We lost the battle; they kicked our butts, but we will win this war. Where we go from here is important. We will go forward now. Hold your heads up high. This was my fault. It will not happen again. We will go over and congratulate the Tafuna players."

Players and coaches lined up and waited for Tafuna to form ranks, then took the long walk to midfield to shake their opponents' hands. Faga'itua players put on their helmets and boarded the bus. They lowered the windows, though the police escort would deter rock throwing as they passed through villages where Tafuna kids lived on the long ride back to the eastern side of the island.

Tafuna's players, meanwhile, performed their *siva tau*. They swelled with pride, moving fluidly and chanting, "I can do anything with the blessing to guide my way. I'm going to war with a big heart. *No fefe*—no fear. *No fefe*—no loss."

After Faga'itua departed, the school's cheerleaders and students waited outside the stadium for rides home. Tafuna students soon surrounded them. A Tafuna parent loaded his truck with Faga'itua students and departed; then a female police officer filled her truck. Her badge did not deter kids who rocked her vehicle as she pulled away. I'm told that rock throwing used to be much worse.

To get another shot at Tafuna, Faga'itua's Vikings had to win their semifinal game against Leone, which had walloped Vo-Tech to cap the regular season. They would play without their best player, Oly Ta'ase, who was suspended for the game because of the punch he threw against Tafuna.

No one felt worse than Oly, who knew how much his actions hurt the team. But Oly prepared that week as if he knew they would beat Leone and he would play in the championship. Pooch prayed more than usual and sought counsel from church elders. "Our best player was out," Pooch wrote me after the game, "but Oly showed the other players that he knew he was going to play in the championship game. The next man stepped up and we made the game plan really simple and basic for him."[8] It worked, and after beating Leone, Pooch told his players, "Have fun!" He emphasized special teams that week and kept players focused and feeling positive.

By game day, the east side was painted red and the west side swathed in maroon; hand-painted signs in front of homes testified to supporters' eternal allegiance to their team. Tafuna's Warriors arrived at the stadium with a sense of invincibility; after all, nobody had beaten them in years. Faga'itua's Vikings were more measured, knowing that they needed to play with the disciplined approach that Pooch preached.

The night before the game, Pooch gathered his players to show them *When the Game Stands Tall*. The movie, about California's De La Salle High School and its football team's record 151-game winning streak, was unavailable on island, but Bone had secured a DVD. Pooch wanted his boys to dream of resilience and victory that night.

Pooch's game plan was to stick to the system he had learned from Kahuku High on O'ahu's North Shore a decade ago: run the ball, emphasize special teams play, and keep your best players on defense. "Only Pooch's kids run the mountains," Okland Salave'a commented before the game. "His approach is modeled after Kahuku and Coach Livai. He runs the ball and tries to tire other teams out. They're not big enough to overpower opposing teams, but they're in better condition." Late in a game in steamy tropical conditions, size can become problematic.

Faga'itua had surrendered big plays on Tafuna's opening drive both times they had played that season. When the defense held this time, Pooch barked, "Stick with the plan; don't lose focus!" They didn't.

And then Faga'itua's defenders blocked a Tafuna punt and smothered it in the end zone for the first score. Though Oly Ta'ase and his backfield mate Anthony Tovia were knocked from the game by injuries, both quickly returned and gained more yards per carry as the game went on. Widening their lead, the Vikings ran the ball to eat the clock. They kept Tafuna off-balance with trick plays that slowed their swarming defense, the island's best.[9]

Meanwhile, Faga'itua stymied Tafuna's passing attack. Late in the fourth quarter, rocks thrown from outside the stadium began falling on Faga'itua fans. The police chased the perpetrators into the bush. Then, with two minutes left to play and Faga'itua leading 24–8, Tafuna struck twice through the air. It pulled within two points, 24–22, with eighteen seconds left to play. On the ensuing kickoff, Tafuna recovered an onside kick and went for the go-ahead score. But Faga'itua held. After Tafuna's final pass fell incomplete, Faga'itua's players slid en masse into the end zone, just as the De La Salle players did in the movie they had watched the night before.

Not everyone was so euphoric about the outcome. The loss, *Samoa News* reporter Tony Gasu wrote, awakened "Tafuna's ugly side." As the Faga'itua team and fans drove off, more rocks flew. But a few miscreants did little to dampen Faga'itua's delight. The team bus led a caravan of vehicles back to the east side, slowly wending their way back home. In each small village, residents danced and shouted in glee as the team paraded the championship trophy beneath a canopy of palm trees and red banners. They went all the way to the end of the road in Tula.

"WE HAD FUN," Pooch emailed the next day. "We old school. It's like they say: 'Defense Wins Championships!'" Florence Salesa, the athletic trainer, was at home a few hours later, relieved that no player had been seriously hurt during the game, when Pooch called. "Flo," he said, "I want to thank you for all your help during the season and making sure our guys stayed healthy. We look forward to working with you next season." She smiled from ear to ear, thinking "What a class guy!"[10]

This time, David toppled Goliath.

11

The Samoan Paradox

A few weeks before he died from a stroke in 1894, Robert Louis Stevenson gathered together the *matai* he had befriended during his time in Samoa. As he feted them at Vailima, his estate on the hillside overlooking Apia, the Scottish author spoke with urgency. He believed that neither he nor they had much time left. His health deteriorating, Stevenson found it harder to shake off the black dog of depression that shadowed him more often than not. And alarmed by European inroads, he worried that Samoans, who had already lost much of their sovereignty, would soon find themselves strangers in their own land. "I see that the day is come now of the great battle . . . by which it shall be decided, whether you are to pass away . . . or to stand fast, and to have your children living on and honouring your memory in the land you received of your fathers. . . . Now is the time for the true champions of Samoa to stand forth."[1]

Stevenson, a true champion of Samoa if ever there was one, did not live to see his friends confront their challenge. Nor could he have foreseen the many-headed hydra on the horizon. Stevenson would have relished knowing that German rule over Western Samoa ended abruptly when the guns of August roared in 1914 and control passed to New Zealand. But he would have doubted that transfer from one foreign power to another would solve much of anything. It would not have surprised him that Samoans resisted New Zealand's protectorate.[2] Their insurgency, the Mau rebellion, embraced a vision of independence that called for *Samoa moa Samoa*, Samoa for Samoans.[3]

Samoans achieved independence in 1962, but it would be a mistake to romanticize what came to pass in either Samoa or American Samoa. Neither Samoa's independence nor American Samoa's territorial status shielded them from the pernicious effects of Western culture or more subtle forms of dependency. The consequences could be seen in sport.

By the late twentieth century, football and rugby had become the means by which Samoans told their story to the world. Images of a stoic Jesse Sapolu, a raging Junior Seau, a free-spirited Troy Polamalu, and Manu Samoa's magnificent warriors striking a *siva tau* broadcast a Samoan presence well beyond the islands. They exemplified a sporting culture defined by work, competitiveness, and physicality, by allegiance to family and team, and most of all, by *fa'a Samoa*.

Their success conveyed a narrative of a people who worked hard and played harder, who lost but persevered, and, in the end, became among the best in the world at what they did. Their story was about toughness, discipline, and humility. Sport also created a solidarity transcending parochial identities. Once off island, you're not just from Leone, Pago, or Apia; you're Samoan. Similarly, identities forged in Kahuku, Punahou, and Oceanside gave way in college to a larger sense of representing all Samoans.

By the twenty-first century, boys growing up in the far-flung Samoan archipelago had tangible role models to emulate, with new ones—Manti Te'o and Marcus Mariota—emerging each season. Closer to home, every boy, whether in the South Pacific or the mainland, seems to have a father, uncle, brother, and eventually a son or three who played football. They bring out one another's athletic best and make success tangible. And if no relative is connected to the game's banyan tree, there are neighbors and classmates who are, linking them to *'aiga* with few degrees of separation. Players excelling in football come home in the off-season, holding camps, bringing gear, and offering encouragement to journey from "the rock," or mainland enclave, to a higher level of play. They make football intimate and real, something achievable rather than an abstraction.

Stevenson might have been heartened by some of what transpired after his death. Foreign entrepreneurs, seeing limited resources to exploit, did not rush in. Benefiting from their relative insignificance, Samoans held on to their land, and few adopted Western ways.[4] In 1920s Samoa, Margaret Mead reported, "Poverty, the wage system, the separation of the worker from his land and from his tools, modern warfare, industrial disease, the abolition of leisure, the irksomeness of bureaucratic government—these have not yet invaded." Mead might have been projecting her own rejection of modern times on what she saw as an almost idyllic way of life. But she was more right than wrong in arguing that "the subtle penalties of civilization" had not yet been imposed.[5]

But during World War II, global forces intruded. By the twenty-first century, their consequences were apparent. Samoans topped world indices for the prevalence of obesity and· diabetes, their longevity and quality of life were at risk, and 'aiga bonds had frayed. The foundation on which Samoans built their microculture of sporting excellence had begun to crack.

What created that foundation in the first place? It is often said that Samoans are naturally gifted for rough, physical sports like football and rugby. Similar arguments can be heard regarding African American sporting dominance. The belief is widespread that Samoans and African Americans possess inherent genetic advantages. A century ago, the opposite view was often advanced—that African Americans were naturally inferior athletes, possessing weak abdominal muscles, lacking endurance, and unable to perform under pressure. Popular wisdom was wrong then, and it's wrong now.[6]

Fa'a Samoa, not genetics, made Samoan sport what it is. While Polynesian bodies appear well suited for contact sports, their achievements are primarily the product of a disciplined physical culture that demands fealty to the family and team. They have been integrated into the global game, an industry injecting resources and incentivizing play. Incubating in a transoceanic context stretching from American Samoa to the States, a microculture of sporting excellence coalesced. Its constituent elements include role models, rivalries, infrastructure, and rewards, as well as a highly competitive culture that prizes athletic excellence and a college degree. Samoans also spend more hours doing chores, walking, and practicing football growing up than their North American peers.

A stronger motivation to succeed might be the fear of failure. "You're taught from when you're little, that when you leave the island you're taking the name of the family, village, and religious community with you," Gabe Sewell declared. "You carry the hopes and dreams of the whole island. You know your parents and grandparents are constantly praying for you to succeed. You cannot let them down."[7] When Simon Mageo left to play for Western Washington University in the 1980s, those fears were paramount. Struggling with classes in English, he stayed up late to complete course work. When his mother came to graduation, she found a calendar that Mageo had kept and asked why so many days were X-ed out. He replied that those were days he pulled all-nighters. Over four years, he had done so more than eighty times.[8]

Meanwhile, Samoan players have been caricatured as wild-haired, ferociously tattooed warriors dancing a *siva tau* or *haka*. They've created their own version of the warrior. For players, that's tied to a willingness to hit and be hit, to sacrifice for the team, and to play with *no fefe* (no fear). "We revere the warrior," one coach stated. "Our attitude is that I'm not afraid of anything. I'm going to conquer whatever comes in my way." That attitude contributes to a racialized, hypermasculine identity exploited as a marketing device, but it's part of how Samoans are coming to terms with their place in a changing world.

The warrior mystique encourages aggressive play. "You don't walk off the island," Rafael Ramírez remarked about Dominican baseball players' willingness to swing at any pitch. Passivity won't get you a minor league contract. You don't walk off these islands either; passivity doesn't earn a scholarship. College coaches, who know that Samoan boys do not shy from contact, speak of the sound made when they collide. But Samoans' emergence in sport and playing with *no fefe* came at a cost—to their health, to *fa'a Samoa*, and to their future.

It would be hard to overstate how cataclysmically Samoan health has changed since the 1950s. The islands were never an epidemiologic paradise and had their share of hookworm, elephantiasis, and parasites, many which resulted from Western contact. But people grew up working hard and eating natural foods. Since World War II, a more sedentary lifestyle has eclipsed that way of life. While Samoans are hugely overrepresented per capita in football and rugby, they are also among the most obese and diabetic people on the planet. This divergence parallels that of other groups, especially

African Americans, who dominate the ranks of several sports despite lower average life expectancy and poorer overall health. That's a pattern in microcultures of sporting excellence—concentrations at both ends of the health and fitness spectrum.

Steve McGarvey has borne witness to these changes since he first came to American Samoa in the 1970s. Already equipped with a doctorate in anthropology, but working on a second degree in epidemiology, McGarvey recognized the proportions of the dilemma early on. Profound changes had visibly eroded Samoan well-being and he realized conditions would worsen before they improved. Obesity, which affected about a third of men and almost 60 percent of women in American Samoa in 1976, soon doubled for men and reached three-quarters of all women. While rates in Samoa lagged behind those in American Samoa, they more than tripled for men, reaching 34.1 percent, and doubled for women, to 58.7 percent, between 1979 and 2003.[9] The South Pacific had become the epicenter of a global crisis.

While on Tutuila in the fall of 2014, McGarvey sat by the sea on a Sunday morning, sipping coffee while birds jauntily welcomed the dawn and whales played offshore.[10] "It was apparent that there was a health crisis when I first came down," McGarvey recalled. He had chosen to investigate Samoa because he was concerned with what globalization meant for smaller, peripheral societies. Infectious diseases declined but noncommunicable diseases associated with lifestyle and nutrition—especially obesity, diabetes, and hypertension—often soared. McGarvey referred to this turn of events as the "epidemiological transition," a term coined by epidemiologist Abdel Omran in 1971.

"I could see how quickly things were changing," McGarvey recounted. "I couldn't necessarily measure it, but could see with my own eyes the profusion of crap foods in the stores." And then KFC, McDonald's, and Carl's Jr. set up shop. The McDonald's that opened on Tutuila in 2000 and operated twenty-four hours a day led the corporation's thirty thousand restaurants in average sales by its fourth year of operation.[11] The results were painfully obvious. But why had the epidemiological transition wrought such exceptional damage among Samoans?

When it came to determining the etiology of this crisis, McGarvey did not skirt the undeniable size of Samoans or the possibility that genetics might be part of the story. "We've spent a lot of taxpayer money, and I've been the principal investigator, trying to ask the question whether we can discern evidence that would allow us to say that the obesity we see in Samoans or other Polynesians is driven by genetic determination. But I cannot say that."

Still, McGarvey noted, "there is good evidence that the body composition of Polynesians is different. I don't know how significant it is, but it is real. You don't want to racialize that, but we've measured frame size and see differences with other people." Nor did McGarvey deny that history favored larger bodies.[12] Early Samoans undertook voyages that tested the limits of endurance. Those with ample body fat and efficient energy metabolism were better able to survive because bulk forestalled starvation and hypothermia during cold nights on open waters. But, McGarvey cautioned, any genes that might cause obesity have been elusive. Instead, he argued that obesity results from a combination of lifestyle and biological susceptibility.[13]

Looking for genetic connections with sport has been as difficult as searching for an obesity gene. David Epstein's *The Sports Gene* identifies genetic patterns conducive to athletic performance, but favorable variations are only part of a complex story.[14] "There's solid evidence that Polynesians have more lean tissue, muscle mass, and bone than Europeans, but does that explain their success as interior linemen and their explosive speed?" McGarvey asked. "I don't know; nobody has gone that far. I think it's trivial against these larger background issues."

Instead, decades of research and a lifetime rooting for his hometown Philadelphia Eagles led McGarvey to conclude that football "fits right into" Samoan culture, which demands service to the 'aiga. "That culture fits so much into the military and into football, where the social mobility possibilities are very fluid, but where the hierarchies are strictly known and people can actually aspire to them." McGarvey also noted that Samoans largely escaped enslavement and colonization. "I've been plenty of places as a global health person where colonialism happened, and you see its weight on people there. But not here; they're very proud of that and very self-confident." That carries over into sport.

So does stoicism about pain. "Around here," he said, "you do not cop to pain from football." Or for that matter, from anything else. Noting that strong psychosocial impulses affect how people express pain, McGarvey shook his head. "During my almost forty years of working with Samoans, it's as if it's not even there. It's unbelievable."

Choosing words carefully, McGarvey stressed an environmental explanation for the catastrophic makeover in Samoan bodies, one rooted in history, a transition in the islands' political economy, and social class. "World War II primed the pump," he explained, "and then big changes really happened with the *Reader's Digest* article about Samoa as the shame of the South Pacific." Within a few decades, American Samoa shifted from subsistence farming and fishing to a wage-labor economy.

During World War II, working for the military supplanted agriculture, and fishing waned. Consequently, imported goods replaced what Samoans had once produced themselves. As population outpaced the territory's ability to grow breadfruit, taro, and coconuts, it became a net food importer.[15] Devastating typhoons in the 1950s and '60s worsened dependency on imported foods. When the government and the Red Cross imported rice, flour, and instant energy foods to prevent starvation, many encountered these foods for the first time. Nor did Samoans return to farming when these emergencies abated. Instead, people became ever more dependent on imported provisions, especially cheap, unhealthy food. Meanwhile, 1960s territory building prompted another wave of government programs from which Samoans have yet to wean themselves.

While agriculture was Tutuila's primary occupation in 1960, only 8 percent of economically active males worked the land fifteen years later and just 3 percent of all adults in 1990.[16] This transition meant that people expended far less energy at work. Studies of Samoans in the islands and in Hawai'i determined that, on average, a Samoan man who weighed 65 kilograms used approximately 6.5 kilocalories per minute while working the land, but only 1.8 when employed in an office. Unsurprisingly, as a sedentary lifestyle became the norm, fitness decreased, especially for women.[17]

The consequences of this shift in the means of production were twofold. People not only expended less energy as agriculture waned; they lost the chance to eat fruits and vegetables they no longer grew. Their diets swung toward processed, store-bought food.[18]

McGarvey underscored the class dimensions of the evolving global health dilemma, especially the paradox that poverty and obesity became so connected. "The social epidemiology of diet and obesity has switched in the last forty years and we have to talk about class to understand that." Those working and commuting long hours for low pay, McGarvey said, have neither the money nor the time to prepare whole foods. "I saw that time had become a precious commodity, even in a place like this." The commodification of time meant that as people took jobs, they spent less time growing and cooking their own food. And as prices dropped due to government subsidies for artificial sweeteners, the obesity epidemic globalized.

"You've had this tsunami—and that word means something out here—of food changes wash over these places." Because these islands are so small, the impact was magnified. "You have this very rapid and very full nutrition transition. You're not talking about a big continental place like India or China where's it happening over time; this happened almost overnight in terms of human history. This is not a big mega-city. In a twenty year period—*kaboom*! You end up with 85 percent obesity in reproductive-age women and 80 percent obesity in men."

Anthropologist James Bindon found that obesity spread more slowly among Samoans retaining a rural way of life but soared when they urbanized. By the early 1990s, they were two to three times more likely to be overweight than adults in the United States. "The most extreme condition," he concluded, "is found among the massively overweight Samoan migrants living in California."[19]

Samoans are not alone in this precipitous turn of events. Tongans and other Pacific Islanders have racked up weight gains almost as mind-boggling. At the dawn of the twenty-first century, the World Health Organization estimated that 8 to 10 percent of all deaths in the Pacific were attributable to obesity.[20]

The epidemiological transition has not yet wrought comparable damage in nearby independent Samoa, but storms are gathering. Samoa is only a thirty-minute flight from American Samoa, and I've been told for years that Samoans are one people with a common culture. Indeed, most people in American Samoa have family and roots in Samoa, and the back-and-forth flow of people, news, and goods is constant and casual. But there are striking differences. A few years ago, Prime Minister Tuilaepa Sailele Malielegaoi unilaterally changed the side of the road on which Samoans drive and moved his island across the International Date Line (it's a day later than in American Samoa). He sought to facilitate relations with New Zealand, the country with which Samoa has the closest connections. He also banned the import of turkey tails, a cheap but nutritionally deficient food, until the World Trade Organization forced him to rescind the decree.[21]

Another difference is easy to see. People are slimmer and far more of them are casting nets in the coves or tilling hillsides than in American Samoa. Agriculture still makes sense in Samoa, which dwarfs American Samoa in arable land, 1,097 to 76.1 square miles.

That's evident in Lauli'i, outside Apia, where Alopati Lolotai grew up much like the boys playing outside the home of his son, Tui'ali'i Motootua Lolotai. Trash cans sit atop wooden platforms to keep pigs away. On Sundays, women in white dresses and hats stroll to church under parasols, clutching Bibles, fans, and the hands of young children. Men in *lavalavas*, white shirts, ties, and flip-flops accompany them. During the 2009 tsunami, water surged up the stream that runs through Lauli'i but stopped short of Motootua's home. It caused damage but no deaths.

When Al and Matilda Lolotai visited in 1972, they adopted Motootua, then fourteen, and brought him to Tutuila in American Samoa.[22] Motootua studied mechanics at the community college while Al taught him how to wrestle well enough to medal in matches against Tonga and Fiji. Returning to Lauli'i in 1979, Motootua worked as a mechanic and farmed *'aiga* land. He still farms, alongside three sons. "All my time, I go to the plantation," he said after getting home and washing up. He grows bananas, yams, coconuts, and taro, which he sells at the Apia market. At low tide, villagers net fish and search for sea urchins, octopus, and shellfish in the cove.

Hymns can be heard from the church nearby. Many of Lauli'i's homes are distressed and the town has less of the landscaping that prettifies many villages along Upolu's coastal road, where the speed limit, never higher than twenty miles an hour, enhances the island's relaxed vibe. His youngest son was playing rugby with friends outside, keeping at it until dark. "We small country, but we love to play," Motootua said, smiling. Like his adoptive father, who wrestled when he was almost sixty, Motootua looks like he still could compete.

So does Tasa Laotele, who carries herself like the triathlete she once was, lean and muscled, with a splay of reddish brown hair. In her fifties, Tasa has competed most of her life. "When I was young," she recalled, "at five p.m., when chores, work, and school were done, everybody played." That's still the case. Games of volleyball, rugby, soccer, and basketball commence each afternoon but Sunday. "There's a lot of laughter in sport here," she added. "A comedian would entertain at cricket games."[23] Tasa displayed a pair of binoculars that her cousin Jesse Sapolu had given her; he had received them in honor of his collegiate career. He told Tasa that she could use them when she flew.

Frank Lloyd Wright has nothing on Tasa in terms of fitting an abode into the landscape. She lives in a bamboo house with a dozen rescue cats and dogs, amid an explosion of pink and red flowers. Apia Park, where Manu Samoa plays, is within hailing distance. The sago palm in her yard provides thatching for her home, including the open-air kitchen. There's another tree she calls the toilet paper tree. Her garden plot includes papaya, lemons, soursop, bananas, taro, coconut palms, and lemongrass. Her diet is similar to what it was when she grew up next door. Her family ate what they grew, trapping fish and gathering sea urchins every Friday night. The Sunday to'ona'i, prepared in an umu, was the fruit of their labor. For Tasa, it still is.

Tasa left Upolu to become the first Polynesian woman to earn a pilot's license. After flying commercially for twenty years, she returned in 2006. Tasa is not at all happy with what happened while she was away. "We've gone from organic and healthy food to processed food," she said, lamenting the devolution of traditional diet and life. But she is determined to regain that way of life for herself and whomever she can influence.

"People here are hungrier than in American Samoa," Tasa declared, referring to the territory's dependence on U.S. federal support. "We've had to work for what we have." That sense of hunger and a willingness to work has driven Samoan sporting success. "Your true colors come out in sport," she offered. "It's why we produce so many good athletes. And it goes back to the soil. We're producing more and more fine athletes. But there's a missing link. Fifty percent of the Pacific population has diabetes. I call them a fading race."

Some of the race is fading away at the LBJ Tropical Medical Center in American Samoa. It's where diabetes, one of obesity's most tragic consequences and the leading cause of end-stage kidney disease, plays out seventeen hours a day. Because those stricken with it can no longer rely on their kidneys to filter and cleanse their blood, dialysis is required.[24] By some estimates, half of the territory's population is diabetic or prediabetic.

After a decade at a hospital in Puerto Escondido on Mexico's Pacific coast,

Michael Gerstenberger knows what it's like running an understaffed, under-resourced facility. LBJ, the island's only full-care hospital, has fewer than half the doctors and a quarter of the registered nurses a facility of its size should have. Gerstenberger projects an easy demeanor, but there's nothing easy about operating a hospital on an island where obesity, diabetes, and multisystem diseases run amok. "We have a twenty-two-unit dialysis center," he said in 2012, "that's not large enough to accommodate the demands we face, so we're doubling its size. If the increase we have seen continues," Gerstenberger warned, "we would have 2,200 dialysis patients on the island by 2025 and it would take 100 percent of the territorial budget simply to care for them."[25] Nor is dialysis a panacea. "The reality is being sentenced to dialysis three days a week, three or four hours a day, with your vascular vessels wearing out after sticking needles in them. The best you can hope for is that you stay the same."

LBJ could neither accommodate nor pay for that many patients. The federal government budgeted $461 per person for island health care in 2010 versus $7,400 per capita in the United States. "We are a Medicare-certified hospital held to the same standard," Gerstenberger said. "Our dilemma is trying to provide $7,400 worth of care for $461."

Diabetes alone makes that impossible; there's also hypertension, gout, coronary heart disease, and end-stage renal disease. "We see far too many patients in their thirties, forties, or fifties who have all of them," Gerstenberger said. According to the World Health Organization, 47.3 percent of Samoans are diabetic, 93.5 percent are overweight or obese, and 99.6 percent exhibit at least one major risk factor for a noncommunicable disease.[26]

Scant funds and inadequate staffing are only part of the dilemma. Patient compliance, prescription costs, and transportation are also barriers. So is language; few doctors speak Samoan, the first and sometimes only language for older people. There's also pervasive fatalism. "A lot of people I've spoken to have simply not taken any responsibility for their own health, and say it's the Lord's will," Gerstenberger said, "then show up dead or nearly dead in the emergency department."

Morbid obesity, he said softly, is often accepted. "We had a seventeen-year-old who died a year ago who weighed 417 pounds. How does your teenager get to be 417 pounds without anyone noticing? It just baffles me." Gerstenberger identified the same culprits as McGarvey—the double whammy of radical change in work and diet—but also stressed culture. "Everything is measured by food," he observed. "Whether it was a successful wedding, a successful baptism, a successful funeral, whatever it is, there are great expectations that a feast will be served. And it has to be a very grand feast, a little sweller than the one we went to last weekend, for the family to keep face." It was one thing when that feast was bananas, taro, fish, and coconuts. "But now every meal has to have pork, has to have fish, has to have chicken, has to have chop suey, has to have breadfruit, has to have taro, has to have rice! You are typically given a six-thousand- or seven-thousand-calorie meal at a function and then you're given an equivalent amount to take home. It's considered very, very offensive if you don't take it home. And if it happens to be a wedding, it's the only culture I'm familiar with where every guest gets a cake!"

It bothers Gerstenberger that many don't see obesity as a problem. "They think there's nothing wrong with being morbidly obese. . . . When doctors say you really have to lose fifty pounds, they say why." But Gerstenberger gets why people have poor diets. "You can understand why lettuce is not consumed when it's $3 or $4 a head, and you have to throw half of it away because it's mushy and been on a boat far too long. Just like the inner city, it's cheaper to buy junk food."

"This is almost completely attributable to large-scale changes from a culture of simple foods, moderate levels of physical activity, and an emphasis on village competition to the worst of what we call obesogenic environments," Steve McGarvey said, using a term coined the 1980s. "Obesogenic environments encourage people to eat unhealthily and not do enough exercise, promoting excessive weight gain. It's a culture of cheap food of poor nutritional quality, and a loss of the spontaneous forms of physical activity associated with subsistence, whether climbing up the hillside to do the taro bed or fishing on the reef." McGarvey does not deny that more research must be done, especially regarding causes. "But look at this nutritional change, at the historical factors," he urged. "That is all the evidence we need! We can't wait to address the issue. The amount of sugared beverage consumption down here is sadly remarkable, like it is in many places in the world."

At the banquet held during Troy Polamalu's camp, Governor Moliga said, "Don't forget to take your pills," before inviting guests to dine. The men at my table laughed, if uneasily. "He's talking about gout—the Polynesian bogeyman," one explains when he saw I didn't understand the governor's remarks. The next day five coaches relaxed in the pool talking about gout. Once known as the disease of kings, it's become more democratic, striking many as a by-product of obesity. The coaches swapped war stories about attacks, describing the pain as worse than anything they had encountered in football. Bulking up to withstand the demands of the NFL, they did not lose that weight afterward, exacerbating the damage their bodies incurred. Many players endure moderate pain daily for the rest of their lives, or worse.

The damage wrought by frequent concussive blows is more pernicious than gout. But they don't talk much about concussions in American Samoa. Playing virtually year-round on rock-hard fields with helmets that would be discarded in the States because they no longer adequately protect the brain, boys incur substantial neurological trauma. Yet there's only one medical trainer working for the schools and no preseason neurological testing to establish a baseline that could be used when concussions occur. Many practice or play when they ought to be sitting quietly on the sidelines.

Education is another sore spot. Though few Samoans play professionally, many leverage football into scholarships, which are especially attractive because there are so few on-island options. A degree enhances the chances of gaining employment with island government, the territory's leading employer. It also helps an individual achieve *matai* status and displays 'aiga power. Nobody knows just how many leave each year to play in college, or how many complete their degrees, because nobody has kept track. It's likely that the number of boys leaving has been exaggerated and their degree of failure understated. "They want to talk about the number of kids who make it to the States to play," coach Pati Pati cautioned, "but they don't ask about the ones who drop out."[27] Perhaps half who leave don't last a year. "Of a hundred kids who go to junior colleges," Mel Purcell estimated, "we're lucky to have fifteen move on to Division I on scholarship. Most drop out or come back."

Youth who drop out are slow to return. "They can't face their parents," Pati Pati explained. "There's a pride we have on the island and you don't want people saying your son went to college and didn't finish." According to educator Li'a Amisone, "Parents say, 'Stay there, don't come back,' when their kids don't make it. Their family is shamed."[28]

Any one of a cluster of economic, cultural, and athletic roadblocks could knock a student-athlete off course. Together, they can be too much to overcome. Success in college tracks closely with family income. Students from better-off backgrounds are finishing college at record rates, while those from less-affluent households are struggling. In 2015, more than three-fourths of youth from families in the top quartile had earned undergraduate degrees by the age of twenty-four, almost double the percentage of well-off students who graduated in 1970. But completion rates hardly budged in the bottom quartile, rising from 6 percent in 1970 to 9 percent in 2013. Though record numbers of lower-income youth enroll in college, few finish.[29] Many doubt it's possible to pay for college. They have no family members with degrees to emulate, nor did their schools equip them with the tools to succeed. Samoans tend to come from that bottom bracket.

Cultural issues compound financial difficulties. It's not hard to see why boys who learned English as a second language and grew up in a culture where tradition prevailed would struggle off island. Samoan remains the default language in most households. "It's the main reason for dropouts," Tafuna principal Beauty Tuiasosopo explained. "It's hard for them to get the required scores on SATs." On the math section of the SATs, Fagaʻitua principal Elvis Liufau said, "We score in the 500 to 600 range, but our reading and writing results are much weaker."

Even if students clear the admissions hurdle by dint of hard work and SAT prep classes, language issues persist. It's harder to puzzle through readings, keep up with overcaffeinated professors in lectures, and write in a second language. At Tafuna, which has more academic success than other public schools, 15 percent go off island each year to continue their education, and another 45 percent attend the island's community college. Many of their classmates try to enlist.

Per capita, it's possible that more Samoans have served in the U.S. armed forces than any other demographic. Likewise, Samoans suffered the highest casualties per capita in Afghanistan and Iraq. Veterans Affairs estimates that 7.3 percent of all U.S. citizens have served or are currently in the military. It could be 20 percent or higher among Samoans; people speak of nine thousand veterans on the island.[30]

There are few alternatives to college and the military. On Tutuila's east side, farming has faded. "Before," Elvis Liufau said, "you could see taro plantations on the mountains; now it's all forests. You just don't see plots of taro anymore." So youth think about enlisting if they don't get an athletic scholarship. The military pays much better than most jobs and offers the best chance for an education.

It's been that way since the military created a volunteer army. In 2014, Tutuila led the army's 885 recruiting centers with 153 recruits, and its Junior ROTC had 1,600 cadets.[31] To enlist, youth take the Armed Services Vocational Aptitude Battery. Acknowledging the language and cultural biases implicit in the battery, the military lowered the passing score for Samoans. But some who pass cannot make weight cutoffs. Faga'itua High has only five hundred students, but they fill all 240 testing slots the school is allotted annually.

Then, once in college, there's the shock of being on one's own. Pati Pati reckons that of the forty boys he's coached who went to college, half dropped out their first year. "First and foremost, they're not used to not having their parents around." Compared to youth in the States, their sense of autonomy is limited. "Kids here don't have the same freedoms growing up, and when they go off island, they don't have their parents telling them what to do."[32]

On the island, children are embedded in *'aiga*, church, and village, with parents, aunties, uncles, reverends, and *matai* exercising control. Rebellion is met swiftly, often with a beating. With lives so regimented, football and rugby provide physical release. But off the field, teenage angst is muted. Even music videos on local television are sweet and gentle. In one, the Samoana student body performs a paean to their school; another is about a family reunion. Both featured extra-large rappers, including the aptly named Big Ice Cream Man and equally large choruses. But that sweetness should not be exaggerated. "One thing about Samoans," Sanele Tuiteleleapaga cautioned. "They're like volcanoes. They're very gentle; they're very patient. But they erupt. When pushed to limits, it comes out."[33]

Eruptions are less likely in American Samoa than in the States. There's no showboating here. Coaches just smiled when I asked what would happen if a boy spiked the ball or showed off after scoring. Kids are told what to do and, for the most part, comply with no questions asked. They don't ask questions in the classroom either; it's how they were brought up. "There's so much emphasis on respect and family here," coach Gabe Sewell stressed, "and kids don't have much freedom." But on their own in college, they tend to drift and often go under.[34]

Nor is there much support in place, especially at a junior college that recruits a hundred boys a season, discarding those who cannot cope. "We're very thankful for opportunities," Elia Savali said, "but there are institutions we discourage our students from attending. It's not so much the freedom they have when they get there but that there's no financial help and really no one to push them academically, someone to confide in, even say get up and go to class when they're tired and sleep in."[35]

To play, boys must be in strict compliance with NCAA Clearinghouse guidelines regarding credits, courses, grades, and exam scores. Island coaches are increasingly attentive to these guidelines, but students fall through the cracks. Athletic careers crash when guidelines are not met.[36]

And then there's the actual football. No matter how much ability, toughness, and desire a boy brings, there's much to learn to make it in college football. Along with daunting challenges to succeed in the classroom and figure out "Amerika," Samoan student-athletes must negotiate the weight room, film study, and practice.[37] Islanders who were never taught correct techniques or how to lift weights properly start at a disadvantage compared to boys who benefited from better facilities, coaching, and nutrition in the States. And even those boys rarely play as freshmen. There's a good reason that most Division I players redshirt a season. They're neither strong enough nor understand the game well enough to hold their own on the field.

Many who currently coach on the island played in the 1980s and 1990s. They speak of football as a vehicle to get a degree, experience life off island, and build relationships they would not otherwise acquire. "But many of the kids I coach now," Gabe Sewell cautioned, "are thinking of the NFL. I am trying to make them understand there's more to life than football."[38]

To confront the dire health problems caused by globalization will require deep-seated cultural shifts. So will succeeding academically and forging sporting careers that enhance lives instead of damaging them. This means thinking differently about food, public health, education, football, and *fa'a Samoa*, as well as how to escape the consequences of dependency on federal funds.

The contrast with independent Samoa is illuminating. Samoa is more self-sufficient in food and has a viable economy, including a tourist sector. Meanwhile, American Samoa is a net food importer and cannot support itself without federal subsidies, substantial transfer payments to veterans, and remittances from abroad.

The two Samoas' trajectories diverged in the 1950s, after the Navy left and American Samoa lapsed into depression. "Its people are unhappy and in some cases hungry," American Samoa governor Lawrence Judd said. But "Western Samoa," he noted, "is booming." More damning was the oft-heard indictment that Washington treated American Samoa as if it were a reservation.

During the 1960s, America's territory-building experiment revamped the economy but undercut self-reliance. After working with the Peace Corps in Samoa and teaching in American Samoa, Robert Shaffer lamented that U.S. influence had overwhelmed the islands' traditional culture. Samoans, he argued, had lost some of their pride and dignity, and latched on to unsavory aspects of American culture in exchange.[39]

Others were more tempered. "It's just like the Berlin Wall," a man in American Samoa said. "We're the same people, the same families even, but we're completely different. Here we feel we're where it's at and think, 'Oh those poor cats, no cars, no money.' And they're saying, 'those guys have lost their heritage and sold out . . . we're poor but we call our own shots.'" When pressed, he added that he thought people in independent Samoa had "a more meaningful and richer life."[40]

Many believe they still do. *Fa'a Samoa* has retained more purchase over daily life, while in American Samoa, people voice growing disenchantment with corruption, dependency, and cultural change. "The sad thing about us today is that we have come to learn the meaning of poor," former governor Togiola Tulafono remarked. "But we only learned the meaning of poor after cash was introduced to us." Before that, he said, the highest chief had no more than the lowest man in the village, both sharing what the *'aiga* provided.

"Dependent mindedness is so ingrained," Tulafono asserted, "that whenever anything comes up, people say, 'Ask the government for it!' And if the government doesn't give it, they say, 'I will take it.' If we continue in these ways, we're never going to be able to take care of ourselves in the ways that we did." Tulafono lauded those who had migrated from Samoa to American Samoa. "They don't let their kids get spoiled, even when things get better. Many of these parents make sure they understand where they came from."[41]

That's the existential question here—can people remember where they came from?

Epilogue

When I run on Tutuila, it's usually late in the day, just before dark. That's soon after sundown this close to the equator. I park at the Korean convenience store past Coconut Point, at the beginning of a stretch of road that winds around Pago Pago Bay. At least, I think it's Korean. They sometimes front for Samoan owners, who find it difficult turning down *'aiga* members asking for something on the shelves. It's not customary to reject such requests.

On one side of the two-lane blacktop, waves slam against a retaining wall of rocks and concrete. On the other, emerald hillsides shoot upward. A small village sits around most bends, with a church invariably the grandest building, towering over the tallest trees and providing a heartfelt soundtrack of hymns most nights of the week on this religious island.

Traffic slackens before sunset in time for *sa*, the brief period set aside for prayer. One day during the Polamalu camp, I was a mile from the end of a run when a volley of clanging sounds erupted in Matua'a, a village where the Polamalus once lived. *'Aumaga* members wearing matching *lavalavas* and white T-shirts were smacking large staves against propane tanks suspended in the air. The tanks once alerted villagers to tsunamis; now they're used to announce *sa*. Young men make sure that people go home or to church when the clanging begins. The first *'aumaga* member I encountered held his stave horizontal to the ground as I approached and indicated I should sit. So I sat cross-legged by the water until *sa* was over, never more a *palagi*.

It's a serene time of day. Traffic flows to a mix of island tunes and hardly anybody speeds or hotdogs. Nor have I seen anything close to road rage. Drivers matter-of-factly let oncoming cars turn in front of them and wave in drivers from sidestreets. Surprisingly cautious, Samoans slow their pickups and SUVs to a crawl if there's gravel on the road or a speed bump. On the other hand, they hurl their bodies around in sport and are less than vigilant about what they put in them.

On one of my first runs on Tutuila, I came across a group of teenage boys sitting on a ledge. As I braced myself, they smiled and greeted me without the slightest edge. I thought of Robert Louis Stevenson remarking that Polynesians were God's sweetest works. Even teenage boys look you in the eye and nod. Almost every female, from the smallest girl to the oldest woman, breaks into a warm smile.

Dogs are another matter. They don't have it good here, and those running loose are sometimes targeted for eradication. Mostly skinny with short brown and white coats, they look like they came from a single pair of parents aboard the *Messenger of Peace*, the ship that brought Christianity to the islands. Extremely territorial, they guard their property from other dogs and passersby. They love to chase cars and, given how slowly people drive, often catch them. As a result, many limp along on three legs. Dogs are not allowed in houses, nor are they considered pets. Fed on scraps, they guard against intruders and *aitu*, the spirit ghosts only they can see.

Pati Pati likes to call the dogs that run onto the field and chase players at practice his speed coaches. I encountered two speed coaches of my own along the coastal road one afternoon. I did what I've been told to do when dogs come at you—bend over and pantomime picking up a rock and throwing it at them. They usually cringe; the only time I threw something, they chased after me. I had broken the code of the shadow war. So I ran. When they're not chasing traffic, dogs sleep on burial crypts erected in front of homes. It's not easy to forget the past when your ancestors are buried in the front yard.

* * *

Kids come out to play this time of day and families cool down in the sea. Boys in uniform, holding their helmets by the face guard, trudge home from practice. They look spent, worn-out by long sun-drenched scrimmages. Still, they swagger a bit, their jerseys and skin stained with mud and speckled with bruises.

Other boys bang into each other Big East–style on basketball courts. Bodies crash and tumble but few fouls are called. A greater number of youth play volleyball in the dirt and sand. Girls, timing their leaps, spike balls across the net with a thwack and a scream. Sometimes, there's football in waist-deep water; one day I saw a teenage girl lay out to catch a pass before disappearing under the waves.

If I run from the Tradewinds Hotel in Ottoville, I hear voices and thuds from rugby and soccer matches on fields near the airport. When I ask the players where they're from, they name villages in Samoa, Fiji, and Tonga. They came here to work so that they could send money back to their families. Their numbers have grown so much in recent years that a majority of Tutuila's current workforce now comes from elsewhere.

On my last trip, I saw younger boys playing tackle in uniforms for the first time. American Youth Football recently organized youth teams. Before, boys tried out in the ninth grade with no experience at organized play; their first encounter came in the bullring with bigger kids more than willing to test them. Walkers, joggers, and runners of all ages, including military personnel, congregate at a track nearby; others take to the path along the ocean. When I first came here, I hardly ever saw another runner. It bodes well.

Half a century ago, Pete Gurr and his mates ran along the ridge and shore to get to and from school. The road snaking along Tutuila's southern coast ends on the east side of the island, in Tula, where a basketball hoop made of a milk crate, its bottom cut out, is affixed to a pole. Tommy Aumua, Troy Polamalu's biological father, who quickly disappeared from his life, is from Tula. On the west side of the island, the road ends at Gurr's farm at Maloata Bay.[1]

Pete grew up here, at the end of the road, during the 1950s and '60s, before moving to California. The Gurrs had been part of Samoan history since their Welsh patriarch arrived in the nineteenth century and married an island girl. Pete's father farmed hillsides that plunge to the beach where green and hawksbill turtles lay eggs. Pete, like his father, catches lobsters in rocky crevices along the cove and visits outer banks for mahi-mahi, wahoo, marlin, and sailfish. Whales congregate offshore to mate during their yearly migrations. Little black birds called *peapea*, or propeller birds, strafe overhead, devouring mosquitos.

Though focused on the future, Pete Gurr believes that Samoa's prospects depend on reprising elements of its agrarian past. Maloata Bay offers a glimpse of that. "My father was a farmer, a great farmer," Pete said, "but we were teased that we were eating weeds, *palagi* food." The Gurrs grew tomatoes, cabbage, and greens. "I was embarrassed about it, but I'm not embarrassed now, because whoever was eating that is much healthier." A youthful-looking fifty-five, Pete is proof positive.

Along with Mel Purcell, Pete Gurr works for the territory's Department of Agriculture, promoting sustainable produce. They organize organic food fairs and campaign to renew community agriculture. "We import about 95 percent of the food that we eat today," Gurr cautioned. "I'm not happy with that; food security in the territory is very fragile. I sing this story wherever I go—what if something happens to the ships, what if there is a war, a shipping strike in Long Beach? I keep saying that we need to return to the land, to become self-sufficient." Gurr linked health woes to dependence on imported foods. Some of the solution, he argued, could come from these very hillsides and the greenhouses where he grows flowers, as well as from the sea.

Never logged, the Maloata valley is thick with dark oak, mahogany, and breadfruit. The latter grows in twenty-one varieties and once sustained villagers when typhoons destroyed plantations and roiled the seas. Breadfruit has recently caught the attention of scientists who see its potential as an underutilized superstaple. Not only does its low glycemic index mean that it does not raise blood sugar, but breadfruit is also high in complex carbohydrates, protein, and micronutrients such as iron and zinc. Nor does it require much maintenance, land, or chemical fertilizer.[2] Gurr identifies trees and plants in the surrounding rain forest and discusses their uses. He's especially proud of the white ginger he cultivates in his greenhouses and sells throughout the island.

A road cut into the hillside connects this remote oasis to the rest of the island. "As I was growing up," Gurr recalled, "there were no cars from my village to 'Amanave, where I went to school." So every morning and then again after school, he ran four miles up and down along dirt paths. If the sea was calm, Pete shortcut the route by paddling a canoe part of the way. "When I was a boy," he said, "we fished and hunted for our food and did chores every day, running up the hillside and cutting bananas and running back down with them. I didn't realize my football career had started."

"Our game was rugby. No rules, just kill the guy with the ball." Following his father's death in the 1960s, Pete and his brother moved to Redondo Beach. When they signed up for Little League, other boys' parents objected and claimed they were overage. They weren't, but they were ripped—bigger, faster, and more muscular than other boys. "It was so embarrassing that I just wanted to run away," Pete remembered. "But Coach said, 'No, we've got your passports, we have your birth certificates, you can play.'"

Pete was not in a gang, but he took on other kids in arranged bouts with money on the line. "We used to go challenge the Mexican kids and they would put up their best fighter," he recalled. Then twelve, he made $5 a fight in twice-a-week matches. "I never was broke," he said, laughing. "We could always go to the movies."

Pete struggled with English when he entered junior high, but he could run like the wind. When the football coach asked him to come out for the team, he didn't know the rules, much less how to play. He hadn't been able to afford Pop Warner, where boys learned the game. The coach said, "Don't worry. We'll just give you the ball and you run with it."

So he ran, stopping when he crossed the goal line or was dragged to the turf. Graduating in 1975, he turned down Division I offers to follow his high school coach to El Camino Junior College. Pete helped El Camino rise to the top of the national rankings his freshman season before injuries abruptly ended his football career. "I was in a state of shock," Pete recalled. "I was tough; I was supposed to be able to take anybody on." At five-nine, 188 pounds, he could bench-press four hundred pounds, but he would never play football again.

Pete threw himself into other ventures and developed serious construction-trade chops, assembling a dynamic Samoan crew. He met Donna, also Samoan, and they married. Returning to the island to catch up with friends and family, they looked at each other and decided to ditch their upwardly mobile California lives. They moved back to Tutuila and have been there ever since.

When their sons entered ninth grade, Pete did not want them playing football. "I know too many Samoan athletes who have paid the price," he said. He spoke of visiting Mosi Tatupu, who had played fifteen seasons in the NFL, weeks before he died. "He had a tear in his eye and told me, 'People don't know the pain I am in. When I get up in the morning, I crawl. I crawl downstairs. I crawl to the kitchen. Pete, people don't know that.' You pay a very big price."

But it wasn't easy convincing his sons, who knew of their father's prowess. "The first week of practice, I looked at their shoulder pads and said, 'No way!' I couldn't believe the straps; they were using fishing rope. The T-hooks were cut off fishing hooks!" After watching Leone practice in sorry-looking gear, Pete went home and ordered equipment. When he dropped it off, Coach Francis Tuitele asked him to coach the backfield. Pete said he would do it for a week, but it was too much fun to quit. He was back in the game.

He still is. Pete coached several years and began establishing contacts with off-island schools. He saw that players who had the talent to succeed in college still needed exposure to be recruited and help to survive in school. Pete and Donna Gurr, Governor Togiola Tulafono, Mel and Moana Purcell, and Kahuku coach Siuaki Livai organized the Samoa Bowl, bringing off-island all-star teams to play against local boys. They began working with players who wanted to give back to the island, facilitating camps and clinics. The Samoa Bowl added volleyball so that girls could leverage sport for education. Their goals—advancing health, diet, and education in tandem with sport—could help define Samoa's future but are not easy to achieve.

"When I began coaching," Pete recalled, "we had a hundred kids come out for a forty-five-man squad. We didn't have enough equipment and had them line up and count off one-two-three-four and said, 'Those with number four, take a hike.' The kids who made it were celebrating, the other kids walking home with their heads dropping. It was cruel and I didn't like it. But that's changed." He sketched the game's evolution here and exclaimed, "This island is going to explode in terms of talent!" He shakes his head about what would happen if football took hold in independent Samoa. "It's a gold mine over there. It's more like we were when we were kids in terms of chores, diet."

Pete said he can tell which boys are from there. "I see their hunger, determination, toughness. I will tell you, if American football goes there, it will be unbelievable."

With the football infrastructure here reaching critical mass, Gurr spends more time on his agricultural portfolio. He's been with the Department of Agriculture since 1993 and feels that efforts to jump-start sustainable farming are gaining momentum. "People really didn't want to work the land when I came back. But for me, it's in the blood. I have to plant something every day." If Pete gets his way, people all over the island will reclaim a healthier diet.

Pete was high on the mountain above the valley with his wife, Donna, when an earthquake rattled Tutuila on September 29, 2009. No alarms sounded but he had recently gone through tsunami training. "I was taught by my father and grandfather how to read the water, to look at the ocean every day and know every pattern. I saw the way the ocean was behaving. I knew it was going to come. I had never been through a tsunami, just hurricanes, but the water tells a story."

He and Donna jumped in his pickup and raced through villages heading toward 'Amanave, honking their horn, blinking their lights, and urging people to higher ground. By then, they could see the waters receding, exposing fringe reef and the ocean floor. Some were paralyzed by fear, unable to run; others were too infirm to walk, much less run. They rescued as many people as they could, cramming them into the pickup and driving up the hill as many times as possible. And then a wall of water, fifteen to twenty feet high, crashed inland for a hundred yards or more, stopping at their truck's tires.

American Samoa and the Samoan diaspora face a cultural and social tsunami that threatens them in slower but deadly ways. But if Samoans can hold on to their past as they make their future, and not allow football to do more damage than good to their sons, just maybe they will continue to be God's sweetest works.

Acknowledgments

After finishing two projects in 2011, I found myself adrift. Having a book to work on is like running for me; I don't feel right when it's not there. Fascinated by locales that develop exceptional cultures of sport, I decided to explore football far from the Friday-night lights of western Pennsylvania. That led me to the South Pacific, where I was struck once more by the universal appeal of sport. At its best, sport offers a vision of an ethical, transparent arena where fairness and performance matter most, where people validate themselves by the strength of their opponents, and celebrate body, mind, and team. I've come to think of it as a republic of play.

But just as the early American republic embraced slavery alongside freedom, the republic of play can be a mean and vicious place—where youth become vulnerable commodities on a global supply chain; the athletes we applaud are traumatized; and sport is used to promote anger and misogyny, bringing out the worst—not the best—in us.

Samoan football is not immune to this paradox, but it shows how much social capital sport can generate. Many who have invested their energy in nurturing football among Polynesians know that being a part of a team in which you have one another's backs and compete with common purpose is one of life's treasures.

I flew to Pago Pago in 2011 on a grant from the World History Center, which colleague Pat Manning created after joining the History Department at the University of Pittsburgh. On this and subsequent trips, I received support from Pitt via the Global Studies Center, a Hewlett International Grant, and the University Center for International Studies.

There might not be a more closely knit sporting fraternity than that of Polynesian football. To find a way in, I turned to Penny Semaia, an anthropology major who played football at Pitt and became its senior associate athletic director. Penny vouched for me with his uncle, Pepine Lauvao, who coached Samoana High to the island title after the 2009 tsunami. Pepine, no longer on the island, connected me to men currently coaching. The day after arriving on Tutuila, I began learning from Lealao Soloata Melila "Mel" Purcell, Pati Pati, Su'aese "Pooch" Ta'ese, Gabe Sewell, Pete Gurr, Pio Grohse, and Simon Mageo. Like a banyan tree, their branches spread to every village on Tutuila, the Manu'a Islands, and independent Samoa, as well as Samoan enclaves in Honolulu, the North Shore, and Oceanside, California.

I also sought counsel from Rich Scaglion and Keith Brown, anthropologists who have spent their lives in the South Pacific and Japan. Simpatico and learned, they provided immeasurable contributions.

The people I spoke with in the islands made me realize why Robert Louis Stevenson called Samoans "God's best, at least his sweetest, works." Elia Savali, an educator and coach, and Lewis Wolman, an expat who found a home on Tutuila's east side, were insightful and forthcoming as they sketched the parameters of Samoan culture and history and made me rethink initial impressions. Mel Purcell traced his own transoceanic journey, clarifying why fa'a Samoa still resonates and the challenges it faces; Pooch Ta'ese, whom Purcell credits for taking island football to a new level, spoke from his heart about coming of age in Faga'itua and San Jose. His Tafuna counterpart, Okland Salave'a, revisited with me the deaths of his close friends Sal Aunese and Junior Seau.

Rob Shaffer, who served in the Peace Corps in Samoa and worked in American Samoa, shared knowledge acquired over decades of commitment to the islands; Evelyn Lili'o-Satele and Judge Satele Lili'o Ali'ita'i welcomed me to their home above Fagasa Bay and taught me much. So did Cheryl

Morales, the director of the Feleti Barstow Public Library, whose resources were critical to this study. Tammy Zielinski was an incredible source of help, first as the Pacific reference librarian at the Barstow and later at the University of Hawai'i. She told me of a dissertation by Lisa Uperesa, now at the University of Auckland. Lisa incisively explores the connections between Samoan culture and football. Learned elders and *matai*, especially Secretary of Samoan Affairs Tufele F. Li'amatua and his deputy director, Sanele Tuiteleleapaga, American Samoa governors Togiola Tulafono and Lolo Moliga, Samoan prime minister Tuilaepa Aiono Sailele Malielegaoi, head of state His Highness Tui Atua Tupua Tamasese Efi and Dr. Malama Meleisea, offered a wealth of knowledge. Ben Kneubuhl Jr. described growing up on Tutuila in the early twentieth century. Li'a Amisone, Tumua Matu'u, and Florence Salesa offered access to the inner workings of island sport.

Football's banyan tree extends to Hawai'i, where Jesse Markham, who authored an eye-opening thesis on Samoan football, helped me understand island culture and the infrastructure underpinning Polynesian football. On O'ahu, Dick Tomey, Cal Lee, and Hugh Yoshida, wise souls all, made me see why football matters so much. Junior Ah You, Rich Miano, Siuaki Livai, Kale Ane, Reggie Torres, Derek Inouchi, Raymond Fujino, and Lee Leslie brought me inside the locker room, figuratively and literally. Malia Ane, the Lolotais, the Anaes, Angel Ramos, and Tanoai Reed brought me into their homes and traced their families' histories. The New Otani Kaimana Beach Hotel was my refuge in Honolulu and the folks who worked there my guides to the island. I later realized that Robert Louis Stevenson stayed on that stretch of beach, at the New Otani's predecessor, the San Souci, and sat under the same hau trees that shaded me every day.

In 2013, when the Troy and Theodora Polamalu Foundation held its second football and volleyball camp on Tutuila, I was in the company of men and women with an inspiring commitment to youth. Though many of them were twice my size and half my age, they welcomed me into their ranks and talked story with me. I owe much to Salu, Kennedy, and Ao Polamalu, Keith Uperesa, Alema and Ma'a Te'o, other coaches, and current and former players at the camp as well as Troy and Theodora Polamalu and their work in American Samoa. Jesse Sapolu, co-founder of the Polynesian Football Hall of Fame, is a man of exceptional gravitas and grace. In Oceanside, Junior and Tony Paopao, Pulu Poumele, Wayne Godinet, and legendary coaches Herb

Meyer and John Carroll reprised their beach town's sporting ascent. Bob Apisa played with *no fefe* and found a second calling on the screen, where he was just as fearless. He and Arlena welcomed me into their home for an unflinchingly honest interview.

When the University of Pittsburgh History Department searched for a professor of sport history soon after my first trip to the islands, I spoke about Samoa for my job talk and was subsequently hired. Dean John Cooper's gracious appointment still seems like a fantasy, but it's one I've embraced. His generous research support made it possible for me to write this book. Neither the position nor the book would have happened without Reid Andrews and Marcus Rediker.

As they have for my previous books, Dave Bear, Mark Cohen, and Marcus Rediker read the manuscript and, as Jamie Dixon would say, made it better. Bear interrogated me as we cycled alongside the Youghiogheny River, as we headed down the Colorado River, and during Steelers games. I kicked the project around with Mark Cohen, my brother since the police brought us together decades ago, while biking and hiking as high as we could in the Rockies. Marcus Rediker, an indomitable historian and better friend, keeps pushing the boundaries of what I think possible. Ted Muller, my collaborator in exploring Pittsburgh's history, pushed this project along over coffee and while hiking out of the Grand Canyon. So did Jay Reifer, my longtime running mate on Schenley Park's trails and city streets. Liann Tsoukas, my energizing, empathizing collaborator on Mal Goode's biography, and Bernie Hagerty, who brings out the best in students and colleagues, were always cheering me up and on.

You could not ask for better friends, or for better colleagues, than Bill Chase, Sy Drescher, Niklas Frykman, Kathy Gibson, Larry Glasco, Wendy Goldman, Janelle Greenberg, Van Beck Hall, Lannie Hammond, Pete Karsten, Patty Landon, Tony Novosel, Pernille Røge, Jonathan Scott, Dick Smethurst, Scott Smith, John Stoner, Gregor Thum, Grace Tomcho, and Molly Warsh. Alex Mountain, Dan Holland, and Cory Brazile, graduate students in history at Pitt, and Anna Tranfaglia helped incorporate this study into my courses. Bob Edelman, Dan Nathan, John Nauright, Dave Wiggins, and Gabby Yearwood—exceptional scholars of sport—and *New Yorker* writer Jonathan Blitzer were welcome comrades along the way. Jamie Miller, a young scholar of tremendous promise, made sure I didn't founder on the cultural shoals of Polynesian history. Stephen McGarvey is working to change Samoan epidemiology's trajectory. Stephen Paciga, Rory Szeto, and Jasper Wilson conducted research as part of Pitt's First Experiences in Research program.

I wanted this book to reach as wide an audience as possible and find an editor who would help me make it better. Marie Brown, a groundbreaking literary agent with infectious energy, did just that by placing it with Carl Bromley at The New Press. Carl understood what I wanted to do with this book and pushed me to realize its potential. He and Ben Woodward, his associate, edited the manuscript with dexterity, and its clarity owes much to their input. A special thanks goes to Eileen Chetti, who copyedited the manuscript, and Emily Albarillo, who guided it through production; they made my writing look better than it really is. My sister Linda's family, the Mittlemans, have made sport part of their lives and mine, and know why it matters.

My son, Alex, who grew up in the City of Champions, and his wife, Alison, made me keep it real. They're part of Pittsburgh's future, one that looks better all the time. So does Maggie Patterson, my partner in life and sidekick in Hawai'i. Somehow, life with her keeps getting sweeter.

Many who crafted this republic of play have passed on. But as Bob Marley said, "Good friends we have, oh, good friends we've lost, along the way. In this great future, you can't forget your past."

Rob Ruck
Meadow Run

Glossary

'afakasi: A person whose ancestry includes both Samoans and non-Samoans.

ahupua'a (Hawaiian): A wedge-shaped piece of land falling from the crest of the mountains to the reefs. Each *ahupua'a*, a political jurisdiction defined by its watershed, was a self-sustaining municipality, under the authority of chiefs, that provided native Hawaiians with a healthy, relatively secure life.

'aiga: The extended and fluid family unit that has long structured Samoan society. The *'aiga* owns its land collectively and was once the means of production and distribution in the village.

'aumaga: Village society of untitled men. Known as the strength of the village, the *'aumaga* serves the *matai*; historically, they fought and labored for the village; instead of fighting with other villages, they now engage in work, row, compete for their villages in rugby, and maintain *sa*.

'ava or *kava*: A mildly stimulating drink shared by those taking part in the highly ritualized *'ava* ceremony.

fa'afafine: A male who lives in the way of a female. *Fa'afafine* are an accepted part of Samoan society and regarded as a third gender.

fa'a lupega: A ceremonial address delivered by a high talking chief as a greeting to visitors from another village or *'aiga*.

fa'a lavelave: The practice of contributing money, labor, or goods when there is a death, wedding, celebration, or collective need in the *'aiga* or village.

fa'a Samoa: In the way of Samoa.

fale: The traditional dwelling. Poles hold up its thatched roof; mats could be lowered to ward off rain and mosquitos. Each village has a *fale* where the *fono*, a gathering of the chiefs, and *'ava* ceremonies are held.

fautasi: Longboats that Samoans modeled after nineteenth-century whalers to work the seas. For more than a century, teams of up to forty men have represented their villages in five-mile-long open-sea races, with honor and prizes as the stakes.

Fita Fita: Guard organized by the U.S. Navy in 1900 to police the island. Its ranks expanded during World War II, when many Samoans enlisted. It was disbanded after World War II. The tradition of military service, however, has continued ever since.

haole (Hawaiian): Island term for those not descended from native Hawaiians.

kirikiti or *kilikiti*: Samoan name for the sport adapted from the British game of cricket and played in the way of Samoa as a village game.

malaga: A traveling party or journey. A traditional visiting party, in which an *'aiga* paid respects to relatives in a distant village might have lasted for weeks, until the hosts' capacity to entertain their visitors was exhausted.

matai: Chiefs. There are talking chiefs, high talking chiefs, paramount chiefs, and the like, each selected by an *'aiga* to lead the family. *Matai* once assigned work and distributed the fruits of their labor afterward; they no longer play such a central economic role.

no fefe: No fear. When Samoans fight for the village, in the military, or for their team, it is often said that they do so with *no fefe*—no fear.

palagi: Foreigners. Samoans called the first Caucasians to arrive in their midst *palagi*, or cloud bursters, because it seemed as if they and their sailing vessels had exploded out of the sky.

pe'a: The traditional male tattoo, which goes from the waist to the knees. The *pe'a* is the work of a master tattooist, who uses a boar's tooth and mallet to ink the designs.

pu'uhonua (Hawaiian): A refuge under the protection of the priests where fugitives and villagers escaping the war could find sanctuary. La'ie was once a *pu'uhonua*.

sa: A period of devotion. *Sa* is observed twice a day, when village life stops for short intervals as people pray.

tatua: The notion of service to family, village, and church that animates *fa'a Samoa*, in the way of Samoa.

to'ona'i: The Sunday meal, cooked in an *umu* or oven made of rocks in the sand, features an array of foods, including taro, coconuts, bananas, seafood, chicken, and lamb.

tui Manu'a: The most prestigious matai title in the Manu'a Islands. The *tui* Manu'a traces its lineage to Tagaloa, the supreme deity who created the Samoan islands.

Notes

Introduction

1. For the sake of readability, I have dispensed with the macron, a diacritical mark (ˉ) placed above certain vowels in words like "Samoa" to indicate a long vowel or a stressed syllable.

2. It's often said that a Samoan is forty times more likely than a member of any other demographic group to make it to the NFL. A documentary about Tongans in Utah, *In Football We Trust* (directed by Tony Vainuku and co-directed by Erika Cohn, 2015), states that Polynesians are twenty-eight times more likely than any other ethnic group to make the NFL. About twenty Tongans join Samoans at NFL camps each July. These men did not learn football in Tonga; they were exposed to it after their parents came to the States, many at the urging of the Church of Jesus Christ of Latter-day Saints. They took to football quickly and learned how to play alongside Samoans at a handful of high schools. Their numbers will likely increase; Tom Reed, "How Cleveland Browns Are Cultivating a Polynesian Brotherhood Thousands of Miles from Home," July 22, 2015, Cleveland.com, www.cleveland.com/browns/index.ssf/2015/07/how_the_cleveland_browns_are_c.html.

3. Clark left Pittsburgh for Washington at season's end, played one more season, and retired. Polamalu retired in April 2015.

4. The territory's total population is about 75,000. That figure includes the 55,000 Samoans who live there as well as many who have migrated to the territory from independent Samoa and other countries.

5. Orwell wrote his oft-quoted essay, "The Sporting Spirit," for the *Tribune* in England in December 1945 after watching the Moscow Dynamo soccer team's tour of England create more animosity than goodwill between the United Kingdom and the USSR.

6. In 2009, *New York Times* journalist Alan Schwarz reported that an NFL-funded study of retired NFL players found that they were nineteen times more likely than other men between the ages of thirty and forty-nine to suffer from dementia and other neurological issues. Since

then, more and more evidence has confirmed the damage caused by concussive blows. A 2016 imaging study of youth football players between the ages of eight and thirteen showed changes associated with traumatic brain injury even though they had not exhibited concussion symptoms. When Boston University's CTE Center examined the brain tissue of sixty-two deceased former NFL players, it found that fifty-nine of them tested positive for chronic traumatic encephalopathy. Another study reported that 40 percent of the retired NFL players tested with advanced scanning technology showed signs of traumatic brain injury, a significantly higher rate than in the general population. The largest published study of CTE reported that 110 of 111 (99 percent) of the brains donated by families of former NFL players showed signs of neurodegenerative disease. It detailed CTE's effects, including depression, confusion, memory loss, acting impulsively and violently, and feelings of hopelessness and anxiety. Alan Schwarz, "Dementia Risk Seen in Players in N.F.L. Study," *New York Times*, September 29, 2009; James Hamblin, "Football Alters the Brains of Kids as Young as 8," *The Atlantic*, October 24, 2016, www.theatlantic.com/health/archive/2016/10/football-kids-heads/504863; "American Football Study Finds Evidence of Brain Injury in Living NFL Veterans," Reuters, April 11, 2016, www.telegraph.co.uk/american-football/2016/04/11/american-football-study-finds -evidence-of-brain-injury-in-living/; Lauren Ezell, "Timeline: The NFL's Concussion Crisis," PBS, October 8, 2013, www.pbs.org/wgbh/pages/frontline/sports/league-of-denial /timeline-the-nfls-concussion-crisis; "NFL Concussions Fast Facts," CNN Library, updated August 1, 2016, edition.cnn.com/2013/08/30/us/nfl-concussions-fast-facts/index.html; Rick Maese, "The Latest Brain Study Examined 111 Former NFL Players," WashingtonPost. com, July 25, 2017, www.washingtonpost.com/sports/the-latest-brain-study-examined-111 -former-nfl-players-only-one-didnt-have-cte/2017/25/07/25/835b49e4-70bc-11-8839 -ec48ec4cae25_story.html.

1: God's Sweetest Work

1. Sidney Colvin, ed., *Biographical Edition of the Works of Robert Louis Stevenson, Letters*, vol. 3 (New York: Charles Scribner's Sons, 1912); Stevenson wrote this in a letter sent from Honolulu, May 10, 1889, to Charles Baxter. This remark has often been changed to read "Samoans" instead of "Polynesians," but Stevenson wrote it before arriving in Samoa.

2. Robert Louis Stevenson, *A Footnote to History: Eight Years of Trouble in Samoa* (New York: Charles Scribner's Sons, 1897), pp. vii–5.

3. Roger Robinson, *Robert Louis Stevenson: His Best Pacific Writings* (Honolulu: Bess Press, 2003), pp. 32, 147.

4. Stevenson, *Footnote to History* (1897), p. 1.

5. H. J. Moors, *With Stevenson in Samoa* (London: Collins' Clear Type Press, n.d.), p. 6.

6. Ibid., pp. 11–13.

7. Ibid., pp. 14–15. Though many thought that Stevenson had consumption (tuberculosis), some medical experts argue that the length of time he lived with these symptoms and the fact that he did not transmit them to people with whom he had close contact suggest another diagnosis, that of hereditary hemorrhagic rupturing of blood vessels; Robinson, *Robert Louis Stevenson*, p. 63.

8. Frank McLynn, *Robert Louis Stevenson: A Biography* (London: Hutchinson, 1993), p. 380.

9. Another explanation for the name Vailima is that it means "water in the hand."

10. Robinson, *Robert Louis Stevenson*, pp. 110–11. It's possible that Stevenson had the bottles refilled in Sydney; New York City seltzer deliverymen rarely left the five boroughs.

11. George Turner, *Nineteen Years in Polynesia: Missionary Life, Travels, and Researches in the Islands of the Pacific* (Apia: J. Snow, 1861), quoted in Jocelyn Linnekin, "Ignoble Savages and Other European Visions: The La Perouse Affair in Samoan History," *Journal of Pacific History* 26, no. 1 (1991): 3; Felix Keesing, *Modern Samoa: Its Government and Changing Life* (Stanford, CA: Stanford University Press, 1934), p. 192.

12. Robert Louis Stevenson, *A Footnote to History: Eight Years of Trouble in Samoa*, with an introduction by Malama Meleisea (Honolulu: University of Hawai'i Press, 1996), p. vii.

13. McLynn, *Robert Louis Stevenson*, pp. 421–22.

14. William B. Churchward, *My Consulate in Samoa: A Record of Four Years' Sojourn in the Navigators Islands, with Personal Experiences of King Malietoa Laupepa, His Country, and His Men* (London: Richard Bentley and Son, 1887), p. 30.

15. Joseph Kennedy, *The Tropical Frontier: America's South Sea Colony* (Mangilao, Guam: Micronesian Area Research Center, University of Guam, 2009).

16. Robinson, *Robert Louis Stevenson*, p. 143.

17. As Samoan historian Malama Meleisea observed, power had long been decentralized, based on the ability of the *matai* to reach consensus. Though conflict often preceded consensus, the talking chiefs usually resolved squabbles over land, titles, and status. But attempts by foreigners and some *matai* to create a more centralized government inspired three decades of conflict in the years preceding Stevenson's arrival; Stevenson, *Footnote to History* (1996), p. xii.

18. Ibid., pp. 103–7.

19. Ibid., p. 118.

20. Ibid., chap. 10.

21. Ibid., pp. 128–29.

22. J. Robert Shaffer, *American Samoa: 100 Years Under the United States Flag* (Honolulu: Island Heritage Publishing, 2000), pp. 100–1.

23. Ibid., pp. 99–105. In the past, Tutuila had been used as a place to exile unwanted Samoans or those who had violated a *matai*'s expectations.

24. Village *matai* met in the *fono* (the village council). Some *matai* were *ali'i* (chiefs), others *tulafale* (talking chiefs). While the paramount chiefs administered family and village life, the high talking chiefs, who carried sennit whisks and staffs as symbols of their authority, spoke for them in village and ceremonial affairs. Beginning deliberations with a *kava* ('*ava*) ceremony, the talking chiefs led the *fono* toward decisions.

25. Stevenson, *Footnote to History* (1996), p. 64.

26. Malama Meleisea, *The Making of Modern Samoa: Traditional Authority and Colonial Administration in the History of Western Samoa* (Suva, Fiji: Institute of Pacific Studies of the University of the South Pacific, 1987), p. 3.

27. Lowell D. Holmes and Ellen Rhoads Holmes, *Samoan Village Then and Now* (Fort Worth, TX: Harcourt Brace Jovanovich, 1992), pp. 99–101; Irving Goldman, *Ancient Polynesian Society* (Chicago: University of Chicago Press, 1970), p. 262. Cultural change, Lowell and Ellen Holmes wrote, occurred the most in societies where the traditional system rewarded only a small number of people. Shaffer, *American Samoa*, pp. 121–22.

28. Frederick Harris Olsen, "The Navy and the White Man's Burden: Naval Administration of American Samoa" (PhD thesis, Washington University, 1976), pp. 144–46.

29. Ibid., p. 157.

30. Ibid., pp. 144–46, 151.

31. Olsen cites No. 1 of January 7, 1907, regulation No. 1-1907, file 3931:649 to 3931:660. Record Group 80. General Records of the Navy Department. Office of the Secretary. General Correspondence, 1897-1940, National Archives; p. 151.

32. Churchward, *My Consulate in Samoa*, p. 142; Andy Bull, "The Spin: Cricket in Samoa: It's Just Not Kilikiti," *The Guardian*, January 26, 2010, https://www.theguardian.com/sport /blog/2010/jan/26/the-spin-cricket-in-samoa.

33. *The Mercury* (Hobart, Tasmania), January 20, 1883, p. 2.

34. Churchward, *My Consulate in Samoa*, pp. 142–45.

35. Ibid., pp. 143–44.

36. Ibid., pp. 145–47. Churchward wrote that Samoans once tried to use cricket to pull off a general strike. Samoan leaders had written England, he related, seeking "British annexation, to put them out of their misery." In order to forestall German interference, "they determined to start a cricket match of such stupendous proportions that it would last until they got an answer" to their pleas from London. It was to no avail; England did not respond. The Germans, however, did and "forbade the King, under dire penalties, to play the game called 'cricket' at his seat of government."

37. The Germans, who dominated Western Samoa until World War I, evinced little interest in introducing sport—especially for the natives. They attempted to ban *kirikiti* and opposed anything that undercut production. Even recreation for German expats was an afterthought, confined to the Concordia club, to which most Germans in Apia and some "respectable settlers" of other nationalities belonged. The social club offered sickness and death benefits along with a circulating library and the chance to fraternize. Members enjoyed its bowling alley but never embraced the more purposeful sporting activities then animating Germany; Thomas Trood, *Island Reminiscences: A Graphic, Detailed Romance of a Life Spent in the South Sea Islands* (Sydney: McCarron, Stewart & Co., 1912), pp. 129–30.

38. Augustin Kramer, *The Samoa Islands: An Outline of a Monograph with Particular Consideration of German Samoa*, vol. 2 (Honolulu: University of Hawai'i Press, 1995), pp. 391–92.

39. W. T. Pritchard, *Polynesian Reminiscences: Or, Life in the South Pacific Islands* (London: Chapman and Hall, 1866), pp. 50–51.

40. Kramer, *Samoa Islands*, pp. 394–95; Napoleone A. Tuiteleleapaga, *Samoa Yesterday, Today and Tomorrow* (Great Neck, NY: Todd & Honeywell, 1980), pp. 132–33.

41. Churchward, *My Consulate in Samoa*, p. 148.

42. "Samoan Kilikiti (Cricket)," Museum of New Zealand, Wellington, New Zealand, https: //collections.tepapa.govt.nz/topic/2069.

43. McLynn, *Robert Louis Stevenson*, p. 404.

44. Stevenson, *Footnote to History* (1996), p. 6.

45. Shaffer, *American Samoa*, pp.145–46.

46. Keesing, *Modern Samoa*, pp. 314, 328, 342.

47. Ibid., p. 31.

48. Ibid., pp. 154–56, 185, 314, 328–42.

49. Robert Gibbings, *Over the Reefs* (London, J. M. Dent & Sons, 1948), pp. 77–81.

50. Keesing, *Modern Samoa*, p. 398.

51. A.S. Farebrother, "Fiji Victors by Six Nil," *Fiji Times and Herald* August 18, 1924; "Fiji Beat Western Samoa in First Test," *Samoa Times*, August 22, 1924.

52. Robinson, *Robert Louis Stevenson*, pp. 143–46.

53. Moors, *With Stevenson in Samoa*, pp. 31–32.

54. Robinson, *Robert Louis Stevenson*, pp. 143–46; Keesing, *Modern Samoa*, pp. 29–31.

55. Robinson, *Robert Louis Stevenson*, pp. 145–47; McLynn, *Robert Louis Stevenson*, p. 500.

56. Robinson, *Robert Louis Stevenson*, pp. 143–50.

57. Ibid., p. 317.

58. Ibid., pp. 10, 318.

2: The War and America Come to Samoa

1. Meade quoted in Peter Karsten, *The Naval Aristocracy* (New York: Free Press, 1972), p. 172.

2. Joseph Kennedy, *The Tropical Frontier: America's South Sea Colony* (Guam: Micronesian Area Research Center, University of Guam, 2009), pp. 55–56.

3. Ibid., p. 57.

4. Ibid., p. 67; J. Robert Shaffer, *American Samoa: 100 Years Under the United States Flag* (Honolulu: Island Heritage, 2000), p. 109.

5. Peter C. Stuart, *Planting the American Flag: Twelve Men Who Expanded the United States Overseas* (Jefferson, N. C., McFarland, 2007), pp. 89–98.

6. Shaffer, *American Samoa*, pp. 107–10; Kennedy, *Tropical Frontier*, p. 70.

7. Kennedy, *Tropical Frontier*, p. 66.

8. Quoted in Shaffer, *American Samoa*, pp. 117, 172.

9. Shaffer, *American Samoa*, p. 118.

10. Though the Germans provoked substantially more resentment in Western Samoa than the Americans did in American Samoa, they did a better job developing an economic infrastructure. Whenever Tilley or later governors asked for funds to build a dispensary, schools, library, or agricultural station, they were ignored or denied. The only Navy activity that extended beyond Fagatogo was road building. Drafted to work as unpaid laborers, Samoans found road-work especially onerous. Not only did the United States fail to deliver the largesse that Samoans anticipated, but Washington had not bothered to sign the Deed of Cession. This slight was finally addressed when President Theodore Roosevelt's 1904 letter acknowledging recognition of the cession was read to the *matai* who had signed the Deed of Cession and they were presented with a medal and a silver watch; Frederick Harris Olsen, "The Navy and the White Man's Burden: Naval Administration of American Samoa" (PhD thesis, Washington University, 1976), p. 154.

11. Shaffer, *American Samoa*, pp. 110–11; Kennedy, *Tropical Frontier*, pp. 134–35.

12. Jack C. Hudson and Kay G. Hudson, "American Samoa in World War II," Final Draft prepared for American Samoa Government Department of Parks and Recreation, June 15, 1994, Seabrook, TX, pp. 8–10, 22; Shaffer, *American Samoa*, pp. 168–70.

13. Lieutenant Commander John Burke, USNA, *The U.S. Naval History of Tutuila, American Samoa* (Pago Pago, American Samoa: Headquarters, South Pacific Area and Force, 1945), p. 27.

14. Hudson and Hudson, "American Samoa in World War II," p. 18; Shaffer, *American Samoa*, p. 171.

15. Olsen, "The Navy and the White Man's Burden," pp. 168–72.

16. Ibid., p. 175; Hudson and Hudson, "American Samoa in World War II," p. 18.

17. Shaffer, *American Samoa*, pp. 172–73; Kennedy, *Tropical Frontier*, p. 207.

18. Quoted in Kennedy, *Tropical Frontier*, pp. 207–8. They were the first American Expeditionary Forces to embark after Congress voted to declare war.

19. Captain J. A. C. Gray, *Amerika Samoa: A History of American Samoa and Its United States Naval Administration* (Annapolis, MD: U.S. Naval Institute, 1960), p. 241; Shaffer, *American Samoa*, pp.171–72.

20. Shaffer, *American Samoa*, pp. 174–75.

21. Other U.S. troops landed in Western Samoa after New Zealand authorized U.S. military control there. The already porous boundaries between Western Samoa and American Samoa became even less consequential, and Samoans traveled back and forth between villages and 'aigas in the two territories.

22. Hudson and Hudson, "American Samoa in World War II," pp. 3–4.

23. "The Samoan Creation Legend," National Park of American Samoa, National Park Service, February 28, 2015, https://www.nps.gov/npsa/learn/historyculture/legendpo.htm.

24. Terry Hunt and Patrick Kirch, *An Archeological Reconnaissance of the Manu'a Islands, American Samoa Final Report*, prepared for Coastal Zone Management Office and American Samoa Government, Seattle, August 1987, pp. 7–9.

25. Shaffer, *American Samoa*, pp. 110–11; Kennedy, *Tropical Frontier*, pp. 70–71. Tilley confronted the limits of U.S. power when his own men were unable to take him ashore. He needed a Manu'an longboat steered by a high chief to pass through the deadly reefs protecting Ta'u.

26. Burke, *U.S. Naval History of Tutuila*, pp. 133, 147.

27. John Enright, "A Closer Look at Tutuila in WWII, It Begins," part 9 in *The Past Surrounds Us: Historic Preservation in American Samoa*, by John Enright and the Staff of the American Samoa Historic Preservation Office, 1997, ashpo.com/index.php?option=com_content&view=article&id=57&Itemid=59.

28. Margaret Mead, *Coming of Age in Samoa* (New York: Blue Ribbon Books, 1928), p. 35.

29. Jim Wexler, *SteelCity Insider.net*, "Bolt from the Blue," November 19, 2011.

30. Mead, *Coming of Age in Samoa*, p. 77. After Pearl Harbor, the Polamalus kept working the land and fishing the seas, as they had for generations. The men knew how to pass safely through the treacherous reefs fringing Ta'u and catch bonito; the women were skilled weavers, fashioning fine mats for decoration and gifts as well as more utilitarian ends. Men planted taro and climbed palm trees, dug *umu* ovens in the sand where meals are prepared, and played rugby and *kirikiti* for the teams representing their village. Their identities were tied more to their 'aiga and village than they were to a larger notion of American Samoa.

31. Toeutu Faaleava, "*Fitafita*: Samoan Landsmen, in the United States Navy, 1900–1951" (PhD diss., University of California, Berkeley, 2003), pp. 161–63, n78.

32. Kennedy, *Tropical Frontier*, p. 216.

33. Ibid., p. 198.

34. Olsen, "The Navy and the White Man's Burden," p. 176; Hudson and Hudson, "American Samoa in World War II," p. 14.

35. Hudson and Hudson, "American Samoa in World War II," pp. 10–22: Faaleava, "*Fitafita*," p. 179.

36. Faaleava, "*Fitafita*," pp. 174–75; Olsen, "The Navy and the White Man's Burden," pp. 179–80.

37. During his senior year at Notre Dame, Manti Te'o was enveloped by a media frenzy when it turned out that his supposed girlfriend, a Stanford University student named Lennay Kekua, with whom he had talked and texted but whom he never met, and whom he thought had died

tragically at the beginning of the season, did not exist. He had been hoaxed by Ronaiah Tuia-sosopo, a member of the Tuiasosopo football family. Perhaps the best explanation I've heard for how this could happen came from Jesse Markham. Markham, who wrote a groundbreaking thesis on the geography of Samoan football, has worked with the AIGA Foundation and other groups seeking to advance Polynesian youth's best interests in play football. He pointed out that Te'o had led a very sheltered life as a result of growing up a member of the Mormon Church in La'ie in Hawai'i. Furthermore, from an early age, Te'o's life had been consumed by training and football. His naïveté might be understood in this context.

38. *The Sporting Life* 68, no. 12 (1916).

39. Faaleava, *"Fitafita,"* p. 178.

40. Quoted in Kennedy, *Tropical Frontier*, p. 208.

41. Hudson and Hudson, "American Samoa in World War II," pp. 16–22.

42. Kennedy, *Tropical Frontier*, pp. 208–15; Hudson and Hudson, "American Samoa in World War II," p. 22.

43. Olsen, "The Navy and the White Man's Burden," p. 176.

44. Others were recruited into the service mostly because they could swing a bat. Burke, *U.S. Naval History of Tutuila*, pp. 216, 239, 242.

45. Kennedy, *Tropical Frontier*, p. 206; Shaffer, *American Samoa*, pp. 120, 137.

46. Hudson and Hudson, "American Samoa in World War II," pp. 31–33.

47. Burke, *U.S. Naval History of Tutuila*, p. 131.

48. Olsen, "The Navy and the White Man's Burden," pp. 176, 179–80.

49. Ibid., pp. 176–78.

50. Kennedy, *Tropical Frontier*, p. 209. In neighboring Western Samoa, where fewer U.S. soldiers were stationed, a 1945 census estimated that U.S. servicemen fathered sixteen hundred children. John Enright and the Staff of the American Samoa Historic Preservation Office, "A Closer Look at Tutuila in WWII, the Impact," part 10 in *The Past Surrounds Us: Historic Preservation in American Samoa*, 1997, ashpo.com/index.php?option=com_content&view=article &id=57&Itemid=59, accessed.

51. Hudson and Hudson, "American Samoa in World War II," p. 176.

52. Burke, *U.S. Naval History of Tutuila*, pp. 88–89.

53. Faaleava, *"Fitafita,"* pp. 174–75.

54. Olsen, "The Navy and the White Man's Burden," p. 179.

55. Hudson and Hudson, "American Samoa in World War II," pp. 12–30.

56. Jesse Markham, "An Evolving Geography of Sport: The Recruitment and Mobility of Samoan Football Players 1998–2006" (MA thesis, University of Hawai'i, 2008), p. 99.

57. "Tuiasosopo: High Chief of American Samoa," Football Zealot, September 14, 2010, footballzealot.com/2010/09/14tuiasosopo-high-chief-of-american-samoa.

58. Shaffer, *American Samoa*, pp. 184–87.

59. Gordon R. Lewthwaite, Cristiane Mainzer, and Patrick J. Holland, "From Polynesia to California: Samoan Migration and Its Sequel," *Journal of Pacific History* 8 (1973): 133–57. In his 1953 annual report, the territory's governor wrote that it was "impossible for the majority of Samoans to maintain the standard of living to which they had become accustomed."

60. Lewthwaite, Mainzer, and Holland, "From Polynesia to California"; Kennedy, *Tropical Frontier*, p. 198.

61. Bernard F. Pierce, "Acculturation of Samoans in the Mormon Village of La'ie, Territory of Hawaii" (MA thesis, University of Hawai'i, June 1956), pp. 20–33.

62. Sanele Tuiteleleapaga, interview with the author, Tutuila, American Samoa, August 2011. Tuiteleleapaga was then deputy director of Samoan Affairs.; Kennedy, *Tropical Frontier*, p. 223; Unasa L. F. Va'a, "Searching for the Good Life: Samoan International Migration" (paper presented at Anthropology Colloquium, Department of Anthropology, University of Hawai'i, Manoa, January 27, 2004).

63. Unasa L. F. Va'a, "Samoan Migrants in Australia" (Institute of Pacific Studies, Univerity of the South Pacific, Suva, and *National University of Samoa, Apia*), p. 59.

64. *Annual Report of the Governor of American Samoa* (Washington, D.C.: USGPO, 1953).

65. Lewthwaite, Mainzer, and Holland, "From Polynesia to California."

66. Governor Lolo Moliga, interview with the author, Tutuila, American Samoa, July 9, 2013.

67. Ibid. A study Don Vargo from the American Samoa Community College prepared, "Prevalence of Overweight in American Samoan Schoolchildren (2007/2008 School Year)" (Department of Health, Department of Education, June 2008), confirms that those on the Manu'a Islands were slimmer overall.

68. Aoata Polamalu, interview with the author, Pottstown, PA, June 2, 2014.

69. Talalupe Pola, telephone interview with the author, June 8, 2014. Some of the Polamalus have used Pola, the shortened version of their name, as their surname.

70. Mead, *Coming of Age in Samoa*, p. 71.

71. *'Ava* (or *kava*) is a mild stimulant prepared by young men and women in a ceremonial fashion. Upon completion, it is offered to visitors and *matai*.

72. Toeolesulusulu Damon Salesa, "An American on the Beach," *Common-Place* 5, no. 2 (January 2005), www.common-place.org; "Oriental and Occidental Northern and Southern Portrait Types of the Midway Plaisance," N. D. Thompson Publishing Co., St. Louis, 1894.

73. *Official Guide New York World's Fair*, www.nywf64.com/polyne01.shtml.

74. Mead, *Coming of Age in Samoa*, p. 42.

75. His son, Maika, enrolled at the Naval Academy to play for Ken Niumatalolo.

76. Kennedy Polamalu, interview with the author, San Bernadino, CA, August 15, 2014.

77. The Seattle Seahawks selected Lofu Tatupu in the second round of the NFL draft in 2005.

78. Mead, *Coming of Age in Samoa*, p. 58.

3: Hawai'i: The North Shore

1. Mike Foley, "City Council Names Ramos a Living Treasure," *Kaleo*, February 26, 1998, nanilaie.info/?p=1163.

2. Angel Ramos, interview with the author, Kahuku, HI, July 13, 2013.

3. The HSPA quoted in Ronald Takaki, *Pau Hana: Plantation Life and Labor in Hawaii, 1835–1920* (Honolulu: University of Hawai'i Press, 1983), pp. 102–4.

4. Montague Lord, "Report of Investigation into Conditions on the Plantations," July 21, 1916, Grove Farm Plantation Records, quoted in Takaki, *Pau Hana*, pp. 103–4.

5. Takaki, *Pau Hana*, pp. 20–21.

6. MSSH 558, box 15, Kahuku Plantation Collection Athletics Records 1934-2939, Joseph F. Smith Library Archives and Special Collections, Brigham Young-Hawai'i Archives.

7. Takaki, *Pau Hana*, pp. 149–75.

8. Letter from Joe Katsunuma, Athletic Director of Kahuku Plantation, March 23, 1938, MSSH 558, box 15 Kahuku Plantation Collection Athletics Records 1934–2939, Joseph F. Smith Library Archives and Special Collections, Brigham Young-Hawai'i University Archives.

9. Junior Ah You, interview with the author, Kahuku, HI, November 17, 2014.

10. Don Johnson and Ronald Oba, *The Ol' Man: Father Kenneth A. Bray* (Honolulu: 'Iolani Boosters Club, 1994), p. 44.

11. Arlene Lum, ed., *At Thy Call We Gather: 'Iolani School* (Honolulu: 'Iolani School, 1997), pp. 48–49, 106.

12. Ibid.

13. Nick Abramo, "Lombardi of Kahuku Started Dynasty," *Honolulu Star-Bulletin*, September 21, 2003, archives.starbulletin.com/2003/09/21/sports/index7.html.

14. Hugh Yoshida, interviews with the author, Honolulu, July 16, 2013, November 3, 2014.

15. Larry Ginoza, interview with the author, Wai'nae, HI, November 16, 2003.

16. After playing for Harold Silva, Leo Reed enrolled at Colorado State University and then spent time with the Houston Oilers, Denver Broncos, and Toronto Argonauts. Returning to Honolulu after retiring from football, Reed became a policeman, then a teacher, and finally a union representative for the Teamsters in Hollywood. During the 1960s, Reed and Ray Schoenke were the only two Samoans playing professionally. Schoenke played at Punahou but finished his high school career in Texas after the Air Force reassigned his father. He went to Southern Methodist University, where he majored in history and won Academic All-American honors. Both the NFL's Dallas Cowboys and the AFL's Oakland Raiders drafted Schoenke in 1963. Signing with Dallas, he played two years there and then a decade with the Washington Redskins. Players in those days needed a job in the off-season, and Schoenke parlayed his into a successful business. Along the way, he gravitated to politics, organizing Athletes for McGovern in 1972 and later backing another Punahou student, Barack Obama.

17. Nick Abramo, "'Lombardi of Kahuku' Started a Dynasty," *Honolulu Star-Bulletin*, September 21, 2003; Stacy Kaneshiro, "Harold Silva, Former 'Iolani, Kahuku Coach," *Honolulu Advertiser*, September 16, 2003, the.honoluluadvertiser.com/article/2003/Sep/16/sp/sp11a.html.

18. Richard Johnston, "Shake 'Em Out of the Coconut Trees," *Sports Illustrated*, August 16, 1976, www.si.com/vault/1976/08/16/613329/shake-em-out-of-the-coconut-trees.

19. Cynthia D. Woolley Compton, "The Making of the *Ahupua'a* of La'ie into a Gathering Place and Plantation: The Creation of an Alternative Space to Capitalism" (PhD thesis, Brigham Young University, 2006), pp. 22, 43, 82.

20. Takaki, *Pau Hana*, pp. 17–21.

21. Compton, "Making of the *Ahupua'a*," pp. 22, 43, 82.

22. Other plantations averaged but 3 percent native workers.

23. Compton, "Making of the *Ahupua'a*," pp. 112–13.

24. Bernard F. Pierce, "Acculturation of Samoans in the Mormon Village of La'ie, Territory of Hawai'i" (MA thesis, University of Hawai'i, 1955), pp. 19–20, 188–200.

25. Ibid., pp. 14–22, 37–40. Samoans supplemented subsistence farming and fishing by working for the church and hawking leis, cowry necklaces, and mats fashioned from pandanus leaves to visitors interested in the temple and indigenous culture. They also worked the *hukilau*, after the church turned the traditional style of fishing into entertainment. In a *hukilau*, after men dropped a long net affixed with leaves into the sea from a canoe, villagers pulled it in to shore and

shared the catch. At LDS *hukilaus*, tourists paid to pull the nets in, then enjoyed food and music afterward on the beach.

26. Compton, "Making of the *Ahupua'a*," pp. 215, 273.

27. Max Stanton, "Samoan Saints: Samoans in the Mormon Village of La'ie, Hawai'i" (PhD thesis, University of Oregon, 1973), pp. 75–79; Junior Ah You, interview with the author, Kahuku, HI, November 17, 2014.

28. Vai Sikahema, "Vai's View: BYU-Hawaii, Prep Football Powerhouses and a Living Legend," *Deseret News*, August 26, 2011, www.deseretnews.com/article/700173908/Vais-View -BYU-Hawaii-prep-football-powerhouses-and-a-living-legend.html?pg=all.

29. *Honolulu Advertiser*, Editorial, November 18, 1965; *Honolulu Advertiser*, Editorial, December 1, 1965.

30. Alice Anae, interview with the author, La'ie, HI, November 12, 2014.

31. Allen Anae, interview with the author, Honolulu, November 19, 2014.

32. Alice Anae interview.

33. Vai Sikahema, "The Robert Anae You May Not Know," *Deseret News*, January 7, 2011, tucson.com/sports/blogs/finley/the-robert-anae-you-may-not-know/article_46645a60 -1ab7-11e0-8ba2-001cc4c002e0.html.

34. Johnston, "Shake 'Em Out."

35. Ibid.

36. When Famika's grandson and namesake knocked on a door in Corpus Christi, Texas, on his mission, the man who opened it looked at the name tag on the six-foot-six, 312-pound young man and asked, "Do you know Famika Anae?" When Famika explained the connection, the man said, "He coached me at Compton Community College, and to this day I consider him the greatest mentor and teacher I ever had." Famika Jr. knew what he meant. His grandfather's approach to sport had been passed down via his father, Robert. "My father is a very hard worker in everything he's done his whole life," Famika Jr. said. "He's been a great mentor. . . . We've been taught in a very strict way and a hands-on way of doing things. Anything short of that was not acceptable." Dick Harmon, "BYU Football: Famika Anae Finally Got His Chance to Live Up to Legacy," *Deseret News*, October 3, 2012, www.deseretnews .com/article/765608951/BYU-football-Famika-Anae-finally-got-his-chance-to-live-up-to -legacy.html?pg=all.

37. Robert Anae also made his mark in coaching and eventually returned to coach at BYU.

38. Rod Ohira, "Kahuku OIA'S Champions," *Honolulu Star-Bulletin*, November 23, 1972, sec. E, p. 1; Andrew Mitsukado, "4th Quarter Rally Does in Leilehua," *Honolulu Advertiser*, November 23, 1972, Sports sec., p. 1.

39. Allen Anae interview.

40. Dennis Anderson, "1972 Thriller a Classic," *Honolulu Advertiser*, August 12, 2007, the.honoluluadvertiser.com/article/2007/Aug/12/sp/hawaii708120365.html. Salanoa later coached at the school, where three of his sons were on championship teams. Finai, like Anae, played at BYU and then spent three seasons in the pros before turning to prizefighting.

41. Pauline Masaniai, interview with the author, Kahuku, HI, November 13, 2014. Masaniai attended Kahuku as a student and returned as the school's principal.

4: Al Lolotai, Charlie Ane, and Bob Apisa

1. Al Costello, "Walton Given Coaching Job with 'Skins," *Washington Post*, November 6, 1945.

2. Al Costello, "Eagles Upset by Redskins," *Washington Post*, October 22, 1945. Costello frequently described Lolotai as a Hawaiian-born Samoan instead of a Samoan-born Hawaiian but at least corrected his earlier references to his name as Jim Lolotai.

3. Al Costello, "Headwork by Baugh, Moore Clinched Eagle Game for Skins," *Washington Post*, October 23, 1945; Al Costello, "$902 Loser's Share Only Bright Item," *Washington Post*, December 18, 1945.

4. Uniform Player's Contract, National Football League, signed February 2, 1945, 'Iolani School Archives.

5. Hokulani Aikau, *Chosen People, a Promised Land: Mormonism and Race in Hawai'i*, First Peoples: New Directions in Indigenous Studies (Minneapolis: University of Minnesota Press, 2012), pp. 83–84.

6. Don Johnson and Ronald Oba, *The Ol' Man: Father Kenneth A. Bray* (Honolulu: 'Iolani Raiders Booster Club, 1994), pp. 71, 187–88.

7. Allen Anae, interview with the author, Honolulu, November 19, 2014.

8. Al Warren, "The Sport Highway," *Ogden Standard-Examiner*, June 6, 1945.

9. *'Iolani School Bulletin*, Fall 1988, p. 19; "Multi-racial Hawaii Is Without Problem," *Los Angeles Times*, December 10, 1965.

10. Charlie Ane's parents were from the villages of Malaeimi and Aloau; Don Cisco, *Hawaii Sports: History, Facts and Statistics* (Honolulu: University of Hawai'i Press, 1999), p. 10.

11. Ben Kneubuhl Jr., telephone interview with the author, September 26, 2012.

12. J. Robert Shaffer, *American Samoa: 100 Years Under the United States Flag* (Honolulu: Island Heritage, 2000), pp. 163–65.

13. Other expatriates who had settled on Tutuila and *'afakasi* (those of mixed racial backgrounds) lived nearby. The Reids, who had connections to New Zealand; the Hallecks, whose German-born patriarch, Max, ran bush stores; and the Scanlons, another *'afakasi* family that developed successful businesses, were the core of the island's commercial class at a time when most Samoans remained part of a subsistence economy.

14. Ben Kneubuhl Jr., telephone interviews with the author, September 26, October 8, and October 9, 2012; John Clark, "Ben Kneubuhl '36," *Punahou Bulletin*, Spring 2008, www.punahou.edu/bulletin/detail/index.aspx?LinkId=1255&Issue=8843f64f-6542-4947-985b-a1b1013ecc72.

15. Kneubuhl Jr. interview, September 26, 2012.

16. Craig Kojima, "Buffanblu Football Runs in Family," *Honolulu Star-Bulletin*, August 3, 1999, starbulletin.com. http://archives.starbulletin.com/1999/08/03/news/story3.html.

17. Jeane Hoffman, "All American in Household," *Los Angeles Times*, October 31, 1952.

18. Ibid.

19. Rob Ruck, Maggie Jones Patterson, and Michael P. Weber, *Rooney: A Sporting Life* (Lincoln: University of Nebraska Press, 2010), p. 310.

20. *Los Angeles Times*, March 29, 1960.

21. "Inflation Calculator," DollarTimes, www.dollartimes.com/inflation/inflation.php?amount=1&year=1960.

22. "Neal Blaisdell Ane," October 21, 2012, *Honolulu Star-Advertiser*, obits.staradvertiser.com/2012/10/21/neal-blaisdell-ane.

23. Ferd Lewis, "Charles Ane, Longtime Coach, Football Legend," *Honolulu Advertiser*, May 11, 2007.

24. Bob Apisa, interview with the author, Granada Hills, CA, August 16, 2014.

25. Ibid.

26. Ibid.

27. Tom Shanahan, *Raye of Light* (Middleton, WI: August Publications, 2014), locations 2801/2801.

28. Robert Bao, "MSU Was a Catalyst for Social Change," *Michigan State University Alumni Magazine*, May 6, 2013, http://alumni.msu.edu/stay-informed/story.cfm?id=515.

29. Shanahan, *Raye of Light*, locations 411/412.

30. Ibid., locations 134–142/4922.

31. William D. Murray, "Duffy Daughterty Took Black Athletes from South to Fame at Michigan State," *Los Angeles Times*, December 14, 1986.

32. Apisa interview.

33. Ma'osi Tuipala Tuitele, "Ia outou Fealofani!" *Tafananai: Se leai ua luva o le a Koso le Pa!* March 1, 2009, 1samoana.com/tafananai/2009/03/01/ia-outou-fealofani-a-short-story.

34. Earl Gutskey, "Roots '66: Former UCLA Defensive Back Bob Stiles and Former Michigan State Fullback Bob Apisa Are Friends Forever Linked by the Key Play in the 1966 Rose Bowl," *Los Angeles Times*, December 28, 2000, articles.latimes.com/2000/dec/28/sports/sp-5575; Shanahan, *Raye of Light*, location 2808.

35. Ibid., location 2850/4922.

36. *Chicago Tribune*, November 17, 1966; *Watertown Daily News*, November 17, 1966.

37. Michael Weinreb, "Remembering Bubba Smith," *The Triangle*, August 4, 2011, grantland.com/the-triangle/remembering-bubba-smith; Johnette Howard, "Bubba Smith's Career: From Big Smash to Big Cash," *Orlando Sentinel*, August 20, 1985, articles.orlandosentinel.com/1985-08-20/sports/0320250299_1_bubba-smith-defensive-lineman-football.

38. Notre Dame tied the score early in the fourth quarter; when it regained possession with 1:10 left to play, coach Ara Parseghian elected to run out the clock. He earned the opprobrium of fans who wanted to see him play for the win, and *Sports Illustrated*'s Dan Jenkins mocked him for his decision to "tie one for the Gipper."

39. *Honolulu Star-Bulletin*, November 19, 1966.

40. *Honolulu Advertiser*, November 17, 1966; *Honolulu Star-Bulletin*, November 19, 1996.

41. *Honolulu Star-Bulletin*, November 19, 1996.

42. Apisa interview.

43. Ibid.

44. Shanahan, *Raye of Light*, locations 2703/4922 and 2733/4922.

5: American Samoa in the 1960s

1. Clarence W. Hall, "America's Shame in the South Seas," *Reader's Digest*, July 1, 1961.

2. Richard MacMillan, *Honolulu Advertiser*, August 6, 1953.

3. Richard Barrett Lowe, *Problems in Paradise: The View from Government House* (New York: Pageant Press, 1967), pp. 8, 73.

4. Hall, "America's Shame in the South Seas."

5. Clarence W. Hall, "Samoa: America's Showplace of the South Seas," *Reader's Digest*, November 1965.

6. Li'a Amisone, interview with the author, Utulei, American Samoa, August 8, 2011; Sikuini Seevaetasi, interview with the author, Ottoville, American Samoa, August 8, 2011.

7. Sanele Tuiteleleapaga, interview with the author, Tutuila, American Samoa, August 1, 2011.

8. *Annual Report of the Governor of American Samoa 1967* (Washington, D.C.: USGPO), p. xi

9. *Annual Report of the Governor of American Samoa 1979* (Washington, D.C.: USGPO), pp. vii–5, 45, 59. There were, and continue to be, a few religiously affiliated schools and private academies, including two—Marist and Kanana Fou—that field football teams.

10. Wilbur Schramm, Lyle M. Nelson, and Mere T. Betham, *Bold Experiment: The Story of Educational Television in American Samoa* (Stanford, CA: Stanford University Press, 1981), pp. vii, 2–4, 45, 108, 149, 155.

11. George Remington, *Honolulu Advertiser*, August 25, 1957.

12. Mort Rosenblum, *Honolulu Star-Bulletin*, June 7, 1973.

13. Judge Satele Lili'o Ali'ita'i, interview with the author, Fagasa, American Samoa, August 10, 2012; Evelyn Lili'o, interview with the author, Tafuna, American Samoa, August 10, 2012.

14. *Daily Bulletin Office of Samoan Information*, November 1, 1966. Archives, Feleti Barstow Public Library, Pago Pago, American Samoa.

15. Mort Rosenblum, *Honolulu Star-Bulletin*, June 7, 1973.

16. *Annual Report of the Governor of American Samoa 1956* (Washington, D.C.: USGPO, 1956.), pp. 23–24, 54; in 1954, the governor reported, recruiters plucked forty-eight "of our best young men" from the 192 who completed their education that year. He lamented that "with the cream of male leadership thus removed, the progress of instruction for the remaining" became problematic.

17. The honorific "Tufele" had been bestowed upon him by the village of Fitiuta when he became its *matai*.

18. Tufele Li'amatua, interview with the author, Tutuila, American Samoa, August 1, 2011.

19. Augustin Kramer, *The Samoan Islands*, vol. 1, trans. Theodore Verhaaren (Auckland, New Zealand: Pasitika Press, 1984), pp. 384–88.

20. Sanele Tuiteleleapaga, interview with the author, Utulei, American Samoa, August 1, 2011.

21. Eneliko R. Sofa'i, *The History of Education in American Samoa to 1984*, EdD thesis, Brigham Young University, 1984, p. 50.

22. Susan Hawkes, "Football in Samoa: The BYH Connection," Brigham Young Academy & Brigham Young University High School, http://www.byhigh.org/History/SportsHistory/SamoanFootball.html.

23. Tusipasi Suiaunoa, interview with the author, Fagasa, American Samoa, August 11, 2011.

24. Mel Purcell, interview with the author, Ottoville, American Samoa, July 30, 2011.

25. Governor Togiola Tulafono, interview with the author, Utulei, American Samoa, August 13, 2012.

26. Sikuini Seevaetasi, interview with the author, Ottoville, American Samoa, August 8, 2011.

27. Riki Reinhart, correspondence with the author, August 8 and October 1, 3, and 11, 2011.

28. Peta Anoai, interview with the author, Alega Beach, American Samoa, August 6, 2011.

29. Gabe Sewell, interview with the author, Ottoville, American Samoa, July 31, 2011.

30. Lewis Wolman, interview with the author, Alega Beach, American Samoa, July 28, 2012.

31. Rob Shaffer, telephone interview with author, June 28, 2012.

32. Governor Togiola Tulafono, interview with the author, Utulei, American Samoa, August 13, 2012.

33. Pati Pati, interview with the author, Leone, American Samoa, August 2, 2011.

34. Sikuini Seevaetasi, interview with the author, Ottoville, American Samoa, August 8, 2011.

35. Simon Mageo, interview with the author, Utulei, American Samoa, July 31, 2011.

6: Jesse Sapolu, Dick Tomey, and *Fa'a Samoa*

1. Jesse Sapolu, *I Gave My Heart to San Francisco* (Newport Beach, CA: Celebrity Publishing, 2012), p. 24.

2. Jesse Sapolu, interview with the author, Ottoville, American Samoa, July 5, 2013.

3. Jesse Sapolu, "Jesse Sapolu: 4-Time Super Bowl Champ Reflects on How Samoan Culture Shaped His Career," *The Post Game*, December 7, 2012, http://www.thepostgame.com/blog/men-action/201212/jesse-sapolu-san-francisco-49ers-heart-samoa-hawaii-nfl.

4. Robert Franco, *Samoans in Hawai'i: A Demographic Portrait* (Honolulu: East-West Population Institute, East-West Center, 1987), pp. 6–8.

5. Kevin Lynch, "Former 49ers Jesse Sapolu Reveals His Secret Ordeal," San Francisco 49ers, *Niner Inside Blog*, SFGate.com, posted August 4, 2012.

6. Sapolu, *I Gave My Heart*, pp. 12–23.

7. Don Cisco, *Hawai'i Sports: History, Facts, and Statistics* (Honolulu: University of Hawai'i Press, 1999), pp. 32, 90–98.

8. Joel Franks, *Crossing Sidelines, Crossing Cultures* (Lanham, MD: University Press of America, 2000), pp. 86–88. He also played for the Hawaiian Warriors in the Pacific Coast Football League; it was a novel, community-owned team supported by backers who owned $10 shares.

9. In 1952, Don Coryell got his first head coaching position at the school. He was an innovator who anticipated the future of pass-oriented offenses. Cisco, *Hawai'i Sports*, p. 133.

10. The Turkey Day game was the most anticipated and significant sporting event of the year, with crowds of 25,000. The Interscholastic League of Honolulu championship, it featured the two best teams at season's end. In 1965, Kamehameha met Farrington. Few gave the Farrington Governors, who had won their only title with Yonamine in 1944, a chance against their private school foes. Kamehameha had already beaten them 25–6 during the regular season. Public schools rarely triumphed, while Kamehameha had won eight titles. The *Honolulu Star-Bulletin*'s Jim Becker, however, figured he would cover the underdogs and profiled the Kalihi kids. For Becker, it was the story of boys from a part of town so tough that thieves one day stripped every car in the school faculty parking lot but the one belonging to Coach Tom Kiyosaki, the husky World War II veteran with two Purple Hearts. Unlike well-heeled Kamehameha, Farrington High could do little for its team. They rode to games in a twenty-year-old bus driven by a garbage collector on his days off. Kiyosaki, worried about crank calls and gamblers bothering his players the night before the game if they stayed with their families in the Kalihi projects, signed an IOU and put them up at the Coco Palms hotel on Waikiki. He signed another to cover the tab for a meal at a restaurant before the game. Most of his boys had never been to a restaurant, much less a hotel, and several took their dinner plates into the kitchen and offered to wash them. Though Kamehameha scored first, Farrington came back to win in a game still celebrated.

11. "Jesse Sapolu Kalihi Disciples Football Teams," YouTube video, 0:57, posted by Lisa Sapolu, May 7, 2014, www.youtube.com/watch?v=w7jAjnGKJzA.

12. Sapolu, *I Gave My Heart*, pp. 71–72.

13. Dick Tomey, interviews with the author, Honolulu, August 15, 2012, and July 14, 2013.

14. Jesse Markham, "An Evolving Geography of Sport: The Recruitment and Mobility of Samoan College Football Players 1998–2006" (MA thesis, University of Hawai'i, 2008), p. 65.

15. Jesse Sapolu, "Post Game," *Samoa News*, December 4, 2012.

16. Nick Abramo, "A Football Family That Keeps Giving," *Honolulu Star-Bulletin*, April 7, 2002, archives.starbulletin.com/2002/02/07/sports/index4.html.

17. Wes Nakama, "Noga Brothers Put a Hurting on the Opposition," *Honolulu Advertiser*, July 26, 2009, the.honoluluadvertiser.com/article/2009/Jul/26/sp/hawaii907260376.html.

18. Rich Miano, interview with the author, Honolulu, July 15, 2013.

19. Abramo, "Football Family That Keeps Giving."

20. The two youngest brothers also played at Farrington, and one of them continued with football at a junior college, but did not join their older siblings in the pros.

21. Gerald Eskenazi, "An Australian in the N.F.L.," *New York Times*, October 23, 1987; "Colin Scotts—a Chat with a Giant," Scotty Cam, May 9, 2013, www.scottycam.com.au/blog/colin-scotts-a-chat-with-a-giant/; Phil Elderkin, "Scotts Is Australia's Gift to the NFL; Saints in First-Ever Title Bid," *Christian Science Monitor*, November 25, 1987, www.csmonitor.com/1987/1125/pcolin.html.

22. "Feature on Rich Milano, Centurians #28," UH Warrior Quotes: Quotes About the University of Hawaii Football Team, July 3, 2009, warriorquotes.wordpress.com/2009/07/03/feature-on-rich; Cal Lee, interviews with the author, July 17, 2013 and November 19, 2014, Honolulu.

23. Simon Mageo, interview with the author, Utelei, American Samoa, August 8, 2012.

24. Stephen Tsai, "American Samoa Becomes Focus for Recruiting," *Honolulu Advertiser*, December 17, 2002, the.honoluluadvertiser.com/article/2002/Dec/17/sp/sp06a.html.

25. Sapolu, *I Gave My Heart*, pp. 23, 71–72.

7: *Fa'a Kalifonia*: Oceanside, California

1. Junior Paopao and Anthony Paopao, interviews with the author, Oceanside, CA, August 11, 2014.

2. Almost three-fourths of the Samoans to play in the NFL by the early twenty-first century were from either Hawai'i or California. Jack "the Throwin' Samoan" Thompson, from Evergreen, Washington, and Washington State, was the third selection in the 1979 NFL draft. But every Samoan to play in the NFL during the decade except for Thompson and Mekeli Ieremia, from Sleepy Hollow, New York, was from either California or Hawai'i.

3. Mike Tuiasosopo, interview with the author, San Bernadino, CA, August 15, 2014.

4. Herb Meyer, interview with the author, Oceanside, CA, August 11, 2014.

5. Pati Pati, interview with the author, Tutuila, American Samoa, August 2, 2011.

6. Maria Newman, "Samoans Strive to Keep Old Ways in New Land," *San Diego Union*, July 9, 1981.

7. Dick Burton, "Paopao Has Rare Talent for Oceanside," *Blade-Tribune* (Oceanside), n.d., Tony Paopao Scrapbook.

8. Sulimoni M. Molifua, *Oceanside Blade Citizen*, January 3, 1993, "Samoan Family Obituaries," compiled by Kristi S. Hawthorne, Oceanside Historical Society.

9. Newman, "Samoans Strive to Keep Old Ways in New Land."

10. John Donner, *Blade-Tribune* (Oceanside), n.d., Tony Paopao Scrapbook.

11. Bill Center, *Blade-Tribune* (Oceanside), n.d., Tony Paopao Scrapbook.

12. *Blade-Tribune* (Oceanside) November 14, 1973, Tony Paopao Scrapbook.

13. Bill Center, *Blade-Tribune* (Oceanside), n.d.; Jerry Magee, *San Diego Union*, March 7, 1974, p. D-1.

14. Steve Scholfield, *Blade-Tribune* (Oceanside), November 14, 1973, Tony Paopao Scrapbook.

15. Earl McRae, *Ottawa Citizen*, November 7, 1981, Tony Paopao Scrapbook.

16. *Blade-Tribune* (Oceanside), November 14, 1973, Tony Paopao Scrapbook.

17. Steve Scholfield, *Blade-Tribune* (Oceanside), November 14, 1973, Tony Paopao Scrapbook.

18. Steve Scholfield, *Blade-Tribune* (Oceanside), n.d., Tony Paopao Scrapbook.

19. Steve Scholfield, *Blade-Tribune* (Oceanside), 1974, Tony Paopao Scrapbook.

20. Richard Fuerstein, *San Diego Union*, July 13, 1978, p. 4.

21. Steve Scholfield, "Oceanside Mourns Paopao," *Oceanside Blade Citizen*, October 24, 1995, "Samoan Family Obituaries," compiled by Kristi S. Hawthorne, Oceanside Historical Society.

22. Steve Scholfield, interview with the author, Oceanside, CA, August 12, 2014.

23. Fuerstein, *San Diego Union*, p. 4; Meyer interview.

24. Fuerstein, *San Diego Union*, p. 4.

8: Kalifonia Dreaming

1. Mel Purcell, interview with the author, Ottoville, American Samoa, July 30, 2011.

2. Ibid.

3. Estimates of the Samoan population range widely; many of those considered of Samoan descent are only partially Samoan. The 2010 U.S. Census put American Samoa's population at 55,519; others believe it was upward of 70,000 by 2014, with many residents from other islands, often living without official documentation. U.S. Census Bureau, 2010 Census for American Samoa, "American Samoa—2010 Census Results: Total Population by County," www.census.gov/2010census/news/pdf/cb11cn177_ia_as_totalpop_2010map.pdf.

4. Oceanside then seemed similar to Pacific City, the name Joan Ablon gave to a Pacific Coast city she described in 1971 as hosting a "virtual Samoan world" that had created an "incredibly active and viable community." She found the first generation of Samoan émigrés successfully negotiating their entry into America; Joan Ablon, "The Social Organization of an Urban Samoan Community," *Southwestern Journal of Anthropology* 27, no. 1 (Spring 1971): 75–96.

5. Craig R. Janes, *Migration, Social Change, and Health: A Samoan Community in Urban California* (Stanford, CA: Stanford University Press, 1990), pp. 63–78.

6. In writing about Aunese, I leaned heavily on a wonderful story written by Tom Friend, "Full Circle," *Outside the Lines, ESPN*, n.d., sports.espn.go.com/espn/eticket/story?page=090925/aunese.

7. Bob Padecky, "Seau Always Knew How Hard Life Could Be," *Press Democrat*, May 3, 2012, www.pressdemocrat.com/news/2312645-181/seau-always-knew-how-hard.

8. Website for the documentary film *Born to Lead: The Sal Aunese Story*, www.salaunese .com/?cat+15.

9. John Gugger, "Seau Sees Light Even in Darkness," *The Blade*, January 28, 1995.

10. Tony Paopao, interview with the author, Oceanside, CA, August 11, 2014.

11. Chris Ello, "Give the Guy a Break," *Los Angeles Times*, San Diego County edition, February 10, 1987.

12. Claire Noland, "Arthur Hemingway Dies at 48," *Los Angeles Times*, March 1, 2009, articles.latimes.com/2009/mar/01/local/me-arthur-hemingway1.

13. Tom Shanahan, "He Was Right There with Them," *Voice of San Diego*, March 19, 2009, https://www.voiceofsandiego.org/topics/news/he-was-right-there-with-them.

14. Bernie Wilson, "Hey Buddy: Seau Fondly Recalled as He Goes into Hall of Fame," Associated Press, August 6, 2015, bigstory.ap.org/article/7986293219be45aabb26c8190552276e /hey-buddy-seau-fondly-recalled-he-goes-hall-fame.

15. Nathaniel Penn, "The Violent and Sudden Death of Junior Seau," *GQ*, September 2013, www.gq.com/entertainment/sports/201309/junior-seau-nfl-death-concussions-brain-injury.

16. Greg Bishop and Mary Pilon, "A Community Recalls a Star Who Never Left," *New York Times*, May 3, 2012.

17. Penny Semaia, email to the author, September 4, 2014.

18. Maria Newman, *San Diego Union*, July 9, 1981.

19. Robert W. Franco, *Samoan Perceptions of Work: Moving Up and Moving Around* (New York: AMS Press, 1991), pp. 248–98, cites U.S. Department of Labor, "Study of Unemployment, Poverty and Training Needs of American Samoans," Washington, D.C. Employment and Training Administration, 1984.

20. Janes, *Migration, Social Change, and Health*, pp. 10, 50–56.

21. Herb Meyer, interview with the author, Oceanside, CA, August 11, 2014.

22. Lieutenant Joe Young, Oceanside police force, in Geoff Bouvier, "To Live and Die in Oceanside," *San Diego Reader*, February 20, 2008, www.sandiegoreader.com/news/2008/feb /20/cover.

23. Ken Belson, "Tackle Football Makes a Comeback," *New York Times*, December 4, 2016.

24. Ryan Wallerson, "Youth Participation Weakens in Basketball, Football, Baseball, Soccer," *Wall Street Journal*, January 31, 2014, online.wsj.com/news/articles /SB10001424052702303519404579350892629229918. The sources for these figures are National Federation of State High School Associations, Sport and Fitness Industry Association, the Physical Activity Council, and Pop Warner; Steve Fainaru and Mark Fainaru-Wada, "Youth Football Participation Drops," ESPN.com, November 14, 2013, espn.go.com/espn/otl/story/_/page/popwarner/pop-warner-youth-football-par ticipation-drops-nfl-concussion-crisis-seen-causal-factor; Gregg Doyel, "Decline of Pop Warner Football Doesn't Bode Well for NFL," CBS Sports, November 14, 2013, www.cbssports.com/general/writer/gregg-doyel/24233232/decline-of-pop-warner -football-doesnt-bode-well-for-nfl; Mike White, "Football Decline Continues," *Pittsburgh Post-Gazette*, August 16, 2015.

25. Mike White, "Endangered Species," *Pittsburgh Post Gazette*, September 23, 2016.

26. "Half of Americans Don't Want Their Sons Playing Football, Poll Says," Bloomberg Politics, December 10, 2014, www.bloomberg.com/politics/articles/2014-12-10/bloomberg -politics-poll-half-of-americans-dont-want-their-sons-playing-football.

27. "RMU Poll Shows Growing Support for Banning Youth Contact Football," December 14, 2014, rmu.edu/news_highlights.aspx?id+817.

28. Ken Belson, "Pop Warner Bans Kickoffs for Youngest Players' Safety," *New York Times*, May 13, 2016.

29. Kalyn Kahler, "The Town That Doesn't Tackle," *Sports Illustrated*, September 19, 2016, p. 7.

30. Belson, "Tackle Football Makes a Comeback."

31. John Maffei, "The 52: Carroll's Exploits Unmatched," *U-T San Diego*, August 1, 2014, www.utsandiego.com/news/2014/aug/01/john-carroll-oceanside-football-coach-52.

32. John Maffei, "Carroll Steps Down as Oceanside Coach," January 7, 2015, hs.utpreps .com/news_article/show/464095. The Oceanside football stadium has been renamed in his honor; he was inducted into the California Coaches Association Hall of Fame a few months later.

9: Back in Hawai'i: Where Football Still Matters

1. Paul Honda, "Private School Pipeline," *Honolulu Star-Advertiser*, November 11, 2014, p. C-5.

2. Ibid.

3. Billy Hull, "Punahou Survives an Emotional Affair," *Hawaii Prep World, Honolulu Star-Advertiser*, November 16, 2014, p. C-9, http://www.hawaiiprepworld.com/football /punahou-survives-an-emotional-affair.

4. *Samoan Population by County, Island and Census Tract in the State of Hawai'i: 2010*; State of Hawai'i, Department of Business, Economic Development & Tourism Research and Economic Analysis Division, Hawai'i State Data Center, February 2012, p. 6, www.ohadatabook.com /HSDC2010-9_Samoan.pdf.

5. Cal Lee, interviews with the author, Honolulu, July 17, 2012, and November 19, 2014.

6. Dave Reardon, "Cal Lee to Step Down," *Honolulu Star-Bulletin*, July 7, 2001, starbulletin.com, http://archives.starbulletin.com/2001/07/07/news/story1.html.

7. Hugh Yoshida, interview with the author, Honolulu, November 3, 2014.

8. Private school domination spearheaded the organization of the Interscholastic League of Honolulu (ILH). Roosevelt, McKinley, Farrington, and a few other public schools had belonged during the 1930s but were at a disadvantage in terms of resources and recruiting. While Honolulu became the game's undisputed center of gravity, rural schools formed their own league in 1940, the Rural O'ahu Interscholastic Association (ROIA).

9. Dan Ciso, *Hawaii Sports: History, Facts and Statistics* (Honolulu: University of Hawai'i Press, 1999), pp. 130–44.

10. Tanoai Reed, interview with the author, Kahuku, HI, November 12, 2014.

11. Lee Leslie, interview with the author, Kahuku, HI, November 18, 2014.

12. Pat Bigold, "Semones Returns to the Big One," *Honolulu Star-Bulletin*, November 26, 1993, D-6.

13. Siuaki Livai, interview with the author, Kahuku, HI, October 30, 2014.

14. Pat Bigold, "Transfers Add Top Talent to Red Raiders," *Honolulu Star-Bulletin*, October 1, 1995, p. A-1.

15. Tom Shanahan, "Three Taken on First Day Connected to San Diego," *Union-Tribune*, April 21, 2002, www.utsandiego.com/sports/nfl/20020421-9999_1s21locdraft.html.

16. Stacy Kaneshiro, "An Appetite for Success," *Honolulu Advertiser*, September 2, 1998, pp. D1, D3.

17. Bruce Feldman, "Rock Star," *ESPN The Magazine*, November 26, 2001, espn.go.com /magazine/vol4no24fonoti.html; Shanahan, "Three Taken on First Day."

18. Stacy Kaneshiro, "Dog Days," *Honolulu Advertiser*, August 15, 1999, pp. C1, C4.

19. Kyle Sakamoto, "Red Raiders Kept Crusaders on the Run," *Honolulu Advertiser*, December 2000.

20. Livai interview.

21. Cal Lee, interview with the author, Honolulu, November 19, 2014.

22. Junior Ah You, interview with the author, Kahuku, HI, November 18, 2014. According to Seamus Fitzgerald, who works at the Polynesian Cultural Center and teaches at BYU-Hawai'i, the team did the Ka Mate *haka* for that game but changed to the Tika Tonu *haka* in 2004. "There are 1000's of different *haka* with different names, words, motions, meanings, and purposes." Fitzgerald, email to the author, January 13, 2015.

23. Ferd Lewis, "A Triumph of Heart and Hope," *Honolulu Advertiser*, December 3, 2000; Sakamoto, "Red Raiders Kept Crusaders."

24. Livai interview.

25. Scott Ishikawa, "Proud Kahuku Throws a Party for State Champs," *Honolulu Advertiser*, December 2, 2000; Kyle Sakamoto and Scott Ishikawa, "Kahuku Rolls Out Red Carpet for Football Champions," *Honolulu Advertiser*, December 3, 2000; Lewis, "Triumph of Heart and Hope"; Sakamoto, "Red Raiders Kept Crusaders."

26. Pauline Masaniai, interview with the author, Kahuku, HI, November 12, 2014.

27. Dave Reardon and Paul Honda, "Livai Leaves a Winner," AIGA Foundation blog, March 28, 2006, aigafoundation.blogspot.com/2006/03/more-on-siuaki-livai-resignation.html.

28. Ibid.

29. Pauline Masaniai, interview with the author, Kahuku, HI, November 12, 2014.

30. Livai interview.

31. Sal Ruibal, "Tiny Hawaii Looms as Giant in Football World," *USA Today*, November 9, 2004, usatoday30.usatoday.com/sports/football/2004-11-09-hawaii-football_x.htm.

32. Reardon and Honda, "Livai Leaves a Winner."

33. "Samoa Bowl IX: Live the Experience Through the Samoa Bowl!," www.samoanews .com/samoa-bowl-ix-live-experience-through-samoa-bowl.

34. Paul Honda, "Livai Bids Aloha to Kahuku Football," *Honolulu Star-Bulletin*, March 28, 2006, archives.starbulletin.com/2006/03/28/news/story04.html.

35. Wes Nakama, "Dynasty Had Humble Start," *Honolulu Advertiser*, July 25, 2009, the.honoluluadvertiser.com/article/2009/Jul/25/sp/hawaii907250327.html.

36. Honda, "Livai Bids Aloha to Kahuku Football."

37. Siuaki Livai, interview with the author, Kahuku, HI, August 16, 2012.

38. Reggie Torres, interview with the author, Kahuku, HI, July 12, 2013.

39. Robert Franco, "International Movement and Samoan Marriage in Hawaii," in *The Business of Marriage: Transformations in Oceanic Matrimony*, ed. Richard A. Marksbury (Pittsburgh, PA: University of Pittsburgh Press, 1993), pp. 238–40. He cites 1990 Samoan Service Provider's Association, "Report to Samoan Community 2000 Conference," Honolulu, 1990, p. 6.

40. Matt Kester, interview with the author, Laʻie, HI, July 11, 2013.

41. Doc Taula, interview with the author, Kahuku, HI, July 12, 2013.

42. Cal Lee, interviews with the author, Honolulu, July 17, 2013, and November 19, 2014.

43. Lee Leslie, interview with the author, Kahuku, HI, November 18, 2014.

44. Jesse Markham, interview with the author, Kailua, HI, November 1, 2014.

45. Jerry Campany, "Kahuku Football Coach Resigns," *Star-Advertiser*, March 19, 2015, www.staradvertiser.com/news/breaking/20150319_Kahuku_football_coach_resigns .html?id=296916491; Brenton Awa, "Lee Leslie Resigns: Kahuku High School in Need of Head Football Coach," KITV.com, March 19, 2015, www.kitv.com/news/lee-leslie-resigns-kahuku -high-school-in-need-of-head-football-coach/31905850. It didn't take Leslie long to line up something closer to home. He coached the following season at the McCall-Donnelly High School in McCall, Idaho. The Vandals were 1–7 the year before, but he'll be back home again; Dani Allsop, "Lee Leslie to Take Over McCall-Donnelly Football Program," April 20, 2015, http://www.ktvb.com/story/sports/high-school/2015/04/26/lee-leslie-to-take-over-mccall -donnelly-high-school-football-program/26430143.

46. Lee Leslie, interview with the author, Kahuku, HI, November 18, 2014.

47. Nick Abramo, "Kahuku Names Tata Football Coach," *Honolulu Star-Advertiser*, April 20, 2015, http://www.staradvertiser.com/2015/04/20/sports/kahuku-names-tata-football-coach.

48. Nick Abramo, "New Kahuku Football Coach Tata Is Big on Grades," *Hawaii Prep World*, May 8, 2015, hawaiiprepworld.com/football/new-kahuku-football-coach-tata-is-big -on-grades/.

49. Nick Abramo, "Tata Out as Kahuku Football Head Coach," *Honolulu Star-Advertiser*, February 10, 2017, www.staradvertiser.com/2017/02/10/sports/sports-breaking/tata-out-as -kahuku-football-head-coach.

50. Austin Murphy, "Tennessee Two-Step," *Sports Illustrated*, May 11, 2015; Cal Lee, interview on *Leahey & Leahey*, PBS Hawaii, October 15, 2014, https://www.youtube.com /watch?v=B7bkpTEt1dI.

10: David and Goliath

1. His Highness Tui Atua Tupua Tamasese Efi, Ottoville, American Samoa, July 7, 2013.

2. Bill Halleck, interview with the author, Fagatogo, American Samoa, July 12, 2013; Judge Satele Liliʻo Aliʻitaʻi, interview with the author, Fagasa, American Samoa, August 10, 2012.

3. Keith Uperesa, interview with the author, Honolulu, July 16, 2013.

4. Okland Salaveʻa, interview with the author, Ottoville, American Samoa, November 9, 2014.

5. Beauty Tuiasosopo, interview with the author, Tafuna, American Samoa, November 6, 2014.

6. Elia Savali, interview with the author, Utulei, American Samoa, July 31, 2012.

7. Tony Gasu, "Players Keep Their Cool, but Not Coaches and Fans," *Samoa News*, November 22, 2014.

8. Pooch Taʻase, email correspondence with the author, November 27, 2014.

9. Tony Gasu, "'Toa o le Vasa' Vikings Are ASHSAA Champs," *Samoa News*, November 24, 2014, www.samoanews.com/"toa-o-le-vasa"-vikings-are-ashsaa-champs.

10. Florence Salesa, email correspondence with the author, November 25, 2014.

11: The Samoan Paradox

1. Roger Robinson, *Robert Louis Stevenson: His Best Pacific Writings* (Honolulu: Bess Press, 2003), pp. 147–48.

2. Malama Meleisea, *Change and Adaptations in Western Samoa* (Christchurch, New Zealand: Macmillan Browne Center for Pacific Studies, University of Canterbury, 1992).

3. Felix Keesing, *Modern Samoa: Its Government and Changing Life* (Stanford, CA: Stanford University Press, 1934), pp. 154–56, 185, 314, 328–42.

4. W. E. H. Stanner, *The South Seas in Transition: A Study of Post-War Rehabilitation and Reconstruction in Three British Pacific Dependencies* (Sydney, Australia: Australasian Publishing Company, 1953), p. 316.

5. Margaret Mead, *Coming of Age in Samoa* (New York: William Morrow & Company, 1928), pp. 276–77; Malama Meleisea, *Change and Adaptations in Western Samoa*, p. 53.

6. See David Wiggins, *Glory Bound: Black Athletes in White America* (Syracuse, NY: Syracuse University Press, 1997), pp. 177–99; and David Epstein, *The Sports Gene: Inside the Science of Extraordinary Athletic Performance* (New York: Current, 2013).

7. Gabe Sewell, interview with the author, Ottoville, American Samoa, July 31, 2011.

8. Simon Mageo, interview with the author, Utulei, American Samoa, July 31, 2011.

9. Ember D. Keighley, Stephen T. McGarvey, Pasa Turituri, and Satupaitea Viali, "Farming and Adiposity in Samoan Adults," *American Journal of Human Biology* 18 (2006): 112–22; these body mass index numbers, defined as >32 kg/m², are based on body composition studies for Polynesians that factor in greater muscle and skeletal mass and are thus set higher than for other groups of people. The BMI threshold for non-Polynesians is >30 kg/m².

10. Stephen T. McGarvey, interview with the author, 'Ili'ili, American Samoa, November 10, 2014; Ember D. Keighley, Stephen T. McGarvey, Christine Quested, Charles McCuddion, Satupaitea Viali, and Uto'ofili A. Maga, "Nutrition and Health in Modernizing Samoans and Adaptive Perspectives," in *Health Change in the Asia-Pacific Region: Biocultural and Epidemiological Approaches*, ed. Ryutaro Ohtsuka and Stanley J. Ulijaszek (Cambridge: Cambridge University Press, 2007).

11. "McDonald's in American Samoa Gets the Top World Wide Rating," Radio New Zealand, February 23, 2004, www.radionz.co.nz/international/pacific-news/147427/mcdonalds-in-american-samoa-gets-the-top-world-wide-rating.

12. "Early anthropologists," McGarvey said, "never measured anything but the size of the goddamned head because that's what the early physical anthropologists were interested in." Nor could they escape the scientific racism that pervaded scholarly thought a century ago and tied intelligence to race. Their failure to record heights and weights prevents researchers from computing historical body mass index (BMI) comparisons.

13. McGarvey interview; Keighley et al., "Nutrition and Health in Modernizing Samoans," pp. 148–49, which cites McGarvey's earlier work on the question.

14. Epstein, *Sports Gene*.

15. James R. Bindon, "Polynesian Responses to Modernization: Overweight and Obesity in the South Pacific," in *Social Aspects of Obesity*, ed. Igor de Garine and Nancy J. Pollock (Abingdon, Oxon, UK: Gordon and Breach Publishers, 1995), p. 233.

16. Keighley et al., "Farming and Adiposity in Samoan Adults," p. 113, cites the 1991 Samoa Census. The shift from farm to office was not as precipitous in neighboring Samoa, where about two-thirds of working adults were subsistence farmers and fishermen in 1991. Within a decade, that number had dropped to 44 percent of men in Samoa.

17. Ibid., p. 112.

18. McGarvey interview; Keighley et al., "Nutrition and Health in Modernizing Samoans," pp. 181–82.

19. Bindon, "Polynesian Responses to Modernization," pp. 227–42; Craig R. Janes, *Migration, Social Change, and Health: A Samoan Community in Urban California* (Stanford, CA: Stanford University Press, 1990), p. 10.

20. Keighley et al., "Farming and Adiposity in Samoan Adults," p. 113.

21. Lanuloa Tusani Tupufia and Zaskiya Lesa, "Turkey Tails Cost Govt. $18m in Annual Health Bill," *Samoa Observer*, October 6, 2012, www.samoaobserver.ws/local-news/75-food /1376-turkey-tails-cost-govt-18m-in-annual-health-bill.

22. Tuiʻaliʻi Motootua Lolotai, interview with the author, Lauliʻi, Samoa, August 6, 2012.

23. Tasa Laotele, interview with the author, Apia, Samoa, July 21, 2012.

24. "Dialysis Reduces Insulin Needs for Patients with Type 2 Diabetes," American Diabetes Association, October 7, 2013, www.diabetes.org/research-and-practice/patient-access-to -research/dialysis-reduces-insulin.html#sthash.6FA2De88.dpuf.

25. Michael Gerstenberger, interview with the author, LBJ Tropical Medical Center, Fagaʻalu, American Samoa, August 13, 2012.

26. Department of Women and Youth Affairs, "Comprehensive Sports Study and Strategic Plan for American Samoa" American Samoan Department of Youth, Women, & Sports (draft, 2014), p. 18.

27. Pati Pati, interviews with the author, Ottoville and Leone, American Samoa, August 2 and 3, 2011.

28. Liʻa Amisone, interview with the author, Utulei, American Samoa, August 7, 2011.

29. Melissa Korn, "Big Gap in College Graduation Rates for Rich and Poor," *Wall Street Journal*, February 3, 2015, www.wsj.com/articles/big-gap-in-college-graduation-rates-for-rich -and-poor-study-finds-1422997677.

30. Mona Chalabi, "What Percentage of Americans Have Served in the Military?" FiveThirtyEight, March 19, 2015, fivethirtyeight.com/datalab/what-percentage-of-americans-have-served -in-the-military.

31. B. Chen, "Local US Army Recruiting Station Ranked #1 in the World," *Samoa News*, www.samoanews.com/content/en/local-us-army-recruiting-station-ranked-1-world; Rachel Kahn Taylor, *Warriors Born: American Samoans in the U.S. Military*, 2010 documentary, 22:42, http://www.rachelkahntaylor.com/portfolio/directed-produce/.

32. Pati Pati interviews.

33. Sanele Tuiteleleapaga, interviews with the author, Utulei, American Samoa, August 1, 2011.

34. Sewell interview.

35. Elia Savali, interview with the author, Ottoville, American Samoa, July 31, 2012.

36. Several groups help coaches, players, and families navigate the NCAA maze. The West Coast–based AIGA Foundation has worked with boys of Polynesian background for almost twenty years, mentoring them, hosting camps, and serving as a go-between with college coaches. Field House 100 also operated on Tutuila for several years. After Brian Smart arrived in 2005, intent on starting an English-language Baptist church, he concluded that he could reach young people through sport. He persuaded his twin, Brandon, who had been coaching in Tennessee, to help him develop a sports ministry. They focused on techniques and academics. "These kids have

the physical potential," Smart argued, "but their technique is awful. They're college-sized kids with a middle school football mentality." Posting clips of players on their website for recruiters to study, the Smarts worked with coaches to find appropriate schools for them. Meanwhile, counseling clarified confusing NCAA eligibility protocols and what going off island would mean. Though dropout rates are notorious, especially at junior colleges, Brian Smart maintained that none of one hundred kids they sent dropped out. "FH 100 Exceeds Its Goal for 2012–2013 to Find College Homes for Local Student-Athletes," *Samoa News*, August 30, 2012. If the seventy student-athletes—mostly football players and girls competing in volleyball and softball—from the 2012 and 2013 graduating classes they helped place complete their education, they will receive a total of $2.5 million in scholarship support. The Smarts decamped in 2013. Brian Smart, interview with the author, Ottoville, American Samoa, August 8, 2012.

37. "America" is often spelled "Amerika" on island because there is no *c* in the Samoan alphabet.

38. Sewell interview.

39. Richard MacMillan, *Honolulu Advertiser*, August 6, 1953; Mort Rosenblum, *Honolulu Star-Bulletin*, June 7, 1973.

40. Rosenblum, *Honolulu Star-Bulletin*. June 7, 1973.

41. Governor Togiola Tulafono, interview with the author, Utulei, American Samoa, July 12, 2012.

Epilogue

1. Pete Gurr, interview with author, Maloata bay, Tutuila, July 31, 2012.

2. Kelsey Nowakowski, "Can Breadfruit Overcome Its Past to Be a Superfood of the Future?" *National Geographic*, July 15, 2015, http://theplate.nationalgeographic.com/2015/07/22/can-breadfruit-overcome-its-past-to-be-a-superfood-of-the-future.

Index

About the Author

Rob Ruck is a professor of history at the University of Pittsburgh. His documentaries include *The Republic of Baseball: Dominican Giants of the American Game* (PBS with Dan Manatt) and the Emmy-winning *Kings on the Hill: Baseball's Forgotten Men* (PBS and NBC). He is the co-author of *Rooney: A Sporting Life* and author of *Raceball: How the Major Leagues Colonized the Black and Latin Game* (a PEN-ESPN Literary Sportswriting Award finalist). He has written for the *New York Times*, the *Washington Post*, and the *Wall Street Journal* and was a member of the 2006 committee that elected Negro Leaguers and Latinos to the National Baseball Hall of Fame. He and his wife and co-author Maggie Patterson live in Pittsburgh, where he has run every Pittsburgh Great Race since its inception in 1977.

Publishing in the Public Interest

Thank you for reading this book published by The New Press. The New Press is a nonprofit, public interest publisher. New Press books and authors play a crucial role in sparking conversations about the key political and social issues of our day.

We hope you enjoyed this book and that you will stay in touch with The New Press. Here are a few ways to stay up to date with our books, events, and the issues we cover:

- Sign up at www.thenewpress.com/subscribe to receive updates on New Press authors and issues and to be notified about local events
- Like us on Facebook: www.facebook.com/newpressbooks
- Follow us on Twitter: www.twitter.com/thenewpress

Please consider buying New Press books for yourself; for friends and family; or to donate to schools, libraries, community centers, prison libraries, and other organizations involved with the issues our authors write about.

The New Press is a 501(c)(3) nonprofit organization. You can also support our work with a tax-deductible gift by visiting www.thenewpress.com/donate.